RIVERS ON FIRE

KHALISTAN STRUGGLE

RIVERS ON FIRE
KHALISTAN STRUGGLE

Jagtar Singh

AAKAR

Rivers on Fire: Khalistan Struggle
Jagtar Singh

First Published 2020
Reprinted 2024

ISBN 978-93-5002-665-6 (Pb)

Published by
AAKAR BOOKS
28 E Pocket IV, Mayur Vihar Phase I
Delhi 110 091 India
aakarbooks@gmail.com

In Association with
Institute for Development and Communication
Sector 38 A, Chandigarh 160 014

Laser Typeset at
Arpit Printographers, Delhi

Printed at
Mudrak, Noida

Contents

Foreword

This book is a sequel to *Khalistan Struggle: A Non-movement*, published in 2011. That book focused largely on the study of the events and role of the political action in the shaping of these events within the canvas of 'Akali Politics', ranging from the moderate to the militant factions. The present book, *Rivers on Fire: Khalistan Struggle* is well researched and comprehensive in its approach. The book has relied extensively on the original documents, interviews with the active militants, policemen engaged in the counter militant operations and the academia in this field.

To revisit the recent past by an actor, in this case, a journalist, who actively covered the decade long politics of the extremes is always fraught with danger. These explorations provide crucial information for historical scrutiny. The process of the reconstruction of the facts involves subjectivity laced with political and ideological positioning. The important question is: which facts are selected and from which standpoint? The standpoint tends to colour the interpretations as these actors themselves are the product of the same historical events which they try to interpret.

The author of this book applies caution, as he puts his facts in the public domain through his popular newspaper writings for feedback and provides evidence of his impressions.

This, perhaps, is among the best evidence-based books. Most of the literature reconstructed their analysis from the outcomes rather than analyzing the process which led to the shaping of these events. The book has captured minute details. It is said that excellence lies in details. In this sense, it is an excellent treatise on the 'Khalistan' phenomenon.

The main argument advanced is to bring a closure to the tragic decade. And, it can only be achieved if the culture of violence is negated and the culture of peace is continuously reconstructed. And that kind of politics which creates conditions for the people to take to violence has to be purged. In that sense, this book is different as it provides insights not only to understand, but also to eliminate the conditions for the re-occurrence of such tragedies in future.

Pramod Kumar
Director
Institute for Development and Communication
Chandigarh

1

Volcanic Punjab

Sikh-dominated Punjab province in north India, bordering Pakistan, witnessed a violent separatist political struggle that dictated political discourse of the country for years beginning in 1980 during which about 40,000 people were killed. This three-phased conflict involving a section of the dynamic and dominant Sikh minority with the Indian state continues to be perceived as a threat despite the claims of it having been wiped out in the early 1990s. The Khalistan narrative resurfaced in 2018.

Union Home Minister Rajnath Singh, while addressing a meeting of police chiefs from all the states in December 2018 in Gujarat, specifically hammered this struggle. "Union Home Minister Rajnath Singh said radical elements based in "Europe and America" and backed by Pakistan are attempting to revive terror in Punjab...recent terror incidents in Punjab indicate concerted efforts by Pakistan establishment and Sikh extremist elements based in Pakistan to revive terrorism in Punjab."[1]

Besides going into various dimensions of Punjab militancy that has been categorised into three phases, the issues that repeatedly surface in the Sikh religio-political narrative have been taken up. One of these aspects is the perceived failure of the Sikh leadership in 1947 to negotiate for a dignified space in this region at the time of the partition of India that led to the creation of Pakistan. The situation in the run-up to the army attack on Darbar Sahib (Golden Temple) code-named Operation Bluestar in June 1984 with focus on dialogue, on the record and off the record, has been dealt with.

There is yet another dimension. Did Sant Jarnail Singh Bhindranwale dictate the actions of Prime Minister Indira Gandhi as part of his strategy and tactics to intensify the struggle for Khalistan, the objective that he otherwise never spelled out unequivocally?

The bombing of Air India plane Kanishka has been one of the

most talked about actions pertaining to this militant struggle but never owned by any militant organization. Nothing conclusive could be proved by the Canadian investigators. The book carries new information.

Pakistan's role has been detailed, based on the experience of the activists.

It is for the first time that details of negotiations leading to signing of the Punjab Accord between then Prime Minister Indira Gandhi and Akali Dal president Sant Harchand Singh Longowal has been documented. Then there is the boycott of the 1992 Punjab assembly elections as the entire story is still to come out.

An important issue that has been part of the militant and general political narrative is the river waters dispute between Punjab and Haryana. An effort has been made to go to its roots based on official documents.

The first phase ended with the brutal army attack on the Golden Temple complex in June 1984. The period after this attack till the second storming code-named Operation Black Thunder-II by the security forces on the shrine in May 1988 can be categorised as Phase II that also marked the start of Phase III when militancy took over the entire Punjab with media terming the Tarn Taran area as the 'liberated zone.' The last major action in Phase III was the assassination of Chief Minister Beant Singh by human bomb Dilawar Singh on August 31, 1995.[2]

Punjab has been witnessing sporadic incidents of political killings and terrorist incidents causing concern to the Indian establishment after a lull spanning about a decade after that assassination. At the political level, the Sikh separatist campaign for the sovereign state of Khalistan has intensified, not in the Indian Punjab but in the countries where the Sikhs have migrated in sizeable numbers including Canada, USA and the UK. Canada has emerged as the second most powerful Sikh region after Indian Punjab and the strategic role to fuel that volatile political dynamics has now been taken over by the Sikh Diaspora.

Violent political struggles are continuing in Kashmir, central and north-eastern India too but strategically, Punjab is perceived to pose a far too serious threat. The main land access from the Indian mainland to disturbed Kashmir is through Punjab. Indian Kashmir is the most garrisoned conflict region on the globe.

The strategic location of Punjab bordering Pakistan, which is India's historically hostile neighbour is an important contributory factor to the turbulence in the Sikh political matrix.

Punjab and Indian Kashmir are the two regions in India where Sikh and Muslim minorities respectively are in a majority. Both these regions share border with Pakistan. Pakistan has strategic interests to keep this region disturbed.

Sikhs, who dominate Indian Punjab, have a unique relationship with Pakistan that is different from the Kashmiris. This relationship is organic as Pakistan is the birth place of Guru Nanak Dev, the founder of this religion who was born at Nankana Sahib and died at Kartarpur Sahib. The Sikh religion originated in the region that is now Pakistan and in that sense, Pakistani Punjab is the native land of the Sikhs while Indian Punjab is their homeland. Sikhs from all over the world visit their shrines in their native land.

It is perhaps in this context that even the genuine demand for re-organization of Punjab along linguistic lines on the pattern of other states was opposed by Prime Minister Jawaharlal Nehru who said in his speech on August 15, 1960 from the ramparts of the Red Fort: "Tamasha (drama) is going on in Delhi and Punjab about the Punjabi Suba...This demand might be good or bad but there were many wrong things in the movement and there is danger to the freedom of the country".[3, 4]

There is another important dimension to the Sikh narrative. The Sikhs are the only native people after Muslims who have ruled over the region from river Satluj to Khyber Pass in a period of about 500 years despite being about 13 per cent of the population at the best of times, and the Sikh Empire was the last to be annexed by the British in 1849. This nostalgia of being the rulers of the land nurtures the ambition to rule. The foundation of the Sikh Raj was laid by Baba Banda Singh Bahadur, the warrior who had been deputed to Punjab by Guru Gobind Singh during his last days at Nanded in Maharasthra, with the conquest of Sirhind province in 1710 that was part of the Mughal Empire.

This nostalgic glory continues to sculpt the Sikh ambitions and aspirations even under the present rapidly changing geo-political situation. At another level, this is what can be called the historical baggage that they carry. The Sikhs were the third entity after Hindus and Muslims in all the negotiations with the British government till the partition. The Sikh leaders were given the option to decide their political destiny during these negotiations.

The organic relationship with Pakistan, locational aspect and ambition to rule are the factors that apart from others have shaped the radical Sikh struggle. Yet another important dimension is the historical revenge psyche.

This Sikh struggle took the life of Prime Minister Indira Gandhi, Sant Jarnail Singh Bhindranwale, Akali Dal President Sant Harchand Singh Longowal, General A.S. Vaidya (retd.) who was the army chief in 1984, besides Chief Minister Beant Singh.

The martyrs' memorial raised in the Golden Temple complex in Amritsar epitomizes that struggle.[5]

This violent confrontation in Punjab that was initially rooted in the Sikh religious dynamics turned anti-state over a period leading to Operation Bluestar. Beant Singh and Satwant Singh, the assassins of Prime Minister Indira Gandhi, were not indoctrinated but were motivated by revenge psyche. This was also the case with Ranjit Singh who gunned down Nirankari chief Gurbachan Singh in 1980 to avenge the killings of the Sikhs on April 13, 1978 in Amritsar.

The demand for Khalistan dominated the second phase of this violent struggle that was mainly in reaction to Operation Bluestar.

The nature of political discourse relating to that period includes the role of the Indian State, the Akali Dal and the militants. The Akali Dal beginning a few years before the partition of the country has been dictated by the fear of the Sikhs getting subsumed by what used to be perceived as the Hindu discourse.

Sant Bhindranwale and the radical organizations perceived the Indian State to be the Brahmin-Bania state that is another name for the Hindu state. This perception diverted the fight from being against the Indian State to the Brahmin-Bania State. It was this perception that pitchforked the Hindus in this fight as a symbol of the Indian State.

The space for the radical ideology to operate was provided by the Akali political discourse that was rooted in the perceived discrimination against the Sikhs. The legitimacy of the use of violence by the radicals to settle religio-political issues was provided by the Akali Dal.[6]

However, the relationship between the Akalis and the radicals changed periodically that also included confrontation. The Akali leaders would be viewed with suspicion. This nature of relationship denied a mass political front to the radicals without which the militant struggle could not be taken forward. This is the difference between Punjab and Kashmir.

The campaign for Khalistan continues but is carried on mainly by the Sikh Diaspora. Dal Khalsa is one organization in Punjab that consistently continues to espouse this political goal, now democratically.

This book is an attempt to unravel what actually happened from

1978 onwards and the interplay of forces, besides the historical factors that shape the Sikh psyche. Even the basic facts relating to this struggle are still to come out.

Question Mark Over the Number of Casualties During Operation Bluestar

Operation Bluestar in June 1984 was the biggest 'peacetime' operation by the Indian army since 1947 against the Indian people, in this case the Sikhs. However, the entire action continues to be shrouded in mystery that includes the total number of civilians including militants who were killed. The Punjab government refused to share the information sought under the Right to Information Act as to who signed the file requisitioning army for action in the Golden Temple complex.

No enumeration has ever been done of the victims of this deadly politics of violence. The Akali Dal came to power in Punjab after Operation Bluestar first in 1985 and then in 1997, 2007 and 2012 but no such effort has ever been made even by this party's government in this regard. The space to radical politics and legitimacy was provided by the Akali political discourse over the years. It was this party that had launched the struggle known as the *Dharamyudh Morcha* on August 4, 1982 on a 15-point demand charter that was practically taken over by Sant Bhindranwale at the time when religio-political violence had already been introduced in Punjab.[7]

The White Paper released by the Union government in the Parliament on July 10, 1984 put the total number of civilians killed in the Golden Temple complex in the three-day operation in 1984 at 493 with 86 injured while in case of the army, the comparative figures were 83 killed and 220 injured. During the same period, 42 other shrines were raided all over Punjab resulting in the killing of 23 civilians and one army personnel. Thirty-eight others were killed during curfew violations and search operations. These people were mainly those who tried to march to Amritsar from the nearby villages.

Record of Deaths and Postmortems Missing

Intriguingly, the entire record of postmortems relating to the said period that included these dead bodies has been reported missing as also the record of cremations. An effort was made to procure the record of the postmortem reports conducted by the office of the Chief Medical Officer, Amritsar from June 3 to 12 and also the total number of cremations during the same period in the city cremation grounds under the Right to Information Act. After several weeks, the CMO office replied under letter No. MRC/RTI/12/3129 dated October 31, 2012 that the said record was stolen in 2004 and the first information report No. 121 dated May 7, 2004 was lodged with the Civil Lines police station. The government has not shared in the communication whether this record is available at any other level also or not.

The controversy about the number of the dead refuses to die down. The bodies of those who were killed in the Darbar Sahib complex were treated like animals while being carried in garbage trucks for postmortem and then to the cremation ground near Gurdwara Shaheed Baba Deep Singh going by the pictures available.

The Akali Dal remains confined to Congress bashing during elections rather than addressing the basic issues when in power. This party repeated the promise to initiate a judicial inquiry into the November 1984 massacre in its manifesto for the 2014 Lok Sabha elections "under a Supreme Court judge to inquire into and expose those who hatched the conspiracy behind the massacre; ditto for those who shielded the guilty." The promise was subject to the BJP, its alliance partner, coming to power at the national level. A similar promise was made in the 1985 manifesto and again in the 1997 Common Minimum Programme with the BJP. However, nothing ever materialized.

The party promised on page 3 of the manifesto for the 2014 Lok Sabha elections:

> When NDA forms the government at the Centre, we will ensure the following to deal with the guilty of the 1984 massacre:
> -Fast track courts to try the ongoing cases.
> -Cases that have been closed are reopened and challans presented in the fast track courts for disposal in a time bound manner.
> -Complaints on which no action has been taken to be acted upon.
> -A commission of inquiry under a judge of the Supreme Court to go into the entire conspiracy behind the massacre, to get at the original sinners. The commission will also go into the reported conspiracy under which the guilty has been shielded.

It was the NDA that came to power at the Centre in 2014 with Narendra Modi as the Prime Minister. Harsimrat Kaur Badal, wife of Akali Dal president Sukhbir Singh Badal, represented the Akali Dal as the cabinet minister in this government. Despite the Akali Dal being part of the NDA government, the promised judicial probe was never ordered.

Yet an earlier promise made by the Akali Dal in the manifesto for the 1996 Lok Sabha elections is important at another level too as this struggle has been described as Congress-abetted 'terrorism.'

It states: "Shiromani Akali Dal is for a probe by a commission comprising Supreme Court judges to probe the role of the Congress in encouraging fissiparous and secessionist tendencies and terrorism so that the misuse of the unbridled power, exploitation, loot and excesses are put to an end forever."

The Akali Dal used the term 'terrorism' as against earlier 'militancy' under the changed scenario when militancy was perceived to have been rooted out.

Killing of Hindus as Collateral Damage

Hundreds of Hindus also became victims of this violence, most of them innocents, just like many of the Sikhs. The targeted killing of Hindus started with the Dhilwan bus shocker on the night of October 5, 1983 but the situation worsened during the post Operation Bluestar period. Of course, the Hindus were killed for the first time by the Sikh militants in reaction to the arrest of Sant Bhindranwale on September 20, 1981 in the case of the assassination of Jalandhar-based owner-editor of the Hind Samachar group of newspapers, Lala Jagat Narain but those were random killings.

Shiromani Akali Dal focuses mainly on Operation Bluestar and the November 1984 killings while overlooking the targeted killing of innocent Hindus. Of course, Akali Dal had been condemning the killing of the Hindus but so did Sant Bhindranwale, on the record in two cases at least.

Significantly, the Hindus as a community were not the target. The Hindus were the collateral damage due to the perception of their being a symbol of the Indian State. This confrontation was with the Indian State.

Congress President Sonia Gandhi in 1998 expressed anguish over Operation Bluestar and the planned November 1984 anti-Sikh mayhem. According to a UNI report dated January 27, 1998, while indirectly referring to Operation Bluestar during an election rally in Chandigarh, Sonia said, "Jo *kuchh June 6 ko hua, uska mujhe dukh hua* (I am anguished by the events of June 6). On the November anti-Sikh riots, Sonia said she could "understand" the pain of Sikhs as she herself had experienced it, losing her husband Rajiv and mother-in-law Indira Gandhi that way. "There is no use recalling what we have collectively lost. No words can balm that pain. Consolation from others always somehow sounds hollow," she said. However, it was far short of an apology.

Dr. Manmohan Singh, the first Sikh Prime Minister who took over in 2004, apologized in the Parliament on August 11, 2005 saying, "I have no hesitation in apologizing to the Sikh community. I apologize not only to the Sikh community, but to the whole Indian nation because what took place in 1984 is the negation of the concept of nationhood enshrined in our Constitution."

More important than apology, however, is fixing accountability.

The Sikh Religion and the Golden Temple

The Sikh religion was founded by Guru Nanak Dev, born at Nankana Sahib (now in Pakistan) in 1469, as a socio-cultural revolution for the creation of an ideal human being and a non-exploitative society that is casteless, classless and compassionate, thereby inclusive with human dignity as its core. Guru Nanak visualized "an ideal social order for mankind".[8] The founding of Sikhism as a socio-political revolution coincided with the establishment of the Mughal Empire in India.

This is the only religion in the world that is lyrical, humanistic and universal. Guru Nanak created Gurbani in Punjabi (Gurmukhi script) in Indian classical ragas. (Punjabi is also written in the Shahmukhi script and this script is used in Punjab that is part of Pakistan). Exception to lyrical dimension is Japji Sahib at the start of Guru Granth Sahib that is described as "the most aphoristic creation of Guru Nanak Dev in which the whole theology, ethics, sociology, religion and philosophy of Sikhism are encapsulated in thirty-eight stanzas of varying length".[9]

Guru Nanak, who spent his last years at Kartarpur, chose Bhai Lehna as his successor ignoring his sons and renamed him as Angad. The idea of Guru Granth Sahib started with Guru Angad Dev who standardised the Gurmukhi script and prepared the *Pothi* (sacred book) of Guru Nanak's creation in that script. The *Pothi* can be described as an early template of Adi Granth.

The writings of the gurus were compiled and edited by Guru Arjan Dev, the fifth Guru, as Adi Granth is based on content and ragas. Adi Granth was accorded the status of a Living Guru, Guru Granth Sahib, by the Tenth Master, Guru Gobind Singh. Adi Granth was first installed in the Golden Temple.

This can be interpreted as the religion that worships knowledge. Democratic ethos is inbuilt in Sikhism, at least at the doctrinal level and is exemplified by the institution of Panj Piaras (Five Beloved Ones) started by Guru Gobind Singh when he created the Khalsa by baptising the Sikhs.

Yet another characteristic unique to this religion is the concept of saint-soldier that underlies the creation of ideal human beings and ideal society in which the exclusive and independent Sikh religio-political identity is rooted. The saint-soldier concept is the synergy of religion and politics.

The revolutionary pro-people dimension of the new religion put it in direct confrontation with the established socio-religious-political order that was exploitative and oppressive. Amritsar subsequently developed as the main centre of this religion.

Guru Nanak Dev spent his last more than 17 years at Kartarpur where he anointed Guru Angad Dev as his successor. Kartarpur did not develop as the Sikh centre. The two sons of Guru Nanak resisted Guru Angad as the successor and hence he shifted to Khadoor Sahib. It may be mentioned that Bhai Lehna had moved to Khadoor Sahib from Harike earlier. Goindwal near Khadoor Sahib emerged as the next centre during the time of Guru Amar Das who succeeded Guru Angad. Work on Goindwal Sahib had started during the later part of Guru Angad's life. It is pertinent to mention that the Guruship was not dynastic earlier.

Finally, Amritsar was conceived as the centre of the Sikh religion. The site was selected on the advice of Guru Amar Das that was originally known as Chak Guru or Ramdaspur.[10] The same account is available in some other works.[11] The construction of Amritsar was started by his successor Guru Ram Das.[12] It was the Fifth Master Guru Arjan Dev who conceptualized and constructed Harmandar Sahib (Golden Temple), also known as Darbar Sahib, amidst the *sarovar* (sacred pool) as the main shrine of this Faith. The construction was completed in 1604.

> Harmandar being a symbol of spiritual and ideological formation has always been a hub of Sikh activities. As a concept in the abstract, it had been conceived even by earlier Gurus, Guru Amar Das and Guru Ram Das. But it blossoming into a full-fledged concept as also its objectification in architectural form took place under Guru Arjan Dev's creative genius. It has always been cynosure of the Sikhs and all those who sought welfare of the whole mankind. Whether it was the process of community formation on basis of equality, dignity, love for all, non-exploitation and non-discrimination, freedom of worship and conscience, honest earning, or of comprehending spiritual truth, or purging humankind of evils, or of galvanising right thinking people into a dynamic force, its role has always been pre-eminent...It embodies as well as reflects Guru Nanak's vision in all its aspects.[13]

The shrine over the years emerged as a symbol of the Sikh identity and ideology. It became an honour to die for the Golden Temple going by the Sikh struggles. It was this historical inspiration that motivated Sant Jarnail Singh Bhindranwale and his associates to sacrifice their lives rather than escape when the Indian army launched a fierce attack in June 1984.

One important dimension of this new city developed by the Gurus was that it was tax free. "Verily, an atmosphere akin to the kingdom of God had come to prevail at Ramdaspur."[14]

It was Guru Arjan Dev who conceived the Golden Temple, whose architecture reflects the essence of the Sikh doctrine. Adi Granth was installed in the Golden Temple on August 1, 1604 and Baba Budha was appointed the first priest (Granthi).

There is an interesting dimension to the installation of Adi Granth in the Golden Temple as "besides serving as a source of divine wisdom, it conferred on the Sikhs a distinct identity on their own." There was reaction. "The orthodox elements within the Hindu community were really upset over the emergence of the definitive edition of the Sikh sacred text...Some of the Muslims were suspicious of the content of the Sikh scripture."[15] The Sikh religio-political dynamics was now entering a new phase. Guru Arjan Dev was subsequently arrested and tortured to death in Lahore by the then Mughal government. The martyrdom of Guru Arjan Dev proved to be the catalyst in militarization of the Sikhs.

The Akal Takht was visualized by the Sixth Master Guru Hargobind as a symbol of the temporal (state) power in front of the Golden Temple. It was constructed as a platform at a certain angle to the Golden Temple by his two main disciples—Baba Buddha and Bhai Gurdas—-with their own hands to translate the vision of the Guru under his direct supervision. No one else was allowed to join in its construction. The Guru used to hold his court on this 'Throne of the Timeless.' "Akal Takht became the seat of the supreme temporal authority of the Sikhs. It symbolised the Sikh sovereignty."[16] The militarization of the Sikhs started with the creation of Akal Takht.[17]

The Sikhs, despite being the third demographic group in size, established their rule at one stage in this region that came to be known as the 'Country of the Sikhs' going by the maps of 'Hindoostan' drawn by British geographer James Rennell after the British took over this land.

Shaping of the Sikh Psyche

An important dimension of the Sikh religious formation is the collective psyche shaped by fierce struggles for survival. Guru Nanak was jailed by Mughal Emperor Babur. Fifth Sikh Master Guru Arjan Dev was martyred in June 1606 after five days of inhuman torture by the rulers in Lahore, now in Pakistan. Guru Tegh Bahadur, the Ninth Guru, was martyred for human rights while the two youngest sons of Guru Gobind Singh, the Tenth Guru, were bricked alive.

The concept of martyrdom is intrinsic to the Sikh religio-political praxis. Sikhs do not look back but they keep their history of struggle alive and remember their martyrs every day in the daily Ardas.[18]

The Sikhs as a community are characterized by the historical tendency of not looking back but at the same time, not sparing the perpetrators of oppression and taking revenge is part of their collective psyche. The attack on the Golden Temple complex has always been avenged. This complex has been destroyed and rebuilt virtually within no time. The history of the Sikhs has been turbulent, especially during the first almost 300 years. It was a struggle for survival amidst extreme repression during which the state announced bounty on the heads of even ordinary Sikhs. The Golden Temple was levelled twice by Afghan invaders in 1759 and again in 1764 but rebuilt by the Sikhs within no time. They retreated to jungles and the desert of Rajasthan to escape persecution, only to strike back. This region is characterized by frequent armed struggles in history. This confrontation between the Sikhs and the Mughals was brutal and bloody but the Sikhs survived.

The assessment of the Sikhs by the British rulers of India is relevant here. The British rulers had rightly assessed that the political discourse of Punjab was different from the rest of India. "Nowhere is the communal feeling potentially so dangerous and so complicated as in Punjab. It is dangerous because of Punjab's hot-headed and virile people and complicated because there is a third and not less obstinate party, the Sikhs, who were more closely knit together than either Hindus or the Muslims, fiercer too and prouder and more dynamic, they never forget that it was from them we conquered the Punjab," wrote Sir Malcolm Darling in his book *At Freedom's Door*.[19]

Punjab as Melting Pot of Civilizations

The Sikhs as a religious community might be about 500 years old but this region has been the cradle of ancient civilization and melting pot of several cultures including Greek, Turkic, Mongol and those from Central Asia due to its strategic location. The Indus Valley Civilization blossomed in this region. The region stretched from Delhi to Peshawar (now in Pakistan) at one time.[20] The Mughals were the last of these tribes to rule over this region followed by the Sikhs and then the British during the last about 1,000 years. This biggest plain in the world was also the most fertile with six rivers flowing through it.

The name Punjab is traced to the writings of Ibn Batūtā who visited the region in the 14th century. This term finds mention again in *Tarikh-e-Sher Shah Suri* dating back to 1580. Abul Fazal also referred to this region as Punjab in *Ain-i-Akbari*. Its origin, however, is in Persian that literally means land of five rivers and used by Turkic invaders. In the ancient period, the name used is Pancha-Nada. Sapta Sindhu too finds mention in ancient texts.

The Separatist Sikh Struggle

This recent struggle was sparked as a religious conflict that turned political but phased out as a law and order problem.

One of the striking aspects of this militant struggle is that its dynamics has been deeply rooted in the political discourse associated with the Shiromani Akali Dal over the years. The demand for Khalistan and political violence were new dimensions associated with this discourse. The issues and concerns that constitute the foundation of the militant struggle have been raised by the Shiromani Gurdwara Parbandhak Committee (SGPC) and Akali Dal from time to time. These issues include the separate and exclusive Sikh identity, autonomous region for the Sikhs, plebiscite and self-determined status. Both the SGPC and the Akali Dal at one stage joined the radicals in raising the demand for Khalistan.

The demand for self-determined status has been raised at different times by the two Akali stalwarts from the grassroots—Master Tara Singh and Gurcharan Singh Tohra. Both these leaders remained untouched by power and pelf. Militant leader Sant Jarnail Singh Bhindranwale who made a violent political intervention in the Sikh religio-political discourse and had a similar spartan lifestyle did not introduce any fresh agenda but inherited that of the Akali Dal. His contribution was phrasing the religio-political discourse in the militant idiom. All the Akali Dal agitations launched from the Golden Temple complex were peaceful but it was Sant Bhindranwale whose armed associates fortified this complex in recent times.

One of the very striking dimension is that the religio-political dynamics in this region during the last about 300 years has been dominated by the Sikh religio-political discourse despite the community being the third demographic component of Punjab, after Muslims and Hindus till 1947. The truncated Indian Punjab turned into a Sikh majority state for the first time in history after its second division in 1966. The Sikhs with an exclusive and separate identity are the most dominant second principal minority at the national level. The community over the years has proliferated as a global community capturing prominent geo-political spaces in countries like Canada, USA, Australia and England. The Hindus, the national majority, are in a minority in Punjab. It is this demographic characteristic that distinguishes the unique political dynamics of this border state from all the other regions in India.

Maharaja Ranjit Singh proclaimed the Khalsa Raj and it was mainly during this period that most of the Hindu families had one member who embraced Sikhism. He was proclaimed as the Maharaja on April 12, 1801 at the young age of 21 with Lahore as the capital.

Changing Dynamics After 1947

The present turbulence in Punjab rooted in the events of 1978 has been shaped by the religio-political dynamics of the Sikhs that goes back to the pre-partition period. It is the Sikh-Hindu dynamics that has defined the political context of Punjab's religio-political-cultural narrative since 1947. The boundaries of this dynamics continue to be redefined. The Akali Dal has experimented with blurring the politico-cultural boundaries dictated by the political dynamics of the times twice since 1966 by raising the slogan of Punjabiat. This has followed the moves to sharpen the boundaries by pressing for exclusive political space for the Sikhs articulated in the demand for Sikhstan and the Anandpur Sahib Resolution.

It was in 1969 that the Akali Dal raised the slogan of Punjabiat in its election manifesto for the first time. This was the fallout of the rejection of the Sikhstan agenda on which the Akali Dal had contested the 1967 assembly elections. The party opted for Punjabiat once again at its 75th anniversary conference at Moga in February 1996 after the Akali Dal had repeatedly supported the demand for a Sikh homeland during the militant struggle.

One of the important factors that has played an active role in constructing the religio-political dynamics in Punjab is globalization. The resurgence of radical Sikh political dynamics is now witnessed in the countries where the Sikhs are settled in sizeable numbers.

The fight for political space for which the Sikh struggle commenced following the 1940 Pakistan Resolution intensified under the changing political scene after 1947 as the majority-minority syndrome started dominating the political landscape and further sharpened after 1966.

The partition uprooted lakhs of people and as the Sikhs started demanding their own religio-political space reminding the Congress of the assurances given to them before 1947, the Hindus perceived these issues to be pushing this region towards another partition. All the three communities (Sikhs, Muslims and Hindus) in Punjab had paid too heavy a price for freedom due to the partition of Punjab. More than one million people perished in Punjab during partition. Every issue raised by the Akali Dal was viewed through the prism of suspicion and distrust by the Hindu leaders owing to the spectre of yet another partition.

The struggle by the Akalis for political space resulted in the geographical boundaries being recast again in 1966, turning Punjab to be demographically Sikh dominated for the first time in history. Both the communities played the politics of victimhood during these agitations.

A notable aspect of the armed struggle in Punjab is that it did not remain localized unlike other militant conflicts including those of Kashmiris or the Nagas and the Mizos but its tremors were felt not just across India but also overseas.

The assassination of Indira Gandhi could have marked closure of Operation Bluestar but the planned carnage of the Sikhs by the Congress in Delhi and some other places,which was triggered within hours, sparked what can be termed as Phase II of the militant struggle.

It was during Phase II that Canada was hit by Sikh radicalism when Air India Flight 182 (Emperor Kanishka) operating on the Toronto-Montreal-London-Delhi route exploded mid-air near the Irish coast over the Atlantic Ocean on June 23, 1985 killing 329 people. A bomb exploded in yet another plane the same day at the Narita Airport in Japan. The second flight was Canadian Pacific Airlines 301 from Vancouver to Tokyo that was to connect to Air India Flight 301 to Bangkok. All the suspects who happened to be Sikhs were subsequently acquitted by a Canadian court in the absence of concrete evidence. These two actions globalised the Sikh militant struggle. The first action associated with this struggle that had caught global attention was hijacking of Indian Airlines planes by young Sikhs from Dal Khalsa to Lahore on September 29, 1981.

The Indian Punjab continues to cast its shadow over Canadian political discourse as evident from the motion adopted by the Ontario Assembly in Canada describing the November 1984 anti-Sikh mayhem in Delhi following the assassination of Indira Gandhi as genocide. The motion was moved by Brampton-Springdale, Member of Provincial Parliament Harinder Malhi supported by Vick Dhillon and Harinder

Takhar from the Liberal Party that was passed after a daylong debate on April 6, 2017 by a majority of 35 members with five members opposing it.[21]

The Sikh radical discourse dominated the Indian media during the weeklong visit of Canadian Prime Minister Justin Trudeau to India including Amritsar beginning on January 19, 2018. The Indian media painted him as a supporter of the Sikh secessionism that he denied subsequently. His visit was cold shouldered by New Delhi but in the process, the Sikh radical discourse hit the media at the global level.

Another country where this issue has surfaced from time to time is the United Kingdom and one of its manifestations was in the Labour Party manifesto for the June, 2017 parliamentary elections. "The Labour Party has committed to an independent inquiry into the role of Britain in Operation Bluestar should it be elected on June 8. This commitment is briefly referenced in the manifesto's section on diplomacy."[22] Earlier, the Labour Party had called on Prime Minister Theresa May to "come clean" on the role played by Britain in Operation Bluestar before her three-day visit to India in November 2016.[23]

Yet another expression of this support for the Sikh radicals was the decision taken by several gurdwaras in USA, Canada, the UK and Australia in January 2018 to block any activity of the Indian officials in these shrines.

It was Sant Bhindranwale who commanded the militant struggle in the 1980s and confronted the Indian Army during Operation Bluestar. He emerged as the embodiment of this struggle as no one could question his commitment to the cause, although one might differ with his strategy and tactics for the achievement of what can be termed as his political objective that he never defined in unequivocal and un-ambivalent terms. One of the important aspects of that bitter confrontation is the permanent scars that this, perhaps the most botched up, Indian army operation left on the collective Sikh consciousness, including among the section that never supported this struggle.

Prime Minister Indira Gandhi fell victim to the revenge psyche as she was gunned down by her two Sikh security guards to avenge the army attack on the morning of October 31, 1984 at her residence, triggering a planned massacre of the Sikhs in Delhi and several other cities in the country engineered by the Congress leaders. Her assassins were not associated with any political formation.

Operation Bluestar and the November 1984 massacre of the Sikhs continue to make headlines, especially during elections. This narrative revives bitter memories and reopens the festering wounds every time the Akalis try to exploit Sikh sentiments for political ends on these sensitive issues.

There is no organized movement but the revenge psyche continues to operate even at the social level.

Lieutenant General Kuldip Singh Brar, who had commanded the troops that attacked the Darbar Sahib complex as Major General, survived a murderous assault by three Sikh activists on the streets of London years later on September 30, 2012.

Lt General Ranjit Singh Dyal, the hero of the famous Haji Pir Pass battle of 1965 war with Pakistan, was then Chief of Staff at the Western Command that had executed Operation Bluestar. Unlike Lt Gen Brar, Lt Gen Dyal maintained Sikh symbols. He was appointed Security Advisor to the Punjab Governor as the army took over the troubled state on June 2, 1984. After his retirement, he shifted to Panchkula in Haryana on the outskirts of Chandigarh. His first death anniversary falling on December 30, 2012, hit the headlines as it was not allowed to be observed by the gurdwara management in the shrine. The *Hindustan Times* quoted his widow Barinder Kaur Dyal who said, "When I went to the gurdwara to ask them to conduct the rituals, they (management) said he should have resigned over Bluestar. I was shocked, I said he had just followed orders".[24]

Interestingly, Lt Gen Dyal too was all praise for the exemplary courage and the fighting spirit exhibited by the militants and he expressed his opinion at an informal evening get together at Amritsar after the army operation on June 8, 1984. This incident has been recalled by Narpinder Singh Rattan, the IAS officer who was on official duty in his capacity as the officiating Commissioner, Jalandhar Division. He had reached Amritsar during the day. Some other Punjab government officers too were present. Earlier, it was Chandigarh based Western Army commander Lt Gen K. Sundarji, who, at a news conference on June 6 at Chandigarh, stated that he wished he had 1,000 such committed warriors. Both the army officers entrusted with this sensitive operation were credited with the same view. Lt Gen Dyal had made the comments in the presence of Lt Gen Brar who counselled his superior against airing his views even at that exclusive gathering.

The attack on Lt Gen Brar was planned by a small Sikh group in London. The Panchkula gurdwara management at its own had refused permission to organize religious service in the memory of Lt Gen Dyal. The ghastly army action has become part of the collective

Sikh psyche. The martyrs' memorial to Operation Bluestar in the Darbar Sahib complex would continue to perpetuate the memories of the army assault for the coming generations.

Counter-Narrative on Operation Bluestar

Operation Bluestar hit the headlines in the run up to the 2014 Lok Sabha elections for yet another reason as former Congress Chief Minister of Punjab Captain Amarinder Singh launched a frontal attack on Parkash Singh Badal alleging his complicity in the army attack, asking him to reveal as to what had transpired at his secret meeting on March 28, 1984 with the then Union Home Minister P.V. Narasimha Rao at a guest house in New Delhi. Badal flatly denied the nine secret meetings the Akali leaders had with the Centre despite the fact that Akali stalwart and then SGPC President Gurcharan Singh Tohra had been on record about the last such meeting which was held on May 26, 1984.[25] The white paper released by the SGPC in 1996 also mentions 26 rounds of talks between the Akalis and the government which include these nine secret meetings.

In the run up to the 2014 Lok Sabha elections, Amarinder produced documents to prove the involvement of the Bharatiya Janata Party (BJP) and Rashtriya Swayamsewak Sangh leaders also in the November 1984 killing of the Sikhs.

The timing of the army action was also a mystery as it coincided with the anniversary of martyrdom of the Fifth Sikh Master Guru Arjan Dev on June 3 when thousands of devotees visited the shrine. Lt Gen Brar, years later, attributed the urgency of the action to the fear of announcement of Khalistan by Sant Bhindranwale. But till then, the maverick leader had never even mentioned Khalistan as demand and his speeches remained confined to the implementation of the Anandpur Sahib Resolution which had been adopted by the Akali Dal way back in 1973.

Historical Tendency to Move On

Sikhs have the historical tendency to move forward but the lingering perception of denial of justice must end. It is said that those who aspire to shape the future live in the present rather than the past. It is a historical fact that they ruled this region. It is a fast changing situation and the future has to be shaped accordingly rather than living under the shadow of the past glory and grief. Most of the issues that fuelled the militant struggle might not be relevant today but bitter memories and wounds of that struggle can not just be wished away. Earlier in history, such memories have become part of the Sikh folklore and collective consciousness.

Radical Discourse Continues to Resurface

The Sikhs have always moved on. However, Sikh radical politics continues to be part of the broader political discourse. Flashes of militant psyche continue to surface periodically.

Large-scale protests erupted once again in Punjab in 2012 when the court ordered the hanging of Balwant Singh Rajoana, accused in the 1995 assassination of Chief Minister Beant Singh. The pressure that was built over the issue forced even Chief Minister Parkash Singh Badal to take a stand in the assembly against the verdict. The statement he read out in the assembly on March 26, 2012, stated, "I deem it mandatory on my part to bring all the facts relating to the most important issue of peace and communal harmony before the people of Punjab through the respectable members in this august house. Before I dwell on the psychological, social and political aspects of this issue, I want to share the details and legal facts related to the case of Bhai Balwant Singh Rajoana. The Supreme Court of India has in several judgements extended the benefit of lesser sentence to the other co-accused although they had not filed an appeal. It is necessary to await the outcome of the matter in the Supreme Court of India before executing the death warrant of Balwant Singh Rajoana. In view of the old cases and rules, it is amply clear that Bhai Balwant Singh Rajoana could also get the same relief to be given to the other accused in this case, whether he has not filed any appeal." The appeal on his behalf was later filed by the SGPC.

Badal's appeal had some deeper ramifications. He was making the appeal from the same bench which Beant Singh used to occupy as the chief minister in the assembly. The Bharatiya Janata Party that respects Beant Singh as a martyr did not make any intervention. The party was in alliance with the Akali Dal. Beant Singh was perceived to be a ruthless oppressor by the Sikhs. Beant Singh was a martyr for the Congress, the BJP and the Hindus and traitor of the Panth for the Akali Dal and the Sikhs in general. Rajoana earlier was conferred the honour of "Zinda Shaheed" (living martyr) by the Akal Takht on March 23, 2012. Punjab turned saffron on March 28, 2012, the like of which used to be seen during militancy, when protests were held across the state against the order on Rajoana. It is this latent psyche in the Sikh community which has the potential to explode on issues associated with this struggle.

It is the role of the Akali Dal, in this case the ruling party at that time, that was very significant as the history was repeating itself. "Badal referred to Balwant Singh Rajoana as "Bhai" Balwant Singh Rajoana. It is perhaps for the first time that a convicted militant has been referred to as "Bhai" by a sitting chief minister in the Vidhan Sabha in recent years. Referring to them by this honorific during militancy was not uncommon. However, doing so on the floor of the house amounts to providing legitimacy to the militant movement."[26] This has to be seen in the context of the Shiromani Akali Dal providing legitimacy to political violence in its August 1980 working committee resolution which hailed the assassination of Nirankari chief Baba Gurbachan Singh. The Akali Dal has invariably been sailing in two boats.

Jagdish Tytler was appointed general secretary in-charge of the Congress in Punjab by Sonia Gandhi on June 12, 2016 but he had to beat a hasty retreat amidst strong reaction in the state.

Akali Dal was never directly part of the militant struggle but the political space for the militant psyche to operate had been created by the politics of this party which had been agitating over the years voicing concerns of the Sikhs, both before and after the partition of India, thereby reinforcing the perception of being discriminated against and victimized. In the post-partition period, the Akali Dal took up the agenda of the recasting of state boundaries on a linguistic basis as was being done in case of other states and it came to be known as the Punjabi Suba (Punjabi-speaking state) agitation that started in 1955 leading to trifurcation of Punjab in 1966, which again created certain problems that continue to remain unresolved till date. These irritants include the transfer of capital city of Chandigarh to Punjab and the river water apportionment dispute with the successor state of Haryana.

Akali Dal demands over the years have ranged from self-determined status for the Sikhs to Sikhstan and to autonomy under Article 370 on the pattern of Jammu and Kashmir during the post-partition period. The party supported the Khalistan demand too at one stage.

At the doctrinal level, the Golden Temple symbolises love, brotherhood and egalitarianism, open to all irrespective of caste and creed, high and low—the values of humanism. Struggle for high human values and human rights are part of Sikh doctrine, not hate. Sikhism is for dignified existence of human beings. It is these values and the doctrine symbolising these values that would define the future of the Sikhs at the global level. Sectarianism and bigotry are anathema to this philosophy.

ENDNOTES

1. December 21, 2018. *The Indian Express.*
2. Beant Singh headed the Congress government that came to power in the February 1992 Assembly elections boycotted by all the main Akali factions. He was killed by human bomb Dilawar Singh. The action was planned by Babbar Khalsa International. Dilawar Singh and his associate Balwant Singh Rajoana, both from Punjab police, who executed it, were not from Babbar Khalsa. This militant organization mainly extended logistical support for which Jagtar Singh Hawara and Jagtar Singh Tara were roped in.
3. Ajit Singh Sarhadi. (1970). *Punjabi Suba,* Delhi: UC Kapur & Sons, p. 331.
4. ShiromaniAkali Dal, the party articulating Sikh concerns, had demanded linguistic re-organization of Punjab on the pattern of other states after partition in 1947and this struggle was known as the Punjabi Suba agitation. The States Re-organization Commission had rejected this demand in 1953 and the first agitation on this issue was started in 1955 when even the 'Punjabi Suba Zindabad' slogan was banned by the Punjab government. This was the first agitation launched by the Akali Dal after partition from the Golden Temple complex. Punjab was finally re-organized on November 1, 1966 to become the Sikh majority state.
5. The first resolution to raise this memorial was adopted by the Akali Dal at its meeting at Amritsar on October 7, 1984. This memorial was inaugurated on April 27, 2013. This is the third memorial in this shrine complex, the earlier two being dedicated to Baba Deep Singh and Baba Gurbax Singh. The Golden Temple complex is managed by the Shiromani Gurdwara Parbandhak Committee that is a statutory body under the Sikh Gurdwara Act, 1925.
6. Jagtar Singh. (2011). *Khalistan Struggle: A Non-movement*. Delhi: Aakar Books, p. 39.
7. List of Akali Dal demands submitted to the government in October, 1981:Unconditional release of Sant Jarnail Singh Bhindranwale and judicial inquiry with regard to police action in connection with Delhi rally (September 7), Chowk Mehta and Chando Kalan, removal of alleged government high handedness in the management of Delhi gurdwaras, holding of democratic elections after removal of forcible control by "one of the government stooges, restoration of the SGPC's right to send pilgrim parties to Pakistan, permission to Sikhs travelling by air to wear kirpan on domestic and international flights, All India Gurdwara Act, grant of holy city status to Amritsar, installation of "Harimandir Radio" at Golden Temple, Amritsar to relay kirtan, renaming Flying Mail as Harimandir Sahib Express, autonomy on the basis of Anandpur Sahib resolution, merger of Punjabi-speaking areas and Chandigarh into Punjab, handing

over of dams and headworks in the state to Punjab and re-apportionment of river waters as per national and international rules, second language status to Punjabi language in Haryana, Delhi, Himachal Pradesh and Rajasthan, end to uprooting of Punjabi farmers from the Terai area of Uttar Pradesh, setting up of a dry port at Amritsar, licence for starting a new bank in place of the Punjab and Sind Bank under Sikh control and fixing of remunerative prices for agricultural produce by linking to the industrial production index.

8. Kirpal Singh and Kharak Singh. (2013). *History of the Sikhs and Their Religion*, Vol. 1. Amritsar: SGPC, p. 57.
9. Ibid., p. 55-56.
10. Ibid., p. 133.
11. Giani Kirpal Singh. (2003). *Sri Harmandar Sahib Da Sunahiri Itihas*, Vol. 1. Amritsar: SGPC, p. 15.
12. *Gazetteer of the Amritsar District, 1883-84* (Reprint 2003). Lahore: Sang-e-Meel Publications.
13. Kirpal Singh and Kharak Singh. (2013). *History of the Sikhs and Their Religion*, Vol. 1. Amritsar: SGPC, pp. 224-25.
14. Ibid., p. 153.
15. Ibid., p. 154.
16. Ibid., p. 171.
17. The Akal Takht was raised by the Sixth Guru, Guru Hargobind, as a symbol of resistance against the state after the Guru Arjan Dev, the Fifth Guru, attained martyrdom following extreme torture by the Lahore Darbar. It was conceptualised as a state within the state, the seat of Sikh temporal power in front of the Golden Temple. At the doctrinal level, this temporal seat was created as subservient to the spiritual seat. The synergy of religion and politics in Sikh doctrine is defined by this unique correlation. Akal Takht is not just another gurdwara but a symbol of state power. Although set up as a symbol of state power, the Akal Takht evolved as a democratic platform for collective decision-making relating to religio-political affairs that subsequently acquired the reputation of being the institution for prayer and politics. The importance of this institution can be assessed from the fact that no other person was allowed to join its construction except Baba Buddha and Bhai Gurdas. The Sikh leaders used to meet here to resolve their issues. This system of collective democracy became part of history after Maharaja Ranjit Singh took over. The Maharaja was summoned at this institution to punish him for his irreligious lifestyle. It was this institution in the Golden Temple complex that was stormed by the Indian army in June 1984 that is known as Operation Bluestar. The code of conduct practised here is different from that at the Golden Temple as it is temporal seat. All the Akali struggles ever since the party came into existence were launched from here. The office of the Akali Dal used to be in the Golden Temple complex till 2008.

18. The concept of martyrdom captures the Sikh mind from an early age as their sacrifices are part of the daily Ardas. These sacrifices have also been kept alive through paintings. The focus in ballads (*Vaars*) is on Sikh struggle and martyrdom. This medium of ballad singing motivates the Sikhs to make any sacrifice and embrace martyrdom. And above all, Gurbani itself prepares a Sikh for such a role. One has to listen to the Gurbani recital in the morning from the Golden Temple on days like the martyrdom anniversary of Guru Arjan Dev, Guru Tegh Bahadur and the two youngest sons of Guru Gobind Singh who were bricked alive and the like to which has now been added the June 6—Operation Bluestar.
19. Kirpal Singh. (2006). *Partition of Punjab– 1947*, New Delhi: National Book Shop. p. x.
20. Delhi was transferred to the Punjab region after the Sepoy Mutiny in 1857 till shifting of capital from Calcutta, now Kolkata. Punjab comprised five administrative divisions including Delhi, Jalandhar, Lahore, Multan and Rawalpindi and several princely states
21. April 8, 2017. *The Tribune.*
22. May 17, 2017. *The Hindu.*
23. November 6, 2016. *The Times of India.*
24. January 21, 2013. *The Hindustan Times.*
25. Jagtar Singh. (2011). *Khalistan Struggle—A Non-movement*, Delhi: Aakar Books, Delhi, pp. 168-69.
26. Jagtar Singh. (April 10, 2012). *The Hindustan Times.*

2

Sikh Identity, Self-Determination and Khalistan

The perception persists that the history ditched the Sikhs, the people who ruled over the land from river Satluj to Khyber Pass till less than a hundred years ago, at the time of the partition in India. The Sikh leadership of that time is blamed for missing the opportunity to restore the lost glory of the valiant community. The chronicle of negotiations at various levels during that period, however, indicates that the Sikh leadership was left with little choice. The issue needs to be settled in the context of the record available as the Sikhs having missed on the opportunity to decide their destiny in 1947 continues to be part of the community's political narrative.

That missed opportunity is the interpretation of the offer made to the Sikhs in 1946 by the Cabinet Mission deputed by the British government to work out modalities for the transfer of power to the Indians.

The Muslim League had already adopted its Pakistan Resolution and the Sikhs were recognised as the third party to the political narrative in the country. The Sikhs were the first to oppose the Pakistan Resolution. The Shiromani Gurdwara Parbandhak Committee and Shiromani Akali Dal came out with the Sikh framework. The only difference is that the Sikh articulation was in reaction to the Muslim League resolution on Pakistan and not an own initiative per se. This point is vital in the entire narrative.

This raucous opposition to the Pakistan demand forced the British rulers to concede space to the Akali Dal to represent the Sikhs as the separate third entity in all negotiations after the Congress, which represented the Hindu concerns, and the Muslim League. This recognition of the Sikhs as the third party to work out a constitutional setup for the freedom of India was evident from the invitation sent out to Master Tara Singh by the Viceroy Lord Wavell for the Shimla Conference in June 1945 as representative of the Sikhs.

Master Tara Singh's opposition to the Muslim League demand was so strong that he went to the extent of taking the stand that, "The Sikhs would demand nothing less than a sovereign Sikh state in the event of Pakistan's demand being conceded".[1] The area that was to be Pakistan was the homeland of the Sikhs. It was in view of his categorical stand that M.A. Jinnah sent feelers to Master Tara Singh through former Amritsar deputy commissioner Penderel Moon and Malik Hardit Singh, a bureaucrat with the Patiala state service.

There are several important resolutions adopted by the Sikh organizations during this period articulating the dominant political thinking.

One such resolution was adopted in February 1946 by a representative gathering of the Sikhs at Lahore in a meeting chaired by Master Tara Singh. It stated: "In order to ensure the free and unfettered growth of the Sikh Panth, the Panth demands the splitting up of the existing province of Punjab, with its unnatural boundaries, so as to constitute a separate autonomous state in those areas of the central, northern, eastern and south-eastern Punjab in which an overwhelming part of the Sikh population is concentrated, and which because of the proprietors in it being mostly Sikhs, and its general character being distinctly Sikh, is also the de facto Sikh homeland—the area, extent, the status and constitutional framework of such a state being left to be settled by negotiations between accredited representatives of the Sikh Panth and other interested parties, such as the British government, the Hindus and the Muslims, further resolving that the above demand is the unconditional, absolute and minimum demand and political objective of the Sikh Panth as a whole.

The Panth visualizes, but this proposed state will be democratic in constitution and will have a socialistic economic structure, with full protection of the culture and rights of the minorities".[2]

The resolution adopted at the general house of the Shiromani Gurdwara Parbandhak Committee on March 9, 1946 stated: "(a) The Shiromani Gurdwara Parbandhak Committee declares that the Sikhs are a separate nation. (b) This meeting is of the opinion that the Sikh state is vital for the maintenance of Sikh shrines, preservation of Sikh traditions and culture, protection of dignity and freedom of the Sikhs and their advancement in future. Therefore, this meeting appeals to the Sikh masses to do everything possible for its creation".[3]

This resolution was reinforced by the Akali Dal at its meeting on March 22, 1946. The resolution stated:

Whereas the Sikhs being attached to the Punjab by intimate bonds of

> holy shrines, property, language tradition and history claim it as their homeland and holy land which the British took as 'trust' from the last Sikh ruler during his minority and whereas the entity of the Sikhs is being threatened by the Muslims on account of the persistent demand of Pakistan and on the other hand the danger of absorption by the Hindus, the executive committee of the Shiromani Akali Dal demands the preservation and protection of the religious, cultural, economic and political rights of the Sikh population and their important sacred shrines and historical gurdwaras with provision for the transfer and exchange of population and property.[4]

The British government in 1946 constituted a three-member commission of cabinet members known as the Cabinet Mission to hold talks with the stakeholders in India for the transfer of power. Headed by Sir Pethick Lawrence, Secretary of State for India, the members included Sir Stafford Cripps, President of the Board of Trade and A.V. Alexander, the First Lord of Admiralty. The Mission arrived in India on March 24, 1946.

The Cabinet Mission made three offers to the Sikhs.

> The mission wished particularly to know whether, if it were given the choice, the Sikh community would prefer the transfer of power to a single body, or to more than one body, if power were to be transferred to two bodies, which of them the Sikh community would wish to join, and if such a thing were practicable and could be arranged, would the Sikhs wish to have a separate autonomous state of their own?[5]

It is the third offer that is interpreted as the sovereign Sikh state.

Menon has provided a detailed account regarding the reaction of the Sikh leaders to the offer.

> Master Tara Singh stood for a united India and some sort of coalition government of all communities. The Hindus and Muslims were not united and would remain antagonistic for some time, in that situation then Sikhs in united India would have a degree of bargaining power. If India were divided the Sikhs would come under the majority of one community or the other, in that case, they would prefer a separate independent state with the right to federate either with Hindustan or Pakistan.
>
> Giani Kartar Singh said that the Sikhs would feel unsafe in united India or in Pakistan. They should have a province of their own where they should be in a dominant, or almost dominant, position. In reply to Sir Stafford Cripps, who asked what would be the area of the proposed Sikh state, Giani Kartar Singh suggested that it should be the whole of Jullundur and Lahore divisions. Together with the Hissar, Karnal, Ambala and Simla districts of the Ambala division and the Montgomery and Lyallpur districts.

> Harnam Singh was opposed to the partition of India. Such a step, he said, would be against the wishes of the community. A divided India would be a prey to foreign invasion and there would be no safeguard except in an independent Sikh state. He advocated the increased representation of Sikhs in the proposed constitution making body and pleaded for a separate one for Sikhs if there were to be more than one constitution-making body.
>
> Baldev Singh, who was a minister in the Punjab government at that time, was interviewed separately. He gave a brief description of the manner in which the position of the Sikh community had deteriorated since 1914 and how impossible it would be for it to exist unless it were given special protection. Sir Stafford Cripps asked specifically how 'Khalistan' could be formed, to which Baldev Singh replied that it would be in the Punjab, excluding the Multan and Rawalpindi divisions, with an approximate boundary along the Chenab river. An area comprising the Ambala division, the Jullundur division and the Lahore division was smallest that could be contemplated. But the Sikhs strongly favoured a united India, they considered the division of India unwise because the smaller states on the frontier would be at the mercy of great powers and so be a source of danger to India. In Baldev Singh's view, the best solution was a united India, with safeguards for minorities in the form of weighted communal proportions in the legislatures. Questioned as to the nature of safeguards, which he would regard as adequate, Baldev Singh said in some of the British Indian provinces, e.g. Bombay, weightage was given to Muslims as against the Hindus. If, in the Punjab legislature, the Muslims were content to have 45 per cent of the seats instead of 51 per cent, and the balance was to be divided between the Hindus and the Sikhs, then Sikh interests would be protected."[6]

The offer for a Sikh homeland had come from the Cabinet Mission but the Sikh leaders' response was not clearly defined despite the fact that the SGPC and the Akali Dal had already unambiguously articulated the demand for the Sikh state. Moreover, there were differences on this issue. At least two of the four Sikh leaders consulted by the Cabinet Mission were from the Akali stream and could have taken the stand in the framework of this resolution. Harnam Singh was a senior advocate. Consensus eluded the Sikh leaders.

The same was not the case with Muslims. Muhammad Ali Jinnah pressed for a sovereign Pakistan on the basis of the Muslim League Resolution of 1940. "Jinnah was entirely immovable in his demand for Pakistan".[7]

The Cabinet Mission after interaction with the Congress and the Muslim League released the draft of proposals on May 16, 1946.

The proposal envisaged the Union of India, embracing both British India and the states dealing with foreign affairs, defence, and communications with powers to raise finances. The Union was to have an executive and a legislature constituted from British India and states' representatives. Any question raising a major communal issue in the legislature will require for decision, a majority of the representatives present and voting of each of the two major communities, as well as a majority of the members present for voting.

The proposal recognised three main communities for constituting this set up that included General, Muslims and the Sikhs. An interim government was to be constituted under the arrangement.

It was claimed that the proposal "offered the Muslims the right to direct their own essential interests, their religion, education, culture, and economic and other concerns in their own way and to their own best advantage. To another great community, the Sikhs, they preserved the unity of their homeland—the Punjab—in which they played, and could still play, so important and influential a part".[8]

> The proposals (May 16) can be divided into two parts—short term and long term arrangements. The short term arrangements envisaged the formation of an interim government consisting of all the political parties. It was to have an equal number of the Congress and Muslim League and other minorities like Sikhs, Christians etc. were to be separately represented. According to the long term arrangements, the Constituent Assembly was to be established with the following compulsory groupings for making the constitution of free India:
>
> Group A: Consisting of Madras, Bombay, Uttar Pradesh, Bihar, the Central Provinces and Orissa.
>
> Group B: Consisting of Punjab, the North Western Frontier province, Sindh and British Baluchistan.
>
> Group C: Bengal and Assam.[9]

Master Tara Singh, in a memorandum submitted to the Cabinet Mission, had stressed: "Before the Mission arrives at a decision on the question (constitution making), we would emphasize that the Sikhs have as good a claim for creation of a separate sovereign state as the Muslims for Pakistan and that Mission would not concede the claim for Pakistan without conceding at the same time claim for a separate state made on behalf of the Sikhs".[10]

The proposal offered nothing special to the Sikhs. They phased out of the bargaining narrative at this very stage in 1946 as the Pakistan narrative started dominating the political discourse. Of course, it was at this stage that the Sikh leaders were given assurances by the

Congress from which the party backtracked after partition. However, the offer made by the Congress was a dimension entirely different from negotiating separate religio-political space from the then rulers.

The Sikh organizations at a two-day conclave at Amritsar beginning on June 9, 1946, constituted the Panthic Pratinidhi Board headed by Col. Niranjan Singh Gill comprising 25 members. However, the opportunity had already slipped. He had been amongst the founders of the Indian National Army which Netaji Subhas Chandra Bose later commanded. The board on July 11 gave a call to the Sikhs to boycott elections to the four Sikh seats in the Constituent Assembly. However, this decision was revised later following an intervention from Pandit Nehru. Here was the turning point. Four Congress Sikh and four Akali MLAs filed their nominations to the Constituent Assembly at the last moment. The Congress Sikhs were Partap Singh Kairon, Partap Singh, Babu Bachan Singh and Shiv Singh while Panthic representatives were Baldev Singh, Ujjal Singh, Narottam Singh and Bawa Harkishan Singh.

"An important change came about in the politics among the Sikhs with this complete alignment of Panthic leadership with Congress politics. It was to cease demanding an independent Sikh state".[11]

The Viceroy and the Cabinet Mission issued a statement on June 16, 1946 on the formation of the interim government having 14 members who were mentioned by name. They included six from the Congress, including a member from the Scheduled Caste, from Muslims, one Sikh, one Indian Christian and one Parsi.

"The Sikhs rejected the interim proposals as they had rejected the long-term plan and refused to agree to any Sikh representative joining the Executive Council".[12]

The Congress at this juncture extended assurance to the Sikhs at its working committee meeting on August 10 stating, "The working committee assures the Sikhs that the Congress will give them all possible support in removing their legitimate grievances and in securing adequate safeguards for the protection of their just interests in Punjab".[13]

The Panthic Pratinidhi Board in turn, on August 14, 1946, accepted the May 16 Cabinet Mission Statement although, like Congress and the Muslim League, with reservation. The resolution stated: "After careful consideration, the Board is of the view that the situation calls for an earnest effort by the Sikhs to give the Constituent Assembly method a fair trial to secure for the Sikhs similar safeguards in the

Union and the provincial spheres as are provided for the majority communities in the long-term proposals".[14]

It was decided to join the government paving the way for the induction of Baldev Singh as the defence minister. Negotiations between the Sikh leaders and Jinnah had failed by that time.

The rest is history.

There is an interesting observation made by Master Tara Singh later for the failure of the Sikhs to get their state, besides other factors.

> Another reason for our inability to put pressure behind the demand for a Sikh state was that we were not fully familiar with the post-war international situation. None of us knew that a separate state could be carved out for a minority community by some other means. There was the case of the Jews who had been given a separate state. I learnt of this only in 1949 when I was detained in a jail in Almora. At that time, I also came to know that the Russian paper *Pravda* had also high lighted the fact that there were just two communities in the world which did not have a state of their own even though they possessed all the marks of a distinct community or nation. These were Jews and Sikhs. The Jews got their state but the Sikhs still remained in the wilderness.[15]

It may be mentioned that the Cabinet Mission members were clear on Sikh issues. The discussion on the Sikh issue in both the House of Lords and the House of Commons on July 18, 1946 is important. In that debate, Lord Pethic-Lawrence, the then Secretary of State for India, and Sir Stafford Cripps stated that in the future constitution of Punjab "special means should be devised for giving the Sikhs a strong position in the affairs of the Sikhs".

Origin of Sikhs as a Separate Religious Identity

The Sikh narrative during the last about one hundred years has oscillated between different shades of demand for autonomy and Khalistan. The formation of the Shiromani Gurdwara Parbandhak Committee on November 15, 1920 as articulation of Sikh assertion was the watershed development in the Sikh religio-political affairs in this context. The SGPC set up the Akali Dal as its volunteer corps on December 14, 1920. The SGPC as the first statutory body of the community was a forceful assertion of the Sikh identity at one level.

Guru Nanak started the new religion by rejecting the prevalent religious traditions when he stated, "There is no Hindu and no Musalman". The first reinforcement of the Sikh identity is traced to standardization of the Gurmukhi script in which *Pothis* (sacred book) containing creations of Guru Nanak. "It imparted a distinct identity to the Sikhs as a separate community from both the Hindus and the Sikhs".[16] The creation of the Khalsa by Guru Gobind Singh in 1699 at Anandpur Sahib was the last stage in this process.

The Sikh identity assertion at the political level was complete when Maharaja Ranjit Singh founded the Sikh Empire that was known as Sarkar-e-Khalsa. The subsequent Sikh struggles during the British rule witnessed this identity assertion.

The demand for referendum, right to self-determination and Khalistan are rooted in separate and exclusive Sikh identity.

Sikh Identity Assertion Post 1947

The demand for Sikh rights made a forceful entry into the Akali political narrative within no time of the partition of India. The radical political discourse during the post-Operation Bluestar period has been moving between right to self-determination and Khalistan.

The Sikh legislators signed a 13-point demand charter on November 15, 1948 demanding adequate protection for the rights of the community. The main issues taken up included 5 per cent representation in the central cabinet with one cabinet minister and a deputy minister being a Sikh, the office of Governor and Chief Minister in Punjab should alternate between a Hindu and a Sikh, Sikhs should get 50 per cent reservation in the state cabinet with 40 per cent reservation in the government jobs. Gurgaon district and Loharu tehsil should be taken out of the state.

The alternative suggested to these demands was to carve out a new state of Punjab, which should include the districts of Hoshiarpur, Jalandhar, Ludhiana, Ferozepur, Amritsar, Gurdaspur and Ambala. The princely states had not been merged with Punjab by that time. It is this demand for a new Punjab, which was perceived by a section of the Hindu leadership as 'Sikhistan', making the Sikhs suspect at this very stage. The only Sikh member who did not sign it was Partap Singh Kairon who later became the Chief Minister heading a Congress government.[17]

The Sikhs identity assertion found expression in the articulation of the demand for Punjabi Suba (Punjabi linguistic state) that was adopted at a convention in Amritsar on April 9, 1949. It is pertinent to mention here that in accordance with the policy decision, 23 Akali MLAs had earlier joined the Congress on March 18, 1948.

The communal cleavage sharpening the identity narrative had started surfacing immediately after partition that is evident from the statement made in the Assembly by Akali Dal MLA Gurbachan Singh

Bajwa who later became finance minister in the Congress government who said, "Prevalence of communalism in services is having serious repercussions on the public life in the province... If we want to avoid a repetition of the past tragedy, the confidence of the minority communities will have to be won by the majority community...It was the reluctance of the majority community (to win over the confidence of the minority) which has brought about the partition; and I am afraid if the majority community again behaved in this manner, the results would be disastrous. The minority would have to face the situation". SGPC chief Udham Singh Nagoke too, took strong notice of the "communal attitude" of the Hindu officials and demanded separate seniority lists for Hindus and Sikhs.[18]

The observations of Master Tara Singh while addressing the Akali conference in Delhi in 1949 are significant in the context of Sikh identity. He asserted: "If the Sikhs accept the rule of the non-Sikhs and especially in the Hindu Raj, Sikhs will not be able to maintain their self-respect, and therefore, they will be absorbed...my first demand is that the Sikh political entity and Sikhs' respect must be preserved. This is the mother of all demands as they can be answered if we have political power. Preservation of our political power is the root of all our demands and all principles".[19] It was in this background that he raised the demand for autonomy stressing, "Not only do we want an area with a majority of the Sikhs but also complete internal autonomy".

This is the first reference to the demand for identity-centric autonomy made by the Akali Dal post-independence.

Master Tara Singh further elaborated this autonomy as similar to the kind given to Jammu and Kashmir extending the logic that under the given dispenzation, the states had been reduced to merely big district boards.

> While justifying the demand for Punjabi Suba, Master Tara Singh, in an article acknowledged that the Akali Dal had decided that such a state was the best method of maintaining the independent existence of the Sikhs. What he wanted, he said, was a state where the Sikhs would be in a majority so that they could escape from Hindu dominance in the legislature. He reiterated that the aim was to free the Sikhs on a provincial basis... He further mentioned that he would like to secure for the Punjabi Suba the internal autonomy of the kind granted to Kashmir since states had now become merely big district boards.[20]

The articulation of this demand found expression in the Akali Dal manifesto for the 1952 General Elections. The party stated:

> The true test of democracy, in the opinion of the Shiromani Akali Dal, is that the minorities should feel that they are really free and partners in the destiny of their community... the Shiromani Akali Dal is in favour of formation of provinces on a linguistic and cultural basis throughout India, but it holds, it is a question of life and death for the Sikhs for a new Punjab to be created immediately. The Shiromani Akali Dal has reasons to believe that a Punjabi-speaking province may give Sikhs the needful security. It believes in a Punjabi-speaking province as an autonomous unit of India.[21]

Carrying his logic further, Master Tara Singh maintained at the 10th All India Akali Conference at Amritsar on February 11, 1956: "If the Punjabi Suba is formed, not only are our culture and language protected, but also our religion will be ensured proper protection and security". For him, the issue at stake was not just political but the very existence itself of the Sikhs in the backdrop of repeated attacks on their separate and exclusive identity.

Self-Determined Status

The demand for self-determined status rooted in Sikh identity was forcefully raised for the first time at the Hari Singh Nalwa Conference at Ludhiana organized under the banner of the Sikh Central Board on July 4, 1965. The resolution moved by Justice Gurnam Singh, retired Judge of the High Court and then leader of the opposition in the Punjab Vidhan Sabha, and seconded by Giani Bhupinder Singh, the then President of the Master Akali Dal, stated:

> This conference in commemoration of Hari Singh Nalua of historic fame reminds all concerned that the Sikh people are makers of history and are conscious of their political destiny in a free India. This conference recalls that the Sikh people agreed to merge into common Indian nationality on the explicit understanding of being accorded the constitutional status of co-sharers in the Indian sovereignty along with the majority community, which solemn understanding now stands totally repudiated by the present rulers of India. Further, the Sikhs have been systematically reduced to sub-political status in their homeland, and to an insignificant position in their motherland, India. The Sikhs are in a position to establish before an international tribunal, uninfluenced by the present Indian rulers, that the law, judicial process and executive action of the Union of India is consistently and heavily weighted against the Sikhs, and is administered with unbandaged eyes, against the Sikh citizens.
>
> This conference, however, resolves after careful thought, that there is left no alternative for the Sikhs in the interest of self-preservation than to frame their political demand for securing a self-determined political status within the republic of the Union of India.[22]

Then there is the thesis propounded by Master Tara Singh after return from Salogora in Shivalik hills ending his self-imposed exile in July 1965. Accompanied by journalist-cum-historian Khushwant Singh, he articulated the demand at a news conference in Delhi saying, "The Sikhs demand a space under the sun of free India wherein they can breathe the air of freedom". The Anandpur Sahib Resolution of 1973 was rooted in this articulation.

Here are excerpts from his statement:

> When India achieved independence in August, 1947 the Sikhs had been justly recognised and accepted as legitimate inheritors of the sovereignty of India, along with Hindus and Muslims. When the country was partitioned, the Sikhs accepted solemn assurances of the Hindu leaders saying that they would be accorded a free political status in a free India through a Constitution with their acceptance. As power passed into the hands of the majority community, these solemn promises were forgotten and cynically repudiated.
>
> The resurgence of militant Hinduism has since 1947 completely taken control of the scene in free India...The threat which this situation poses assumes most alarming proportions in the case of the Sikhs, for they have their cultural roots and social integration with the Hindus. Precisely on this account, there has been an open conspiracy during the last 18 years to suppress and absorb the Sikhs into the inchoate mass of Hindus. The Sikh people are makers of history, and the community's identity cannot be wiped out in the name of national unity.
>
> The Sikhs demand a space in the sun of free India, wherein they can breathe the air of freedom. In the traditions of Sikhism, and in the teachings of their gurus, there is no room for inter-communal strife or inter-communal discrimination.[23]

Sikhstan on Jammu and Kashmir Status

It was in this background that the Akali Dal contested the 1967 Assembly election on the agenda of Sikhstan.

This manifesto states: "After such bitter experience, the Shiromani Akali Dal has decided to articulate its political aim as the setting up of Sikhstan, which would include the region as specified in Resolution No. I of the 17th All India Akali Conference at Ludhiana which say:

"This 17th All India Conference of the Akali Dal held at Ranjit Nagar, Ludhiana on December 11, 1966 hereby ratifies and adopts Resolution No. 2 passed at the Delhi convention on July 20, 1966."

After going into the miserable plight of the Sikhs in free India, the party has arrived at the conclusion that the Hindu rulers are bent upon heaping indignities upon the Sikhs and weakening them to push them out of the mainstream and it is under this design that the state has been re-organized in such a way to create a truncated Punjab to corner the Sikhs on the pattern of the treatment meted out to the Jews in Europe in the middle ages and the subjugation of coloured races by the whites even now.

Accordingly, the Sikhs resolve to confront such designs and forcefully counter all such heinous attacks on the Panth. Therefore, the Sikhs demand that the following steps be taken immediately so that the Sikhs can live a dignified life as Indian citizens:

The areas which have been deliberately kept out of Punjab like Dalhousie in Gurdaspur district, Chandigarh, Pinjore and Kalka Sadar of Ambala district, Una tehsil of Hoshiarpur district, the area of Nalagarh known as 'Des', Tehsil Sirsa, sub-tehsils of Guhla and Tohana, Ratia block of Hissar district, Shahbad block of Karnal district and Ganganagar district of Rajasthan be merged with Punjab.

"This would pave the way for the creation of Sikh homeland that is Sikhstan under the Indian Constitution."

"This region should be accorded the same status as given to Jammu and Kashmir under the Indian Constitution in 1950."

"Reservation should be made for the Sikhs in Assemblies, courts and police in other states of the country to put an end to the excesses against the Sikhs."

The Batala Resolution

Continuing with this narrative, the Akali Dal under the leadership of Sant Fateh Singh in 1969 came up with the Batala Resolution that advocated autonomy.

The text of the Batala Resolution is as follows:

> This conference of the Shiromani Akali Dal strongly feels that great changes have come in the political field of the country during the last 20 years and, as such, new considerations have cropped up, necessitating reconsideration of the State-Central relationship under the changed conditions. Many non-Congress governments have come in several states of the country, and the Congress party in power has abused the Constitution to the detriment of the non-Congress Governments, and uses its power for its party interest. Therefore, it has become necessary in the light of the experience gained that the Constitution of Bharat should be reconsidered and changes made in the State-Centre relationship to fit in with new conditions. The Shiromani Akali Dal demands that the Constitution of India should be on a correct federal basis and that the states should have greater autonomy. The Shiromani Akali Dal feels

> that the Central Government's interference in the internal affairs of the states, and the obstacles it places in the proper functioning of the state machinery, are detrimental to the unity and the integrity of the country; therefore, whereas this conference demands of the Central Government that necessary changes should be brought in the Constitution, there it also appeals to the State Governments to raise their voice to protect and safeguard their rights so that the country may be able to go smoothly on the federal system and progress by maintaining unity and entity.[24]

However, the diktats of the electoral dynamics pushed the Sikh identity assertion into the background. The problem is not with the Sikh identity per se as the Sikh religion is inclusive. The perception that the Sikh identity created was that of exclusivity. The compulsions of electoral dynamics now dictated the Akali Dal to adopt the agenda of Punjabiat.

The 1969 manifesto of the Akali Dal released on January 1, 1969 started with reference to Punjabi unity stating: "The Shiromani Akali Dal is committed to the unity of Punjabis, strengthening the bonds between different communities and to provide equal opportunities to all Punjabis."

The Anandpur Sahib Resolution 1973

However, out of power, the Akali Dal reverted to the identity narrative and the outcome was the Anandpur Sahib Resolution. The Anandpur Sahib Resolution of 1973 is perceived to be the most radical Akali Dal articulation till Operation Bluestar. What differentiated the Anandpur Sahib Resolution from the Sikhstan demand was thrust on Sikh identity. The Sikhstan articulation called for special status on Jammu and Kashmir for Sikhstan, the region that was to be created after re-organization of Punjab while the Anandpur Sahib Resolution talked of "pre-eminence of the Khalsa" in that region.

It is the political objective as delineated in the Anandpur Sahib Resolution that is significant:

> The political goal of the Panth, without doubt, is enshrined in the commandments of the Tenth Lord, in the pages of the Sikh history and in the very heart of the Khalsa Panth, the ultimate objective of which is the pre-eminence of the Khalsa. The fundamental policy of the Shiromani Akali Dal is to seek realization of this birth right of the Khalsa through creation of a geo-political environment and a political set up.

This radical programme was adopted by the committee, which was headed by not much eminent but moderate leader Surjit Singh Barnala who rose to be the Chief Minister in 1985. The socio- economic agenda that was part of the resolution was like that of any other Left of the Centre progressive party. It was this resolution, which years later, was dubbed as secessionist.

SGPC on Sikh Identity and Self-Determination

Two resolutions on self-determination and identity articulation separated by about 21 years are important. The body that raised this issue in 1979 was the SGPC.

This resolution was moved in May 1979 by Gurcharan Singh Tohra at the general house meeting in which he was again elected as the president following its general election in which the Akali Dal had received a massive mandate. Tohra earned the moniker of "*Panth Da Roshan Dimag* (Intellectual powerhouse of the Sikhs)" over the years.

Here is the articulation on exclusive and separate identity states:

> 2-Ensuring Political Identity of the Sikh nation within Indian unity: The SGPC would provide ideological lead to the Sikh community in its historical crusade for preserving its political identity as a nation—a quest that has been continuously operative in Sikh history in various forms and through various means depending upon the exigencies of the situations. In the context of contemporary realities, this quest has taken the form of our demand for autonomy of the states in a federalized set-up, which is essential and necessary for preserving the being and identity of the nations, nationalities and minorities that constitute the fabric of multi-national Indian society. This is the only way to abiding national unity and integrity of the country.

The issue of self-determined status was raised in introduction to this five-point agenda maintaining, "It was the SGPC that set up the Shiromani Akali Dal as the central body to knit together and command the various Akali 'jathas' that were springing up in the form and spirit of volunteers corps for the emancipation of the Sikh shrines; the Akali Dal in due course emerged as the main political platform of the Sikhs under the guidance of this religious Parliament that has remained in the forefront of all battles and crusades fought by the Sikh community by preserving the sovereign self-identity of Sikhism and securing for itself an honourable self-determined status within India."[25]

Although the parameters of the self-determined status were not specified, there was no ambiguity about the relationship of Sikhs with India as such a region was to be within the country.

Here was the agenda that was to shape the course of Sikh religio-political dynamics.

The demand for self-determined status next was reiterated by the

Akali Dal and SGPC on December 26, 1990 at its Fatehgarh Sahib Conference.

The resolution states:

> This massive gathering of Sikhs unanimously resolves that in view of the continuous injustice, discrimination and undemocratic attitude of the successive central governments towards Sikhs ever since Independence and in the light of this background and in view of the attitude of central leadership, Sikhs should be given the right to self-determination to decide about their future, which is in accordance with the constitutional and international treaties and agreements. The Sikhs will not be satisfied by anything less than this because the successive central governments have been treating the Sikhs in India as second class citizens by enacting black and draconian laws as a result of which Sikhs have lost faith in the Indian governments since Independence.

The resolution to this effect was moved by Tohra and seconded by Parkash Singh Badal to formalize the proposal mooted by then Akali Dal president Simranjit Singh Mann. The demand for self-determination made at this conference differed from the one made by the SGPC in 1979. This right was to be exercised by the Sikhs to decide whether they wanted to live with India or not.

"Mann specified the demand as a separate state, which would act as a buffer between India and Pakistan. The right to self-determination was to be exercised for this purpose. The Sikhs were to act as a balancing force between 'Hindu India' and 'Muslim Pakistan'."[26]

This issue was referred to by Mann in his letter to Prime Minister Chandra Shekhar who had opened channels for talks. It states: "Therefore, the Sikhs have no choice but to safeguard their religion, political and other interests. This is only possible if they invoke the right of self-determination permitted by the international law recognised by India."[27]

Earlier, Mann on April 13, 1990 had talked of plebiscite under the UN supervision to decide whether the "Sikhs wanted to live in this country". He raised this issue at the Baisakhi Conference at Talwandi Sabo.[28]

This was followed up with a letter to US Ambassador to India, William Clarke on August 9, 1990. Mann sought US intervention in this letter on the issue of self-determination. The letter said,

> We have no choice but to press for the right of self-determination for the people of Punjab. United Nations' Universal Declaration on Human Rights, and more specifically, the International Covenant of Civil and Political Rights, which were ratified by the Indian government on March

> 27, 1979 stipulates that all people have the right to self-determination...It is need of the hour to exert diplomatic pressure on India so that it respects all norms of International law. (Quoted from the original).

The Panthic Committee associated with Dr. Sohan Singh, however, hit back in a statement on August 20, 1990 and questioned the demand for self-determination. The statement said, "We are of the firm view that those who rejected the Anandpur Sahib Resolution in favour of right to self-determination are not clear about the difference between the two. They have neither initiated serious discussion on this issue, nor do they deem it necessary".

The Babbar Khalsa too joined with Mann on this issue saying it could not be termed as a political goal, as self-determination was simply a device or a method to determine something.[29]

Khalistan Post-1947

The Sikh homeland slogan for the first time after partition was articulated by some Sikh leaders with an Akali background in the early 1970s in the UK and this issue gained currency after it was taken up by another Sikh leader Dr. Jagjit Singh Chohan. The author of the Sikh homeland was Charan Singh Panchhi, then president of the UK unit of Shiromani Akali Dal based in Birmingham. His group included Giani Bakshish Singh and Sohan Singh Birmingham, Gulwant Singh Sandhu, Swaran Singh, Onkar Singh, Sohan Singh, Avtar Singh Azad, Jaswant Singh Dhadi and Sohan Singh Dhesi. Some of them also later joined Dr. Chohan.

Panchhi argued: Sikhs have to realize that there is no future in India dominated by Hindus. The honour and prestige of the community cannot be maintained without state power. Sooner we realize this challenge, better it will be for us to set our objective of establishing a sovereign Sikh state in the Punjab. We cannot keep ourselves in bondage forever...[30, 31]

There is yet another version, according to which, Davindar Singh Parmar was the first person to raise the Sikh homeland demand at that time. He along with Panchhi set up the Sikh Homeland Front.

However, Dr. Chohan and US based Ganga Singh Dhillon were the first Sikh activists with whom Pakistan established links. Pakistan was the launching pad for Dr. Chohan who never looked back. That was the period of high tension between India and Pakistan.

Dr. Chohan, a popular medical practitioner, was elected to the Punjab Assembly for the first time from Tanda in Hoshiarpur district on the Republican Party of India ticket in 1967 and became Deputy

Speaker of the Assembly when the first ever Akali Dal-led coalition Government took office in Punjab headed by Justice Gurnam Singh (retd). However, as Lachhman Singh Gill replaced Justice Gurnam Singh after the split in the party, Dr. Chohan joined him and was inducted as the Finance Minister. He lost in the 1969 Assembly. He played a major role in former Akali leader Darshan Singh Pheruman's undertaking fast unto death on August 15, 1969 for transfer of Chandigarh to Punjab, who died on October 27 on the 74th day of his fast. Pheruman raised the issue of "Azad Panth-Sikh Homeland" in "Azad Hindustan" in his will.

Dr. Chohan, who later visited USA and Canada, placed a half-page advertisement in *The New York Times* of October 13, 1971 on the Sikh homeland:

> At the time of partition of the Indian subcontinent in 1947 it was agreed that the Sikhs shall have an area in which they will have complete freedom to shape their lives according to their beliefs. On the basis of the assurances received, the Sikhs agreed to throw their lot with India, hoping for the fulfilment of their dream of an independent, sovereign Sikh homeland, the Punjab.

Dr. Chohan and Panchhi were taken to Lahore in 1971 during the Indo-Pak war to use them in the psychological war. This psychological war was related to the Nankana Sahib shrine, the birthplace of Guru Nanak Dev. The Pakistan authorities wanted to give the impression that the Nankana Sahib shrine had been handed over to the Sikhs for management. Pakistan TV telecast the handing over ceremony with Dr. Chohan as the custodian of the shrine. At the same time, he made an appeal to the Sikh soldiers in the Indian Army to rebel against India as Pakistan had done such a big favour to the Sikhs. However, there was nothing like Sikh struggle on the ground in Indian Punjab at that time and his appeal went unnoticed.[32]

Pakistan's intervention in Sikh affairs was the fallout of the 1971 war leading to dismemberment of that country leading to creation of Bangladesh.

In India, however, the Sikh Homeland Akali Dal had already been formed in 1969 with Hargurnad Singh as president and Manmohan Singh as the president of the Chandigarh chapter.

Some young Sikhs in Chandigarh including Manmohan Singh and Harsimran Singh in the early 1970s too raised the Khalistan slogan. These political activists subsequently on August 6, 1978 constituted Dal Khalsa with setting up of Khalistan as the political objective.

Harsimran Singh shared the information that Sikh leaders from UK contacted him around 1972 and they included Giani Bakhshish Singh, Iqbal Singh and Sohan Singh Patara. Bakhshish Singh visited India in 1972 and met Harsimran who was already active along with senior leader Hargurnad Singh.

Khalistan as Conceptualised by Dr. Jagjit Singh Chohan

The National Council of Khalistan that was announced by Balbir Singh Sandhu on behalf of Dr. Jagjit Singh Chohan in the Golden Temple complex on June 16, 1980 provides an outline of Khalistan.

This declaration states that the independent Sikh state would include Punjab and Punjabi-speaking and Sikh-dominated areas of Haryana, Rajasthan and Himachal Pradesh.[33]

Punjabi would be the official language of this independent Sikh state. All the communities would enjoy full religious freedom. Everyone would be free to worship in accordance with their religious beliefs. However, the Sikh religion would be the state religion.

The Khalistan government would be committed to provide full employment. Providing food, clothing, housing, educational and health facilities to everyone would be the responsibility of the government in the independent Sikh state. Child care and looking after the old would also be the responsibility of the Khalistan government. The Sikh state would be committed to the creation of an ideal and welfare state in accordance with the teachings of Guru Nanak and Guru Gobind Singh and this responsibility would be performed firmly and sincerely.

There would be no place for exploitation in such a state. Anti-people forces would be completely eradicated from this state. The Sikh state would follow the principle of dignity of labour and distribution of the fruits of labour and would not encourage unnecessary accumulation of wealth in the hands of the people. There would be no place for unequal distribution of wealth in the Khalsa Raj. The international relationship would be based on humility, peace and truthfulness.

The demand for Khalistan was globalized for the first time with the hijacking of the Indian Airlines plane to Lahore in Pakistan by Dal Khalsa on September 29, 1981 to demand the release of Sant Jarnail Singh Bhindranwale in the Lala Jagat Narain murder case. The banner headline in *The Indian Express* of September 30 stated: "Khalistan men hijack Boeing to Lahore".

Satnam Singh Paonta Sahib and Jaswant Singh Thekedar from the Dal Khalsa had called on Sant Bhindranwale two days prior to his arrest. During this interaction, Sant Bhindranwale said, "The killing of Lala has enraged the Hindus. They have rewarded him in his death with such protests. Now I would see how my community reacts to my arrest". (*Main dekhanga ki meri qaum mera ki mul paondi hai*). These two young Sikhs assured him that he could count on them for action. They said, "You are precious to us and the Qaum. We assure you to take the necessary measures following your arrest".

The five Dal Khalsa people who hijacked the plane on September 29 included Gajinder Singh, Satnam Singh, Tejinderpal Singh, Jasbir Singh and Karan Singh. This was the first major action of the Dal Khalsa and the first hijack associated with the militant Sikh struggle.

This demand for Khalistan emerged as the main agenda of the radicals in the post Operation Bluestar period when armed struggle intensified during phase II. Phase I had ended with storming of the Golden Temple by the army in June 1984.

This dimension of political objectives of the struggle was referred to but discreetly for the first time in phase II in the Sarbat Khalsa Resolution at Akal Takht in January 1986 by the radicals. This reference was in the last para that stated:

> This conclave expresses serious concern over the death sentence awarded to Bhai Satwant Singh, Bhai Balbir Singh and Bhai Kehar Singh and calls upon the Indian rulers to withdraw it. Pakistan government is urged to immediately release all the hijackers, three of whom including Parminder Singh Harfanmaula, Bhai Harminder Singh and Bhai Dalip Singh have been sentenced to death. In case any of them is martyred, they would be regarded as the martyrs of Khalistan.

The Khalistan demand was formally announced on April 29, 1986 from the Golden Temple complex by the five-member Panthic Committee constituted at this Sarbat Khalsa.

The Khalistan Declaration stated:

> The Panth Khalsa, founded by Sahib Sri Guru Gobind Singh on the Baisakhi of 1699, as per Guru's ordained dictum *Raj Karega Khalsa* (the Khalsa shall rule), through the five-member Panthic Committee nominated by the Sarbat Khalsa on January 26, 1986, fulfils the most cherished dream of the Sikhs (by this declaration) of 'Khalistan'.
>
> On this auspicious day, from the Holy Akal Takht Sahib, it is hereby declared before all the nations and governments and notified to them that from today onwards, the Khalsa Panth shall have its own Home, the Khalistan, wherein will ever remain high in the air the flags, towers and posts of the Sikhs and wherein the writ of the Khalsa will run supreme.

The Khalistan narrative formally entered the militant discourse with this declaration.

Khalistan Memorandum to the UN

The demand was taken up by the SGPC and Akali Dal at the global level in 1992 through a memorandum. The 11-page letter was submitted by the Shiromani Akali Dal and the Shiromani Gurdwara Parbandhak Committee to the United Nations' Secretary General Boutrous Boutrous-Ghali during his visit to New Delhi on April 22, 1992 through his representative.

The operative part of this memorandum on Khalistan states:

> The Sikh Nation represented by the Shiromani Akali Dal and the SGPC are convinced that the Indian state is incapable of holding independent elections in the state of Punjab and has recently foisted a quisling regime which could barely get eight per cent votes. In this hour of crisis, the Sikh nation appeals through you to the nations of the world to satisfy the quest and yearnings of the Sikh people by allowing the people's will to manifest in an appropriate manner.
>
> Demilitarization and decolonization of the Punjab is crucial and indispensable to enable the Sikh people to enjoy full freedom to exercise their economic, social and cultural rights. Like all free people of the world, the Sikh Nation, in accordance with the UN Declaration on the granting of independence to colonial countries and people seek an independent and sovereign state to break the shackles of apartheid, slavery, colonialism and a retrograde political system and structure.

This para was inserted by Simranjit Singh Mann towards the end of the draft prepared by his associate, Prof. Jagmohan Singh.

It was signed by Mann, Parkash Singh Badal, Gurcharan Singh Tohra, Sukhbir Singh Khalsa, Inderpal Singh Khalsa, Harcharan Singh (Dilli) and Rajinder Singh Monga.

This significance of this memorandum is that it was for the first time since the partition of India that the demand for Khalistan had been taken up by the Shiromani Gurdwara Parbandhak Committee that is a constitutional body under the Sikh Gurdwara Act, 1925.

The last resolution associated with that phase of struggle that is part of the Sikh identity and Khalistan narrative is the Amritsar Declaration adopted by the Akali factions at Akal Takht on May 1, 1994.

This resolution states:

> The Shiromani Akali Dal reiterates its commitment to work within

> democratic parameters and renew its struggle for the creation of a separate region for the Sikhs where they, as the avant-garde of Punjabi national culture, based on the holy Guru Granth Sahib, can enjoy the glow of freedom. The envisaged region, promised by the Indian National Congress before partition (of India in 1947) but never created, will fulfil not only the aspirations of the Sikh nation and Punjabis, but also help the minorities in it to realize their potential.
>
> At this juncture of history, when the entire South East Asia is in turmoil and Western nations are also looking for a stable value system and new model for reorganizing their cultures, a region based on Sri Guru Granth Sahib's ideas of cosmic harmony, dialogue, poetry and non-exploitative politics free from negative hegemonic power to subordinate, will serve as a centre of light to other cultures.
>
> The Sikh ethos, translated into distinct religious, economic, political and social institutions in this region, apart from incarnating the original consciousness of people, will give them an opportunity, denied in recent past, to reveal their best and make a vital contribution to world culture.
>
> The Shiromani Akali Dal is of the view that Hindustan (India) is a subcontinent of diverse national cultures, each with its heritage and mainstream. The subcontinent needs to be reorganized with a confederal structure so that each culture could flower according to its genius and add a unique fragrance to the garden of world cultures. If such a confederal re-organization is not accepted by the Hindustani (Indian) rulers (Government of India), the Shiromani Akali Dal will have no other option than to demand and struggle for an independent and sovereign Sikh state.

It was signed by Capt. Amarinder Singh, Jagdev Singh Talwandi, Simranjit Singh Mann, Col. Jasmer Singh Bala, Bhai Manjit Singh and Surjit Singh Barnala.

Drafted by Dr. Gurbhagat Singh of Punjabi University, Patiala, the initiative for this resolution had come from Tohra.

Sikh State Issue in the Pre-Partition Period

The term Sikh Land appeared in the geo-political lexicon relating to this region for the first time in 1859 in *Linguistic and Oriental Essays* by Robert Needham Cust, ICS, Secretary to the Royal Asiatic Society and at one time, assistant to the Political Agent, Punjab. He wrote,

> By a mere chance, by the fancy of a great man, by a fatality of circumstances, the writer found himself after a lapse of seven years again among a people whom he loved so well and in a position to study the character of the residents and visit the great cities of the rich tract which lies between the rivers Chenab and Beas, the original Sikh Land, the cradle of the Sikh faith

> and the nursery of the chivalry of the followers of the Guru.[34]

The term 'Sikh nation' first surfaced in the communication of the East India Company's British administration. Lord Dalhousie in his April 7, 1849 communication addressed to the Secret Committee repeatedly used the term 'Sikh Nation'.[35]

There is another significant reference in this document on page 39 that states:

> We have no admissible alternative that as the only mode which is now left to us of preventing the recurrence of perpetual and devastating wars, we must resolve on the entire subjection of the Sikh people and on its extinction as an Independent Nation. We have been for the second time engaged in war with the most formidable enemy, we have yet encountered in India. They have resisted us through the course of a protracted and severe campaign.

The Khalistan articulation is traced to Dr. Vir Singh Bhatti of Ludhiana who conceptualised it within no time of adoption of the Lahore Resolution by the Muslim League on March 23, 1940 demanding Pakistan.[36] He proposed it as a buffer state between India and Pakistan on the presumption of the two neighbours being hostile.

The area that was to be included in Khalistan included the districts of Amritsar, Lahore, Lyallpur, Gujranwala, Sheikhupura, Montgomery, Ambala, Ludhiana, Jalandhar, Hisar, Rohtak and Karnal, besides the princely states of Patiala, Nabha, Jind, Faridkot, Kalsia and Malerkotla, and Simla. The head of this proposed Sikh homeland was to be the Maharaja of Patiala.

Significantly, the leader who initially opposed the Khalistan proposal was Master Tara Singh, who was not only president of Shiromani Akali Dal but also a member of the Punjab Congress working committee. Several Sikh leaders were in both these parties for some time during that period. He said, "While opposing the Pakistan scheme, some Sikhs have lost their head and they are preaching the establishment of Sikh rule. This will simply result in adding to the confusion already created by the Muslim League...Swaraj is the only solution to our country's misfortune".[37, 38]

He elaborated his concept of Swaraj at the 'Pahali Lasaani Sikh Shaheed Akali Dharmak Conference' at Bhawanigarh in Patiala state on October 12, 1940, stating, "I want independence and not slavery of the British, the Muslims, the Hindus, the Germans or the Russians. ...We want Swaraj (self-rule) in which all are equal, not the one in which the Sikhs are slaves". He was also president of the Shiromani

Gurdwara Parbandhak Committee at that time.

The All India Akali Conference held at Attari in 1940 announced its vociferous opposition to the demand for Pakistan. Master Tara Singh and Giani Kartar Singh declared that Pakistan would be formed over their dead bodies.[39]

The most vociferous opposition to the Pakistan demand had come from the SGPC in 1940 itself. This body took a forceful stand against the Pakistan demand and on the protection of Sikh religion and identity.

The SGPC at its general body meeting on April 3, 1940 through a resolution moved by Dalip Singh Doabia and seconded by Giani Kartar Singh and Amar Singh condemned the Pakistan demand.

The Khalsa National Party of which Punjab minister Sunder Singh Majithia was a leader, adopted a resolution within a week of the Pakistan Resolution in 1940 that said, "It would be the height of audacity for anyone to imagine that the Sikhs would tolerate for a single day undiluted communal Raj of any community in Punjab which is not only their homeland but also their holy land".[40]

The Sikh homeland issue thus surfaced before 1947 essentially in reaction to the Muslim League demand for Pakistan.

The demand for the Sikh homeland was first raised at the All India Akali Conference at Vahila Kalan (District Lyallpur in Pakistan) on July 12, 1942.

This state was to be known as Azad Punjab and this demand was formally adopted by the Akali Dal at its working committee meeting on June 7, 1943. The resolution adopted by the party to this aspect stated:

> The Shiromani Akali Dal hereby declares that in Azad Punjab the boundaries shall be fixed after taking into consideration population, property, land revenue and historical traditions of each community...if the new demarcations are effected on the above mentioned principles, then the Azad Punjab shall comprise Ambala, Jullundur, Lahore Divisions and out of the Multan Division, Lyallpur district and some portions of Montgomery and Multan districts.[41]

Earlier, Giani Kartar Singh had asserted that the Azad Punjab demand was to confront the demand for Pakistan.

The Azad Punjab idea originated with Master Tara Singh and Giani Kartar Singh in 1930 when they were in Gujarat jail (now Pakistan) in connection with the Congress Civil Disobedience movement. Sindh was separated from Bombay province on the demand of the Muslims around that time.

This demand was raised formally for the first time at the First Round Table Conference in 1930 in London by Sikh representatives Ujjal Singh and Sampuran Singh by way of re-drawing of boundaries of Punjab. The idea was to carve out a state for Sikh consolidation on the premise that geographical space was the prerequisite for preservation of the Sikh identity. It was this proposal that was followed up as reflected in the 1940 articulation on Khalistan and Azad Punjab.

> The Azad Punjab scheme made territory as a key to the preservation of the Sikh community. In fact, it was this scheme which paved the way for partition of Punjab in case the demand for creation of Pakistan was conceded. The significance of Azad Punjab scheme lies in the fact that it set a pattern for the Sikh polity that continued to remain in political limelight for about two decades even after the partition. The Sikhs as a whole came to believe that only territorial re-arrangement could ensure the survival of Sikh community as a religious minority in the emerging democratic political system. Both the Hindus and Muslims strongly opposed Azad Punjab proposal and refused to concede any political space to the Sikhs. For Master Tara Singh and his colleague Sikh leaders, this came as a rude shock.[42]

For the Sikh leadership, the crisis was now that of preserving exclusive identity of the community in a defined geographical space. The slogan of "Panth in danger" given by Master Tara Singh was rooted in this apprehension of once the rulers of the land getting marginalized.

The demand for the creation of Pakistan was most vociferously opposed by the Akali Dal and the SGPC and not the Congress.

"In order to counter the Muslim League demand for a sovereign Muslim state, the Shiromani Akali Dal put forward the demand of the Sikh state. The main aim and the most important feature of this demand was to insist upon the partition of Punjab".[43]

It was the statutory SGPC which took the most vociferous stand against Pakistan and raised the counter demand, which can be interpreted as the first step by a powerful Sikh organization towards articulation of the Sikh state at its general house meeting on February 27, 1943 at Amritsar, presided over by Master Tara Singh.

This resolution moved by Sher Singh states:

> Keeping in view the danger being perceived to the Sikh religion, this meeting of the SGPC resolves as under:
>
> For the protection of the Sikh religion, it is imperative that such a state be created where maximum of the Sikh population can be accommodated. Neither the Sikhs, nor the Hindus or the Muslims should be in a majority

in this state.

This meeting is of the considered opinion that creation of Pakistan would be highly detrimental.

After this re-organization to carve out the Sikh areas, the Muslim dominated areas could form a separate state or merged in neighbouring state. In this Muslim dominated state, the Sikhs would have the same rights as enjoyed by the Sikhs and the Hindus in Frontier province and Muslims in Central Province.

Permanent protection should be granted to all religious communities in the country.

Master Tara Singh raised the demand for a separate Sikh state subject to creation of Pakistan at the Shimla Conference convened by the Viceroy on June 25, 1945.

The Sikh state demand was adopted by the SGPC in 1946. The resolution to this effect moved by Basant Singh Kukkar Pind at the general body meeting of the SGPC on March 9, 1946 stated:

> Keeping in view the current political situation in the country and the state of mind of the nationalities and the repercussions thereof which have the potential to adversely affect the Sikhs and the likely revolutionary changes in the country, and in this context realizing the need to maintain independent identity of the Sikhs:
>
> a. The Shiromani Gurdwara Parbandhak Committee declares that the Sikhs are a separate nation.
>
> b. This meeting is of the opinion that the Sikh state is imperative for maintenance of Sikh shrines, Sikh traditions and culture, protection of dignity and freedom of the Sikhs and advancement of the Sikhs in future. Therefore, this meeting appeals to the Sikh masses to do everything possible for its achievement.
>
> Amar Singh Dosanjh, who seconded the resolution, said a separate Sikh state had become a necessity for the protection of Sikh religion and its propagation. "Sikhs are definitely a separate nation and fulfil all the conditions to qualify for the same. We are projected as branch of the big Hindu tree to mislead us. I maintain that this is being done to assimilate us. We can't prosper by being slave to another nation. Our minority status cannot come in the way of our attaining statehood. Being a separate nation, we should be treated at par with other communities.[44]

The demand for a Sikh state was forcefully advocated in the memorandum submitted by the Sikh leaders to the Sapru Committee too. The position of the Sikhs stated in this memorandum was in reaction to the proposal for the creation of Pakistan.

The Sapru Committee in para 176 of its report on Constitutional Proposals in 1945 states:

> The Hindus claim the Punjab to be as much their homeland as of the Muslims. The Hindus have been there since the dawn of history. As for the Sikhs, if a community can lay special claim to the Punjab as its homeland, it is they. They were the last rulers of the Punjab and their most important shrines stretch from Sirhind on the one side to Panja Sahib on the other, with the Golden Temple in Amritsar in the centre of the Province. It is not only the homeland but the holy land of the Sikhs, to which they are attached by all intimate bonds of religion, history and tradition.[45]

The Sikh leaders pressed for a Sikh state "which included the largest possible number of Sikhs, their important religious and historical shrines and to facilitate this, we demand the transfer of the Sikh population and their properties".

Following this resolution, Master Tara Singh declared on March 22, 1946:

> Whereas the Sikhs being attached to Punjab by intimate bonds of holy shrines, property, language, traditions and history claim it as their homeland and holy land which the British took as trust from the last Sikh ruler during his minority and whereas the community of the Sikhs is being threatened on account of the persistent demand of Pakistan by the Muslims on the one hand and of danger of absorption by the Hindus on the other, the executive committee of the Shiromani Akali Dal demands for the preservation and protection of the religious, cultural and economic and political rights of the Sikh nation, the creation of the Sikh state which would include a substantial majority of the Sikh population and their sacred shrines and historical gurdwaras with provision for the transfer and exchange of population and property.[46]

There is an interesting observation made by Master Tara Singh later for the failure of the Sikhs to get their state, besides other factors.

> Another reason for our inability to put pressure behind the demand for a Sikh state was that we were not fully familiar with the post-war international situation. None of us knew that a separate state could be carved out for a minority community by some other means. There was the case of the Jews who had been given a separate state. I learnt of this only in 1949 when I was detained in a jail in Almora. At that time, I also came to know that the Russian paper *Pravda* had also high-lighted the fact that there were just two communities in the world which did not have a state of their own even though they possessed all the marks of a distinct community or nation. These were Jews and Sikhs. The Jews got their state but the Sikhs still remained in the wilderness.[47]

Communists and the Sikh State

Within months, yet another significant development took place relating to the Sikhs but outside their religio-political matrix. This was the thesis propounded by Dr. Gangadhar Adhikari of the Communist Party of India on the Sikh homeland proposing Amritsar as the capital of the new state to be carved out on the basis of the right to self-determination.[48] Although the thesis was the formulation of Dr. Adhikari, it was the Communist leader from Punjab, Harkishan Singh Surjeet who was said to be the brain behind it and he admitted this decades later.[49]

There is another vital historical dimension in the context of the Sikh assertion and that is the annexation of Punjab by the East India Company in 1849. In case the Sikhs had won, the history of India might have been different and as such, the 1849 war must be treated as India's first war of independence rather than the 1857 rebellion that was confined to a few pockets, sparked by purely local issues and led by local chieftains, who lacked coordination among each other. In the two Anglo-Sikh wars, the first being in 1846, the Indians sided with the British as the British Indian Army then known as the Bengal Army consisted mainly of the natives from Bengal, Bihar and other such areas. This aspect has to be taken into account while referring to the role of Punjab during the 1857 sepoy mutiny. These very people who revolted in 1857 had sided with the British rulers against the Sikhs only eight years back and now they could not expect sympathy from them.

ENDNOTES

1. Kapur, Prithipal Singh. (2015). *Master Tara Singh and His Reminiscences*. Amritsar: Singh Brothers, p. 51.
2. Kirpal Singh. (2006). *Partition of Punjab-1947*. New Delhi: National Book Shop, pp. 12-13.
3. Ashok, Shamsher Singh. (1982). *SGPC Da Panjah Saala Itihas*. Sikh History Research Board, Amritsar: SGPC, pp. 230-31.
4. Riar, Sukhmani Bal, (2006). *The Politics of the Sikhs*. Chandigarh: Unistar, p. 95.
5. Menon, V.P. (1957). *Transfer of Power in India*. Delhi: Orient Longman, pp. 242-43.
6. Ibid. Menon was a bureaucrat who worked as the Constitutional Adviser and Political Reforms Commissioner to the last three Viceroys during British rule in India and hence an insider to the negotiations during that period.
7. Ibid., p. 254
8. Ibid., p. 268.

9. Kirpal Singh. (1946). *The Sikhs and Transfer of Power*, p. 31.
10. Ibid., p. 32, cited *Indian Annual Register*, Vol. 1. p. 200.
11. Riar, Sukhmani Bal. *The Politics of the Sikhs*. Chandigarh: Unistar, pp. 120-21.
12. Menon, V.P. (1957). *Transfer of Power in India*. Delhi: Orient Longmans, p. 276.
13. Riar, Sukhmani Bal. *The Politics of the Sikhs*. Chandigarh: Unistar, p. 122.
14. Kirpal Singh. (1946). *The Sikhs and Transfer of Power*, pp. 36-37.
15. Kapur, Prithipal Singh. *Master Tara Singh and His Reminiscences*. Amritsar: Singh Brothers, p. 242.
16. Kirpal Singh and Kharak Singh. *History of the Sikhs and Their Religion*, Vol. 1. Amritsar: SGPC, p. 112.
17. Sarhadi, Ajit Singh. (1970). *Punjabi Suba*. Delhi: UC Kapur and Sons, p. 167.
18. Ibid., p. 158, quoted from File No. 16, May 21, 1949 with SGPC.
19. Ajit Singh. (2005). *Shiromani Akali Dal*. Kapurthala: Arman Publications. p. 95.
20. Ibid., p. 97 cited Gurcharan Singh. (1950). *Sikh Kya Chahtey Hain?* Delhi: New India Publications, p. 122.
21. Ajit Singh. (2005). *Shiromani Akali Dal*. Kapurthala: Arman Publications, pp. 96-97.
22. Sarhadi, Ajit Singh. (1970). *Punjabi Suba*. Delhi: UC Kapur and Sons, pp. 401-02.
23. Ibid., pp. 405-06.
24. Ibid., pp. 465-66.
25. This meeting of the general house was held after elections to the general house of the SGPC in March 1979 in which the Akali Dal was opposed by the group led by Sant Jarnail Singh Bhindranwale. This resolution was adopted under the presidency of Gurcharan Singh Tohra.
26. Jagtar Singh. (2011). *Khalistan Struggle: A Non-movement*. Delhi: Aakar Books, p. 347.
27. Chandra Shekhar was the Prime Minister between November 10, 1990 and June 21, 1991
28. Jagtar Singh. (2011). *Khalistan Struggle: A Non-movement*. Delhi: Aakar Books. p. 333.
29. January 25, 1991. *The Tribune*.
30. December 12, 1971. *Des Pardes*.
31. Tatla, Darshan Singh. *Imagining Punjab: Narratives of Nationhood and Homeland Among the Sikh Diaspora*.
32. The gurdwaras in Pakistan remained neglected for years after partition in 1947 and most of these Sikh shrines were shut down as the Sikhs migrated. The Sikhs of Nankana too deserted the birthplace of Guru

Nanak. Nankana Sahib was among the first gurdwaras that were re-opened by Pakistan. Several Sikh families were subsequently brought from Peshawar and settled at Nankana Sahib to manage this shrine. This arrangement was worked out after the SGPC chief Gurcharan Singh Tohra took up this issue with Pakistan

33. Going by this concept, Khalistan would have been Hindu-dominated as the majority of Punjabi-speaking people in these states are Punjabi Hindus.
34. Kirpal Singh. (2006). *Partition of Punjab-1947*. New Delhi: National Book Shop, p. 238.
35. Bhai Nahar Singh and Bhai Kirpal Singh. *Rebels Against the British Raj*, Vol 2. New Delhi: Atlantic Publishers, pp. 24-40.
36. Riar, Sukhmani Bal. (2006). *The Politics of the Sikhs*. Chandigarh: Unistar, p. 53.
37. Ibid., p. 57.
38. April 18, 1940. *The Tribune*.
39. Ajit Singh. (2005). *Shiromani Akali*. Kapurthala: Arman Publications, p. 34.
40. Kirpal Singh. (2006). *Partition of Punjab-1947*. New Delhi: National Book Shop, p. xiv.
41. Harbans Singh. (1983). *The Heritage of the Sikhs*. New Delhi: Manohar Publications, p. 301.
42. Kapur, Prithipal Singh. *Master Tara Singh and His Reminiscences*. Amritsar: Singh Brothers, p. 48.
43. Kirpal Singh. (2006). *Partition of Punjab-1947*. New Delhi: National Book Shop, p. XV.
44. Ashok, Shamsher Singh. (1982). *SGPC Da Panjah Saala Itihas*. Amritsar: SGPC, pp. 230-31.
45. Kirpal Singh. (2006). *Partition of Punjab-1947*. New Delhi: National Book Shop, p. 237.
46. Harbans Singh. (1983). *The Heritage of the Sikhs*. New Delhi: Manohar Publications, p. 302.
47. Kapur, Prithipal Singh. *Master Tara Singh and His Reminiscences*. Amritsar: Singh Brothers, p. 242.
48. Adhikari, Gangadhar. (1946). *Sikh Deshbhoomian*. CPI.
49. November 6, 2000. *The Hindu*.

3

Sant Jarnail Singh Bhindranwale: Warrior from the Past

Radical militant discourse in Indian Punjab in the 1980s is synonymous with one person—Sant Jarnail Singh Khalsa Bhindranwale. He was from that class of leaders in the world who are loved and hated in equal measure. Martyrs' memorial in the Golden Temple complex commemorates the struggle that he waged against the Indian state. This is the third memorial associated with the Sikh warriors in this most sacred shrine of the community, the earlier two being dedicated to Baba Deep Singh and Baba Gurbax Singh.[1]

This lanky man with a commanding voice looked like warriors from the earlier Sikh times having transcended space and time, lacking in formal education but gifted with perception shaped by the Sikh history and psyche. He nurtured the dream to sculpt the destiny of his community in modern times. Burdened by history, his biggest asset was his unwavering commitment and dedication to the Sikh Panth.

Attired in a long robe like earlier Sikh combatants, he would carry a 9 mm Mauser, the only symbol of contemporary times, along with a metallic arrow. He had kept the pistol long before he displayed it publicly. It would normally be hidden in the brass pot (gadva) carried by his attendant.

He took over as the chief of the seminary Damdami Taksal headquartered in Gurdwara Gurdarshan Parkash at Mehta Chowk in Amritsar district on August 25, 1977 when India for the first time since independence had been ruled by a non-Congress dispensation.

The rise of Sant Bhindranwale as a rebel-warrior can facilitate the understanding of the recent Sikh religio-political dynamics in which militant struggle is rooted. Here was a man who otherwise did not make any outstanding ideological contribution to the religio-political discourse of the Sikhs but he as an indefatigable fighter is the source of inspiration for his followers.

He opted to lay down his life for the cause for which he took up the arms, the cause that he never defined unambiguously. He never categorically raised the demand for Khalistan, the Sikh homeland.

The path of armed struggle he had chosen could not just be for the implementation of the Anandpur Sahib Resolution adopted by the Akali Dal working committee way back in October 1973 that called for autonomous Punjab with special rights to the Sikhs, the realization of which he used to vouch for. The two related demands that he added to this resolution were recognition of Sikhs as a separate nation and separate personal law. These were the issues that had already been raised by the SGPC.

He never wavered from this demand although he is the embodiment of the struggle for Khalistan, the sovereign Sikh state. Had this maverick leader resolved to sacrifice his life just for the implementation of the Anandpur Sahib Resolution whose political objective is "creating a geo-political environment and political set up" with special rights to the Sikhs that can be interpreted as autonomy for Punjab within the Indian state? This vague political objective would not justify the type of the powerful armed struggle that he commanded. It was a war in which the commanders of both the armies were gunned down, the other being Prime Minister Indira Gandhi.

On the record, Sant Bhindranwale advocated armed struggle for the objective that was the Anandpur Sahib Resolution. Looking back, the armed struggle just for the implementation of an autonomous Sikh state cannot be justified.

Sant Bhindranwale was unequivocal on one political dimension of his struggle. For him, political power was the inalienable right of the Sikhs and would quote history in support of his arguments. After all, the Sikhs have been the rulers of the region from Satluj to Khyber Pass at one time in history. He was dictated by nostalgic glory of the past.

However, he would make it clear in private that his goal was Khalistan. He had shared his objective in an interaction with former finance minister Balwant Singh too but the information has surfaced only now. The Akali Dal leader was of the view that the situation might result in attack by the Indian army on the Golden Temple complex and the Sikh homeland was not possible. However, what is important is the political objective that he hammered on the record.

Sant Bhindranwale then expressed the confidence of Pakistan's intervention and said his people would capture Delhi. Balwant Singh tried to convince him that the losers would be the Sikhs and the agitation should remain within the ambit of the Constitution. Balwant

Singh had gone to Amritsar to meet Akali Dal president Sant Harchand Singh Longowal where he got the message from Sant Bhindranwale.

Sant Bhindranwale had clarified his stand on March 11, 1984 saying, "I have neither opposed Khalistan nor supported it. We are to live in this country. Those who tell us to leave are mistaken" (*Mein na taan Khalistan da virodh kita ate na aje hamait kiti aa. Des vich ee aapaan rahna, jihre lok kahende aa na des chon nikal jao, ih uhna nu bada bhari bhulekha*).[2]

His earlier speech at Manji Sahib Hall on May 18, 1983 also provides some insight into his thinking. Here is another articulation of his thesis when he said, "We should keep in mind only one thing that we got freedom to Hindus in 1947 and now we too want to be free. We can't live under this slavery". (*Iko ik gall chete karo ki asin 1947 vich topi ate janeu nu azad karvaia, hun asin pagg azad karvaoni hai*").[3]

Although he never elaborated this objective, he might have been dictating the actions of Prime Minister Indira Gandhi as part of this deadly politics and she just walked into his trap. Sant Bhindranwale's strategy envisaged a mass upsurge in Punjab in reaction against the army attack on Darbar Sahib followed by intervention from Pakistan. This could have paved the way for the achievement of Khalistan. The situation would have been different had his strategy succeeded.

Sant Bhindranwale had not assessed the might of the Indian state and this was his fatal miscalculation.

Dignified existence for the Sikhs was the issue that surfaces repeatedly in the narrative of those times and it was born out of experience after 1947.

The timing of adoption of the Anandpur Sahib Resolution by the general house of the Akali Dal is important as this was the period when the Khalistan slogan had already been introduced in the Sikh religio-political matrix via England. This was also the period when the Sikh organizations were coming into confrontation with the Nirankaris, a heterodox sect with its headquarters in Delhi that was patronized by the ruling Congress in the national capital and a section of bureaucracy in Punjab.

Here was a leader with a handful of committed armed followers who gave the severest of jolts to the Indian state during those times. He emerged as the leader with mass following within no time but he never identified himself with the parallel peaceful struggle led by the Akali Dal for the same avowed objective of the implementation of the Anandpur Sahib Resolution despite contributing to its success. His enigmatic public life as the Damdami Taksal chief lasted a little more than seven years including three and a half years of the armed struggle.

He started dictating the narrative after he was involved by the Akali Dal leadership in mobilising volunteers to court arrest during the Dharamyudh morcha.

The seminary tradition, with which the Damdami Taksal is associated, is said to have originated with Baba Deep Singh, one of the two main disciples of the Tenth Sikh Master Guru Gobind Singh, the other being Bhai Mani Singh who used to teach Gurbani and was the first priest of the Golden Temple.

The Damdami Taksal at one stage in history was set up at Bhinder Kalan near Moga by Baba Sunder Singh who belonged to that village. The seminary at Mehta Chowk, about 20 kms from Amritsar, came up in 1969 where Sant Kartar Singh shifted as a section of the Sikhs had refused to recognise him as the successor of Baba Gurbachan Singh who was cremated at this place. This resulted in the split with Sant Mohan Singh having been appointed as the head of the seminary at Bhinder Kalan.

It was the Akali Minister Sohan Singh Bassi who was opposed to the taking over of Taksal by Sant Kartar Singh as he was perceived to be a hardliner in the Sikh religious stream. Bassi managed to get Sant Mohan Singh installed. This was the major institution for the training of granthis and preachers and thus had a large network in the religious domain.

According to one version, Sant Kartar Singh left Bhinder Kalan along with a handful of associates. He used to be dressed in the long robe that he left behind in Bhinder Kalan. The group had limited funds at that time. It was at Sarhali that Baba Tara Singh gave him Rs. 1,000 from where he proceeded to Mehta Chowk.

Baba Gurbachan Singh used to stay at Mehta Chowk at the house of a family that was settled in China (possibly Hong Kong). The house was looked after by a member of that family. Sant Kartar Singh also stayed there after leaving Bhinder Kalan.

He worked hard to emerge as one of the most powerful religious preachers of his times. He succeeded in establishing around 30 base areas or centres (manjis) in Punjab where he used to stay during tours to propagate Sikhism. He organized 37 massive nagar kirtans (religious processions) in Punjab and Delhi. It was during this period that he came into confrontation with the Nirankaris and then Indira Gandhi.

Sant Kartar Singh confronted the Nirankaris in the religious space and Indira Gandhi in the political domain. Sant Bhindranwale inherited not only this discord but also the large support base that had been created by his predecessor.

The Nirankari sect originally had come up against distortions that had crept into the Sikh religion. This sect, to maintain the pure form of Sikhism, was started by Peshawar-born Sehajdhari Sikh Baba Dyal (1783-1855) who shifted to Rawalpindi at the age of 30. It was during the time when Baba Gurdit Singh headed this sect that one of his devotees Buta Singh set up his parallel Nirankari faction in league with one Avtar Singh at Peshawar. This came up as a heretical sect by introducing perversions and un-Sikh practices. Avtar Singh took over as its chief after the death of Buta Singh in 1943. He shifted to Delhi at the time of partition of the country in 1947. Avtar Singh started posing as the guru. He was succeeded by Gurbachan Singh.

This sect began attracting non-Sikhs too over the years as it was no more a Sikh sect in the strict sense of the term. The Sikh organizations started opposing practices followed by Gurbachan Singh that amounted to denigration of Guru Granth Sahib. With the following of the sect growing, the Congress government at the Centre started patronising the Nirankaris as part of the vote bank politics. The followers also included bureaucrats. Punjab chief secretary H.S. Chhina at the time of the Sikh-Nirankari clash in 1978 was a Nirankari of this brand.

Sant Bhindranwale on His Successor

Here was a man who had the premonition that he would not live long and this is on record. This was in August 1981, the time when the discourse on a separate Sikh identity and related issues intensified.

Sant Bhindranwale authorized Baba Thakar Singh who was amongst the senior most persons in Damdami Taksal, to nominate his successor in case such a situation arose. The occasion was his address to the congregation at Narangwal in Ludhiana district on August 25, 1981. Here is what he said,

> The farmer can make out when east winds start blowing that there could be clouds. Whether it would rain or not depends upon the clouds. It is keeping such a situation in view that I have made this request as one can't predict about the future. One has to be fully prepared as otherwise, this can create problems. I request all of you to cooperate with Baba Thakar Singh if such a situation arises. You should support whoever is considered to be suitable by him.[4] (*Main saarian sangataan nu benati karanga koi aisa sama ban jaave te saarian sangataan ne Baba Thakar Singh nu sahyog dena...*

Jis nu uh yog te laik samajhange, us naal mil karke saare jathe ne challan di koshish karni.)

This was not some kneejerk reaction. Earlier in interaction with this author in 1979, he had expressed his resolve with folded hands and bowed head to make every sacrifice for the Panth.[5] It is pertinent to recall the caption of his interview carried in *The Indian Express* in 1981: 'Maverick in Quest of Martyrdom'.[6]

Both Sant Bhindranwale and Prime Minister Indira Gandhi were leaders with the death wish. Despite their calibrated confrontational path, both of them carried on secret negotiations till the very end even when the army had moved to Amritsar. It may be mentioned that army units are permanently stationed in Amritsar due to proximity to the border but the troops, who were part of the operations to storm the Golden Temple complex, were inducted from other cantonments.

By the time of his death on June 6, 1984, Sant Bhindranwale had emerged as a leader with a mass following. His phenomenal rise was rooted in the religio-political dynamics of that period rather than just being part of some deeper design. One has to travel back in time to 1977 to understand the dynamics.

Sant Bhindranwale Takes Over as Taksal Chief

The Damdami Taksal with its headquarters at Gurdwara Gurdarshan Parkash at Mehta Chowk is a residential seminary for training preachers. Most of the students of this seminary come from a rural background, mainly semi-literate so far as formal education is concerned and mainly from lower middle class families. Sant Bhindranwale was the 14th head of this seminary as claimed by this organization.

His predecessor Sant Kartar Singh, who was critically injured in a car accident near Ludhiana on August 3, 1977, died on August 16 and cremated at Mehta Chowk on August 21. Two groups had emerged in the Taksal on the succession issue. While one group favoured Jathedar Ram Singh Chauladha, the other group backed Bhai Amrik Singh, son of Sant Kartar Singh. Sant Bhindranwale was said to have emerged as the compromising candidate. Jathedar Chauladha and Bhai Amrik Singh continued to function as his most trusted lieutenants till death during Operation Bluestar. Jathedar Chauladha, the operations man, always maintained a low profile.

The other narrative of his succession is that he was the choice of Sant Kartar Singh.

One of the seven brothers, born on June 2, 1947, Jarnail Singh, an unknown young man till then, was entrusted with the responsibility of leading the Taksal on August 25, 1977 at the bhog ceremony (memorial service) of Sant Kartar Singh at Mehta Chowk. Also present on the occasion were Chief Minister Parkash Singh Badal and Shiromani Gurdwara Parbandhak Committee President Gurcharan Singh Tohra, both of whom honoured him with a turban in their official capacities as per the tradition.

He had his training with Taksal from 1964 to 1967 and lived in his village after marriage with Pritam Kaur of Bilaspur village, about 30 kms from Rode on the Moga-Barnala road. As per the arrangement, he would spend about six months a year to look after farming and family. This period would be divided into three months each during Rabi and Kharif. His son Ishar Singh was born in 1971 and Inderjit Singh in 1975.

Sant Kartar Singh visited Narangwal near Ludhiana in July 1976 as part of religious programmes. He stayed there for a few days. Jarnail Singh accompanied by his nephew Jasbir Singh (Rode) went to Narangwal who too was to be introduced to Taksal. Sant Kartar Singh drew a line on the ground with his arrow that he used to carry and asked Jarnail to take a final decision about offering his services to the Panth permanently and shift to Mehta Chowk when called. According to Jasbir, his uncle did not even blink and crossed the line. The decision had been taken. He started devoting more time to the Taksal affairs.

Sant Kartar Singh visited Rode in July 30, 1977 while returning from the Muktsar side. It was around midnight. He told Jarnail he might have to shoulder some bigger responsibility and at the same time, advised him against seeking financial help and visiting the residence of any minister while carrying out that duty. He told him not to worry about money to run the Taksal affairs. Then he took him aside and talked to him for about three minutes. Jarnail promised that he would wrap up within 3-4 days and join him at Mehta Chowk.

It was around 8 pm on August 3 that Bhan Singh of Damru village near Rode conveyed to him about Sant Kartar Singh having met with an accident. He took along Jasbir and reached the main Kotkapura-Moga road about three kms away. There would be very few vehicles on the road those days after sunset. As they were waiting for some truck, a bus approached and they signalled it to stop. There was no other passenger in the bus that took them to Ludhiana. This bus on the Abohar-Ludhiana route had broken down near Muktsar earlier in the day and was being brought to Ludhiana for the return trip the next morning. They were the only two passengers in that bus.

A brief background of another influential Taksal man Jathedar Chauladha is necessary in the context of certain watershed events and developments in the run up to Operation Bluestar. He was known to be associated with some major incidents that dictated the political discourse during those times. Born in 1948, Chauladha joined Damdami Taksal at an early age and rose to become a teacher in the seminary. He was the first person in Damdami Taksal who was allowed the luxury of a wristwatch. Till then, wearing of a wristwatch was not permitted in Taksal and only some senior teachers were allowed to carry a pocket watch. He was the only person in the Taksal whom Sant Kartar Singh would address as Jathedar (chief), such was his status.

This background corroborated by those who were part of Taksal during that period debunk the thesis that Sant Bhindranwale was the choice of Sanjay Gandhi whom Indira Gandhi was grooming as a successor but died in a plane crash on June 23, 1980. The timing and circumstances under which Sant Bhindranwale took over are significant in this regard.

Sant Bhindranwale a Congress Creation?

The first 11-year rule of Indira Gandhi as the Prime Minister ended on March 24, 1977. She resigned on March 22 following defeat of the Congress in the Lok Sabha elections and was succeeded by Morarji Desai who was sworn in on March 24 to head the Janata Party government. It was during the Emergency imposed on June 25, 1975 that Sanjay had emerged as a powerful leader and extra-constitutional authority. The Emergency was withdrawn on March 21, 1977. Indira Gandhi on January 16, 1977 called fresh elections to the Lok Sabha and released all political prisoners.

Both Indira Gandhi and Sanjay lost the elections as the Congress was wiped out in Northern India facing a humiliating defeat. The polling was spread over four days from March 16 to 19. The counting of votes started on March 20 and the results began coming in late in the evening. Sanjay Gandhi quit the AICC and active politics within days. He said, "As I have already announced that I do not intend to take part in active politics, I see no reason to continue as a member of the AICC".[7]

Could Sanjay Gandhi have been looking for a person to oppose the Akali Dal within weeks after the humiliating exit from power and politics when the mother and son were being hounded by the Janata Party government ruling at the Centre? Could that have been the first priority of Sanjay Gandhi in that situation? Moreover, could he have engineered the accident that took the life of Sant Kartar Singh? It was for the first time that the Congress had been thrown out by the people at the Centre since independence.

The Janata government arrested Indira Gandhi on October 3, 1977 on the charge of misuse of authority and corruption. However, she was ordered to be released the next day by additional chief metropolitan magistrate R. Dayal.

Indira Gandhi was fighting for survival even within the Congress. A section of the senior Congress leaders led by party president K. Brahammananda Reddy on January 1, 1978 announced the sack of Indira Gandhi. At a convention on January 2, 1978 in New Delhi, Indira Gandhi announced the launch of Congress (Indira).

Did the Congress leaders loyal to Indira Gandhi including Giani Zail Singh conspire to confront the Akalis by patronising Sant Bhindranwale and formation of Dal Khalsa in August 1978 during that crisis for survival?

Yet another defeat awaited the Congress in Punjab. With the change at the Centre, the Congress government headed by Giani Zail Singh in Punjab was ousted on April 30, 1977 when the state came under President's Rule followed by the assembly election on June 12, 1977. The Akali Dal-Janata Party combine swept to power and Parkash Singh Badal took over as the chief minister on June 20, 1977.

By the time Indira Gandhi returned as the Prime Minister again on January 14, 1980, Sant Bhindranwale was a well-known figure, although not prominent. This marked the beginning of another phase in the Punjab political discourse. It is a different matter as to who used whom when the Congress returned to power at the Centre.

Thus by the time Sant Kartar Singh died in the road accident and Sant Bhindranwale was chosen as his successor, the Congress was neither in power at the Centre nor in Punjab and was rather in disarray. The facts do not substantiate the thesis, rather the propaganda, including by a section of the Akali Dal, that he was the creation of the Congress.

Institutionalized Legitimacy to Sant Bhindranwale

What made Sant Bhindranwale different from the traditional politicians was his integrity which, unlike the contemporary ruling Akali leaders barring Tohra, was unimpeachable, above suspicion and perceived to be committed to whatever cause he espoused. His radical politics is a different issue.

Sant Bhindranwale was provided legitimacy in the beginning by three main institutions in the religio-political stream and these were the SGPC, the Akal Takht and the Akali Dal. The SGPC support to him was articulated through Tohra.

Akal Takht Jathedar Gurdial Singh Ajnoha was the second pillar of strength for Sant Bhindranwale. It is pertinent to refer to a conference addressed by Sant Bhindranwale in Chandigarh on the birth tercentenary of Baba Deep Singh on February 14, 1982. He called upon the Sikh officers and policemen "not to be a party to inhuman treatment being meted out to the innocent Sikhs." This call was repeated by Ajnoha who addressed the congregation after him.[8]

It was the main Akali Dal that provided him the much-needed space in the political domain. His arrest on September 20, 1981 in the Lala Jagat Narain murder case brought Sant Bhindranwale on the agenda of the Akali Dal as the party threatened to launch an agitation in case he was not released by October 17.

The release of Sant Bhindranwale and judicial probe into police firing at Mehta chowk after his arrest topped the Akali demands to be taken up with the Prime Minister scheduled for October 16 for which the invitation was delivered to Sant Longowal in the afternoon on October 13 by a special messenger. The release of Sant Bhindranwale was finalized at a meeting the Prime Minister had with home minister Giani Zail Singh and Punjab Chief Minister Darbara Singh on the evening of October 14.

Sant Bhindranwale was released on October 15 on the orders issued by trial court magistrate in Ludhiana, G.K. Rai, who held special court in Ferozepur where the former had been detained.

The court order stated:

> On September 9, 1981, Lala Jagat Narain was murdered in the area of Sadar police station, Ludhiana. Nachhatar Singh, one of the accused persons, was arrested on the spot. Sant Jarnail Singh Bhindranwale was also arrested on September 20. He was remanded in police custody and judicial custody from time to time at the request of the police. Today the date of remand of the suspect in judicial custody ends. In the present application the request of the police is that they do not require his remand.
>
> This necessarily implies that there is no evidence to justify his further detention in judicial custody. Under such circumstances, I am left with no alternative but to allow the police request, which automatically means the release of the suspect from judicial custody.[9] The proceedings lasted 15 minutes.

He was taken to Amritsar by Tohra in a procession.

The Akali Dal yielded political space to Sant Bhindranwale as he virtually took over the party from the second week of October 1982. The party faced difficulties in mobilizing party workers to court arrest every day as part of the Dharamyudh Morcha. The broader platform to Sant Bhindranwale was thus provided by the Akali Dal. He started addressing Akali volunteers going to court arrest from the Manji Sahib Diwan Hall stage along with Sant Longowal. He subsequently began dominating the Akali narrative.

His tone, tenor and idiom, however, would be different from that of Sant Longowal. His speech would be interactive and he would directly connect with the audience. "Sant Harchand Singh Longowal is known to be the dictator of the morcha but it is the younger Sant who really seems to run the show.[10]

His audience did not comprise people just from the rural areas but included retired army generals, people from academics and other such fields.

By the time he arrived on the scene, an independent group comprising people, several of whom associated with the Akhand Kirtani Jatha, had come up to protect the religion. They were part of what came to be known as the Nagoke group. Both Sant Bhindranwale and this group had the common objective of avenging the Sikh-Nirankari clash but were working independently. It is pertinent to mention that the AKJ as an organization was not involved so far as the operations part of this group was concerned.

SGPC First to Object to Nirankaris

Much before the Damdami Taksal and the AKJ, it was the Shiromani Gurdwara Parbandhak Committee, known as the mini-parliament of the Sikhs, that was the first to object to certain practices of the Nirankaris perceived to be distortion and denigration of Sikhism. Taking strong notice, the general house of the SGPC at its meeting on November 28, 1973 cautioned the Sikhs against the "tactics and practices" of Nirankari chief Gurbachan Singh. Here was the starting point for confrontation between the Sikhs and the Nirankaris.[11]

Both Taksal and AKJ were confined to religious activities with no direct involvement in political affairs. These two bodies otherwise had differences with each other over some basic Sikh doctrinal issues and practices.

Despite such differences, Sant Kartar Singh from Taksal and Mohinder Singh of AKJ had come closer through Baba Harnam Singh Rampur Kherewale on some common issues confronting the Sikhs.

Also associated with them was Baba Sohan Singh of the Bidhichand sect with headquarters in the border village of Sursingh (now in Tarn Taran) in Amritsar district. All three objected to anti-Sikh practices of the Nirankaris as pointed out by the SGPC.

During the buildup to this confrontation between these Sikh organizations and the Nirankaris, the Gurdaspur Deputy Commissioner happened to be Naranjan Singh who was among the top hierarchy of the Nirankari Mandal. It was perhaps this reason that the Taksal organized several congregations in this district during that period. Mehta Chowk, where Taksal headquarters Gurdwara Gurdarshan Parkash is located, borders Gurdaspur district. The next function after Ghuman was at Qadian in that district. These functions provoked Sant Kartar Singh. It was this ongoing confrontation that Sant Bhindranwale inherited when he took over as Taksal chief. The clash on the Baisakhi of 1978 was the flashpoint of this ongoing confrontation.

Eye-Witness Account of April 13, 1978 Tragedy

The genesis of political violence that is known as the Sikh militancy is rooted in the Sikh-Nirankari clash of 1978 in which 18 persons including 13 Sikh protesters were killed. The most enigmatic are the developments immediately following this tragedy. Some forces had come into operation going by the failure of the police to act. The Nirankari function was allowed to continue as if nothing had happened. The Nirankari chief was later safely escorted out of the state.

The comments made by Karnal sessions Judge R.S. Gupta who acquitted all the accused are revealing in this context. Here is the crux: "In his 282-page judgement, Mr. Gupta said that the case of the prosecution was "intrinsically wrong." It was all a frame-up and afterthought. The judge observed that the case was trumped up after long deliberations by the "police officers concerned changing the whole genesis and substratum of the matter."[12]

The chief minister at that time of the Baisakhi tragedy was Parkash Singh Badal who headed the Akali-Janata coalition. The same coalition was in power at the Centre with Morarji Desai as the Prime Minister. The senior superintendent of police (district police chief) was Gurbachan Jagat with Kuldip Singh Janjua being the deputy commissioner heading the civil administration. The duty magistrate on the spot was the sub-divisional magistrate Baj Singh Bhullar.

The Nirankaris decided to organize their annual function at

Amritsar on Baisakhi on April 13, 1978, the anniversary of the birth of the Khalsa created in 1699 at Anandpur Sahib by Guru Gobind Singh. Sikh devotees in large numbers visit the Golden Temple that day. Here was a provocation in the making. The basic issue arises as to why this function was allowed by the district administration and that too on Baisakhi. The Nirankaris took out a huge procession through the main areas that passed off peacefully before the main function.

An effort has been made to reconstruct the scene that day based on the account provided by several eye-witnesses who were part of the protest.

A Sikh congregation is held on Baisakhi every year at Manji Sahib Diwan Hall in the Golden Temple complex. Sant Bhindranwale was also present there on April 13, 1978. The issue of Nirankaris organizing their function also came up and Sant Bhindranwale announced to lead a group of protesters. Before that, he had some heated exchanges with Revenue Minister Jiwan Singh Umranangal present there who made it clear that the government could not stop the Nirankari function at that late stage.

Sant Bhindranwale and his associates then shifted to a small hall in nearby Guru Ram Dass Serai and a message was sent to the AKJ people as that organization was also holding a function at Ajit Nagar in Amritsar, less than two kms from the shrine complex. The AKJ people rushed to the Golden Temple, many of them barefoot, after getting the message. This group was led by Fauja Singh who was a graduate in agriculture from Punjab Agricultural University (PAU), Ludhiana with total commitment to his organization and the Sikh Panth. He was busy preparing langar (food) for the congregation. This organization had no programme of its own to protest against the Nirankari conclave that day and had only responded to the call given by Sant Bhindranwale.

Significantly, some members of the Akhand Kirtani Jatha had already constituted the Dusht Maru Khalsa Dal to peacefully confront anti-Sikh activities of the sects and groups like the Nirankaris. Among those who rushed to the Golden Temple and later to the venue included 84-year-old Avtar Singh. In case the protest had been planned to be violent, people of the age of 84 years could not have been part of it.

Amarjit Kaur, widow of Fauja Singh who is a former school teacher, is the person on whose mind that day has remained etched forever. She recalled during interaction in the later part of 2016 at her residence in the Golden Temple complex above the office of Akal Takht Jathedar that Fauja Singh used to talk of being in the ninth incarnation. He would say that he attained martyrdom for the first time while fighting in the army of the sixth Sikh Master Guru Hargobind and that battle was fought at Lohgarh from where the spot where the Sikhs and Nirankaris clashed is not far. Leading the protesters, Fauja Singh was the first to be shot in 1978. He perceived himself in the martyr mould. Amarjit said he would even describe to her the wounds on his dead body when he would die. He would also give the deadline of Baisakhi, 1978 of his ninth martyrdom, such was his mental make-up.

She hurriedly handed over some lathis and gandasas (traditional weapons) that were available at her home to the activists rushing to the Golden Temple. She maintained that in that sense, the AKJ people were not completely unarmed. Fauja Singh carried his traditional shield with him tied to his back. Some of them carried kirpans that even otherwise was normal for these people. According to another version, around 30 people had traditional weapons and lathis while one person had .12 bore gun.

As they reached Guru Ram Dass serai, Sant Bhindranwale sarcastically asked Fauja Singh, "You people only recite Waheguru but in this case you might have to sacrifice your life (*Waheguru, Waheguru karanwale ho, shaheed hona pai sakda hai*)." According to Prof. Manjit Singh who had come with the AKJ group, Fauja Singh's face turned red at this insolence. "Jarnail Singhaa (You Jarnail Singh), we are prepared for any eventuality, he shot back. Sant Bhindranwale perhaps did not realize that here was another maverick seeking martyrdom. So was Sant Bhindranwale as he revealed his mind in 1979.[13] The differences between the two groups were visible in this terse exchange. But then this reaction substantiates Amarjit's version that her husband carried the perceived aura of martyrdom.

Prof. Manjit Singh was later elevated to the high office of Akal Takht Jathedar (chief) after militancy had been contained. He was among the protesters.

As people from AKJ and Taksal started for the venue of the Nirankari meet, less than 200 in number, none knew what was the agenda or why they were going there. There is a difference between going there to stop the Nirankari congregation that was massive as compared to their strength or warn them against denigrating the Sikh religion and gurus. The venue of the Nirankari meet was at a distance of about three kms from the Golden Temple.

They were stopped by the small police contingent near the venue of the Nirankari meet that was being held on the ground near the fort but about 100 metres from the road.

There are two versions about what happened at this point. According to one version, they were stopped by Inspector Anup Singh who was accompanied by four or five policemen and warned them that the Nirankaris were fully prepared. They told him that they had come not to fight but only to lodge their protest against denigration of the Sikh faith and their gurus.

According to the other version, it was deputy superintendent of police O.D. Joshi who stopped them. Fauja Singh who was in command told Joshi that they had come to warn the Nirankari to stop his anti-Sikh tirade. Joshi promised to convey their protest. Fauja Singh assured him that they would disperse after that. Joshi came back saying he had delivered their message. The protesters wanted to be sure and stayed put to listen to what was being said from the Nirankari stage. They were too small in numbers to force the Nirankaris to stop the function. This continued for about half an hour during which the protesters scattered but stayed near the venue.

According to another version, some of them broke through the police cordon. However, the Nirankari chief was not present on the stage at that time as he was at the local Nirankari Bhavan. This perhaps was not known to the protesters.

Suddenly, all hell broke loose while they were listening to the speeches to be sure that the Nirankaris were not speaking against the Sikhs. They came under attack from the Nirankaris who carried lathis. However, several of the members of AKJ trained in Sikh martial art Gatka confronted them. Some sharp-edged weapons too were used. The second group of Nirankaris started throwing stones at them. About 50 protesters were engaged in this clash that had initiated from the Nirankari side.

It was during this chaos that the Sikhs came under fire. Sikh protesters were under attack from all sides. Some people received both bullet and sword injuries. Fauja Singh asked the ex-serviceman with him to return fire. Prof. Manjit Singh managed to take with him the badly injured Mohan Singh to the Golden Temple complex. Many of the protesters took shelter behind the trucks parked there.

The shield carried by Fauja Singh has several bullet marks. Years later, Amarjit Kaur handed it over to the SGPC to be kept in the central Sikh museum in the Golden Temple complex.

"The police, which had made elaborate arrangements to maintain law and order during Nirankaris' procession, felt relieved when it terminated peacefully. Therefore, when the anti-Nirankari jatha marched towards the Nirankari congregation venue, it was intercepted only by a small police contingent. The jatha had little difficulty in breaking through the cordon. This was the signal for both sides to start throwing brickbats at each other. The police lobbed tear gas shells and fired in the air but to no result. Gun shots were being fired from several directions and lathis and swords were also used... Mr Gobind Singh, Punjab Pratinidhi of the Nirankari Mission said they had remained peaceful. The casualties in the other camp might have occurred from police firing. However, he could not give a straight reply to a question why more than a dozen persons armed with guns and rifles were camping in the tent near the reception enclosure."[14]

Here is a question mark over the Badal government. In case the Nirankaris had made preparations apprehending trouble, how is it that the state agencies concerned and the district police lacked information, took no precaution and just slept over the situation?

The Sadar police station was only about 10 minutes' drive from the venue of the clash and preventive steps could have been taken when the Sikhs rushed to the place.

Going by the version provided by then Amritsar Deputy Commissioner Kuldip Singh Janjua, a police constable had come rushing to his residence to hand over to him the intelligence assessment when he was stepping into the car to reach the spot after the tragedy had occurred.[15]

Significantly, the Nirankari chief reached the stage after the clash and left only after addressing the congregation as if nothing had happened.

Police Version as Per the FIR

The first information report (FIR) was registered in the "D" division police station under Sections 302, 307, 332, 353, 148, 149 and 120-B of the IPC and Sections 25, 54 and 59 of the Arms Act.[16]

According to the FIR, the Nirankaris' procession started at 7.30 am on April 13 from their Bhavan in Rani Ka Bagh and concluded at the railway stadium at about 11.30 am where the main function was to be held. According to the police, about 20,000 to 25,000 people participated in the procession.

A police party including inspectors Inderjit Singh and Darshan Singh had been deployed at the venue of the main congregation that was to start at 1 pm. The armed police and the tear gas reserve under the charge of Deputy Superintendent of Police O.D. Joshi and Duty Magistrate Baj Singh were present on the spot.

As per the FIR, news was received around 12.15 pm that about 200 Nihangs with traditional weapons and led by Avtar Singh, Gurbachan Singh and Ranbir Singh were coming to disrupt the congregation. The police party stopped them at a distance near Rego bridge. However after about half an hour they succeeded in breaking the police cordon to move ahead and managed to reach about 200 metres from the gate of the venue.

> Meanwhile, a group of 5,000 to 6,000 Nirankaris, armed with kirpans, lathis and guns, led by Mr. Gobind Singh, came out of their pandal and challenged them. The police party tried to separate them. But they started brick batting. Mr. Baj Singh warned them and ordered them to disperse. But he failed in his attempt and ordered the use of 37 teargas shells.
>
> The rival groups separated for a little while. However, within minutes, the Nirankaris started firing on the Nihangs and some firing was also made from the other side. The advancing group started clashing. The police tried to stop the clash and in the process arrested 32 persons on the spot. The firing from the side of the Nihangs was made by Ranbir Singh with his licensed gun in self-defense but he was killed in the clash.[17]

The FIR was of two pages. The challan that was put up in the court also had a 4-page annexure.

Here are the excerpts reported in *The Tribune* on June 20, 1978:

> According to the 4-page report attached to the challan file, at about 12.15 pm, Mr. O.D. Joshi and Mr. Baj Singh were present near the Sammellan pandal along with the tear gas squad and the armed police. On getting information at 1 pm that about 200 followers of Sant Bhindranwale and Sant Randhir Singh were coming towards the Nirankari pandal in protest against the Nirankari propaganda against Sikhism, the police went and stopped them but in the process they reached within 200 yards of the main gate of the Nirankari Sammellan.
>
> At that time, Partap Singh, Mukh Sikhshik of the Nirankaris, announced from the pandal stage that all volunteers should reach the gate with their arms because the Singhs were coming to disrupt their sammellan. About 5,000 to 6,000 Nirankaris armed with guns, revolvers, lathis and kirpans came challenging to the main gate and advanced towards Rego bridge. When they came about 200 yards out of their main gate, the police pushed them away. The Nirankaris were raising slogans.
>
> Having failed to disperse them, the police used tear gas and they retreated. At this stage, Mr. Niranjan Singh, IAS, exhorted the Nirankaris not to allow the Sikhs to go back alive. The Nirankaris started firing and about half a dozen men of the Jatha died on the spot. Ranbir Singh on

behalf of Sant Bhindranwale fired on the Nirankaris with his licensed gun. As a result, 13 persons died on the spot.

The Nirankaris carried away their injured. The injured Sikh Jatha members were also removed to the hospital. In all, about 18 persons were killed, out of whom 13 belonged to the Sikh Jatha, three to the Nirankaris while the rest were members of the public. About 77 persons were injured, while 32 were arrested on the spot....

Giving the background of the case, the report said that in September 1977, Nirankari Bachint Singh, one of the witnesses, observed that the Nirankaris had decided that in future Sammelans they must come prepared to teach the Akalis a lesson in their strongholds. It was also decided at that Nirankari get-together of a few persons to bring the maximum number of weapons.

"Nirankari Resham Singh who later turned approver fired with his carbine on the day of the clash. Before the start of the procession, Baba Gurbachan Singh made certain that the procession should not be stopped even if they had to shoot down the Sikhs."

There was no mention of the Nirankari chief's whereabouts in the FIR or any effort to arrest him. Joshi was placed under suspension for mishandling the situation.

The Sikh protesters who were killed included Fauja Singh, Avtar Singh, Harbhajan Singh, Piara Singh, Raghbir Singh, Gurcharan Singh, Gurdial Singh, Amrik Singh, Dharambir Singh, Kewal Singh, Hari Singh, Ranbir Singh and Darshan Singh.

The official statement on the tragic incident issued on April 16 put the number of deaths at 17. It stated: "A case (FIR No 88) dated April 13 under Sections 302, 307, 148, 149, 25, 54, 59, 332 etc. of the IPC had been registered at "D" Division police station in which 17 persons were killed and over 40 injured."[18]

Sant Bhindranwale was aghast when Manjit Singh returned and told him about the shocking attack. Perhaps none from the Sikh bodies had expected such vicious retaliation. However, the Nirankaris were fully prepared for every eventuality. Of the 13 Sikh protesters who were killed, nine belonged to the Akhand Kirtani Jatha and four to Taksal. The media reports described the protesters as 'Nihang Akalis' which they were not.

It was a spot decision by Sant Bhindranwale and AKJ to protest against the Nirankaris as the Akali minister present had expressed his helplessness to intervene.

It was this incident with which then virtually unknown Sant Bhindranwale was catapulted into the limelight for the first time after taking over as the Taksal chief, never to look back. He had come into confrontation with the Akali rulers even before the protesters had started from the Golden Temple complex.

The Akali Dal working committee at its meeting on April 15 at Amritsar condemned the "ghastly murder of innocent, unarmed and peaceful Sikhs who had gone to the Nirankari sammelan to plead with organizers to refrain from speaking or doing anything against fundamental tenets of Sikhism. The Sikhs were fired at while on the way and mercilessly butchered in a pre-planned conspiracy by the armed volunteers of the Nirankari sect."[19]

Badal was conspicuous by his absence at this meeting.

There are several questions that remain unanswered. Going by the chronology of this tragedy, it seems the administration at the district level just collapsed. The most intriguing part is that the Nirankari chief was escorted out of the state after the function was over. Could this be possible without political involvement? The function continued as if nothing had happened and going by Janjua's version, there was no police intervention. The function should not have been allowed to continue after such a tragedy. Who was responsible for this state of affairs characterized by brazen callousness?

The safe passage provided by the district police to Gurbachan Singh is a mystery. It was Janjua who was the first to reach the Nirankari stage persuading Gurbachan Singh to stop the function. He was the only senior official who opened up years later for the first time to recall the tragedy.[20]

Badal was in Bombay on the day of the tragedy. The Punjab Police chief was B.S. Danewalia with R.C. Kapila as the home secretary and Gurbachan Jagat as the SSP. The state chief secretary Hardev Singh Chhina was a Nirankari. There is a question mark on the investigation also as the prosecution case was too weak leading to the acquittal of all the 62 accused. Was the district administration dictated from above, in this case Badal, to escort the Nirankari chief? Was there any other force pulling the strings?

The country subsequently paid a heavy price for what happened in Amritsar on April 13, 1978. The Punjab government never fixed accountability for blatant mishandling by the police except taking action against Joshi, a junior official.

For years, Punjab was not the same again after the April 13, 1978 tragedy that was avoidable. The basic issues involved the permission granted to the Nirankaris to organize this function at Amritsar on Baisakhi and later facilitating the Nirankari Chief's escape. What complicated the situation was first the mishandling and later the investigation.

This confrontation between the Sikhs and the Nirankaris was fuelled in the post-April 1978 period by the June 10, 1978 edict (Hukamnama) issued from the Akal Takht calling upon the Sikhs to sever socio-economic relations with the members of the Nirankari sect. The Akal Takht is also referred to as the supreme institution for prayer and politics.

This edict was issued from the Akal Takht following the recommendation made at a meeting of Sikh organizations and individuals by the SGPC on May 17. This meet set up a seven-member committee to prepare the draft. The members included Sirdar Kapur Singh, Giani Lal Singh, Giani Gurdit Singh, Giani Partap Singh, Prof. Satbir Singh, Prof. Parkash Singh and Giani Sadhu Singh Bhaura. It was this draft that was issued as Hukamnama from the Akal Takht on June 10, 1978 directing the Sikhs to sever all socio-economic relations with the Nirankaris, meaning total boycott.

June 10 was the martyrdom anniversary of the Fifth Guru, Guru Arjan Dev.

The edict was read out by the Akal Takht Jathedar Giani Sadhu Singh Bhaura. Those present included former Akal Takht chief Giani Partap Singh, former Golden Temple head priest Giani Chet Singh and former Akali Dal president Mohan Singh Tur, MP. Those who were conspicuous by their absence included Sant Bhindranwale, Gurcharan Singh Tohra and Akali Dal president Jagdev Singh Talwandi.

This is how a section of the media reacted to the Akal Takht directive:

> The command for a social boycott of the Sant Nirankari sect impinges on territory wider than religious faith and practice. This interpretation is supported by further directive from the Akal Takht that the Nirankaris should not be allowed to "grow and flourish" and that they should be treated as "enemies" of dharma and social morality. These are strong words against a group of citizens who, despite their several possible failings, have not been outlawed by the government of the day. They have doubtless caused irritation to the Sikh community over a period and the general reaction among the community has been a powerful resentment against what many regard as sacrilege. But resentment, however strong, takes a risky form when it crosses the boundary of legal propriety. Displeasure, even when it is valid, must not be allowed to assume the proportions of incitement. In the present context the Hukamnama could well be cited by opponents of the Akali party as the cause of a certain

> sense of insecurity among the Nirankaris that led to the tragic killings in Amritsar on Baisakhi day. Prudence demands that the application of the Hukamnama should be tempered with wisdom, keeping in view the potential dangers of a lateral or radical implementation of the edict.[21]

The working committee of the Akali Dal at a meeting in Chandigarh on June 20, 1978, while welcoming the Hukamnama, expressed concern that "some people, sections of the press and "stooges of Nirankaris" had criticized the Hukamnama and shown disrespect to it. Their action amounted to "interference in the internal affairs of the Sikhs." Those who abstained included Revenue Minister Jiwan Singh Umranangal.[22]

Sant Bhindranwale assumed the role to monitor implementation of this edict that brought him into direct confrontation with the Badal government. Badal came under attack from Tohra for soft-pedalling the issue. Permutations and combinations were changing in the Sikh political matrix. It was in this situation that Sant Bhindranwale emerged as the symbol of fight against the Nirankaris. It is Badal's role as the chief minister during that period that is questionable.

Although it was the state versus the Nirankaris, Sant Bhindranwale too engaged lawyers to fight this case in the court that was later shifted to Karnal in Haryana. The Karnal sessions court acquitted the Nirankari chief and his associates on January 4, 1980 but the Punjab government did not go in for appeal against the verdict. The judicial process was scuttled by the government. The prosecution failed to present a strong case because of shoddy investigation. Here was another turning point in Punjab's religio-political discourse.

The Officials Surrendered

The scathing commentary on the civil and police administration came from the trial court in the judgement. The court castigated the civil and police administration stating, "All these police officers and, for that matter, the executive magistrate surrendered their conscience to the pulls and pressures from those who could make or mar their career."[23]

At the time the verdict was announced, Badal was the chief minister whose government was dismissed on February 17, 1980 after the Congress returned to power at the centre on January 14, 1980 with Indira Gandhi as the Prime Minister. Punjab was among the total of eight state governments dismissed the same day where non-Congress parties were in power.

This judgement is a telling commentary on the people's role in the state government which, it is clear, had some deeper design to sabotage the case at the stage of writing the First Information Report itself.

The judgement held the Sikh protesters responsible for violence. The judgement stated: "The Nirankaris were justified in the lawful exercise of the right of self-defence to kill the invaders and to throw them back till the danger was completely removed...to make preparations for replying to a sudden attack by an enemy was no conspiracy at all".[24]

Here are the relevant details from the judgement:

"The *jatha* (Sikhs) opened a wanton, violent and capricious attack on the Nirankaris killing some of them and causing injuries to many others. Even the meagre police posse which was available there was pushed back...None of the firearms in the possession of the Nirankaris was illicit. If they used those firearms against the violent aggressors for saving their lives including the women and children, it could not be said that they committed any illegal act of offence."

"The Nirankaris were lawfully justified in the exercise of their right of self-defence... the *jatha* of Singhs with the said deadly weapons made a violent attack on the Nirankaris and they were left with no alternative but to repel the violent attack with firearms. Further, the Nirankaris were lawfully justified in the use of violence till such time as the danger from the *jatha* was completely removed."

Here is what the court observed on the account provided by the witnesses: "As regards the account given by the *jatha* and those who suffered injuries, they were all partisan witnesses whose paramount interest was to project themselves as innocent and victims of aggression at the hands of the Nirankaris... it would not at all be safe to rely on the evidence that clashes had taken place at a distance of 200 yards from the main gate of the pandal...after being pushed back by the scanty police force, the *jatha* of Akalis went berserk and rushed to the main gate of the pandal and attacked the Nirankaris...It seems to me that their differences with the Nirankaris in the matter of religion had the better of them, that they threw all discretion to the winds and in flagrant subversion of law and order went to the Nirankari pandal determined to uproot their *samagam* and to punish them."

However, the protesters were not Akalis as stated by the session judge but members of two different groups from within the Sikh stream. The protesters included people from all ages. In case they had gone to attack the Nirankaris, would old men be accompanying them or several of them would be barefoot. Moreover, it is just illogical to assume that less than 200 people had proceeded to attack a gathering of more than 50,000 people who were fully guarded by armed men.

Then there is a disparaging observation on the registration of the FIR:

> The relevant entries in the daily diary of the police station showing that the FIR had been recorded by 3.20 pm and 32 of the arrested Nirankaris had been brought to the police station on the day at 5 pm were forged and fostered ones. The arrested Nirankaris must have been brought to the police station much later...the clumsy replacing of the relevant pages in the daily diary had been done in an attempt to show that the FIR had been received in the police station a few minutes after 3 pm...here is a case where certain police officers have committed a serious crime inside the police station. I hope the Punjab government take due notice of it.

The judgement is self-revealing how everything was manipulated in favour of the Nirankaris by the police. Who were the people behind all this?

It is in this context that it is relevant to quote a para from the charge-sheet dated September 27, 1979 submitted to the Akal Takht against Badal by Tohra and Talwandi who said,

> A very tragic incident took place on April 13, 1978 at Amritsar. The fake Nirankaris killed 13 Sikhs that day. This resulted in strong resentment and anger among the Sikhs. Mr. Badal and the state Chief Secretary managed safe passage for Nirankari chief Gurbachan Singh from Punjab under police protection. The issue of the role of the Chief Secretary and ban on the books of Nirankaris continued to crop up in the meetings of the Akali Dal working committee. However, in an effort to appease anti-Sikh forces, the Chief Minister and some of his cabinet colleagues adopted the policy of dilly-dallying that continues even today.

The Punjab special public prosecutor on January 13, 1980 recommended the filing of appeal against the verdict and the state home department gave its consent on January 15. The chief minister cleared the file the same day to go in for appeal. However, instead of filing an appeal immediately, a proposal came up to engage a top lawyer for this job. The file got delayed in the bureaucratic rigmarole. In the meantime, the Badal government was dismissed on February 17, 1980. The Nirankaris approached Governor Jaisukh Lal Hathi during President's rule against the filing of appeal. The Governor issued instructions on February 23 that the matter should be re-examined and it was decided to seek the opinion of an eminent criminal lawyer. In the meanwhile, a new advocate general was appointed who expressed his opinion on March 15, 1980 against the filing of appeal. The same was discussed by the government and the opinion was accepted on April 1, 1980. The state government closed the file.

This was to open another file that is still waiting to be closed. The grenade attack on Rajasansi Nirankari Bhavan in November 2018 killing three Nirankaris added another page to that voluminous file.

The Punjab and Haryana High Court rejected the petition on April 8, 1980 filed by Lal Singh, father of Dharambir Singh who was killed on April 13, 1978, against acquittal of the accused.

Within days, Nirankari chief Gurbachan Singh was gunned down on April 24, 1980. The historical revenge Sikh psyche had come into operation. This was the first killing relating to the violent religio-political conflict that hit Punjab and dictated the political discourse of India at one time. Here was institutional failure of the Indian state to provide justice to the victims of April 1978.

Assassination Planned Before Acquittal of Nirankaris

Sant Bhindranwale made up his mind to avenge the April 13 killings by targeting Gurbachan Singh and assigned the task to men in Taksal. The Taksal men also had some licensed weapons. They would go to Delhi to explore the possibility, do the recce and return without any success. They had also stocked some hand grenades in Delhi, besides weapons. They would stay at the Dera of Baba Harbans Singh in Gurdwara Rakab Ganj in the capital. Those who were assigned this operation included Dalbir Singh Abhiyasi, Swaran Singh, Bhola Singh and Lakha Singh Nagoke.

Ranjit Singh, an unknown devout Sikh from Amritsar district settled in Delhi, too had resolved to target the Nirankari chief after his acquittal. He was dictated by the historical revenge psyche. He was a lone wolf who intended to execute the operation at a place where the target could not be missed and the best place was the residence of Gurbachan Singh in the otherwise heavily fortified Nirankari colony. It was as part of his plan to gain access that Ranjit Singh made his entry in the Nirankari colony as a carpenter and succeeded in winning over confidence of the people manning the affairs within a few days. However, he did not have the kind of assault weapon and the search for it brought him to Sant Bhindranwale. Besides weapons, he was promised other logistics like a vehicle to escape. He was offered financial help that Ranjit Singh declined.

Ranjit Singh had a narrow time window to execute his mission as Gurbachan Singh was to proceed on a foreign tour for about eight months from May 2.

Ranjit Singh was a member of the Baba Deep Singh Ranjit Gatka Akhara, a Sikh martial art academy run by Gian Singh in Delhi. The members of this Akhara used to organize demonstrations against Nirankaris after the 1978 Amritsar clash. There were two people who bore the name of Gian Singh, senior and junior. He took Gian Singh Senior into confidence who was married in village Nagoke in Amritsar district. Ranjit Singh had earlier got hold of a .303 country-made pistol but it could fire only a single bullet and had to be re-loaded. He needed a semi-automatic weapon.

Gian Singh and Ranjit Singh reached Nagoke and took along Lakhwinder Singh Lakha from Nagoke Akhara to meet Sant Bhindranwale. Sant Bhindranwale was in Bathinda that night and Ranjit Singh returned by the night bus to be in the Nirankari colony in the morning. He was taking every precaution to ensure that his movements should not be suspected. He returned to Amritsar the very next night after getting the message.

They succeeded in meeting Sant Bhindranwale on their second visit and discussed details of the operation. Sant Bhindranwale was convinced that here was the right man who could carry out the job. He arranged the logistics but at the same time, lay down the condition that one of his associates from Taksal, Kabul Singh, would accompany him. Ranjit Singh agreed but reluctantly as it was not easy to take a stranger to the Nirankari colony.

Sant Bhindranwale first offered to accompany Ranjit Singh to carry out the assassination. However, Ranjit Singh made it clear to him that he would have to discard his long robe and wear normal clothes. The matter ended there.

As per the plan, he was delivered weapons at a pre-determined place in Delhi that had been brought in a gunny bag. His choice was a .30 semi-automatic carbine and a revolver from the lot. He was also given two hand grenades with the assurance that Kabul Singh knew how to detonate them. He was in favour of a stolen motorcycle to escape but Sant Bhindranwale insisted on a car that he had arranged. A person cannot be traced easily from a stolen vehicle.

The plan was to target Gurbachan Singh while leaving his residence as part of his routine to address the weekly Nirankari congregation. The problem was of smuggling weapons and grenades safely to the Nirankari colony. As he was working there as a carpenter, he prepared an improvized box from a log to conceal the weapons. No one suspected when he took it to the colony and placed it among other logs that had been stocked there for woodwork. The operation could not be carried out as Gurbachan Singh had already left to address the weekly Nirankari congregation at Paharganj.

He was now left with only one chance and that was his return. He had selected room No. 14 in the guest house to execute the plan as it overlooked the entrance to the Nirankari chief's residence. It was normal for him to spend the night in the guest house at times as part of his strategy. The grill of a bathroom had been loosened earlier during the day under the escape plan. He had taken along Kabul Singh to the colony at about 4 pm and introduced him as his cousin.

As Gurbachan Singh alighted from his 1972 make black Mercedes car, Ranjit Singh fired the first shot. It was about 10.35 pm. However, he had never fired a weapon at night and did not know that it would emit strong flare too. His location in the guest house opposite the residence was spotted immediately due to this flash and the alert security men returned the fire. He fired more shots and saw Nirankari chief falling. Partap Singh, the body guard accompanying Gurbachan Singh was also killed in the firing. The hand grenades that were part of the escape plan did not explode and were later defused by the army. The escape plan did not work as planned. The grenades were to be exploded to create confusion and escape easily under that cover. However, Kabul Singh had hurled them without removing the pin.

The plan was to chop off Gurbachan Singh's head during the confusion caused by the explosion for which they had also brought in a sword in the log box. The head was to be taken away while escaping. It is pertinent to mention that Sukha Singh and Mahtab Singh in August 1740 had severed the head of Massa Ranghar, the Mughal commandant of Amritsar, who had taken over the Golden Temple and brought dancing girls there. The severed head was taken by them to the Buddha Johar on the Rajasthan border near Sri Ganganagar where the Sikhs were camping.

Ranjit Singh escaped along with Kabul Singh from the back. However, the car was not at a pre-decided location. The arrangement was to keep the car parked at a place from where gunshots could be heard and bring it near the crime spot after hearing the first shot. The escape plan had gone haywire as the grenades did not explode. They escaped on foot. Finally, they reached the nearby drain on the outskirts of Delhi and found the spot from where it could be crossed. They threw weapons in that drain. The carbine was never recovered. They managed to reach Panipat the next day from where they took the train to Ludhiana. However, it was much later that he took shelter in the Golden Temple complex where he stayed for about six months before negotiating his surrender with the CBI. During the underground period, it was Sant Bhindranwale who arranged a safe house for him before his stay at the Golden Temple complex.

Those who were assigned the job to pick them up in the car included Dalbir Singh, Swaran Singh, Bhola and Lakha Singh Nagoke. They went to Gurdwara Sis Ganj in Chandni Chowk to spend the night and parked the car in the gurdwara parking. Within hours, the police were searching the gurdwaras, including Sis Ganj.

Gian Singh Junior, also from the Akhara who had a motor garage, sent his nephew to pick up the car from parking. They first dumped the remaining weapons in the Yamuna river and then parked the car in the parking area of Delhi railway station from where it was traced. It was the arrest of Giani Singh Junior that the case was solved.

There was another evidence that pointed to involvement of Ranjit Singh. It was the long screw driver left behind in the action that gave him away. He had taken that screw driver from an electrician Ajit Singh in the complex to open the log box containing weapons. That screw driver was recovered from the room from where Ranjit Singh had fired at the Nirankari chief.

Delhi police Chief Pritam Singh Bhinder reportedly commented later: "This is the best planned murder I have come across in my 22-year police career. It has been executed like a commando operation."

Gian Singh Senior left Delhi immediately and died in mysterious circumstances at the residence of Ujjal Singh in Malsian village of Jalandhar district. The rumour was that he had been poisoned and his body thrown into the Satluj river. This led to the rift between Ranjit Singh and Sant Bhindranwale.

Indira Gandhi's Offer to Bhai Ranjit Singh

During his underground period, there was a very interesting and important development at the political level. Ranjit Singh was known to Delhi Akali leader and Delhi Sikh Gurdwara Management Committee chief Santokh Singh who was close to Indira Gandhi. It was Santokh Singh who sanctioned the pension for Ranjit Singh's mother and Kabul Singh's wife from DSGMC.

He received an offer from the Prime Minister through Santokh Singh promising that he would be acquitted within about two years in case he surrendered. She had her own calculations. Ranjit Singh consulted Sant Bhindranwale who did not favour this offer. It was later when their differences deepened that Ranjit Singh negotiated with the CBI. However, contrary to an earlier impression, Akali leader

Surjit Singh Barnala had no role to play in his surrender. It may be mentioned that it was Santokh Singh whose speech was the most provocative on September 20, 1981 when Sant Bhindranwale offered himself for arrest at a big function on his own terms at Mehta Chowk in the case of the assassination of press baron Lala Jagat Narain.

Ranjit had managed to contact CBI chief J.S. Bawa who had visited Darbar Sahib after the murder of Deputy Inspector General of Police Avtar Singh Atwal on April 25, 1983 at the main gate of the shrine. The surrender was negotiated through him. Bawa handed him over to the authorities concerned in October 1983 in Delhi.

The FIR in the killing of Gurbachan Singh was registered about 10 hours after the action. There was no eyewitness and it was a blind case. The FIR in a murder case has to be sent to the court concerned within 24 hours but this was not done. His conviction was based on circumstantial evidence. He was convicted on March 26, 1993 and sentenced on March 27, 1993.

He was convicted and sentenced under six heads: First, conspiracy to kill Gurbachan Singh under Section 120-B IPC; second, murder of Gurbachan Singh in pursuance of the conspiracy under Section 302 read with Section 120-B IPC; third, murder of Partap Singh under Section 302 with Section 34 IPC; fourth, attempt to murder Kuldip Singh Walia under Section 307; fifth, conspiring to cause explosion of hand grenades to endanger life and property under Section 4 of the Explosive Substances Act, 1908 and lastly, for possessing arms and ammunition with intent to use the same for unlawful purposes under Section 27 of the Arms Act, 1959. On each of the first three heads, he was sentenced to imprisonment for life and fine of Rs. 4,000 and in default of payment of fine, rigorous imprisonment for an additional year. In respect of each of the other heads, sentence had been passed for vigorous imprisonment for seven years and fine of Rs. 4,000 and in default of payment of fine rigorous imprisonment for one year. His sentence under the first three heads was directed to be concurrent.

It was while in jail that he was appointed the Jathedar of the Akal Takht by the Shiromani Gurdwara Parbandhak Committee on June 9, 1990. He finally came out on parole on October 12, 1996 and took over as the Akal Takht Jathedar on December 31 the same year. His remaining sentence was remitted with the Delhi High Court giving permission to the executive to release him when his parole was about to end. The order was issued by the President of India on November 9, 1997.

Punjab witnessed a similar confrontation between the Sikhs and

Dera Sacha Sauda chief Gurmeet Ram Rahim Singh beginning in 2007 when his pictures appeared in the media attired like the 10th Sikh Lord, Guru Gobind Singh. As in the Nirankari case, the Sikh high priests issued an edict after a congregation at Talwandi Sabo on May 17, 2007 directing the Sikhs to boycott followers of this sect with its headquarters at nearby Sirsa in Haryana. Several people were killed as this confrontation continued till the high priests, apparently under political pressure, pardoned Ram Rahim on September 24, 2015 on the basis of an explanation sent in writing which fell short of an apology. The chief minister again happened to be Parkash Singh Badal.

Violating all norms, the Akal Takht Jathedar Giani Gurbachan Singh and his associates had been summoned to the official residence of Badal in Chandigarh to engineer this issue of pardon. The exoneration was announced through a press release on September 24, 2015 triggering shock waves among the community as the procedure adopted was in violation of the Akal Takht norms.

This pardon sparked angry protests among the Sikhs and had to be revoked on October 16, 2015. The Sikh institutions of Akal Takht and the SGPC suffered irretrievable damage in the process. The functioning, legitimacy and credibility of the top Sikh clergy came under question.

It was Badal in 1978 and Badal and his son Sukhbir Singh Badal in 2015.

The gunning down of Nirankari chief in 1980 to avenge the killing of 13 Sikhs should have marked the closure of the April 13, 1978 tragedy. However, by the time Gurbachan Singh was shot, several forces had already been unleashed in Punjab. Moreover, there was strong reaction to the killing of the Nirankari chief in Punjabi and Hindi media in Punjab leading to polarization that triggered social tension. The security forces started indiscriminate arrests of the Sikhs.

The detention of innocent Sikhs and police repression following this killing provoked a strong reaction and contributed to fuelling of militancy.

The second killing was that of Nirankari sect leader Shadi Lal Angra on August 5, 1981 at Anandpur Sahib that was carried out by Sukhdev Singh and others. Sukhdev Singh later headed the Babbar Khalsa, the other militant organization functioning from the Golden Temple complex along with Sant Bhindranwale. By the time Jalandhar-based press baron Lala Jagat Narain was murdered on September 9, 1981, militancy had arrived in Punjab.

Sant Bhindranwale negotiated his arrest in the Jagat Narain murder case. He courted arrest at a big function at his headquarters at Mehta Chowk on September 20, 1981. He went to the police station in his own vehicle. Yet another of his vehicles was permitted to follow the caravan. Sitting on the back seat, his hand touched his 'Gadva'. He suddenly realized that the utensil had his pistol in it. He managed to transfer it to the other vehicle. This was known only to his personal attendant that he used to carry the weapon. However, no one knew from when. He was accompanied by his personal attendant in jail who was allowed to stay with him. Here was a special concession granted to him as part of the negotiated surrender with the Darbara Singh government.

Sant Bhindranwale had emerged as the man of the masses and symbol of confrontation with the Indira Gandhi government by the time differences with Babbars surfaced in 1983. He was perceived to be fighting to restore the Sikh dignity and get the community a rightful place. He was the face of the militant struggle, although most of the early killings had been carried out by the people associated with AKJ who later formed the Babbar Khalsa.

Despite his conflict with Babbar Khalsa, Sant Bhindranwale continued to be in touch with Bibi Amarjit Kaur till the very end. The Babbar Khalsa finally came into open confrontation with Sant Bhindranwale due to which he shifted from Guru Nanak Niwas to the Akal Takht. However, as usual, he continued to visit her. "The converzation would be the standard one. He would come, inquire about my well-being and would ask if I needed anything. He would not sit. This was part of his routine till the end," Bibi Amarjit Kaur disclosed years later.

She was the common link between Sant Bhindranwale and Akali Dal President and Morcha Dictator Sant Harchand Singh Longowal who used to reside in Teja Singh Samundari Hall. Babbar Khalsa backed Sant Longowal.

At the time when the relationships between the two Sants were very tense, she wanted to take both of them along to pay obeisance at the sanctum sanctorum of the shrine after taking its round. That might have helped in ending all misunderstandings and give out the right signals. However, there were some others who were not inclined for this patch up.

On the night of June 5 when the shrine was under intense firing, she moved from her room on the first floor, went down to the verandah of the Golden Temple and managed to reach Teja Singh Samundari Hall to join Sant Longowal and Tohra from where she was taken into custody by the army along with these leaders.

Sant Bhindranwale was the leader who completely dominated the Sikh religio-political discourse till Operation Bluestar and dictated it after his death. He had emerged as the mass leader unmatched by any of his contemporaries. It was Sant Bhindranwale who infused fresh blood into the agitation launched by the Akali Dal. His avowed political objective was no different from that set by the Akali Dal and that was implementation of the Anandpur Sahib Resolution. However, his tactics differed from that of the Akali Dal as he advocated armed struggle.

His legacy could be contentious too as he is also perceived to be the product partly shaped by competing political interests of the time, the controversy that he trashed by opting for martyrdom. His logic would be simple. He saw no wrong in a person in case he or she supported his agenda.

With his memorial in the Golden Temple complex, Sant Bhindranwale has earned his place in Sikh history. At one level, his resolve to confront the Indian army till the end thereby attaining the status of the martyr has legitimized his fight.

ENDNOTES

1. Baba Deep Singh and Baba Gurbax Singh sacrificed their lives in the confrontation against the Afghan army of Ahmed Shah Durrani. Both Baba Deep Singh and Baba Gurbax Singh are part of the Sikh folklore. Afghan Emperor Durrani (also known as Ahmad Shah Abdali) who attacked the region in 1757 looted Amritsar and ravaged the Darbar Sahib complex. The sacred pool was filled up. Baba Deep Singh was in Talwandi Sabo at that time. He was a warrior-scholar chosen for the task by Guru Gobind Singh. Punjab came under control of the Sikhs coinciding with the fall of the Mughal Empire and the region was divided into 12 autonomous zones or confederacies known as Misls. Baba Deep Singh headed Misl Shaheedan.

   As the news about the Golden Temple having been desecrated reached him, he mobilized Sikh fighters to liberate the shrine. The battle between the Sikhs and Afghans took place near Gohalwar, about ten kilometres from Amritsar, in March 1757. Baba Deep Singh was injured grievously but he managed to reach Darbar Sahib where he breathed his last. He was around 75 at that time. His memorial in the shrine was raised at the spot where he breathed his last. He had resolved to die in Darbar Sahib.

   Baba Gurbax Singh and about 30 of his associate Nihangs sacrificed their lives while fighting the forces of Ahmad Shah Durrani during his seventh invasion of India in 1764. They were staying at Akal Takht for the protection of the shrine. The invaders attacked the shrine to throw out the Sikhs. Baba Gurbaksh Singh and his associates came out to confront the invaders who were in strength. All of them died in this battle. Baba Gurbaksh Singh's memorial is near Akal Takht.

2. Narain Singh (ed.). (2008). *Singh Garj*. Amritsar: Gurmat Pustak Bhandar, p. 513.
3. Ibid., p. 200.
4. Ibid., pp. 105-06.
5. Jagtar Singh. (2011). *Khalistan Struggle: A Non-movement*. Delhi: Aakar Books, pp. 30-31.
6. June 27, 1981. *The Indian Express*.
7. March 31, 1977. *The Indian Express*.
8. February 15, 1982. *The Indian Express*.
9. October 16, 1981. *The Tribune*.
10. Jagtar Singh. (October 17, 1982). *The Indian Express*.
11. Ashok, Shamsher Singh. *SGPC Da Panjah Saala Itihas*. Amritsar: SGPC, p. 454.
12. January 5, 1980. *The Tribune*.
13. Jagtar Singh. (2011). *Khalistan Struggle: A Non-movement*. Delhi: Aakar Books, pp. 30-31.
14. April 14, 1978. *The Tribune*.
15. Jagtar Singh. (2011). *Khalistan Struggle: A Non-movement*. Delhi: Aakar Books, p. 34.
16. June 20, 1978. *The Tribune*.
17. Ibid.
18. April 17, 1978. *The Tribune*.
19. April 16, 1978. *The Indian Express*.
20. Detailed version in *Khalistan Struggle: A Non-movement* by Jagtar Singh.
21. June 12, 1978. *The Tribune*.
22. June 21, 1978. *The Tribune*.
23. January 5, 1980. *The Tribune*.
24. Ibid.

4

Genesis of Militancy

The recent Sikh militancy can broadly be categorised into three phases. The first phase ended with Operation Bluestar in June 1984 while the second phase includes the period from Operation Bluestar to Operation Blackthunder in 1988. Phase III covers the period from Operation Blackthunder to 1995.

The architect of the dynamics of militancy is considered to be Sant Jarnail Singh Bhindranwale. There were several radical and militant organizations that surfaced during Phase I. These include the Council of Khalistan headed by Dr. Jagjit Singh Chohan, the Dal Khalsa, the Babbar Khalsa that was formalized in December 1983, although the members of this outfit were active since 1978, the All India Sikh Student Federation (AISSF) and the Dashmesh Regiment. The Dashment Regiment is also known as the militant wing of the AISSF. The AISSF and Dashmesh Regiment were part of Sant Bhindranwale's set up.

The emergence of the earlier groups and formations is rooted in the Sikh-Nirankari clash on April 13, 1978. It was the killing of 13 Sikh protesters (nine from Akhand Kirtani Jatha and four from Damdami Taksal led by Sant Bhindranwale) that sparked the Sikh historical revenge psyche. The single point agenda of all these groups was avenging the killings of the Sikhs on Baisakhi.

Phase I

The first group of militants having two sub-groups was known as the Nagoke group. The nucleus for this group was Gatka Akhara, the Sikh martial art academy at Nagoke village in Amritsar district. Those from the first group of militants included Surinder Singh Nagoke, Gurmit Singh, Anokh Singh and Sukhdev Singh. The other group was organized around the same time by Talwinder Singh Parmar and the people who were associated with him included Tarsem Singh, Wadhawa Singh, Amarjit Singh Khemkaran, Gurnam Singh Havaldar and Sewa Singh. Parmar had returned from Canada.

They were committed to the single cause that was the protection of the Sikh faith. It was this cause that bonded them. The militant struggle initially was rooted in this single cause.

The members cooperated and coordinated with each other. Most of them were associated with the Akhand Kirtani Jatha.The members of this group also interacted with Sant Bhindranwale.The roots of Babbar Khalsa are traced to these informal groups.The Babbar Khalsa was formalized in December 1983 following differences with Sant Bhindranwale. Sukhdev Singh was entrusted with the responsibility to command this organization. He was supported by Gurmeet Singh and Anokh Singh. Talwinder Singh Parmar and Wadhawa Singh had left India following the shootout at Daheru village in Ludhiana district on November 19, 1981 in which three police officials were killed. Parmar later organized his own outfit that was known as Babbar Khalsa Canada. He formally joined the Babbar Khalsa in Pakistan some time in 1990-91 after his return from Canada and was appointed its vice-president. He was also accommodated as a member of the Panthic Committee. He left this organization after about nine months to launch Babbar Khalsa (Talwinder).

The first killing, however, was carried out not by a member either of Damdami Taksal or the Nagoke group but an individual who approached the Nagoke group for logistic support that was provided by Sant Bhindranwale. He was Ranjit Singh who gunned down Nirankari chief Gurbachan Singh.

Even these two groups witnessed a power struggle in the beginning that influenced the decision of Surinder Singh Nagoke to shift to the Sant Bhindranwale camp in 1981. Sukhdev Singh moved up to head the Babbar Khalsa mainly because of Surinder's exit.

It may be mentioned that it was this Nagoke village from where the killing of Muslims started during the partition of India in 1947 and the reason advanced was to settle the Punjabis coming to this side from Pakistani Punjab.

The remaining members of the two Nagoke groups later joined hands and functioned as a loose group till it was formally declared Babbar Khalsa in December 1983. What is important that it was after its formal announcement that the Babbar Khalsa entered the political domain with Khalistan as the objective. This group till then had targeted mainly the Nirankaris and their supporters and not political activists.

Another group that came up rooted in this narrative was the Dal Khalsa that comprised mainly the Sikh youth. The brain behind the formation of Dal Khalsa included Harsimran Singh and Gajinder Singh who were active in the AISSF. Satnam Singh who joined them was the general secretary of the Akali Dal in Himachal Pradesh at that time.

It emerged during interaction of these people with Sirdar Kapur Singh, a former ICS officer turned Sikh activist, that a meeting should be called of the Sikh youth. Accordingly, the first meeting was held in a Sector 35 Gurdwara in Chandigarh on August 6, 1978. The name Dal Khalsa that was borrowed from Sikh history was proposed by Sirdar Kapur Singh. Dr. Jagjit Singh Chohan was also present at this meet. This outfit was formally announced on August 13, 1978 at Aroma Hotel in Chandigarh.

The main feature of militancy in Phase I was total commitment of the militants to the cause. There was no financial support.

The supply of weapons by Pakistan was almost free during this phase. However, most of the weapons captured during Operation Bluestar were of Indian origin. Pakistan was supplying only a limited quantity.

This phase ended with the assassination of Prime Minister Indira Gandhi on October 31, 1984.

Phase II

The three-day planned carnage of the Sikhs from November 1, 1984 in Delhi and other places in India can be treated as the cut-off period for the beginning of Phase II. This brutalized polity was the initial catalyst for triggering this phase.

An important development was the release of Shiromani Gurdwara Parbandhak Committee president Gurcharan Singh Tohra from Jodhpur jail on April 19, 1985. After reaching Amritsar on April 22, he made the all-important announcement that the Akal Takht repaired by the government would be rebuilt. It was this decision that paved the way for the formal return of the Damdami Taksal to the shrine complex as the project was handed over to this seminary.

Tohra's release was followed by that of Parkash Singh Badal on April 25 from Panchmarhi jail.

The first major action under this phase were the series of transistor bomb blasts that rocked India's capital and several other cities beginning on May 10, 1985. This was the beginning of the revenge for the massacre of Sikhs in November, 1984. The transistor bomb blasts in Delhi were organized by Manmohan Singh Khalsa and others of the Babbar Khalsa.

The decision to hit Delhi and other cities to avenge the November 1984 Sikh carnage was taken by the Babbar Khalsa whose leaders had shifted to Pakistan at that time. Those who were assigned the task included Manmohan Singh, Anokh Singh, Iqbal Singh and Avtar Singh Pehlwan. All four of them belonged to Amritsar. They returned to India. Their contact persons in Delhi were Kartar Singh Narang and Mohinder Singh. Narang later headed the Babbar Akali Dal. Jimmy Narang, son of Kartar Singh Narang, too was in Pakistan at that time. The material for these explosive devices was sourced locally in India.

The first targeted killing during this period was of Congress MP Lalit Makan who was gunned down by Harjinder Singh Jinda, Sukhdev Singh Sukha and Ranjit Singh Kuki in Delhi on July 31, 1985. His name had surfaced in this conspiratorial violence against the Sikhs. The next killing in this series was of Congress leader Arjan Dass in Delhi on September 4, 1985. This action again was executed by Jinda and Sukha.

This was the time when the militants were still getting re-organized.

The first major action in Punjab was the gunning down of the former MLA, Chaudhary Balbir Singh in Hoshiarpur on July 10, 1985.

However, it was the gunning down of Akali Dal president Sant Harchand Singh Longowal in Sangrur district on August 20, 1985 that fuelled the revival of the militant struggle.

The group that planned and carried out the killing of Sant Longowal included Gian Singh Leel who was a third generation Akali, Jarnail Singh Hawara, Harjinder Singh Leelan, Charanjit Singh Channi, Dr. Gurmail Singh, formerly from the Leftist Punjab Students Union, Charanjit Singh Halwara, Jasbir Singh and Darshan Singh. They used .455 calibre weapons. This was the first major action in Punjab associated with the revival of militancy.

The .455 weapon was provided to one of the people who was part of the group by Anokh Singh. By the time Longowal entered into negotiations with Rajiv Gandhi, Anokh was already in India. He was contacted by Sant Longowal to seek his support but he refused. It may be mentioned that the Babbar Khalsa was perceived to have a soft corner for Sant Longowal before Operation Bluestar.

The return of the radical political discourse with the base that was the Darbar Sahib complex was marked with the Conclave organized by the Damdami Taksal and the All India Sikh Students Federation (AISSF) on October 31, 1985 that coincided with the first death anniversary of Indira Gandhi's assassin Beant Singh. The idea was to mobilize the families of the militant leaders to intensify the political part of the struggle. Those who were honoured included the families of Sant Bhindranwale, Bhai Amrik Singh, Bhai Thara Singh, Beant Singh, Satwant Singh and others.

It is pertinent to mention that in the Assembly election held in September 1985, the Akali Dal government headed by Surjit Singh Barnala was facilitated into power as part of the secret deal under the Punjab Accord.

The move to organize the Shaheedi Conclave originated with the underground leaders and implemented by AISSF president Harinder Singh Kahlon, its secretary Charanjit Singh Channi alias Talwandi, Baldev Singh Hothian and others. They mobilized Rs. 10,000 from the shopkeepers around the Darbar Sahib Complex as Baba Joginder Singh, father of Sant Bhindranwale who had been brought to Amritsar, refused to provide funds. Another Rs. 1 lakh was contributed by militant leaders Manbir Singh Chaheru and his associates who had visited the shrine in the evening. It was after this Conclave that symbolic demolition of the government repaired Akal Takht was carried out.

The radicals took over the Complex with the Sarbat Khalsa at the Akal Takht on January 26, 1986 organized by Damdami Taksal and attended by thousands of Sikhs at the first such gathering at Akal Takht since Operation Bluestar. The resolution adopted at this Conclave became the magna carta of the struggle.

The five-member Panthic Committee as the umbrella organization of militants was constituted at this Sarbat Khalsa with the Khalistan Commando Force (KCF) as its military wing. The first general of KCF was Manbir Singh Chaheru after whose elimination in a fake encounter, General Labh Singh took over. His real name was Sukhdev Singh, also known as Sukha Sipahi, as he had resigned from the police to join the struggle before the Operation Bluestar period. Wassan Singh and Kanwaljit Singh also headed this organization. The outfit has survived with Paramjit Singh Panjwar being its current head but based in Pakistan.

Gurbachan Singh Manochahal after the split in KCF formed his Bhindranwale Tiger Force of Khalistan and its formation was announced by claiming responsibility for the killing of Sukhdev Singh Umranangal, son of former Akali minister Jiwan Singh Umranangal.

There is yet another dimension. Armed Akali activists led by Gaganjit Singh Barnala, son of Chief Minister Surjit Singh Barnala, opened fire at Akali Takht to throw out Damdami Taksal and AISSF militants on January 19, 1986. They had to beat a hasty retreat amidst strong opposition.

Barnala Provides Legitimacy to Operation Bluestar

It was this Panthic Committee that announced Khalistan as the political objective unequivocally and unambiguously from the Akal Takht on April 29, 1986. The Panthic Committee members escaped from the Complex within minutes after making the announcement. Now the drama to provide legitimacy to Operation Bluestar started in Delhi.

> The security forces entered the Darbar Sahib Complex around 4.50 pm on April 30, a few hours after the announcement had been made, to flush out the militants, thus in a way providing the retrospective legitimacy to Operation Bluestar. The Centre, in a subtle move, had got the justification from an Akali government. The National Security Guards commandos were assigned the task of clearing the Complex. History had repeated itself. The security forces also raided Gurdwara Saheedan at Amritsar and Gurdwara Darbar Sahib, Tarn Taran.The members of the Panthic Committee had already escaped after making the announcement.[1]

Barnala was dictated to send security forces in the Complex at a high level meeting in Delhi which among others was attended by the then Union Home Minister P.V. Narasimha Rao.

Other militant bodies that appeared on the stage in Phase II included Tat Khalsa, Dashmesh Regiment after its re-organization, Khalistan National Army, Khalistan Armed Police and Khalistan Armed Force. These bodies later joined hands and got re-organized as Khalistan Liberation Force headed by Aroor Singh. Avtar Singh Brahma took over on March 5, 1987 after Aroor Singh's arrest.

The militant leaders who commanded KLF included Gurjant Singh Budhsinghwala, Navneet Singh Qadian and Dr. Pritam Singh Sekhon. Sekhon committed suicide in Pakistan while Gurjant and Navneet were killed by the police.

The Khalistan Liberation Organization was constituted by Atinderpal Singh after he fell out with the AISSF in 1985. This outfit was active for a limited period.

The AISSF that resurfaced as the political wing, later got split into four factions with at least one section resorting to militant actions. These factions were headed by Harinder Singh Kahlon, Gurjit Singh, Bhai Manjit Singh and Daljit Singh. The Mehta-Chawla faction virtually replaced AISSF (Manjit) after the assassination of its leader Harminder Singh Sandhu. The SSF (Daljit) was among the most important militant organizations that were part of the Panthic Committee associated with Dr. Sohan Singh.

The Akal Federation was headed by Kanwar Singh Dhami and Narain Singh.

The International Sikh Youth Federation headed by Jasbir Singh Rode was formed overseas after 1984. This organization was banned by several countries. Six of its members from Canada entered India via Pakistan to fight under its banner but were killed by the police over the period. This organization is currently headed by Lakhbir Singh Rode. The second Council of Khalistan headed by Gurmit Singh Aulakh was floated on the US soil during Phase II.

An important development in 1988 was the split in the Khalistan Commando Force with one section going with Charanjit Singh Talwandi, who was not its head but mentor. This split was going to impact developments during the third phase. Talwandi played an important role in re-organizing militant organizations in Phase III.

The AK 47 assault rifle was made available by Pakistan to the Sikh militants around 1987 but only on payment.

This phase ended in May 1988 when the security forces launched another attack on the Darbar Sahib Complex to flush out militants. This exercise was code-named Operation Black Thunder. The Sikhs did not protest this time as distortions crept in, with people being summoned even to the shrine for extortions.

The action began on May 9, 1988 when CRPF DIG S.S. Virk was fired upon from the western side of the Akal Takht when he was on inspection of the area. He was targeted by Sakattar Singh, an associate of Uttam Singh of Khadoor Sahib.

Here is an interesting background to this incident mentioned by journalist Mohinder Singh.

> The militants fighting for the achievement of Khalistan had started taking precautions after the reality of Jasbir Singh Rode (Akal Takht Jathedar) had surfaced and started avoiding him...handlers of Rode in central agencies instructed him to form a group to attack these militants. He was provided both money and weapons for this purpose...the attack was planned for May 11. It was for the implementation of this design and Virk had gone to recce the situation.[2 & 3]

Special Forces were inducted subsequently and the entire operation was carried out in full view of the media. The operation ended on May 18. Some so-called 'Warriors of Khalistan' took shelter in the sanctum sanctorum of Darbar Sahib, something that never happened even during Operation Bluestar.

What happened in the sanctum sanctorum during that period was shocking. "The holiest of the holy shrine had been desecrated by those who claimed to be fighting for the dignity and honour of the Sikhs. The utensils kept inside the shrine were full of human excreta. The sanctity of the shrine stood defiled beyond imagination, not by the security forces but by the militants."[4]

Yet another shocking dimension was revealed with the discovery of 41 mutilated and decomposed bodies of men, women and children from the debris of Akal Takht that had been dumped in the open groud between the Langar building and Manji Sahib Dewan Hall. These bodies were recovered during cleansing operations after Operation Black Thunder.

"Several terrorists confessed to torturing and killing people who had opposed them or refused to give them money," said a senior security official in Amritsar. Other officials said the victims were people accused by the extremists of being police informants.[5]

No militant organization explained these killings in the Darbar Sahib Complex. These killings could not be blamed on agencies. The dumping of these bodies was even known to everybody who mattered in the Darbar Sahib Complex at that time.

Such issues cannot be swept under the carpet, or say the debris.

Phase III

It was phase III that witnessed increasing brutalization from both the sides after the militants had been thrown out of the Darbar Sahib Complex. The main militant organizations active in this last phase were rooted in the earlier two phases although there were several splinter groups. These organizations included Bhindranwale Tiger Force of Khalistan headed by Sukhwinder Singh Sangha, KCF (Wassan Singh Zaffarwal) that included Gurjant Singh Rajasthani, Khalistan Zindabad Force headed by Ranjit Singh Neeta who is still active, Rangretta Liberation Force, Dusht Sodh Commando Force and Khalistan National Army headed by Balkar Singh Canadian.

Among the people active in this period were Charanjit Singh Channi alias Charanjit Singh Talwandi and his associates. The Babbars floated Babbar Sikh Vidyarthi Jathebandi.

This phase is important in terms of availability of weapons with the militants and increase in manpower. The supply of weapons from Pakistan peaked in 1990 despite the border in Punjab having been fenced. Ammunition was also smuggled in from Rajasthan and Jammu borders. The 1990-91 period witnessed a spurt in killings and extortions.The ammunition was exhausted at one stage in 1991.

It was due to the army deployment in late 1990 that the supply of arms and ammunition from across the border was checked. It was this squeeze that led to shortage of ammunition. The other reason was the spurt in killings.

Money from Punjabi NRIs started flowing in Phase III. The militants-cum-terrorists resorted to extortions, lootings and bank robberies. Pakistan did not extend much financial assistance. It was in kind as weapons.

The bomb blasts during the post-Operation Bluestar period were carried out mainly by the Babbar Khalsa while the killings of Hindu passengers in buses were executed by the KCF.

Sant Bhindranwale and Indira Gandhi

The religio-political dynamics of Punjab in the first phase revolves mainly around two main players: Prime Minister Indira Gandhi and Sant Jarnail Singh Bhindranwale. They perished in the very fire that was sparked by their vicious and deadly politics. The build-up to their final showdown that was Operation Bluestar was slow and steady. The statesmanship that was required to avoid this fatal collision was either missing as both of them were reacting to each other at the same level or their actions were dictated by their deeper designs or deeper forces. However, this is just one dimension of the Sikh militant struggle. On the face of it, they seemed to be walking on the calibrated path.

One of the most important factors that played the key role in unleashing the dynamics of militancy is the historical collective Sikh psyche. It would not be an oversimplification to say that the phenomenon triggered in April 1978 is rooted deep in this psyche. This psyche historically can be articulated as not sparing the wrong-doer, or in plain words, avenging any wrong perpetrated upon Sikhs as a community. This revenge psyche also plays out at an individual level in Punjab. This psyche is rooted in the fierce Sikh struggle for survival.

It is this significant dimension that is overlooked while studying this militant struggle.

The historical revenge psyche was unleashed when Guru Gobind Singh appointed Baba Banda Singh Bahadur as the commander of the Khalsa. Banda Bahadur avenged the barbaric killing of Sahibzada Zorawar Singh, aged about 9, and Sahibzada Fateh Singh, aged about 7, the two youngest sons of Guru Gobind Singh, who were bricked alive by the Sirhind provincial governor Wazir Khan. He killed Wazir Khan in the battle at Chappar Chiri laying the foundation of Khalsa Raj in May 1710. The Sikh history is replete with such examples. The

Sikhs rebuilt the Golden Temple within no time after it was destroyed by Afghan invader Ahmed Shah Durrani who attacked this region repeatedly.[6]

Massa Ranghar, the commander of Amritsar who defiled Darbar Sahib, was beheaded in the sanctum sactorum of the shrine by Sukha Singh and Mehtab Singh who escaped with his chopped head to Budha Johar village in Rajasthan in 1740 where a group of Sikhs had taken sanctuary after being hounded in Punjab. They had come from that very place for this specific purpose. Massa Ranghar would use the sanctum sanctorum of the Golden Temple for amusement with dancing girls. The Golden Temple was under siege of the Lahore Darbar at that time.

The historical Sikh psyche is one of the crucial dimensions that underline the Sikh militant struggle at different stages. It is this psyche that did not accept the Akal Takht rebuilt by the government after Operation Bluestar.

The role of the lethal and compromizing politics played by various players and the socio-economic dynamics are the aspects that are different from this sensitive dimension without which this struggle cannot be studied in the right perspective.

It was this revenge psyche that was sparked by the Sikh-Nirankari clash of April 13, 1978.

"The fault line in Punjab did not erupt suddenly. In the first stage, the Sikh militancy fed on revenge psyche triggered by Sikh-Nirankari clash."[7]

The competing factions in the Punjab Congress, of course, played an obnoxious role in political dynamics of the time but that period starts later after the party returned to power in 1980. Sant Bhindranwale had himself confided in some people that Congress leaders Zail Singh and Buta Singh used to visit him frequently as Union Ministers. (*Ik uthda hai, duja aa behnda hai*). It is pertinent to mention that he moved to the Golden Temple permanently only on July 19, 1982. He never went out even for a day after that.[8]

Another player in this Congress political arena was Chief Minister Darbara Singh. He instigated the non-Sikh forces. It was Darbara Singh who had played a role in Hindu organizations staging the pro-tobacco march through the main markets in Amritsar on May 29, 1981. He had visited Amritsar clandestinely to meet some leaders for this purpose during that period. There are several other incidents with which his name is associated. Both these factions in the Congress were functioning at cross purposes. However, it is the role of Indira Gandhi in not controlling this deadly play of forces that is questionable. How did she allow these Punjab Congress leaders to play havoc in the state?

Sant Bhindranwale might not be a willing tool in their nefarious designs but their bitter factional fight suited him and he exploited the situation to his advantage. Finally, it turned into Indira Gandhi vs Sant Bhindranwale following the dismissal of the Darbara Singh government on October 6, 1983.

Operationalization of Revenge Psyche in Reaction to the 1978 Clash

Two centres had emerged dictated by the revenge psyche following the 1978 Sikh-Nirankari clash.These centres were the Damdami Taksal and the Nagoke group having several members from the Akhand Kirtani Jatha (AKJ). Both Damdami Taksal and the AKJ had jointly carried on the campaign against the Nirankaris for years.

The Nirankari Mandal was being patronized by the Indian state as were some other sects that had come out of Sikhism. The latest case is that of Dera Sacha Sauda and Dera Radha Soami with headquarters in Beas in Amritsar district.

It is this aspect that turned the dynamics from Sikhs vs the Nirankaris to the Sikhs vs the Indian state. The state patronage to these sects is a strategic dimension in the relationship of Sikhs with the Indian state.

The stand taken by Akali Dal on Nirankaris in 1978 after the clash is very important. The party working committee at its meeting on June 20, 1978 at Amritsar slammed the Nirankaris as "anti-social, anti-national and anti-religious."[9]

Locational Dimension of Militancy

Yet another strategic dimension is locational as Punjab is a border state where the Sikhs have been in a majority since 1966 after reorganization on the so-called linguistic basis. This locational dimension, however, is independent of Sikhs being in a majority in this border state.

Closely linked to this strategic dimension is the unique organic relationship that the Sikhs have with Pakistan as it is the land of the birth of Sikhism. Guru Nanak Dev, the founder of the Sikh religion, was born at Nankana Sahib and died at Kartarpur Sahib, both in Pakistan. It is a relationship that cannot be wished away. Pakistan Punjab is the native land of the Sikhs and the Indian Punjab, their homeland. It is because of Pakistan Punjab being their native land that the Sikhs were the first to vehemently oppose the Muslim League

Resolution on Pakistan in 1940. The Sikhs migrated to the Indian side at the time of partition.

The 1967 manifesto of the Akali Dal is very significant in the context of this relationship. This resolution demanded: "(xii)-The party is of the considered view that defence forces should be strengthened to defend the freedom of the country. The boundaries of the country should be redrawn keeping in view the earlier natural, historical and geographical boundaries and the areas, which had to be left out at the time of partition after August 15, 1947 should be transferred back."

At the same time, this manifesto also called for "free access to their shrines left out in the West and East of the country (West and East Pakistan that is now Bangladesh)."

One has to relate this dimension of the Sikh-Pakistan relationship to the present in the context of raising a lot of heat and dust at the national level in India unlike in Pakistan over the construction of the 4-km corridor that is to provide direct access to Sikhs from Dera Baba Nanak on the Indian side to Kartarpur Sahib shrine across the river Ravi.[10]

The locational aspect is one of the important dimensions in this India-Pakistan-Sikh dynamics. A strong Sikh community in a border state of Indian Punjab organically linked to the region that is now Pakistan is perceived at one level to be of security concerns by the Indian establishment. This dimension can be neutralised only by cordial relations between these two hostile neighbours that is a necessary condition but may not be sufficient.

The dynamics could be one of the factors dictating India's policy in this region that is perceived to be dividing the Sikhs as a political power using the instrument of patronage to the 'deras' that have proliferated in this part of the country over the years.These 'deras' also decentralize the Sikh political power with their role in elections.

It is pertinent to mention that Sikhs constitute following of the sects like Dera Sacha Sauda, Radha Soami and earlier the Nirankari Mission are sizeable in number. Punjab is dotted by hundreds of 'deras'.

The relationship of Sikhs with the Hindus constitutes one more dimension.

The political domain in Punjab is dominated by Sikh religio-political dynamics but the electoral politics is dictated by Hindu dynamics. Dalits constitute about 32 per cent of the population but lack independent assertion.

The Sikhs and the Hindus share the same composite cultural

heritage but the problem with the Hindus is that at times many of them just do not own it up triggering fault lines. If Punjab today is a Sikh majority state, it is due to this dimension of disowning the common heritage of which Punjabi language is a part.[11]

The Nirankaris were supported by the Hindu leaders in Punjab as the Sikh organizations started confronting them. At the political level, the Congress, the Janata Party that included the erstwhile Jan Sangh and the Communists sided with the Nirankaris. Significantly, it is the Congress that has been articulating the Hindu concerns in Punjab. It is pertinent to mention that Lala Jagat Narain, a Congress leader and owner-editor of the Hind Samachar group of Jalandhar-based newspapers that advocates the Hindu interests, was to attend the Nirankari congregation at Amritsar on Baisakhi and was accorded the status of state guest by the state government. Two Hindu ministers from alliance partner Janata Party too, were to participate in this Nirankari conclave.[12]

The Hindu dynamics can be better understood by relating it to the situation in 2018 when an agitation was launched at Bargari on June 1 by a section of the Sikhs with background from militant struggle to seek action against culprits responsible for sacrilege of Guru Granth Sahib in 2015 when Punjab was ruled by the Akali Dal-BJP government headed by Parkash Singh Badal.

The Bargari agitation was perceived to be a threat to communal harmony despite its being against sacrilege of the holy scripture, Guru Granth Sahib. This was the most peaceful agitation witnessed in Punjab over the years that ended on December 10, after 192 days during which not a single untoward incident was reported, it was perceived to be a threat to the social fabric of Punjab. This agitation was in no way against the Hindus and the main demand was action against culprits responsible for sacrilege of Guru Granth Sahib. Ironically, Badal too attacked this agitation as a threat to amity and harmony. His problem was that the issue of sacrilege was related to his fifth term as the Chief Minister.

All those arrested in these cases of sacrilege are associated with Dera Sacha Sauda.

This situation can help in understanding the condition post-1978, which was not triggered as Sikhs vs Hindus but Sikh vs Nirankaris conflict and ended up as Sikhs-vs-Nirankaris-vs-Hindus-vs-the Indian state as revenge psyche was unleashed in 1980.

The next killing after the assassination of the Nirankari chief too was associated with sacrilege of the Sikh religion but it was treated as a routine crime in the police record. This was the first killing carried out in 1981 by Sukhdev Singh, who subsequently headed the Babbar Khalsa. The target was the mahant (priest) of a 'dera' under the Ghal Kalan police station near Moga. The mahant was hacked to death. The mahant had put his foot on the Granth Sahib after getting drunk and tore its pages. The action was carried out by about eight people. They had walked from the Patti side for about 25 kms to reach the 'dera'. Sukhdev himself had later disclosed this action.

Hindus as a Symbol of the Indian State

The Hindus were targeted as a community as a part of a design for the first time on the night of October 5, 1983 that is known as Dhilwan killings, in which six Hindu passengers were killed. This killing of innocents was not rooted in any psyche but to create terror. This was the first planned action to terrorise the Hindus in Punjab. The situation was already being polarized by that time.

At the political level, this action of killing Hindu bus passengers was an attack on New Delhi. The government at the centre was perceived to be a Hindu government and it was believed that such actions would shake Delhi. This perception subsequently got reinforced as the Darbara Singh government in Punjab was dismissed within hours of this action. The dismissal of the Congress government after the killing of Hindus further strengthened Sant Bhindranwale's narrative of discrimination as no action had been taken in case of killings of the Sikhs.

The first Hindu leader to be killed was Lala Jagat Narain on September 9, 1981 and that action was carried out by the Damdami Taksal people. He was targeted for not being a Hindu Congress leader per se but for opposing the Sikhs in confrontation with the Nirankaris and tarnishing the image of the Sikh religio-political leaders.

Of course, four Hindus were gunned down in a Jalandhar market on September 20, 1981 within hours of the arrest of Sant Bhindranwale in the Lala Jagat Narain murder case but this action carried out by the Nagoke group was not a planned one. This group opened fire the next day in the Tarn Taran market, killing one Hindu.

The Babbar Khalsa claimed responsibility in December 1983 for killing of 35 Nirankaris over the period after differences with Sant Bhindranwale surfaced.

These early killings were rooted in religious dynamics and dictated only by revenge psyche and there was no political agenda, this despite the fact that the slogan of Khalistan had already been raised and Pakistan had started patronising Sikh leaders like Dr. Jagjit Singh Chohan and Ganga Singh Dhillon.

Dal Khalsa was another player whose main action was hijacking the Indian Airlines plane to Lahore on September 29, 1981 to protest the arrest of Sant Bhindranwale. This organization also added to communal flare-up through its actions.

The people from Babbar Khalsa used to participate in Dal Khalsa meetings and vice versa in the beginning. Here was another convergence of the radical religious mission and radical political agenda. This was one section in the Sikh stream with a radical religio-political agenda.

Another aspect of violence was related to functional dynamics within Damdami Taksal. The two leaders who used to be in the forefront in confrontation with the Nirankaris under Sant Kartar Singh were Jathedar Ram Singh Chauladha and Bhai Thara Singh. On the surface, Jathedar Chauladha was committed to the leadership of Sant Bhindranwale but at another level, he considered himself to be superior to his leader and wanted to prove that through actions.

The link of killing of bus passengers at Dhilwan and that of Deputy Inspector General of Police, A.S. Atwal by Major Singh Nagoke while coming out of the Golden Temple complex is traced upto Chauladha.

The Dhilwan killings and gunning down of Atwal sharpened the confrontation leading to Operation Bluestar. However, what is intriguing is why the security forces did not enter the Golden Temple Complex immediately after Atwal's killing and allowed the confrontation to build up over time.

The targeted killing of innocent Hindus raises one important question in the context of basic teachings of love and universal brotherhood propounded by Guru Nanak.

The anti-Hindu narrative was contextualized in the perception of the Indian state being a 'Brahmin-Bania' state.

Congress Returns to Power in Punjab in 1980

The Congress government headed by Darbara Singh took over in Punjab on June 6, 1980.

This is the period when the first religio-political killing associated with this struggle had already taken place. Turbulence was triggered in the Sikh religio-political matrix in the period following this killing with the apprehension that Sant Bhindranwale could be arrested in this case.

Dal Khalsa, the organization that functioned in a limited space till then, jumped into the fray with its leader Harsimran Singh on June 22, warning against the arrest of Sant Bhindranwale. Sant Longowal too, on July 6 threatened a protest on this issue.

It is the Akali Dal that provided legitimacy to him at this very stage itself. The issues like separate Sikh identity and 'Sikhs are a Nation' had already entered the main Sikh religio-political discourse.

The formation of the National Council of Khalistan was announced on behalf of Dr. Chohan from within the Golden Temple Complex on June 16, 1980 by his associate Balbir Singh Sandhu, a former part-time journalist.

The Sikh militancy had thus been unleashed as a religio-emotional response to attack the Sikh religion by sects like Nirankaris and there was no other political agenda initially.

Babbar Khalsa chief Sukhdev Singh clarified in December 1983 that his organization was resorting to killings to "free Sikhism from the onslaught of the Nirankaris."[13]

Dal Khalsa spokesman Kanwarpal Singh contends that Sukhdev had announced Khalistan as the political objective while claiming the killing of 35 persons on December 20, 1983 but media focused only on the killings. Babbar Khalsa was formally announced by Sukhdev, Anokh Singh and Gurmit Singh around this time only. Tarsem Singh and Wadhawa Singh, who were also members of this group, had escaped to Europe earlier, while Amarjit Singh and Gurnam Singh had joined the Sant Bhindranwale camp. Talwinder too, had gone back the same year.

However, weeks before Sukhdev claimed responsibility for these killings, his associate Anokh Singh Babbar had already made the announcement but that went unnoticed.

The statement in Punjabi issued by Anokh Singh Babbar in Tarn Taran in Amritsar district on August 27, 1983 stated: "Babbar Khalsa wishes to make it clear to the government that it owns responsibilityfor killing of all Nirankaris and anti-Panthic elements in Punjab."[14] This statement had been issued in the context of killing the Nirankari leaders, Ratan Chand Khurana and Avtar Singh. One line in this statement was important: "The Babbar Khalsa always leaves its insignia and pamphlets at the spot of the incident".

Within the Sikh religio-political matrix, the Babbars sided with Sant Longowal till the killing of Surinder Singh Sodhi, the right hand man of Sant Bhindranwale, on April 14, 1984. However, Sukhdev Singh refused to provide protection that Sant Longowal had sought following this killing. The suspect in this case was Sant Longowal's secretary Gurcharan Singh.

Sant Bhindranwale as 'Congress Agent'

The narrative of Sant Bhindranwale being a Congress agent is traced to the general house election of the Shiromani Gurdwara Parbandhak Committee held on March 31, 1979. The Shiromani Akali Dal was opposed by various radical groups including Dal Khalsa, All India Sikh Students Federation and Panth Khalsa Dal organized by Dr. Jagjit Singh Chohan. The AISSF was headed by Sant Bhindranwale's associate Amrik Singh. The Congress extended support to this group.

It is pertinent to mention that Sant Bhindranwale had put up some pre-conditions to the Akali Dal to withdraw his candidates that were rejected. The last one was to withdraw the candidature of cabinet minister Jiwan Singh Umranangal who had been put up from Beas. Badal did not agree.[15]

This was the only political activity at that time directly involving Sant Bhindranwale during the remaining period of the Badal government that was dismissed on February 17, 1980.

Down and out after facing defeat in the assembly elections in June 1980, it was the Akali Dal that provided legitimacy to the unleashing of revenge psyche and sought legitimacy for itself by hailing the killing of the Nirankari chief at its working committee meeting on August 20, 1980.[16] Here was a paradigm shift in the Akali political domain after the party was pushed out of power and in the process, provided religio-political legitimacy to Sant Bhindranwale.

Hereafter, Sant Bhindranwale and the Akali Dal started sharing the same religio-political domain and this is an important dimension of the political dynamics in the build-up leading to Operation Bluestar.

The statement of Gurcharan Singh Tohra in November 1981 describing Sant Bhindranwale as a "missionary" is highly significant. He has been quoted as saying, "The Sant was a Sikh missionary and was pursuing the religious goal of the Akali Dal (L)...The Akali Dal (L) was duty bound to protect the Sant if he faced any trouble while preaching the Sikh faith."[17]

Punjab entered into a phase during this period when the Akali politics shifted more towards Sikh identity issues and the radicals talked of Khalistan. The Punjab volcano had started simmering. Sant Bhindranwale, who belonged to a traditional Akali family, confined to the religious domain had maintained this profile for a long time.

His one-liner on September 19, 1982 is significant in this context that he said in an interview: "I shall accept what the Akali leadership decides." This was in reaction to a question on the proposal to refer the Anandpur Sahib Resolution to a high-powered commission after the Dharamyudh Morcha had been launched.[18] At the political level, the Akali Dal and Sant Bhindranwale were supplementing each other till the differences erupted.

The same man later came under attack from the Akali leaders for being an instrument of the Congress. He was already challenging Indira Gandhi by that time.

Importantly, the Indira Gandhi government admitted in the Parliament that the government had been lenient to the Sant at one stage. Union Home Minister P.C. Sethi said in the Lok Sabha on March 21, 1983 while replying to a call attention motion:

> As pointed out earlier in the past, certain leniency was shown and with the result, Bhindranwala became a hero. Whatever mistakes might have been committed in the past, I do not hold a brief for them. But I can assure him that in view of the feelings expressed by the honourable members of this House, we will try to tell the Punjab government to deal with the matter very firmly.[19]

The Indira Gandhi government was on the receiving end in the Lok Sabha on December 2, 1983 for "creating Bhindranwala." "Accusing the Congress (I) of having created "this Frankenstein," they told that it would be disastrous if it continued to treat Bhindranwala with kid gloves." The debate was in reaction to Sant Bhindranwale's threat to kill Hindus.[20]

Sant Bhindranwale had threatened on December 1 that if the Sikhs living in Rajasthan or any other place were kicked out, the Hindus would have to pay a heavy price. This was in reaction to an ultimatum from Jai Hindu Sangh asking the Sikhs to leave Rajasthan by December 5. He said, "This was another attack on the Sikhs." He said, "Since independence, the Sikhs had never asked the Hindus to leave Punjab. If the Sikhs living in other states were evicted, the Hindus in Punjab should be prepared for the worst."[21] The context to this threat had been provided by the Hindu fanatics.

Referring to an attack on him in the Parliament, he said on December 5: "I am a true Sikh. I never hit first with tongue, sword or bullet." He said real harm came to the country from persons like the Prime Minister who had warned the Sikhs to think of those Sikhs living outside Punjab.[22]

Here is another instance of attack on the government in the Lok Sabha on this issue on December 5, 1983: "You have created Bhindranwala," said Prof. Satya Sadhan Chakraborty of the CPI-M during the six-hour debate in the Lok Sabha.[23]

The BJP, however, had already started blaming the Congress for politics of complicity. Party secretary Krishan Lal Sharma said in Chandigarh: "The Congress-I is in league with Sikh leader Sant Jarnail Singh Bhindranwale, and using him and his followers to serve its ulterior political motives."[24]

Akalis Attack Sant Bhindranwale as Congress Agent

Sant Bhindranwale was publicly criticized allegedly for being an agent of the Congress by a section of the Akali leaders for the first time in the second half of 1983. This was in a statement issued by Sucha Singh Chhotepur, Hari Singh Zira and Talib Singh Sandhu, district presidents of Gurdaspur, Ferozepur and Ludhiana respectively and Jaswant Singh from Bathinda.[25]

This was a day after a meeting of the district presidents of the Akali Dal at Amritsar. Significantly, the hint to this effect was thrown by party president Sant Harchand Singh Longowal while addressing this meeting. Without naming Sant Jarnail Singh Bhindranwale or dissident leader Jagdev Singh Talwandi and Sukhjinder Singh, the Akali chief accused them of playing into the hands of the government.[26]

This perception of his being a Congress agent was rooted in that party's support to the candidates put up by Sant Bhindranwale much earlier in the March 1979 election to the general house of the Shiromani Gurdwara Parbandhak Committee. The Punjab Congress, on March 16, opted for indirect intervention in these elections by extending support to the candidates opposing the ruling Akali Dal candidates. On March 29, Finance Minister Balwant Singh attacked the Congress for supporting the candidates put up by Sant Bhindranwale and Dal Khalsa.[27]

However, he had already cautioned people against such propaganda in his speech much earlier on May 23, 1983 from the stage of Manji Sahib Diwan Hall saying, "Who has not levelled these accuzations since 1979 (against me), except Longowal, of being a rascal, criminal, crook, scoundrel, pleasure-loving, Congressman, henchman of Indira (Gandhi)?"[28]

He scoffed at these allegations again in March 1984 saying,

> It is everyday propaganda that I am a government agent, that I have joined hands with the Congress. He speaks against this person, is creation of that person. I am creation of Guru Gobind Singh, his son. None should be under any illusion that some leader or minister can win me over...some say Bhindranwala has joined hands with so and so. Bhindranwala has been bought over by so and so...the day this Taksal (Damdami) is won

> over, entire world would be bought over. Who can buy Bhindranwala...it is now routinely being alleged that Bhindranwala is sarkari, Bhindranwala is creation of the Congress, Bhindranwala is traitor of the Panth.[29]

Then again on April 1, 1984:

> Akali Dal secretary gets license (arms) under Congress government but even then he is Akali. The licenses of Bhindranwala are cancelled by the Congress government and he still is Congress agent...If any representative of Congress meets me here or partake Amrit from Panj Piaras here, he is not labelled as Bhindranwale's man but it is Bhindranwala who is slammed as Congress agent.
>
> Tell me. Have I ever met Indira Gandhi or Rajiv Gandhi? On the other hand, every one of these Akali leaders has met them. These people who meet her regularly are still Akalis but the person (Bhindranwale) who refused to meet her even for two minutes is a Congress agent... Indira and Rajiv tried their level best to meet me. They offered to meet me at some private residence. I made it clear to them that they should either come here or meet me in the gurdwara, not in a kothi. I refused to give them even a second but still I am being labelled as the Congress agent... these people are dubbing that Bhindranwalaas the Congress agent who is the 14th head of the organization whose founder was martyred. On the other, the organization (Akali Dal) whose none of the 14 presidents has made supreme sacrifice is labelled as the organization of martyrs.[30]

He had a recording in which Sant Longowal too had dubbed him as a Congress agent. This is how he referred to it in his speech on May 13, 1984:

> Some boys asked why Bhindranwala is not being allowed to speak from Manji Sahib stage. Longowal said this is the Akali Dal stage from where government agents are not allowed to speak.[31]

He took up this issue with the five-member committee of the high priests saying,

> You give your verdict whether I am a Congress man. If that is so, then why am I have been allowed to stay here? You tell me I am a Congress agent, I will leave immediately.[32]

His politics in the 1979 SGPC elections suited the Congress as the situation had brought him in confrontation with then Chief Minister Parkash Singh Badal but here was the man who received total support from SGPC chief Gurcharan Singh Tohra and Akal Takht chief Jathedar Gurdial Singh Ajnoha. The support from these two most powerful Sikh institutions in the beginning itself just cannot be overlooked in his rise.

Moreover, he was inducted into the democratic Akali struggle that was Dharamyudh Morcha at the time when the support for this agitation was on the decline. It was Sant Bhindranwale who took over the Akali Dal stage at Manji Sahib and re-energised the struggle. The differences with Sant Longowal cropped up in the later part of 1983.

The one leader with whom Sant Bhindranwale did not interact was Badal. The one leader with whom he continued to have cordial relations till the last was Tohra.

It is pertinent to mention that it was the Akali Dal that listed his release as among the main demands while initiating talks with the government in October 1981.

Confrontation with the Government

His entry into the religio-political discourse is rooted in the Sikh-Nirankari clash that also brought him in direct confrontation with Badal. This confrontation further sharpened in March 1979 during the SGPC general house election. His spectacular rise, however, started after the killing of the Nirankari chief.

He alread had direct interaction by that time with the Sikh masses that he started mobilising with his Amrit Parchar campaign. The AISSF functioned as his vanguard among the Sikh youth.

This is how he visualized his role in his interview in 1981: "A Khalsa, said the militant leader, is always a thorn in the flesh of the oppressor: he is born to fight oppression."[33] His contradiction with the Akali Dal is also summed up in these lines: "Politically Sant Jarnail Singh has always been a maverick whom the Akalis can never take for granted." He had become the voice of the victims of state repression that had been unleashed with the killing of the Nirankari chief in April 1980.

His main point of discord with the Akali Dal was on strategy and tactics as he advocated armed struggle and was non-compromising on the issue of the Anandpur Sahib Resolution.

However, the legitimacy to the use of violence for conflict resolution was repeatedly provided by the Akali Dal beginning with 1980. The Akali Dal continued to articulate justification for violence in 1983 going by what Sant Longowal stated at a meeting with the Gandhi Peace Foundation leader Dr. Sushila Nayar: "The Sant (Longowal) justified the punishment being meted out to known guilty persons by the people when the government failed to bring them to book because of reasons best known to itself."[34] This was with reference to the decision of the Punjab government not to go in for appeal against the acquittal of Nirankari chief Gurbachan Singh whose killing was the first case of use of violence as a tool for conflict resolution.

Sant Bhindranwale's Attitude Towards Hindus

The Nirankaris were the main target of religio-political violence that got unleashed in Punjab but this violent discourse also turned against the Hindu leaders when they jumped into the fray in support of Nirankaris.

Although he used to deny animosity with the Hindus, his tone and tenor betrayed his attitude towards the community that was unflattering. He would use the term "Born in a Pandit family" for Indira Gandhi ("*Panditaan de ghare jammi bibi*"). He would use terms "*Chhalli Ram*" and "*Gulli Ram*" for Hindus and that was humiliating.

Here is his threat to the Hindus on April 13, 1984 in case the Golden Temple complex is attacked: "Here is my request. Take this message to every village. Don't wait for my letter or newspaper report when the police enter (the Golden Temple). Not a single *Chhalli Ram* (Hindu) should be seen around."[35]

His first threat to the Hindus, in reaction to the warning given by Indira Gandhi with reference to the Sikhs outside Punjab, was in a speech in February 1983 whereby he talked of "Thirty Hindus per Sikh."[36]

It was this threat from Indira Gandhi that sharpened the confrontation despite the secret talks between her and the Akali leaders. Even otherwise, she started expressing the apprehension even during non-political interactions saying: "What should I do with Bhindranwala?"

The killing of six Hindu bus passengers near Dhilwan and then the threat from the Prime Minister to the Sikhs outside Punjab are two important stages in the build-up that ended in the Operation Bluestar.

It was his threat to kill 5,000 Hindus that triggered a furore at the national level. This was in reaction to the seizure of the Taksal bus that had gone to fetch Labh Kaur, mother of Sant Kartar Singh, from Jhindwala village near Muktsar for his death anniversary function. He gave the ultimatum to release the bus by 5 on August 16, 1983 failing which 5,000 Hindus would be killed. "Release the bus by 5, otherwise 5,000 Hindus would be killed in one hour. Don't forget it," he warned.[37]

This ultimatum rocked both houses of Parliament on August 24 with members pressing the government for strong action. In the Lok Sabha, "Mr. Charan Singh and Mr. Mani Ram Bagri and other opposition members urged the government to take serious note of the reported threat to the lives of Hindus...In the Rajya Sabha, BJP leader L.K. Advani demanded that Punjab should be placed under the President's Rule for some time as the state government had failed to its basic duty to ensure safety of people."[38]

He was so overconfident that he did not realize the might of the Indian state. He said, "In case we unite, Indira Gandhi would herself come to Amritsar. The Sikhs should not be scared of the power of the government at the centre. This power can't suppress the Sikhs." He was speaking at a two-day conclave of the 'Clean-hearted Sikhs.'[39]

His last warning to the government against storming of the Golden Temple too was accompanied by the threat to the Hindus that he issued on May 13, 1984 saying, "When the police and army enter this place, no *Chhalli* Ram and *Gulli Ram* (Hindus) should be left alive in nearby towns and cities, but only after confirmation...don't start action just on the basis of rumours. We have otherwise no enmity with the Hindus but in case the power-drunk Hindus commit the blunder of raiding Darbar Sahib, a befitting reply will be given. This will be world example. Don't worry about me. One lakh will be killed in the first round. By that time you in the villages will rise and come into action."[40]

Sant Bhindranwale and Khalistan

Sant Bhindranwale never directly raised the demand for Khalistan. However, several of his statements clearly indicate that his struggle was for Khalistan. It is a different matter that he was willing to withdraw himself from the scene in case of an 'honourable settlement with the Akalis.'

His March 27, 1983 statement that is quoted to reinforce the demand for Khalistan was in the context of storming the Golden Temple by the police and was in reaction to a speech by Chief Minister Darbara Singh. He said, "The day police attack, establishment of Khalistan would become an example in the world. Khalistan would definitely be created that day." (*"Jiden is asthan te police wallon hamla hoiya te ih duniya ch missal banegi ki Khalistan baniya. Us din zaroor Khalistan banega"*).[41]

He articulated his political objective in a speech on May 31, 1983. He stated:

> We are for unity and integrity of the country. Cooperate with each other. If the government wants peace, then it should accept the Anandpur Sahib Resolution. Peace can't be restored without implementation of the

> Anandpur Sahib Resolution. It is for government to decide whether peace is to be maintained or disturbed...we are neither in favour of Khalistan nor opposed to it. We want to remain in this country. The central government should tell us whether we are to be kept in this country or not. In case Khalistan is offered this time, we would heartily accept it, would definitely have it and not repeat the mistake of 1947. We don't demand it but would not refuse it.[42]

His statement on offer to the Sikhs was in the context of the partition in 1947. Sir Stafford Cripps, who was part of the Cabinet Mission in 1946, had used the term Khalistan at a meeting with Baldev Singh who was a minister in Punjab.[43]

Months before the army attack, he defined his minimum parameters as the acceptance of the Anandpur Sahib Resolution, separate personal law for the Sikhs and recognition of Sikhs as a separate nation. Interestingly, this was the agenda of the Akali Dal. At the same time, he maintained at a meeting of 'clean-hearted Sikhs' that the Anandpur Sahib Resolution was not the ultimate demand saying, "We can go further." ("*Agge vee jaiya ja sakda hai*").[44,45]

He repeated his earlier articulation on demand for Khalistan in the same speech: "I am asked about my views almost daily, by foreign journalists, about Khalistan.We neither oppose it nor support it; we are silent. However, it is certain that in case this offer is made by the queen of Hindustan (Indira Gandhi), we would definitely accept it, would not commit the blunder of 1947 but we don't demand it as yet."

He referred to this issue in his speech on May 18, 1983 too saying, "We got freedom to Hindus (topis and janeu) in 1947 and now we have to liberate our turban. This slavery of the turban would be ended." (*Asin 1947 vich topi te janeu nu azad karvaiya, hun asin pagg azad karvaoni hai. Ih gulami thalle nahin rehan deni*).[46]

His shift on the issue was clear in his speech on March 11, 1984 that amounted to distancing from it. He said, "I have so far neither opposed nor supported Khalistan. We have to live in this country. The people who say that we should leave this country are highly mistaken." ("*Mein na tan Khalistan da virodh kita ate na aje hamait kiti aa. Des vich ee apaan rehana, jihre lok kehnde aa na des chon nikal jao, ih unha nu bada bhari bhulekha*").[47]

The demand for Khalistan was about a decade old by the time Sant Bhindranwale made an effective intervention in Punjab's religio-political discourse.

The official logic advanced in favour of immediate army action that Sant Bhindranwale was about to announce Khalistan holds no ground.

The number of killings was not important as compared to the pattern till the Operation Bluestar. Here is the data on the killings revealed by the Punjab government in the assembly in reply to a question from Congress MLA Tarlochan Singh on October 10, 2005. According to this information, 15 people were killed by the militants in 1982 and 64 in 1983 in Punjab. According to the Union Home Ministry data, the number was 13 (Hindus 10, Sikhs 3) in 1981, 13 (8 Hindus, 5 Sikhs) in 1982 and 75 (35 Hindus, 40 Sikhs) in 1983.[48] This is one aspect. More important is the fear psychosis that engulfed the state, especially following the killing of six Hindu bus passengers near Dhilwan on October 5, 1983. The coming up of bunkers and morchas in the Golden Temple complex coincided with this action.

Militancy During Phase II

The Phase II of militancy started with the assassination of Indira Gandhi on October 31, 1984 and dictated by revenge psyche, this action was planned and executed by people who otherwise were apolitical. She was killed by Beant Singh and Satwant Singh, both Sikhs, in her security detail. The Damdami Taksal had a role in this killing but at a different level.

The second most important killing during this period was that of Akali Dal chief Sant Harchand Singh Longowal on August 20, 1985 for signing the Punjab Accord with Prime Minister Rajiv Gandhi on July 24, 1985.

The militants returned to Darbar Sahib towards the later part of 1985.

The Phase II was again dominated by the Damdami Taksal and the first assertion was the Sarbat Khalsa organized by this outfit at the Akal Takht on January 26, 1986. This conclave was preceded by several developments leading to the revival of militancy. The main highlight of this Sarbat Khalsa was the formation of a five-member Panthic Committee that was to function as an umbrella organization of all Sikh bodies, both political and militant.

The decision to demolish the Akal Takht reconstructed by the government too was executed by the Damdami Taksal.[49]

The centre had tried to rope in highly respected Baba Kharak Singh but he refused saying, "Kar Sewa will be done only when desired by the Sikh Sangat. Kharak Singh does not take orders from the government."[50] He had been approached by Union Minister Buta

Singh. Baba Harbans Singh too refused to undertake the job for the same reasons.

The demolition of the Akal Takht by the Taksal paved the way for the return of the militants to the Golden Temple complex.[51]

It was during this period that the intelligence agencies succeeded in penetrating the Darbar Sahib complex and supplied weapons to their moles. AISSF chief Gurjit Singh admitted that anti-social elements had penetrated the Golden Temple complex.[52]

The targeted killing of Hindus in this phase started around May 1986 beginning with Fatehabad in Haryana and Tarn Taran then in Amritsar district. Posters appeared in Moga in the name of Khalistan Commando Force threatening the Hindus to leave Punjab within five days failing which they would meet the fate of Hindus in Fatehabad and Tarn Taran. The migration of Hindus from rural areas in the border districts was triggered by the Fatehabad killings. This threat was followed up with action, including mass killings of Hindu bus passengers.

This phase ended in May 1988 when the security forces carried out another operation in the Golden Temple complex to flush out the militants whose activities had become questionable. There is yet another dimension. All those arrested during this operation were subsequently acquitted.

Contrary to the general perception, the only Babbar Khalsa activist in the Darbar Sahib complex during the Operation Blackthunder was Kuldip Singh. The firing on CRPF DIG S.S. Virk outside Darbar Sahib that triggered the Operation Blackthunder is ascribed to Babbar Khalsa but he was attacked by militants associated with the Damdami Taksal.

The total number of killings ascribed to the militants in 1985 was 99 that rose to 438 in 1986. This figure went up to 754 the next year and jumped to 1,773 in 1988.

Phase III

This phase during which virtually the entire Punjab turned into killing fields was dominated by non-Taksal leaders. This phase is also characterized by total submission of Akali leaders of various shades to the radicals.

This phase dominated by the Panthic Committee associated with Dr. Sohan Singh started in 1988 after the Operation Blackthunder. This Panthic Committee was formed in the first week of November 1988, possibly on November 3. The original members of this committee included Dr. Sohan Singh, Wadhawa Singh, Mehal Singh,

Satinderpal Singh and Jaspal Singh. Jaspal Singh was later replaced by Harminder Singh Sultanwind. It was after this reorganization that Dr. Sohan Singh went underground for the first time. He functioned openly till then.

This reorganization was preceded in 1987 by coming together of four militant organizations that subsequently functioned under this committee. These bodies included Babbar Khalsa, Sikh Students Federation, Khalistan Commando Force and Khalistan Liberation Force. These bodies started executing action in cooperation and consultation with each other.

These organizations were then headed by Sukhdev Singh (Babbar Khalsa), Gurjant Singh Budhsinghwala (Khalistan Liberation Force), Daljit Singh (Sikh Students Federation) and Paramjit Singh Panjwar (KCF).

The leader who was instrumental in this re-organization was Charanjit Singh Talwandi who was also known as Charanjit Singh Channi. He was part of the Khalistan Commando Force then headed by Labh Singh. However, the de facto chief was Talwandi. Paramjit Singh Panjwar headed the KCF after the killing of Kanwarjit Singh Sultanwind.

This Panthic Committee marked a tactical shift in its operations at two levels. This committee decided to eliminate the old guard in the Akali Dal as these people were perceived to be a hurdle in their struggle for Khalistan.

The leaders who were targeted under this formulation included Gurcharan Singh Tohra, Jagdev Singh Talwandi and Mal Singh Ghuman. Tohra survived the attack on May 14, 1990. The Akali leaders subsequently submitted to the radicals. Total thrust on violence was part of this strategy.

The killing of radical leader Harminder Singh Sandhu was also part of this design but the Babbar Khalsa differed in this case. This action originated with Panjwar and he was supported by KLF and SSF. Sandhu was the general secretary of the AISSF and functioned as an aide of Sant Bhindranwale till the Operation Bluestar. He was shot on January 24, 1990 within weeks of his release from jail. Panjwar owned the killing.

This Panthic Committee expressed its absolute disgust with Simranjit Singh Mann on December 4, 1989 who had won the Lok Sabha election days earlier with a massive margin of more than four lakh votes from Tarn Taran. This body decided against using political methods even as strategy. With the rejection of political methods, the total thrust shifted to armed struggle. This was one of the reasons for increase in killings.

The militant organizations that were part of the Panthic Committee associated with Dr. Sohan Singh had their own distinct style of functioning although there could also be exceptions.

So far as the targeting of the Hindus was concerned, the killings of Hindu bus passengers during this phase were carried out by the Khalistan Commando Force while the Khalistan Liberation Force killed at random. The killings, of course, were not confined to the Hindus. The objective, however, was the same as the Hindus were perceived to be the representatives of the government. The Babbar Khalsa during this phase was involved mainly in bomb blasts and targeted killings.

The second part of this strategy was that the killings should convey a message. The Bhakra Beas Management Board chairman Major General B.N. Kumar was earlier targeted after the September 1988 floods in Punjab as part of this agenda that had been unleashed by KCF even before re-organization of the Panthic Committee. Kumar was perceived to be responsible for the sudden release of water from the dam that flooded vast areas in Punjab in September 1988.

The killing of Dr. D.S. Tyagi, chairman, Agriculture Price Commission, in May 1992 is one of the killings that was executed to protest against the farm policy of the centre. "The Babbars were trying to mobilize the support of the peasantry through such targeted killings. It was the Punjab countryside which was the main recruiting ground for the armed struggle."[53]

The Babbar Khalsa in a statement dated May 11, 1992 justified the killing of Dr. Tyagi on the logic of exploitation of the Punjab farmers by the Indian state. "We have given out the message by killing Dr. Tyagi that Punjab farmers can't be made part of the Indian market," it stated. The organization asserted Punjab farmers had the right to sell their produce in the international market. It is pertinent to mention that the centre procures wheat and paddy from Punjab at the minimum support price fixed by the price commission. The Babbars also referred to the exploitation of the rivers of Punjab whose water has been diverted to non-Riparian Rajasthan and Haryana.

This target was decided by Sukhdev Singh in consultation with the Bharti Kisan Union leaders and planned by Major S.S. Walia (Retd.) who lived in Mohali. He was associated with the Babbar Khalsa. It was executed by the Batala unit of the Babbar Khalsa. These three members of the Batala unit led by Tarlok Singh were staying in Delhi at that time.

Posing as a school principal from Punjab, Walia telephoned Dr. Tyagi inviting him to preside over a function and sought an appointment to extend a formal invitation. Dr. Tyagi was busy with the marriage arrangements of his daughter but agreed to receive him only for the invitation. The BKI militants went at the appointed time on the pretext of handing over the invitation and shot him.

Walia subsequently disappeared in mid-1992, never to be traced. His was the case of what is known as the 'forced disappearance.'

In an earlier statement issued on April 16, 1992, the Babbar Khalsa had claimed responsibility for the gunning down of irrigation engineers and a contractor engaged in the repair of the Bhakra Mail Line Canal questioning as to why 75 per cent of the water from rivers in Punjab was flowing out to Rajasthan and Haryana while the farmers in the state were depending on tubewells. The statement said, "River water is our lifeline. We are here to defend the rights of our people. The ownership (of river waters) rests with the people of Punjab. At the same time, we make it clear that we have no enmity with the people of Haryana or Rajasthan. We would not allow water to flow in the BML Canal or the SYL Canal."

The work the SYL Canal was earlier abandoned due to the gunning down of its chief engineer M.L. Sekhri and superintending engineer Avtar Singh Aulakh by the militants on July 23, 1990 in their office in Chandigarh. By that time, about 90 per cent of the work had already been completed. The action was planned by four militant organizations associated with the Panthic Committee (Dr. Sohan Singh) and assigned to the Khalistan Commando Force but was carried out by the Babbar Khalsa.

The brain behind the ideas for action relating to the peasantry-related issues carried out by the Babbars had originated with a leader from a dominant faction of the Bharti Kisan Union.

Normally, all the four organizations would jointly own the action but the press release at times would be released by the organization that executed it. Former finance minister and senior Akali Dal leader Balwant Singh was assassinated on July 10, 1990 in Chandigarh by Gurjant Singh Budhsinghwala and associates from KLF and the press note too was released by this organization but in the name of all the outfits.

This broadly was the pattern of killings by these dominant militant organizations during Phase III.

Yet another dimension was unlimited supply of weapons from across the borders. The militants staying in Pakistan were given the signal that they could arrange any quantity of weapons that were freely available in the Frontier area. These weapons were coming from Afghanistan then under the Soviet Union's occupation.

Sikh militants, however, refused to be mercenaries. This development relates to some time in 1990. That was the period when militancy was not strong in Kashmir. The target was to be former Jammu and Kashmir governor Jagmohan who had left for Delhi in 1989. His term was associated with state repression. Some Kashmiri leaders in Pakistan approached Babbar Khalsa chief Sukhdev Singh Babbar, who had gone to Pakistan during that period, seeking his help to carry out the operation in Delhi as the Babbars had a strong base in the capital. He refused saying his people would not act as mercenaries.

Politics of Targeting the Hindus

Here is one aspect of Sant Bhindranwale's personality that is not much known. He contributed to the construction of two Hindu temples—one in Gurdaspur jail and the other at Mehta Chowk. He used to refer to the Gurdaspur jail temple in particular in his speeches to counter the attack on him of being anti-Hindu.

The Hindus as a community were not targeted for more than three years after militancy was triggered with the killing of Nirankari chief Gurbachan Singh on April 24, 1980. The design in the killing of Hindus was unleashed with the Dhilwan tragedy in which six Hindu bus passengers travelling in the Amritsar-Delhi bus were segregated and killed sending shock waves across India. The Congress government headed by Darbara Singh in Punjab was unceremoniously sacked within hours. This action of dismissal of the state government by the Indira Gandhi government reinforced the political design of the killing of Hindus as symbols of the government that continued for years.

The Hindus were not targeted for just being Hindus but as a symbol of the government at the centre. The objective was not purging Punjab of the Hindus but shaking the government at the centre. It is for this reason that a spurt in the killing of Hindu bus and rail passengers was witnessed in Punjab and Haryana after the declaration of Khalistan by the Panthic Committee on April 29, 1986. The Hindus were perceived to be the symbol of the Indian state.

The first such incident after the Operation Bluestar was reported on July 25, 1986 when 14 Hindu passengers travelling by the Muktsar-

Chandigarh bus were gunned down on the Muktsar-Sadiq Road. Twenty-two Hindu bus passengers were killed on November 30, 1986 in a Faridkot-Pathankot bus.

The reaction of Sant Bhindranwale on October 16, 1983 to the killing of six bus passengers at Dhilwan earlier on October 5 can be quoted in this context.

He said,

> Somebody killed six or seven persons belonging to the Hindu community. This was condemned by every Sikh but despite such condemnation, she (Indira Gandhi) is shaken. On the other hand, the killing of 150 Sikhs during the last sixteen months since the Morcha was launched does not move her. If our (of Sikhs) blood is spilled, no action is taken for sixteen months but if the blood of a Topiwala (the Hindu) is spilled, action is taken within no time and the ministry is sacked.[54]

This fight was against the centre and not the Hindus as such but the Hindus got caught in the cross fire.

Of course, the indifference of the Hindus as a community to the issues taken up by the Akali Dal that articulated the Sikh concerns over the years contributed in shaping this perception, beginning with the language issue. Even the river water dispute was associated with the Sikhs.

There is yet another aspect. The Hindu leaders sided with the Nirankaris who were patronised by the government at the centre. The Sikhs had come into confrontation on purely religious issues against the Nirankaris. The killing of Hindus was an attack on the centre.

It is pertinent to take note of the pattern of killings in the state in this context as per the figures provided by the Home Ministry. A total of 3,871 Hindus were killed by the militants in the period 1981-91 while the number of Sikhs was 6,177. The targeted killings were of the Nirankaris (both Hindus and Sikhs) till the Dhilwan killings and not the Hindus as a community. However, the perception that got created in India was that the Sikhs were killing Hindus. This perception played a major role in the planned carnage of the Sikhs in Delhi and at other places in November 1984 following the assassination of Indira Gandhi.

Sharing But Not Owning Composite Culture

This problem can be understood at yet another level.

Both the Sikhs and the Hindus in this region share a composite culture. However, the Hindus by and large do not own this heritage or identify with it. The Punjabi language is part of the composite culture but was disowned by a major chunk of the Hindus in Punjab during the 1961 Census. This perversion impacted the Punjab's political and Sikh-Hindu dynamics in the long run.

Interestingly, this owning up has been taking place since about 2010 at another level and that is in the field of entertainment. The Punjabi language and culture has succeeded in making a forceful intervention in Bollywood, mainly through music. It is a different matter that the Punjabis have dominated this field from the beginning but this language and culture did not find such expression earlier.

Violence Just for Autonomy?

The political demand on record raised by Sant Bhindranwale was implementation of the Anandpur Sahib Resolution that called for autonomy and not an independent Sikh state. The violence that initially was rooted in the revenge psyche later got transformed into violent political conflict. Was this violence just for autonomy justified? There seems to be no justification for taking up the arms to get the demand for autonomy implemented.

The state repression that was unleashed to confront the revenge psyche proved to be a catalyst in this conflict.

Over time, the Darbar Sahib complex turned into a fortification and this was given as the excuse for the bloody attack. Of course, 42 other gurdwaras were also raided. Would the army have attacked if the militants were not operating from there?

These are the issues that need to be objectively debated dispassionately and objectively.

ENDNOTES

1. Jagtar Singh. (2011). *Khalistan Struggle: A Non-movement*. Delhi: Aakar Books, p. 258.
2. Mohinder Singh. *Neeh Rakhi Gayee*, p. 270.
3. The person who dealt with Jasbir Singh Rode was Intelligence Bureau official Maloy Krishna Dhar who retired as its joint director. He has detailed this operation in his book *Open Secrets*.
4. Jagtar Singh. (2011). *Khalistan Struggle: A Non-movement*. Delhi: Aakar Books, p. 309.
5. August 8, 1988. *The New York Times*.
6. Baba Banda Singh Bahadur was given the responsibility by Guru Gobind Singh in 1709 during his last days at Nanded, now in Maharashtra. The Guru deputed five of his Sikhs with him along with his authorization symbolised by his five arrows. He was finally captured by the Mughal army, taken to Delhi and tortured to death along with his teenage son. He

was the first ruler to transfer land ownership rights to the tiller. Chappar Chiri is located in Mohali near Chandigarh.

7. Jagtar Singh. (2011). *Khalistan Struggle: A Non-movement*. Delhi: Aakar Books, p. 32.
8. He lived at his headquarters at Damdami Taksal in Gurdwara Gurdarshan Parkash at Mehta Chowk till then. He shifted to the Darbar Sahib on July 19 after he received information about the arrest of his close associates Bhai Amritk Singh, president of the All India Sikh Students Federation and Baba Thara Singh by the Amritsar police. Congress MP from Amritsar Raghunandan Lal Bhatia was waiting to meet him when Sant Bhindranwale received the news. Sant Bhindranwale was running a temperature that day and was having a bath in the evening when Bhatia reached Gurdwara Gurdarshan Parkash. They only exchanged pleasantries as he had to rush.
9. June 21, 1978. *The Tribune.*
10. The border town of Dera Baba Nanak was earlier connected to Pakistan by rail-cum-road-bridge that was damaged in the 1971 war.
11. Hindi was never the language of this region. However, the Congress-dominated municipal committee, Jalandhar, in February, 1948 introduced Hindi as the medium of instruction in the schools run by it thereby triggering the language crisis.
12. Jagtar Singh. (2011). *Khalistan Struggle–A Non-movement*. Delhi: Aakar Books, p. 33.
13. December 21, 1983. *The Tribune.*
14. August 28, 1983. *The Indian Express.*
15. Jagtar Singh. (2011). *Khalistan Struggle: A Non-movement*. Delhi: Aakar Books, p. 36.
16. Ibid., p. 39.
17. November 14, 1981. *The Tribune.*
18. September 30, 1982. *The Tribune.*
19. March 23, 1983. *The Indian Express.*
20. December 3, 1983. *The Indian Express.*
21. December 2, 1983. *The Tribune.*
22. December 6, 1983. *The Tribune.*
23. December 6, 1983. *The Indian Express.*
24. September 6, 1983. *The Indian Express.*
25. September 6, 1983. *Ajit.*
26. September 6, 1983. *The Tribune.*
27. Jagtar Singh. (2011). *Khalistan Struggle: A Non-movement*. Delhi: Aakar Books, p. 36.
28. Narain Singh (ed.). (2008). *Singh Garj*. Amritsar: Gurmat Pustak Bhandar. p. 242.

29. Ibid., p. 493.
30. Ibid., pp. 525-27.
31. Ibid., p. 567.
32. Ibid.
33. Jagtar Singh (June 26, 1981). Maverick in Quest of Martyrdom. *The Indian Express*.
34. September 15, 1983. *The Tribune*.
35. Narain Singh (ed.). (2008). *Singh Garj*. Amritsar: Gurmat Pustak Bhandar. p. 540.
36. Ibid., p. 124.
37. Ibid., p. 376.
38. August 25, 1983. *The Indian Express*.
39. September 5, 1983. *Akali Patrika*.
40. Narain Singh (ed.). (2008). *Singh Garj*. Amritsar: Gurmat Pustak Bhandar. p. 589.
41. Ibid., p. 165.
42. Ibid., p. 252.
43. Menon, V.P. (1957). *The Transfer of Power in India*. Delhi: Orient Longman. p. 243.
44. September 5, 1983. *Akali Patrika*.
45. Narain Singh (ed.). *Singh Garj*. Amritsar: Gurmat Pustak Bhandar. p. 165.
46. Ibid., p. 220.
47. Ibid., p. 513.
48. February 9, 1992. *The Times of India*.
49. This building was severely damaged during Operation Bluestar. It was repaired by the government with the help of a Nihang sect headed by Santa Singh who was subsequently ex-communicated for this action from the Sikh religion, to be re-admitted years later after he apologized. The construction or repair of buildings in the complex can only be undertaken through Kar Sewa (voluntary service) and not through hired labour.
50. Brigadier Onkar Singh Goraya. *Operation Bluestar*, 2013, p. 115.
51. The symbolic Kar Sewa to demolish Akal Takht repaired by the government was undertaken by the Taksal and AISSF activists on October 31, 1985 at the first death anniversary of Beant Singh, assassin of Prime Minister Indira Gandhi in the Darbar Sahib Temple complex. The formal decision to this effect was taken later on January 26, 1986 Sarbat Khalsa. This Kar Sewa was thus part of the broader design.

51\. April 26, 1988. *The Indian Express*.

52\. Jagtar Singh. (2011). *Khalistan Struggle: A Non-movement*. Delhi: Aakar Books, p. 381.

53\. Narain Singh (ed.). (2008). *Singh Garj*. Amritsar: Gurmat Pustak Bhandar. p. 415.

5

The Fatal Bus Journey: Dhilwan to Operation Bluestar

As the luxury deluxe bus of the Raj Transport Company with registration number PNZ 197, plying on tourist permit, left the Amritsar bus stand for Delhi with 28 passengers, two drivers and a conductor on the portentous night of October 5, 1983 around 10. 30 pm, no one would have visualized that this ill-fated bus would take Punjab, one of the most prosperous and progressive states, into a dark tunnel from where it would take more than a decade to emerge and horrifically impact the country's political discourse.

For years, Punjab was never to be the same again after that terrible night, the night whose tremors continued to be felt for long not only in Punjab but throughout the country.

This bus was to crush under its vicious wheels militant Sikh leader Sant Jarnail Singh Bhindranwale as well as Prime Minister Indira Gandhi, in that order. However, the idea that was Sant Bhindranwale survived.

By that time, militancy in the state was more than three years old. The catastrophic journey of this doomed bus, months later, catalysed Operation Bluestar, the brutal Indian army attack on the Golden Temple complex, the holiest of the holy Sikh shrines, in the first week of June 1984. Its journey ended on October 31, 1984 when Indira Gandhi was gunned down by her two Sikh security guards to avenge this attack as per the Sikh tradition. The aftershocks from this tectonic disturbance continued to be felt for a long time, impacting a generation. That tectonic activity has still not subsided. Punjab continues to be the seismic zone.

Three persons rose from their seats, one of them forced the driver to stop at gunpoint and the second one occupied the driver's seat as the ill-fated bus crossed river Beas and approached Dhilwan in

Kapurthala district on the Amritsar-Delhi national highway after about 45 minutes into the journey. He diverted the bus to a deserted place on a link road near Gudana village, about 3 kms from the national highway, and as it stopped, the gunmen asked the Hindu passengers to step out one by one. They were lined up. One of these passengers was accompanied by his ageing mother. They shot six of them in the head in cold blood. Vijay Kumar, the seventh Hindu passenger, was attacked with a sword. Believing him dead, they left him. The old mother begged for mercy for her son. His life was spared.

Six people lay dead and this was for the first time that the Hindus had been targeted in this way in a group ever since militancy had hit the region with the killing of the Nirankari sect chief Gurbachan Singh in Delhi on April 24, 1980. Of course, this was not the first killing of the Hindus but the first killing of Hindus as a group to produce high voltage shock waves that shook the entire country. There might have been ethnic killings in the turbulent North-East but not much information came out from those states.

After their task was accomplished, the assailants drove the bus to the nearby Bhullar village, ordered the shocked passengers to get down and headed back towards Amritsar. They abandoned the bus a few kilometres from Amritsar on a link road and escaped. The traumatised passengers spent the night in the fields and it was in the morning that Punjab woke up to this grim tragedy.

The action was planned very precisely going by the deserted link road where the bus was taken immediately after crossing the river.

The Congress government headed by Darbara Singh in Punjab was dismissed within hours of the gory bloodbath the next morning on October 6, 1983.

Those killers were never identified. Two of them were subsequently killed—one on April 14, 1984 in Amritsar and the second on July 12, 1988 near Tanda. Years after this incident, some other people who were gunned down by the Punjab police near Batala in a so-called encounter were shown to have been involved in this macabre incident. This was the routine with security forces in the state during that period. The file of this case was closed.

However, Sukhdev Singh Sukha Kakkar, one of the three persons who carried out the dastardly attack, is alive and leading a normal life in Kasel village, adjoining his native border village of Kakkar in the Lopoke sector of Amritsar district. Kakkar is the last village on that road from Amritsar to the international border via Chogawan and Lopoke. The land of this village is divided by the border fence. He shifted to the farmhouse of his friend Tega Singh of Kasel where he also constructed his two-room house.

Killer's Account of the Dhilwan Bus Massacre

Sukha is now 68. Retrospectively, he justifies the armed struggle and has no regrets for the Dhilwan killings. He is all for the cause taken up by Sant Bhindranwale and swears by his leader's unflinching commitment, unquestioned honesty and total dedication.

However, he is apologetic about another killing carried out in the market of nearby Lopoke as it was the case of mistaken religious identity. This victim was Sumit Singh known as Shammi to his friends, a jovial clean-shaven Leftist Sikh from Preetnagar, the first and only of its kind township of litterateurs near Lopoke that had come up in pre-partition days. Years later in July 2015, Sukha Singh reconstructed the events sitting in the house of his friend in Kasel village.

Accompanying Sukha on that fatal night were Surinder Singh Sodhi and Sukhdev Singh Sukha Sipahi who later headed the Khalistan Commando Force under the name of General Labh Singh. Sodhi, the close confidante and Sant Bhindranwale's right hand man, drove the bus.

Sukhdev had booked tickets in the name of Labh Singh, the name that had been given to him by Sant Bhindranwale. Belonging to Panjwar village, he joined the Punjab police in 1971 and resigned after 12 years to jump into the militant struggle. Initially, he used to be treated with an element of suspicion due to his police background. He passed the crucial loyalty test in Dhilwan.

Sukha was a clean-shaven small-time smuggler, a normal activity in the border villages during those days. The international border with Pakistan used to be open and was fenced years later in 1988. A new station house officer had taken over at Lopoke police station. He warned that he would break Sukha's legs in case he was caught. "I never gave him that chance. I sent back the message that you would do it only in case you get me. The time never came. I was in touch with Kuldip Singh Kohla who introduced me to Sodhi and others. Being clean-shaven, I was told not to go before Sant Bhindranwale. I was accommodated in Guru Ramdas serai in the Golden Temple complex," he said. He was admitted to the ranks of the hit men without any reservation. Here was a man who had no ideological roots or commitment.

It is pertinent to mention that Kohla's name appeared in the FIR that the army registered after Operation Bluestar in June 1984. Kohla was among those who used to arrange weapons and ammunition from Pakistan for the militants.

One of the first actions in which Sukha was involved was the looting of the Home Guards (a semi-police organization set up for civil defence) armoury at Ferozepur. The militants had used the then popular Premier Padmini car in this operation. They carted away as many weapons including some sten guns as the car could carry. According to him, they came across police barricades (nakas) at some places including the one at Harike bridge over the Satluj river but no one stopped their car and they managed to reach the Golden Temple complex safely. "We were ready to open fire in case stopped," he said.

During investigations of the Dhilwan killings, it was found that the weapons used were the same as had been stolen from Ferozepur.

The background to the Dhilwan killings was provided by Bhai Mohkam Singh, one of the associates of Sant Bhindranwale who functioned as one of the two spokesmen of the militants during the post-Operation Bluestar period. He was surprised about the meeting of this author with Sukha less than an hour earlier, saying no one knew about him except a few select persons. Mohkam Singh narrated the provocation for the strategy to target Hindus in a group. That might have been the immediate reason and just the half-truth but part of a broader design. Here is the version provided by Sukha Singh that was corroborated by Bhai Mohkam Singh. The New Bank of India branch at Bhatnura Lubana village near Bullowal on the Jalandhar-Hoshiarpur road in Jalandhar district was allegedly robbed by four persons on October 1, 1983. The police response was quick as information reached the nearest police station. While escaping, the tyre of the motorcycle of the robbers got punctured and they took shelter in a sugarcane field in Bullowal village. They were surrounded by the police and heavy firing continued for about five hours. The police lobbed hand grenades. Later half-burnt bodies of four people were recovered. The bank employees could not identify them.

Akali Dal President Sant Harchand Singh Longowal and Sant Bhindranwale described the encounter as fake, saying these four persons were already with the police. It was after about two weeks that they were identified by the police as Roop Singh of Sultanwind, Bahadur Singh of Verowal, Swaran Singh of Chheharta and Malagar Singh.

This author had visited the scene of encounter on October 9 as *The Indian Express* staffer. The villagers raised questions about the four persons having been killed in the encounter being the same men who had robbed the bank. Even the bank cashier stated that he could not recognize the robbers as he got so scared he did not look up. The cash recovered from the spot, of course, was from the same bank branch. The scene did not corroborate the police version of exchange of heavy firing barring the signs of burning at the spot from where the bodies were recovered.

The Akali Dal, at a meeting of its district jathedars (presidents), MPs and MLAs on October 11, condemned the killings of four Sikhs at Bullowal in a fake encounter as "murder." At the same time, the meeting strongly criticized the killing of six innocent Hindus at Dhilwan.

One of the four alleged robbers, Malagar Singh was close to Jathedar Ram Singh Chauladha, who was considered to be Sant Bhindranwale's second-in-command. Jathedar Chauladha was the man who coordinated with the militants and provided them with weapons for Operation Dhilwan. Bullowal was also the village where Sodhi had grown up.

The Bullowal killings in general and that of Malagar Singh in particular had angered Jathedar Chauladha. The bhog of all four people, significantly, was performed at Manji Sahib Hall in the Golden Temple complex by the Akali Dal.

Jathedar Chauladha took up the issue of taking revenge with Sodhi and they planned the killing of Hindus in retaliation. It was Sodhi who roped in the other two and they decided upon the night service bus at random.

What is not known is whether Jathedar Chauladha had taken Sant Bhindranwale into confidence on this sensitive issue or not. Sukha was only a hit man and this part was not known to him. But then such a major action could not have been executed without keeping Sant Bhindranwale informed.

A day earlier, Jagtar Singh Nagoke from the Nagoke group had said in Guru Nanak Niwas: "The Mukh Vaak today is that about half a dozen lalas (Hindus) would be no more by tomorrow." This information was shared on the condition of maintaining anonymity by the source who subsequently rose to an important position in the Sikh religio-political hierarchy. This reference was to Sant Bhindranwale.

Sukha has been spending his time unknown to the people that he was one of the three men whose action effected a paradigm shift in the militant struggle under the leadership of Sant Bhindranwale and changed the nature of political discourse at the national level. Sant Bhindranwale strongly condemned this incident in the morning as his personal assistant Rachhpal Singh broke the news in the presence of this writer saying, "*Sant ji, Chhe Turk jhatka te*". (Santji, six Hindus have been killed). This was the reference to the first ever killing of a group of Hindus travelling in the bus. Sant did not react and nothing could be read from his face but he betrayed no element of surprise.

From the detailed account now available, the assailants had reached the shrine by that time.

The killing of Hindus in a group had the potential of the community's migration from Punjab and retaliation against the Sikhs in other states. This amounted to polarizing the situation and coming into direct confrontation with the Indian state.

Sukha Kakkar was one of those faceless non-ideological gun-toting hit men who were never in the limelight. He continued to be faceless, not known even next door that he had been a macabre killing machine once.

As per the information available about the command structure in the Bhindranwale camp, the target would be assigned mostly by Jathedar Chauladha or by Rachhpal Singh, the soft spoken personal assistant of Sant Bhindranwale, who would also provide weapons for the action.

Sukha was also part of the group that was assigned to target then Haryana Chief Minister Bhajan Lal who was considered to be notoriously anti-Sikh. He was to be attacked at Gharaunda where he was to address a public meeting. The action was carried out near Panipat in the second week of March 1984 but the person turned out to be Deputy Speaker of the Haryana Assembly Ved Pal, who was injured in the attack. It was a case of mistaken identity. According to one report, they were in that area for three days.[1]

The assailants returned to Amritsar. Some time later, they were contacted by one Bhagat Singh and taken to Mumbai to target the son of former Chief Minister Darbara Singh settled in Asansol in West Bengal. Also with them was one of the militants from the group who had attacked Ved Pal. They carried out a robbery too during that period. They were arrested just by chance and his associate later broke down and disclosed details of the Ved Pal case. He spent time in jails in Maharashtra and Gujarat before being shifted to Haryana. They were subsequently acquitted in the Ved Pal case in 1995 in the absence of witnesses. He had been bailed out in November 1993. Militancy had petered out by that time and he started a new life.

However, he continued to face police harassment for some time as he was summoned occasionally to the police station. Finally, he made up his mind and approached Superintendent of Police Sukhdev Singh Chhina at Amritsar. He disclosed his involvement in the Dhilwan bus massacre. He was advised to keep his mouth shut as some others had already been named in that incident and killed in a fake police encounter. The police official intervened to end his harassment.

It was the Dhilwan killings that not only changed the entire political discourse but also the perception about the Akalis at the national level who now came to be identified with the militants. This had not happened earlier, although the Hindus had not been targeted for the first time. One of the national newspapers stated in its editorial titled 'Under President's Rule': "The stake in Punjab is extremely high—the country's security. The Centre should spare no effort and shirk no decision, however unpleasant, if it is to restore respect for authority. Obviously, the Akali murder squads are well-organized, well-trained, well-armed and well financed. This must change. Apparently, the intelligence agencies too have not performed well in Punjab... Finally, the Akali leaders should be left in no doubt that the government means business."[2] The Akalis were perceived as terrorists overnight. This was one extreme. A section of the media was already clamouring for tough action. The ground was now being prepared for the army attack.

Within hours of this action, trenches and pill boxes were seen coming up in the Golden Temple complex.

Opposition's Advice to Suspend Agitation

The opposition parties, following the Dhilwan tragedy, advised the Akali Dal to suspend the agitation (morcha) that was turned down by the party at a meeting of its district jathedars, MPs and MLAs on October 11. The Opposition, till then, had supported the Akali agitation. Coinciding with the Dhilwan killing was the two-day conclave of the opposition parties at Srinagar where the Akali Dal was represented by Parkash Singh Badal and Surjit Singh Barnala. The suggestion to the Akali Dal to suspend agitation was made at this conclave.

The Akali Dal, while rejecting this appeal, decided to convene a meeting of the opposition parties to involve them in finding a solution to the issues concerned and strengthen the forces of amity and communal harmony. Yet another objective was to "expose the ruling party's game of encouraging communal and divisive forces." The only leader in favour of suspending the morcha was Parkash Singh Majitha but he was not part of the top hierarchy. Former finance minister Balwant Singh was of the opinion that the suspension of the morcha after so much sufferings and sacrifices and at the time when the Sikhs were engaged in a do-or-die battle for the Panthic cause would not only amount to gross betrayal of the faith reposed in them but would be nothing short of committing political harakiri by the Akali leadership. It was Balwant Singh who two years later was instrumental in the signing of the settlement that is known as the Punjab Accord between Prime Minister Rajiv Gandhi and Sant Longowal.

The offer from Sant Longowal to quit as morcha dictator too was rejected unanimously. It has been the norm in the Akali Dal to designate a leader as the morcha dictator during the entire period of an agitation. That leader is not supposed to leave the Golden Temple complex except to court arrest.

The morcha could have been withdrawn earlier when Deputy Inspector General of Police A.S. Atwal was gunned down while coming out of the Golden Temple on April 25, 1983. The security forces could have entered the complex that day without any protests from the Sikhs. Sant Longowal failed to live up to the responsibility he was entrusted with as the morcha dictator. The second time was after the Dhilwan killings.

Prime Minister Indira Gandhi too started identifying Akalis with the militants as evident from her two-hour long press conference on October 15, 1983 at Vigyan Bhavan in Delhi where she asserted, "Until the Akalis dissociate themselves from the activities of extremists and terrorists and ended the atmosphere of confrontation, nothing tangible would come out. There can be no settlement when the Akalis want to dictate terms."[3]

She reacted sharply to Sant Bhindranwale's statement that she imposed President's Rule only when the Hindus were killed and never reacted when the victims were the Sikhs. "Who killed Sikhs? Who prepared the hit list which included Sikhs also?" she asked.

Sant Bhindranwale hit back the next day on October 16 saying, "Let Indira Gandhi provide the proof that I prepared the hit list. I will offer my head to the Sangat or leave Guru Nanak Niwas and go out (of the Golden Temple complex). In case she is just levelling allegations without any proof, she should resign as the Prime Minister." At the same time, he asserted that despite the fact that all sections of the Sikh society condemned the Dhilwan killing, she was never moved at the killing of 150 Sikhs and the morcha going on for the last 16 months the way she was shaken by the killing of six Hindus and dismissed the government of Darbara Singh within no time. This was because her government could not tolerate the Sikhs. "In case six topiwalas (Hindus) are killed, the government is dismissed within no time but no action has been taken for the killings of the Sikhs during the last 16 months," he added. This was in reaction to Indira Gandhi and here was a challenge thrown to her publicly to prove her allegation or quit.

Here is the excerpt from his original speech at Manji Sahib stage on October 16, 1983 in reaction to the Prime Minister's press conference:

> Mediapersons asked (Indira Gandhi at her news conference) that Sant Bhindranwale has said that the Punjab Chief Minister has not been removed despite the court arrest by 1.70 lakh Singhs (as part of Akali agitation) and martyrdom by another 150, what is the reason? The only reason is that she wanted to humiliate the entire community through this so called Sikh chief minister. So long as he was doing her bidding and Sikhs continued to be insulted, Sikh women dishonoured and she kept on giving ultimatums, nothing was done. Then the time came when six or seven Hindus were killed. This incident was condemned by all the Sikhs. Despite this condemnation, she got a rude shock, the like of which she had not felt, although the blood of 150 Sikhs had been spilled. The 16-month long morcha did not move her. She refused to change this one man (Darbara Singh). In case our (Sikhs) blood is spilled, nothing is done for 16 months but in case these topiwalas (Hindus) are killed, the government is dismissed within no time.[4]

Sant Longowal's reaction too was sharp. "Mr. Longowal alleged that the Prime Minister was deliberately misleading the people and trying to incite the neighbouring states against the just demands of the people of Punjab...he also questioned the sincerity of the Prime Minister's remarks that she was deeply concerned over the loss of life over the wake of violence in Punjab and asked what she had done for those who had been killed in fake encounters and in incidents of communal violence in Haryana and those killed at Mehta Chowk firing near Amritsar... Mr. Longowal strongly condemned the recent bomb explosions in Delhi, Chandigarh and Ludhiana in which at least eight lives were lost. He said that his party was strongly opposed to these acts of violence which, he felt, were being organized to torpedo the struggle for the common interests of all sections of people of Punjab."[5]

Killing of Sumit Singh

Yet another major action involving Sukha was the killing of Sumit Singh on February 22, 1984, grandson of eminent progressive Punjabi writer and founder of the popular Punjabi magazine *Preetlari*, Gurbaksh

Singh, who conceptualized the first planned settlement for writers and artists in association with film personality Balraj Sahni in 1936. This settlement now, close to the international border near Lopoke known as Preet Nagar, is in ruins. Sumit was a clean-shaven Sikh and could thus safely cross Haryana while coming back to Amritsar from Delhi during the anti-Sikh turbulence in that state during those days. Anti-Sikh violence had hit Haryana from February 15 to 20, 1984 against the killings in Punjab during which Sikh travellers were killed, harassed and humiliated. Sumit's was one of the four retaliatory killings.

"I was given instructions to kill Hindus at random in retaliation for what was happening in Haryana. We went to Lopoke market. I did not know Sumit. He was clean-shaven and pillion riding on a scooter driven by a Sikh friend. His Sikh friend kept pleading not to kill him but never said that he too was a Sikh. I regret this killing for which I am prepared to publicly apologize," he said. Sumit, being clean-shaven, had crossed Haryana during that troubled period without facing any harassment, never realizing that death awaited him near his own home. It was Sumit's brother who was driving the scooter.

The signal to target Hindus in this case was given by otherwise soft-spoken Rachhpal Singh, personal assistant to Sant Bhindranwale.

Sumit's too was the case of random killing.

Within days of the Dhilwan killings, the BJP too at a meeting of its national executive on October 22, 1983 at Lucknow adopted a resolution calling upon the Akali Dal to withdraw its agitation and blamed both the Akali Dal and the Congress (I) for the deteriorating situation in Punjab. The Party General Secretary L.K. Advani said while the Congress (I) government failed to take action against those responsible for violence in Punjab, the Akali Dal was equally responsible as the party had not delinked itself from extremists and separatists.

The problem with the Akali Dal was that after the Prime Minister clubbed the party leaders with the militants, they were left with no option despite Sant Longowal condemning such killings. That was the time when Mrs. Gandhi should have provided an escape route to the Akali leaders by negotiating an honourable settlement with the party. She did not exercise this option but allowed the situation to flare up. It is this approach of Indira Gandhi that is intriguing and can be viewed as an indication of the broader design of some forces that might be using even her.

Sant Bhindranwale could be one player in this broader design as the issue was not just the implementation of the Anandpur Sahib Resolution of 1973 as pressed by him, which essentially was the demand of the Akali Dal. There has been no controversy about this resolution of the Akali Dal for years that essentially called for an autonomous region. The public posture, at the other level, was to fight for restoration of Sikh dignity, whatever it meant. However, there was no need to consciously target Hindus for the achievement of that objective.

The design was perhaps destabilization of the region as that could have delinked Jammu and Kashmir too from India. At another level, this can be interpreted as the creation of the independent Sikh state.

It is this design that needs to be probed and that is possible only by thorough investigation based on official records of that period in case still available. The files pertaining to that period, from 1978 and 1992, must be de-classified.

This killing of the innocents raises some basic questions about the ideological framework in the context of the Sikh doctrine. Can such actions be justified on the anvil of the Sikh doctrine as codified in the Guru Granth Sahib? Just condemnation by Sant Longowal and Sant Bhindranwale was not enough. The most important aspect of the Sikh doctrine is its universality as the emphasis is on life discipline. The Golden Temple was conceptualized by the gurus as the shrine open to all irrespective of any caste or creed, high or low. The misuse of such a shrine that emanates this message to humanity as a sanctuary by armed militants cannot be justified by any logic. The Sikh doctrine exhorts people to fight for the rights and justice and not kill innocent persons.

It was Sant Longowal who ultimately raised this very issue of Sikh doctrine in the context of such killings when yet another similar gruesome tragedy took place as four Hindu bus passengers were gunned down near Khabbe Rajputan village, about 45 kms from Amritsar, on November 18, 1983, the second such shocking incident. The bus was on its way to Moga from Amritsar. The modus operandi was the same as the Dhilwan killings as the assailants, who had boarded the bus as passengers, stopped it near that village and asked the Hindu passengers to get down and shot them. The rest of the passengers were told to get down about 400 metres from the spot of killings and one of the militants drove the bus away that was found next morning near Chatiwind village on Amritsar's outskirts.

Both the Sants condemned the killings in strong terms. Sant Bhindranwale described it as an inhuman act that should be condemned by all while Sant Longowal said the perpetrators of the crime had done something contrary to the teachings of the Sikh gurus and basic principles of Sikhism.

He said, "The crime could not be pardoned since it was an inhuman act. Those who had indulged in such a cowardly act or those who had instigated it had done something which was contrary to the teachings of the Sikh gurus and the basic principles of Sikhism. Those responsible for the killings were traitors and enemies of the country".

He had raised the issue in the right perspective but his solitary voice was drowned in the deafening noise of the gun fire from both sides. In case the issues had been publicly discussed and debated in this very framework, the fateful journey of the Dhilwan bus could have been stopped there and then.

Another Aspect of Sant Bhindranwale

In the context of the relationship with Hindus, there is an interesting aspect of the personality of Sant Bhindranwale contrary to the popular perception. Mehta Chowk used to be a small place with a few shops on the intersection of two roads when he had taken over as the Taksal chief. One day, the Hindu shopkeepers approached him with an unusual request. It was about the construction of a temple as the community members had no place for worship in that area. Their problem was both the site and money as they were just petty shopkeepers. Sant Bhindranwale agreed immediately and advised them to select a site of their choice. The Taksal funded the construction of the temple. It may be mentioned that he was also instrumental in getting a temple constructed in Gurdaspur central jail which already had a gurdwara.

There is another dimension in the context of targeting of the Hindus as all along, Sant Bhindranwale and his so-called advisers used to blame the "Brahmin-Bania" rule for the perceived discrimination against the Sikhs. This narrative continued till militancy was crushed. On the other hand, it is the Hindu leaders like Atal Behari Vajpayee who raised their voice against the hanging of Kehar Singh on January 6, 1989 in the case of Indira Gandhi's assassination. The illustration carried by *The Indian Express* that day was the most scathing commentary on the functioning of the judiciary with reference to this hanging.

> Four senior opposition leaders, including Atal Behari Vajpayee (BJP), K.P. Unnikrishnan (Congress-S), Lt General Jagjit Singh Aurora (Akali Dal) and Surendra Mohan (Janata Dal) came out against the hanging of

> Kehar Singh hours before the execution of death sentence. They tried to reach Prime Minister Rajiv Gandhi to prevent what they said would be 'senseless, inhuman and judicial murder.' They wanted to meet the Prime Minister to ask him to convene an emergency meeting of the cabinet to review the earlier decision rejecting the mercy petition of Kehar Singh, as President R. Venkataraman had made it known that he was bound by the advice of the council of ministers. Rajiv Gandhi was out of Delhi. As they tried to contact Home Minister Buta Singh, they were told that he had already gone to sleep.[6]

Here were the Hindu leaders, including a person like Vajpayee from the Sangh Parivar, who were making every effort to save a Sikh, that too in the case of assassination of a Prime Minister, from being sent to the gallows. This single action of these leaders strikes at the very root of articulation of India as a Hindu state targeting the Sikhs.

Fatehabad Bus Killings

This was the first case of killing of innocent bus passengers by the Punjab terrorists in neighbouring Haryana. Thirty-four bus passengers in two buses were shot dead in cold blood by five persons who had arrived in two vehicles.

This happened late in the evening on July 7, 1987 near Fatehabad then in Hisar district. The incident took place virtually within hours of 32 bus passengers having been gunned down near Lalru in Punjab on Chandigarh-Ambala highway. According to the official version, five terrorists travelling in a car and a jeep stopped a bus on a bridge near Fatehabad around 11 pm killing 30 passengers. They then stopped another bus coming from the opposite side killing four passengers. One of the buses headed for Sirsa and the other to Delhi.

One of the terrorists involved was Ranjit Singh Rana of Tharu village near Tarn Taran. He confessed his crime to the police during interrogation.

According to the information available, he operated from Bathinda and lived with his brother and two women as a family. However, they were overcautious while mixing with people in that area and could be seen only when out to fetch milk or other household items. This raised suspicion among the neighbours who informed the police.

The SSP at Bathinda at that time was Rajdeep Singh Gill. The house was raided and those staying there taken into custody. It was during interrogation that Rana broke down and disclosed his involvement in the killing of bus passengers near Fatehabad.

Director General of Police J.F. Ribeiro was informed. The SSP was told to eliminate Rana but he refused. He was handed over to SSP Gobind Ram who was notorious for killings in fake encounters.

Gill subsequently recruited the two women in the police on the plea of rehabilitation.

Rana's name had first surfaced in the assassination of Sukhdev Singh Umranangal, son of Akali leader Jiwan Singh Umranangal. Rana had joined the Bhindranwale Tiger Force of Khalistan in 1987. He had crossed over to Pakistan like several other young men after Operation Bluestar and was detained in Faislabad jail for six months before returning to India.

Hours earlier, 38 Hindu passengers travelling in the Chandigarh-Rishikesh bus HYE 1735 were gunned down by the militants near Lalru on the Chandigarh-Ambala highway around 9.30 pm on July 6, 1987. The action was owned by the Khalistan Commando Force.

These two buses were targeted to avenge the killing of militant leader Mathura Singh from the top hierarchy of the KCF. A student of Khalsa College in Amritsar, he came into contact with Sant Bhindranwale in 1983. He was arrested from the house of Gian Singh Nagoke on July 1, 1987 and taken to the Jandiala Guru police station in Amritsar district. He was killed at night in the police station and shown to have been killed in an encounter, the usual modus operandi of the police in Punjab. The police station in-charge was Inspector Harcharan Singh Suri.

The KCF decided to retaliate. The note left in the Lalru bus warned of killing one hundred Hindus for every killing of a Sikh in fake encounters by the security forces.

Inspector Suri was later killed in February 1990 by the Babbar Khalsa in a bomb attack at Punjab Police Academy, Phillaur where he was undergoing training following promotion as the deputy superintendent of police.

Killing of Train Passengers Near Ludhiana

More than 80 passengers were gunned downs in two trains in Ludhiana district on June 16, 1991. These were Ferozepur-Ludhiana and Ludhiana-Hisar via Dhuri trains. In the first incident, armed persons stopped a train near Baddowal and opened indiscriminate fire. The second train was targeted near Kila Raipur.

The responsibility for these massacres were taken by the Khalistan Commando Force headed by Gurjant Singh Budhsinghwala at a meeting called to condole the killing of its members Jagroop Singh Kalakh and Jagjit Singh Dakha on June 25, 1991 in Bunga village near Mandi Ahmedgarh. It was a news item dated June 30 datelined Amritsar that referred to this meeting.

"The meeting took strong note of those who condemned the train massacre. It was stated at the meeting that the people condemning these actions should confine their thinking to themselves. They said the action was executed to kill army men in the train and the killing of civilian passengers was a collateral damage."[7]

As per this report, the meeting was attended by Budhsinghwala, Nishan Singh, Karaj Singh, Anar Singh Pahra, Mukhjit Singh Bhikhiwind, Harbhajan Singh Mand Dargapur and Jangpreet Singh.

It was the Babbar Khalsa that had condemned the train killings at a meeting attended by its chief Sukhdev Singh, Wadhawa Singh, Dharam Singh Kashtiwal, Dalip Singh Chachowali, Talwinder Singh and Charat Singh. "Bhai Chachowali condemned the killing of train killings near Baddowal and Kila Raipur and attributed the same to penetration by government agents."[8] This report datelined Baba Bakala did not mention that date and place of the Babbar Khalsa meeting.

ENDNOTES

1. April 13, 1984. *The Tribune*.
2. October 8, 1983. *The Times of India*.
3. October 16, 1983. *The Tribune*.
4. Narain Singh (ed.). (2003). *Singh Garj*. Amritsar: Gurmat Pustak Bhandar. p. 415.
5. October 17, 1983. *The Indian Express*.
6. Jagtar Singh. (2011). *Khalistan Struggle: A Non-movement*. Delhi: Aakar Books, p. 320.
7. July 1, 1991. *Daily Ajit*.
8. July 2, 1991. *Daily Ajit*.

6

Operation Bluestar: Indira Gandhi's Fatal Blunder

The unprecedented storming of the Darbar Sahib (Golden Temple) complex by the Indian army in the first week of June 1984 ended as the worst blunder of Prime Minister Indira Gandhi that boomeranged at various levels, including the personal one. While Operation Bluestar redefined India's relations with the Sikhs, Punjab turned into a permanent fault line on the border with Pakistan. For the Indian army, this unprecedented action was a self-inflicted disaster.

However, there is no mention of this attack in the manifestos of the Shiromani Akali Dal in the 1985 Assembly election, 1996 Lok Sabha election and 1997 Assembly election. Surjit Singh Barnala headed the main Akali faction then known as Akali Dal (Longowal) in 1985 while the party president in 1996 and 1997 was Parkash Singh Badal. Operation Bluestar, the code name for this army operation, is missing in these documents.

Indira Gandhi's decision resulting from appropriation of all powers by her turned Punjab into a killing field for years. This was the second time that she had rigged the entire system, the first being the imposition of the Emergency in 1975.

This army attack enigmatically coincided with the Martyrdom Day anniversary of the Fifth Sikh Guru, Guru Arjan Dev on June 3 when people in large numbers visited Darbar Sahib. It was the Fifth Guru who had conceived and constructed this most sacred shrine of the Sikhs.

Operation Bluestar had been in the making for a long time. The build-up started virtually within weeks of the Akali Dal launching the Dharamyudh Morcha on August 4, 1982. The Sikhs were made to realize that they were aliens in India when they were insulted and humiliated while passing through Haryana in the third week of November in 1982 during the Asian Games in New Delhi. Here was the beginning of the confrontation between the Sikhs and the government.

The Sikhs were harassed and humiliated on the directions of Haryana Chief Minister Bhajan Lal on the basis of a story datelined Amritsar, planted by the UNI, stating that the Akalis would gherao the Asiad (the Asian Games). The decision of the Akali Dal to stage a demonstration in Delhi during the Asian Games announced at the political conference in Manji Sahib Diwan Hall in the Darbar Sahib complex on November 4 was distorted by this news agency as gherao. The clarification issued by Akali Dal chief Sant Harchand Singh Longowal made no difference at all. This could have been avoided had the Prime Minister intervened. This treatment to the Sikhs in Haryana provided legitimacy to Sant Jarnail Singh Bhindranwale and reinforced the Akali narrative of the Sikhs being discriminated against in India.[1,2]

The only official record that is available on this darkest chapter of free India is not of the Government of India but the UK. This record that became part of the public domain only in 2014 provides some insight into the situation as India had sought consultancy from the UK. India has not released any part of the record pertaining to Operation Bluestar and all attempts to seek even part of the information have remained futile.

The record clearly indicates that Indira Gandhi had decided on this course of action in February 1984. "The UK High Commission in Delhi reported in February that the revised plan had been approved by Mrs. Gandhi", it is stated in the document.

It can be safely inferred from this record that months had gone into the preparation for storming of the Darbar Sahib complex by the Indian army. The storming of Darbar Sahib by the army, in the first such operation in free India, was not due to some sudden provocation but strategized over a period.

It is significant that Indira Gandhi did not hold any meeting with the Akali representatives after November 26, 1981 and that was much before the party launched its agitation.

The situation was allowed to flare up and the killing of six Hindu bus passengers near Dhilwan on the night intervening October 5-6, 1983 resulted in strengthening the perception among the people in the country that the only way out was the use of force. The humiliation of Sikhs in Haryana and the Dhilwan killings are the two very important dimensions in the run-up to Operation Bluestar.

As per this record, the UK received the request on January 30, 1984 from the Indian Intelligence Coordinator for operational advice to assist with the ongoing situation in the temple complex.

The timing of this request trashes the urgency arguments in support of the timing of the army action coinciding with martyrdom of Guru Arjan Dev on June 3. There was no immediate provocation from the militants requiring quick action.

The British government's political assessment of India during that period is also an important dimension, especially one sentence on page two of this brief that states, "Present trends suggest however that whenever election takes place Congress (I) would win though with a reduced majority. However, Congress, even at the height of its popularity has never won more than 46 per cent of votes in a general election. It cannot therefore be assumed that Mrs. Gandhi will still lead the Indian government 12 months hence."

This brief further strengthens the assumption that playing the Sikh card to win the next Lok Sabha elections due in December 1984 was part of Indira Gandhi's design. The sequence of events reinforces this perception as the situation was allowed to build up by not taking the negotiations to the logical conclusion.

The February 3 note prepared by the UK Foreign and Commonwealth Office states:

> The Indian intelligence coordinator... has sent an urgent request to... for advice on an Indian plan for possible action against dissident Sikhs currently occupying parts of the Golden Temple in Amritsar. The Foreign Secretary believes that the Prime Minister would wish to be aware of the approach and our proposed response.[3]

The SAS officer's assessment was that this type of operation should only be put into effect as a last resort when all other courses of negotiation have failed.

Another UK report on this visit notes:

> He made a ground reconnaissance of the Golden Temple complex in Amritsar on February 10, flown there by a special helicopter. It was clear to the officer that the Indians had not given much thought to how they should root out the extremists, beyond applying the 'sledgehammer to crack a nut' principle.

The UK military adviser was in India between February 8 and 17 and submitted his report to the Indian authorities on February 13.

> With a view to reducing casualties, the UK military adviser recommended assaulting all objectives simultaneously, thereby assuring surprise

> and momentum. The advice given to the Indian authorities identified sufficient helicopters, and the capability to insert troops by helicopter, as critical requirements for this approach. The UK advice also focused on command and control arrangements, and nighttime coordination of paramilitary with Indian Special Group forces.[4]

This advice was not put into operation by India.

The Indian Army Operation

The vicious army attack on the Darbar Sahib complex in Amritsar code named Operation Bluestar beginning June 4, 1984 early morning and ending on June 6 to flush out Sikh militancy icon Sant Jarnail Singh Bhindranwale and his well-entrenched armed associates determined to lay down their lives rather than surrender or escape is a subject matter of research and debate both at the political as well as the strategic level. The 72 hours that this operation supported by tanks and artillery guns lasted could well be the longest 72 hours for the Indian army since Partition in 1947.

In this unprecedented operation, India committed about 70,000 troops, including those deployed all over Punjab. It was a situation never witnessed in any region in India since partition as the entire Punjab was ordered to a screeching halt for 72 hours at 8 pm on June 3, 1984 with the announcement of curfew that covered even villages. Punjab was cut off from the rest of India as communication lines were snapped. Newsmen working for foreign agencies were ordered to leave. It was as if India had attacked not just Darbar Sahib but the entire Punjab. The Golden Temple area had come under curfew earlier on June 1 that was lifted in between when the security forces opened heavy fire on the shrine killing 12 people, mainly innocent devotees.

The Indian Army equipped with tanks and artillery guns was pitted against the 'Army of Faith' of about 200 persons determined to defend this holiest of the holy shrine in an area of a few acres rather than escape. It is a different issue as to why they were holed up there. This battle was not the first in the history of the Darbar Sahib complex that had two memorials dedicated to Baba Deep Singh and Baba Gurbax Singh who had sacrificed their lives while fighting the Afghan invaders.[5]

Commanding the 'Warriors of Faith' was Sant Jarnail Singh Bhindranwale, the maverick, with Major General Shabeg Singh (retd), India's hero of the Bangladesh war of 1971, as what can be described as his director general (military operations). His rival in the Indian army leading the attack was Major General Kuldip Singh Brar, once his junior, the man who was blinded by arrogance and guided by the perception that the 'Warriors of Faith' would surrender at the firing of the first shell.

He ignored the brief by Amritsar Intelligence Bureau chief M.P.S. Aulakh at the very first meeting he held that they would fight to the finish. General Brar and his superiors overlooked the most important aspect—here were the highly motivated people with the death wish who could not be terrorized into submission by the display of military power. Here were the people who had opted for death rather than escape. Of course, the Babbar Khalsa fighters decided to leave but with the objective to carry on the struggle post-Bluestar. It was realized years later that it was a tactical blunder that denied the halo of martyrdom to the leaders of this militant organization.

There is an interesting correlation between General Shabeg Singh and General Brar. Shabeg was his company commander when Brar joined the army as Second Lieutenant, the lowest rank at the entry level then. They were together again when Brar was battalion chief with Shabeg as his brigade commander. Thus both knew the working of the other's mind. Brar played being overconfident.

General Shabeg Singh had been pushed into the situation due to petty rivalry among his colleagues in the army and he was cashiered on concocted corruption charges. By the time his honour was restored by the Supreme Court, this hero of the Bangladesh war had turned 'anti-national.' General Shabeg Singh was the Indian army officer who had organized the Mukti Bahini, the guerrilla resistance in East Pakistan that is now Bangladesh.

At the highest level, it was a battle between Sant Bhindranwale and Indira Gandhi.

The intensity of the war that was fought in this small geographical area is evident from the eye witness account by an army officer who was posted as Colonel (Admn) with Amritsar-based 15 Division but not directly involved with this operation. "Dead bodies were lying everywhere—in the verandahs next to Parikarma, in most of the rooms occupied by the pilgrims in the Serai complex, its courtyard and in the open space in front of the Akal Takht. Some could be seen floating in the Sarovar. I had participated in the active fighting in the 1965 and 1971 wars with Pakistan. Each lasted for about 16 days. I saw more dead bodies in the Golden Temple on 6th June than in the 32 days of both these wars put together."[6] He has described Operation Bluestar as a "worthless encounter."[7]

The space between Darshani Deodi and the Akal Takht turned into a graveyard for the army.

The army suffered such high casualties despite the fact that the main attack was preceded by bombardment by tanks and artillery guns.

> The tanks were positioned near B Division police station and a mountain gun in the open space of Jallianwala Bagh...A number of rounds had to be fired on each target. Those that missed the target even by a small margin landed miles away, somewhere in the opposite corner of the town. One round landed on a portion of the Divisional Canteen in the Cantonment. A large splinter landed in my bungalow which was nearby.[8]

Sant Bhindranwale dictated the course of events on one side with Prime Minister Indira Gandhi on the other. It was a battle in which he virtually dictated Indira Gandhi to fight at his turf and that was her major tactical blunder. However, the reaction among the Sikh masses and at the international level was not as per the calculations of his strategists. For him, it was a calculated gamble and so was the case with Indira Gandhi. Both failed.

Surprisingly, both sides were interacting till the end.

One such effort was made by Amritsar Intelligence Bureau chief M.P.S. Aulakh who brought the Akali leaders and the government representatives to the negotiating table but the secret talks ended in futility.

This meeting in Chandigarh beginning March 27, with the last round on March 29, were part of this exercise. However, in between, Parkash Singh Badal was flown to Delhi alone on March 28 to meet union home minister P.V. Narasimha Rao. Aulakh had met Sant Longowal twice to assess his mind before this exercise was initiated. The Akali Dal chief made it clear that he was open to talks.

Aulakh, although comparatively a junior officer at that time, made every effort to avert a show down till the last. He made it clear to his seniors in Delhi that any drastic action in the Golden Temple complex would alienate the Sikhs at least for 10 years. Here was an earnest officer who understood the Sikh psyche.

Aulakh conveyed Longowal's mind to his superiors who summoned him to Delhi and the situation was discussed with top officials concerned including the cabinet secretary. Aulakh and Abinashi Singh, the all-powerful personal assistant to the SGPC president, too were in Chandigarh to facilitate these meetings. Those who participated in these meetings from the Akali side included Tohra, Badal, Surjit Singh Barnala and Balwant Singh. The official team comprised Narasimha Rao and officials C.R. Krishnaswamy Rao Sahib, P.C. Alexander, M.M.K. Wali and Prem Kumar. T.C. Gupta, a

Punjab officer on deputation with the Chandigarh administration, coordinated the arrangements as inspector general, jail.

Tohra, years later in 1994, disclosed that feelers had been sent to him before Operation Bluestar to meet the Prime Minister secretly.

> He disclosed that four attempts were made to persuade him to "secretly" meet Mrs. Gandhi when he was a member of the Rajya Sabha and had been staying at his residence on 12 Bishamber Dass Road. Two attempts were made by Mr. Buta Singh, the then Union Minister, who met him by chance at Bangla Sahib gurdwara, once by a VIP of Amritsar and once by Mr. Darbara Singh, the then Chief Minister, who himself drove his car to his Bishamber Dass Road residence...He told everyone that he would meet Mrs. Gandhi only on the directive of his party chief, Sant Harchand Singh Longowal.[9]

He also revealed the details of the secret meetings held between the Akali leaders and representatives of Indira Gandhi.

> He said when he was in Burail jail at Chandigarh, Raghbir Singh, an IAS officer from Haryana, and Mr. T.C. Gupta, now Deputy Commissioner of Patiala, who were Deputy Commissioner and SDM respectively of Chandigarh at that time met him in jail with a letter from Sant Harchand Singh asking him to accompany them. The two officers told him that Mr. Parkash Singh Badal would also be brought from Tihar jail, Delhi and Mr. P.V. Narasimha Rao, then a Union minister, would visit on that late night to see them. Mr. Tohra said he again refused to do so till Mr. Surjit Singh Barnala, Mr. Balwant Singh Ramoowalia and Mr. Randhir Singh Cheema also accompanied him...Pointing out that three secret meetings were held at Chandigarh, Mr. Tohra disclosed that the fourth meeting was held at a guest house in Delhi...The three member Akali team comprised of Mr. Badal, Mr. Barnala and himself.

On the surface, the problem with the Indira Gandhi government could be lack of perception and trust. Sant Bhindranwale was not averse to a negotiated settlement. It is for this reason that a high level probe must be ordered into the army action and the situation leading to that bloody showdown to uncover the design.

Military solution should have been the last option after trying for democratic means to confront Sant Bhindranwale in such a small place. Mobilization of the people in general and the Sikhs in particular against radicals occupying the Golden Temple complex after entering into a dignified settlement with the Akali Dal could have been the better democratic choice with Indira Gandhi.

Not just by the officer on the spot in the Intelligence Bureau, Indira Gandhi had been advised even by one of her senior cabinet colleagues, Pranab Mukherjee, against attacking the Golden Temple complex. He was one of the interlocutors deputed by her to engage the Akalis. He was later elevated to the highest office of the President of the country.

Mukherjee, who had been part of the negotiating team before Operation Bluestar, recalled on May 13, 2017 how Indira Gandhi was convinced of the unavoidability of her decision to send the army to flush out militants from the shrine. "As a student of history, I was afraid to do anything with the Golden Temple...I recalled (at a cabinet meeting) how Ahmad Shah Abdali had to face serious consequences after the Third Battle of Panipat when he did something wrong with the Golden Temple," he said. He quoted Mrs. Gandhi's reply, "Sometimes history demands some action to be taken which may not prove correct later on but perhaps is most relevant at that time. This decision cannot be avoided." He described it as her "most dangerous decision."[10]

Former Intelligence Bureau chief T.V. Rajeswar too in his book *India: The Crucial Years* has revealed how the Prime Minister overlooked his four-page note to end the conflict. Rajeswar has claimed that Operation Bluestar could have been averted had the then Prime Minister Indira Gandhi agreed to a deal proposed by a "senior Akali Dal functionary" in 1982. The ex-IB chief, who did not name the leader, said the Akalis had suggested that Mrs. Gandhi ask the then Punjab Chief Minister Darbara Singh to step down and install a coalition government led by an Akali CM in his place, thus effectively neutralizing Jarnail Singh Bhindranwale. "I prepared a four-page note, outlining the offer and gave it to the PM. I told her the offer seemed sincere. I also asked her not to discuss the offer with Gianiji (Zail Singh) and take an independent decision," Rajeshwar says. However, he adds that Gandhi turned down the offer and the situation in Punjab became more explosive, leading to Operation Bluestar in which 492 civilians were killed, according to official estimates."[11]

Indira Gandhi Wanted Sant Bhindranwale's Surrender

Yet another item of information has now surfaced about the thinking of Indira Gandhi.

She convened a meeting of the Punjab Congress leaders days before the army attack on the Golden Temple complex and those who attended included Santokh Singh Randhawa, Captain Amarinder Singh, Bir Devinder Singh, Jagdev Singh Jassowal, Shamsher Singh

Dullo and Dilbagh Singh. The agenda was the situation in the Golden Temple complex.

Indira Gandhi looked very tense as she entered the room and spelled out the agenda: "The situation in the Golden Temple has now deteriorated. I am under pressure both from within the country and outside for decisive action and apparently, only the army can undertake such an exercise. However, I am of the view that such a situation can be averted if 'Bhindaranwala' surrenders. Can you people help in this?" she asked. There was pin-drop silence in the room. "Surrender can be on his terms if Bhindaranwala agrees," she said after a brief pause.[12]

The army strategists might have miscalculated that Sant Bhindranwale would surrender rather than face the military might. In case the Sant had surrendered, she might have emerged as the Durga once again like after the Bangladesh war.[13]

It may be mentioned that in an hour long interaction with this writer at Akal Takht on May 25, 1984, Sant Bhindranwale had made it absolutely clear that he would go back to his headquarters at Mehta Chowk provided the Prime Minister entered into an 'honourable settlement' with the Akali Dal and announce amnesty for his men.[14]

When Indira Gandhi Expressed Helplessness

There is another meeting towards April end that provides an insight into her thinking and sense of insecurity. This was about a 75-minute interaction on the Punjab agenda that she had with some eminent academics on April 29, 1984. They included historian Prof. Bipan Chandra, Prof. M.S. Agwani, Vice-Chancellor, Jawaharlal Nehru University, economist Prof. G.S. Bhalla and researcher Dr. Pramod Kumar.

According to the eye witness account, she appeared to be highly agitated. Her eyelids twitched as she appeared to be apprehensive. A peon came to replace her glass of water. She picked up the intercom and snubbed R.K. Dhawan (her personal secretary) for sending the person in, although she did not ask for water. Apparently, she was feeling so insecure that she did not even trust her personal staff as her apprehension was that these people were spying on her.

On the issue of a negotiated settlement, she said how could she deal with a person who talked of killing 1,100 Hindus? She asked expressing her helplessness, "What can I do under such a situation?" A democratic way out suggested was that she should lead a peaceful march of 10 lakh people to the Golden Temple. She did not favour this line of democratic assertion through mass action.

"I am totally helpless," she said. There was pin-drop silence as she uttered these words.

She was asked whether she was negotiating with Sant Bhindranwale to which she replied in the negative. She said the issues like transfer of Chandigarh to Punjab had turned irrelevant under the given situation.

Dr. Pramod Kumar commented, "Madam Prime Minister, you are known for the art of the impossible." She just smiled and looked away.

In between, she said to her secretary Pandey, "Don't tell your father about this meeting." He was the son of B.D. Pande, then Governor of Punjab.

The situation would have been different in case she had taken such a bold initiative in the democratic domain. However, the army action had already been planned for which she had sought expert "advice" from the UK.

Dr. Pramod inferred from this interaction that he shared with others at that time that the army action was inevitable.

Here was a most powerful leader, who had damaged democratic institutions with her autocratic style of functioning, feeling helpless and powerless in the face of the Punjab crisis.

Last Minute Talks

As the army units were taking positions, efforts were on till the last days to find a way out of the crisis despite tough public posturing. This initiative was undertaken after the last abortive secret meeting on May 26 attended by Tohra, Badal and Barnala from the Akali Dal and Union Ministers Narasimha Rao, Shiv Shankar and Pranab Mukherjee at a guest house in New Delhi.[15]

Apart from this meeting with the Akali leaders, two representatives from the Centre had a two-hour meeting with Sant Bhindranwale at Akal Takht on June 1 before heavy firing was opened by the paramilitary forces on the complex around noon that continued for about seven hours. This meeting is significant in the context that during his last interaction with this writer, he was for conditional safe passage. However, Indira Gandhi wanted him to surrender. Not to mention the talk of surrender, he did not even escape. It is this aspect of the Sikh psyche that she did not comprehend.

He deputed Bhai Amrik Singh, Harminder Singh Sandhu and Harinder Singh Kahlon to escort them out of the complex. The three did not know the identity of these people. From among those three people deputed by Sant Bhindranwale, only Kahlon is alive.

As they moved towards their car in the then parking of the

Golden Temple complex towards Ghanta Ghar, intense firing started. The firing had been opened by the CRPF deployed on the buildings surrounding the shrine. One of them got separated in that confusion. The other one commented, "How can this woman (Indira Gandhi) be trusted?" The second person too later managed to reach the parking. Kahlon stayed with them. They left when the firing stopped around 7 pm. Kahlon escorted them to Mohan International Hotel. Curfew had been imposed in the walled city by the time they reached the hotel.

Earlier, Congress leader Tarlochan Singh Riyasti too met him on May 27 and recorded the conversation. It was confirmed by another senior Congress leader from Amritsar Raghunandan Lal Bhatia that the recording was sent to the Prime Minister. Bhatia used to interact with Sant Bhindranwale even before he had shifted to the Golden Temple complex.

That the two adversaries exchanged letters at one stage is on the record. Their intermediary was Jalandhar-based Akali leader-cum--senior journalist Bharpur Singh Balbir, popularly known as Netaji, who had a copy of the letter written by Indira Gandhi to Sant Bhindranwale. She wrote on February 23, 1983:

> "Respected Santji,
>
> Sardar Bharpur Singh Balbir Netaji has brought me your letter dated February 19, 1983.
>
> I agree with your view that every person should sincerely follow one's religion.
>
> Sardar Bharpur Singh Balbir Netaji spoke to me about your religious programme and also gave me detailed information about your sect. As you know, I am concerned with the unity and strength of our country. That is why it is important to discuss and settle all differences peacefully. Religious leaders can help in this.
>
> The differences which have arisen between the Sikhs and the Nirankaris are causing trouble to a large section of our society. Please try to normalize them. I send my regards and best wishes.
> Indira Gandhi".

Balbir released the letter to the Hindi daily *Dainik Bhaskar* that appeared on February 6, 2014. The letter was in her handwriting. He had been talking about this correspondence for years.

Sant Bhindranwale in his letter to 'Bibi Indiraji' listed injustice and excesses against the Sikhs over the years since independence.

It was some time in the aftermath of this exchange of correspondence that the Gurdaspur deputy commissioner Gurdev Singh Brar received a message to secure a safe house for the secret visit by the Prime Minister. This ostensibly was for meeting Sant Bhindranwale in case the negotiations were to be taken to the logical conclusion. The message conveyed directly from Delhi was not on the record. This exercise did not make any headway. According to Bhai Mohkam Singh, Union Minister Shiv Shankar visited Amritsar some time in the winter of 1983 to establish contact with Sant Bhindranwale. Brar was later shifted to Amritsar to be replaced by Ramesh Inder Singh on the eve of Operation Bluestar.

Home Secretary Pooni Requisitioned Army

The decision to attack Darbar Sahib complex was taken by only one person and that person was Indira Gandhi and in such a situation, the technicalities such as formal requisitioning of the army 'in aid of civil administration' was a minor issue but at the same time, this dimension calls for details.

An official spokesman of the Punjab government in the afternoon of June 1, 1984 "denied reports that Army units were poised for action against terrorists in the state."[16] The spokesman further said that the movement of troops was "unconnected with the requirement of law and order."

Also present at that press conference was the state police Chief Pritam Singh Bhinder.

Troops had already taken positions all over Punjab by that time.

"9 Infantry Div was based in Meerut and moved to Amritsar in the last week of May 1984. In the afternoon of 29th May, as I was proceeding to my office, I was surprised to see a number of vehicles bearing the sign of Pine Tree, parked in the open space around the Panther Stadium in the Cantonment."[17]

Officially, there was no intimation with the state government till then. However, the Army official took over on June 2 within hours of the denial by the state government.

The announcement to this effect was made in Delhi and Indira Gandhi went on air at 8 pm.

The announcement made it clear that the army had been called out on the recommendation of Governor B.D. Pande.

The text of the official announcement is as follows:

> In view of the escalating violence by terrorists in Punjab, the Governor of Punjab has asked the central government for the assistance of the army to help in restoring law and order. Government have accepted

> the Governor's recommendation. The army has been called in aid of the civil authority and Lt General Ranjit Singh Dayal, Chief of Staff, Western Command, has taken over as adviser (security) to the Governor of Punjab. The para-military forces deployed in Punjab will continue to work but under the overall command of the army.

Earlier in the day on June 2, state chief secretary K.D. Vasudeva and home secretary Amrik Singh Pooni were conveyed the message to reach Punjab Bhavan to meet the Governor who was returning from New Delhi.

Vasudeva disclosed 35 years later in 2019 and quoted Pande while speaking on camera: "I have decided to call the army. General Sundarji (Chandimandir-based Western Army Commander Lt General K. Sundarji) is reaching here. He reached there shortly. The Governor instructed us to keep the letter prepared to requisition the army. Pooni prepared the letter. The letter was handed over to General Sundarji. Only the Governor knew what happened during his visit to Delhi. That was Pande's decision and we only implemented it. President Giani Zail Singh too landed at Chandigarh airport that day (He was to go to Himachal Pradesh but his trip was cancelled.) He asked Pande as to what was happening and was he sleeping? The President returned to Delhi."

Vasudeva denied that IAS officer Ramesh Inder Singh, who took over as Amritsar deputy commissioner on June 4 replacing Gurdev Singh Brar, had signed the requisition. He said Brar had already applied for ex-India leave in April. He was to go to the USA and boarded the flight on June 8. He left Amritsar for Delhi on June 5 under escort provided by Amritsar district police Chief Chaudhary Sube Singh.

The army had already moved to Amritsar by the time Ramesh Inder Singh joined as deputy commissioner.

The army officers held a three-hour meeting with the Governor at Raj Bhavan after the formality of requisitioning the army had been completed on June 2. Those who attended included Surendra Nath who had been sent to Chandigarh as adviser to the Governor, Pooni and Bhinder. Western Army Command Chief of Staff and 2-I-C to General Sundarji was appointed security adviser to the Governor.

Lt Gen Dyal added what in hindsight can be termed as a comic touch by maintaining on June 3 at a news conference in the Punjab civil secretariat that "Armed forces had not been deployed in Punjab so far. Troops would be deployed wherever and whenever felt necessary in Punjab as well as Chandigarh."[18]

The whole of Punjab was placed under unprecedented curfew from June 3 evening with movements even in the countryside having been banned. Punjab came to a screeching halt with only the army vehicles on the roads. All telephone networks in Punjab were disconnected and this included the residential telephone of the Amritsar deputy commissioner too.

The official statement with regard to the situation in Punjab issued on June 2 by the Union government stated, "In view of the escalating violence by terrorists in Punjab, the Governor of Punjab has asked the central government for the assistance of the army to help in restoring law and order."

Pooni proceeded on leave for a few days after signing the file. It may be mentioned that the army deployment had been requisitioned for the entire state and not just Amritsar, and this was the reason for the Home Secretary signing the file. The recommendation was routed through the Governor. The Union Home Ministry on June 2 had referred to the army help sought by the Punjab Governor "to help in restoring law and order."

The army also raided 42 other gurdwaras in Punjab. No exact figure is available about how many people were killed during raids on these gurdwaras.

The Centre and the Punjab government were approached seeking information under the Right to Information Act seeking details on the requisitioning of the army. The Union Home Ministry, in a letter on February 27, 2013, stated: "The information sought by you is not available in the records under the purview of the undersigned CPIO. Further the information sought by you pertains to the event occurring 20 years ago. As such, the same is not covered under the RTI Act, 2005".

The office of the Punjab Governor vide letter No. PRB-3G-2013/4802 dated July 9, 2013 denied this information, citing the clause of 20 years.

It is in 2019 that the officers concerned have spoken out.

Amritsar under curfew from 11 am on June 3

Here is one of the most intriguing dimensions of the timing of the army invasion of the Darbar Sahib complex.

Amritsar was placed under curfew at 11 am by deputy commissioner Gurdev Singh Brar before it was imposed in the rest of Punjab at 9 pm that day. The walled city had earlier remained under 32-hour curfew from 9 pm on June 1 when the security forces opened heavy fire on the Darbar Sahib complex. Ramesh Inder Singh, who replaced Brar, has stated: "Later, he told me that he had done so at the direction of the Punjab home secretary".

It is the timing that is critical as June 3 was the martyrdom day anniversary of Guru Arjan Dev, the Fifth Sikh Master who had conceived and constructed Darbar Sahib. Hundreds of devotees visit the shrine during such occasions. The devotees had already gathered in large numbers by the time curfew was imposed on the directions from Chandigarh. However, the home secretary had only been reduced to the post office with the deployment of the army and appointment of Lt Gen Dyal as the security adviser.

Curfew was relaxed for a few hours to facilitate the entry of devotees to the Darbar Sahib complex beginning in the evening of June 2 to 11 am on June 3. Why was this relaxation allowed when the army was to launch the most ferocious attack within a few hours and not just search operations? Was it part of the design to cause maximum damage in terms of human lives? The number of militants staying in the shrine was known to the intelligence agencies. Most of the men and women killed by the army were devotees.

No explanation has so far been provided by the government why June 3 was finalized when hundreds of devotees were inside the complex as the day for starting the operation. Firing was opened early in the morning of June 4. Most of the devotees would have left by the evening had relaxation been given in curfew in Amritsar. Was this assault strategically timed with this martyrdom day to cause maximum casualties and teach the Sikhs a lesson?

This is one of the questions related to Operation Bluestar that must be answered by the Government of India. Of course, there are several others.

This is the reason that accountability for this attack must be fixed after a credible probe.

Going by the sequence of events, none in Punjab had any information about the impending action. The decision was that of only one person and that person was Prime Minister Indira Gandhi. She had again been taken over by the authoritarian streak that had earlier resulted in the disaster that was imposition of the Emergency and that too in June 1975.

She denied autonomy of decision-making at every level and became a victim of her own style of functioning that was dictatorial. She paid the cost of this worst decision with her own life as she was assassinated on October 31, 1984 to avenge Operation Bluestar. Total concentration of power made her the most powerful leader but at the same time, the most vulnerable. She had isolated herself completely with her style of centralized governance. Such a system of governance has always produced tragedies.

It was her decision to hand over Punjab to the army that turned this border state into the vast killing field. When Prime Minister Narendra Modi started talking of the threat from terrorists after taking over in 2014, he perhaps deliberately overlooked the fact that more than 40,000 people had been killed in Punjab in the turbulence that hit the state in 1978 and petered out in 1995. However, there is no closure. Intelligence agencies even in 2019 raised the spectre of militant threat.

When the Akali Dal launched its political struggle on August 4, 1982 to recapture the political space, one of the main demands was the Anandpur Sahib Resolution seeking autonomy for the state. The issue of autonomy had appeared on the agenda of the Akali Dal with the adoption of the Batala Resolution in 1969 and the Anandpur Sahib Resolution passed by the party's working committee in October 1973 was its updated version. No one talked about it till it was taken up by the party again in August 1980 and included as one of the demands underlying the 1982 struggle.

It was this resolution whose implementation was taken up by Sant Jarnail Singh Bhindranwale, maintaining that the Akali leaders would not be allowed to backtrack from it. It was this Akali Dal struggle that provided political space to Sant Bhindranwale initially. He went too far at times on the issue of the Anandpur Sahib Resolution as evident from his call to the people to arm themselves: "There is no need for a license for keeping even a carbine. If anybody asks for a license, show him the Anandpur Sahib Resolution...Read para six of the Anandpur Sahib Resolution."[19] This was ridiculous.

Indira Gandhi responded to the demand for autonomy by resorting to centralization of power. The re-emergence of the centralization tendency in her can be interpreted as her strategy to counter the Anandpur Sahib Resolution that produced the ultimate tragedy.

The two main players in this tragic drama were Indira Gandhi and Sant Jarnail Singh Bhindranwale and both ridiculed each other. At one level, both had the similar streaks.

In the process, Sant Bhindranwale dictated her to come to his turf to fight the ultimate battle that was much bigger than Operation Bluestar. This is the one battle in which both the players failed. Both of them ended up as martyrs but for a different set of people. Both are heroes as well as villains. In case Sant Bhindranwale's strategy had worked out, the situation would have been different.

Indira Gandhi made the moderate politics redundant. Ironically, this suited Sant Bhindranwale too as her politics pushed the ideologically moderate Akali Dal to the margins. The only people who were relevant were Indira Gandhi and Sant Bhindranwale. This precisely is the reason that the people and the politics who turned redundant by them cannot provide the right answers.

This also explains why the ninth and the last secret meeting between the Akali leaders and the ministers of Indira Gandhi in Delhi on May 26 in New Delhi failed. This explains why the ministers told the waiting Akalis, "Very sorry. Madam does not agree."[20]

The first phase of politics of violence that was triggered even before the Akali Dal launched the Dharamyudh Morcha on August 4, 1982, ended with Operation Bluestar. For the understanding of the phenomenon, it is necessary to have insight into the situation during the last hours of the life of Sant Bhindranwale due to which he has left his footprints on the pages of Sikh history. The issue here is not agreeing or disagreeing with his brand of politics and the strategy and tactics associated with that politics.

Eyewitness Account of Last Minutes of Sant Bhindranwale

The army resorted to heavy shelling and firing on the Golden Temple complex in the early morning of June 4, 1984 beginning around 4.40 am. The whole of Punjab and the Union Territory of Chandigarh had been placed under curfew earlier on June 3 beginning 8 pm with no movement being allowed even in the countryside. With the communication lines having been snapped, Punjab was cut off from the rest of the country. It was an all-out war between India and her 'own people.' The shrine had hundreds of innocent devotees, men and women of all ages and children, at that time. Sant Bhindranwale was in the Akal Takht where he had been staying for about eight months.

The army units had started preparing for the attack around May 27 or 28 by way of laying infrastructure like communication lines.

One light machine gun each was manned by Sukhdev Singh Sukha Sipahi alias Labh Singh and Kabul Singh positioned in the two pill boxes on the front side in the basement of the Akal Takht. These two slits had been opened by cutting the thick marble wall of the basement.

The troops entered the shrine on June 5 around 9.30 pm beginning with the main entrance on the Ghanta Ghar side and the serai area after heavy shelling and intense firing had started on June 4 early in the morning. Three attempts by them to storm the Akal Takht were neutralized by heavy firing from the basement. The troops from 10 Guards who entered from the Ghanta Ghar side suffered heavy casualties, beginning with the stairs going down to the Parikarma. The rooms on both sides had ventilators towards these stairs where militants with automatics had taken positions.

The next major hurdle that was encountered by the army was that the Akal Takht was not in direct firing line while the two pill boxes in the basement of that building covered both sides. It was in front of the Akal Takht that the army suffered maximum causalities. Firing stopped at one point from both the sides as the commanders reassessed the situation.

There were no manholes from which the militants would come out to attack and withdraw as was widely reported in the papers at that time. There are no manholes but only a small size covered floodwater drain all around in the Parikarma.

As the army faced unanticipated resistance, tanks were brought into the complex around 11.30 pm on June 5. The earlier attempt to reach the Akal Takht using an armoured personnel carrier was thwarted as it was hit in the Parikarma by a rocket launcher. The armoured vehicle fitted with medium machine guns was later also inducted and placed at strategic points near the Akal Takht to make a direct hit. The tanks targeted the upper portion of the Akal Takht building but firing continued from the basement. On the other side, there could be no replenishment of men and ammunition in the Akal Takht basement.

It was on June 5 that Sant Bhindranwale tried to convince AISSF chief Bhai Amrik Singh to leave the complex as his successor to carry on the struggle later. However, he did not agree.

Several announcements were made by the administration for the pilgrims to come out and to the militants to surrender beginning on June 4 till around 4 pm and the last around 5 am on June 6 when firing was stopped for some time. However, the van of the public relations department making the announcements had been stationed at a distance from the main entrance.

General Shabeg Singh, who monitored the posts manned by militants, started walking towards the Akal Takht as the firing stopped after some time on the first day. He was not that fortunate as he came under fire near the flag posts but managed to enter the Akal Takht. He was taken to the basement to Sant Bhindranwale. Sant Bhindranwale placed his head in his lap. General Shabeg Singh uttered the last words saying he was proud of the fact that he was laying down his life for the defence of Darbar Sahib. "Had I been killed during the Bangladesh war, that would have been immaterial. Now I am dying at the Takht created by Guru Hargobind in the complex founded by Guru Ram Das," were his last words.

Shabeg was a decorated military officer who had played a major role during the 1971 war with Pakistan that resulted in liberation of then East Pakistan now known as Bangladesh. There were a number of retired army officers who supported the armed struggle but they were not active like General Shabeg Singh.

As per the first-hand account provided by Balwinder Singh Khojkipur, Sant Bhindranwale gathered all his associates who were at the Akal Takht around 8.30 in the morning of June 6. It was blood all over the complex. Every inch in the area between Darshani Deodi of the Darbar Sahib and Akal Takht was covered with dead bodies. He said now it would be a hand-to-hand fight as ammunition had been exhausted and those who wanted to leave could go. No one left and all of them prayed for the last time and performed Ardas. The escape passage was from the back of the Akal Takht through narrow lanes. This area was later demolished in the name of beautification. Amrik was ahead when they came out of the Akal Takht from the front. He was the first to be hit. Sant Bhindranwale's driver Gurmukh Singh was also hit. Bhai Parsa Singh, Bhai Joga Singh, Bhai Dhanna Singh and Balwinder Singh Khojkipur, all injured, were handed over by the army to the Border Security Force and taken to Sri Guru Tegh Bahadur Hospital from where they were shifted to a camp about a week later. Khojkipur, one of his personal bodyguards, is among the survivors.

Sant Bhindranwale was near the flag post when he was hit by MMG fire. Before that, he had paid his obeisance with his face towards Darbar Sahib. Khojkipur who was with him too was hit and injured in the leg. He had come under the range of the armoured vehicle-mounted MMG stationed nearby. It was due to MMG firing that one side of Sant Bhindranwale's head was blown away.

One militant Major Singh Warring remained in hiding during combing operations and was killed when he fired at the President of India Giani Zail Singh during his visit to the shrine on June 8.

According to the information available, Sant Bhindranwale tried to contact Pakistan over the wireless set that was with his people at the Akal Takht when the attack began. However, it did not work. It had never been tested ever since it was smuggled in by Baba Devinder Singh.

Sant Bhindranwale sent a message to the Baba staying in Guru Nanak Niwas who brought along the Babbar Khalsa activist Mehal Singh. Mehal Singh, who had been with the Indian Air Force and conversant with the operation of such equipment, said some parts were missing.

His entire strategy was based on intervention by the Pakistan army and this was his biggest miscalculation.

Thus both Indira Gandhi and Sant Bhindranwale had miscalculated. While her design was his surrender, he in turn erred in depending on Pakistan's support.

The Sikhs in Command

When the Indian army carried out its most controversial and the biggest peacetime operation in the country since Independence, most of the senior officers manning key positions were Sikhs. The operation was in the area of Western Command whose Chief of Staff and thus second-in-command happened to be Lt Gen R.S. Dyal, a Sikh. At the ground level, it was yet another Sikh officer Major General Kuldip Singh Brar who commanded the assault. The first to be hit by the bullets of the militants also happened to be a young Sikh officer Captain J.S. Raina. Southern Army Commander Lt Gen Tirath Singh Oberoi too was inducted at some stage. The President of the country at the time was Giani Zail Singh, a devout Sikh, who was also the titular Supreme Commander of the Armed Forces. Was it coincidence?

Army Chief General A.S. Vaidya was gunned down after his retirement on August 10, 1986 in Pune by Harjinder Singh Jinda and Sukhdev Singh Sukha to avenge Operation Bluestar. It may be mentioned that he did not accompany Giani Zail Singh when he visited Darbar Sahib after the Operation. He went to the war scene much later on June 19 and was accompanied by Lt Gen K. Sundarji and Maj Gen Brar.

The Prime Minister visited the shrine on June 23.

Brigadier Goraya (retd) has referred to the presence of Gen Oberoi in Amritsar stating: "The unbroken sequence of visitors increased our workload. The biggest problem was the shortage of accommodation for overnight stay. The three guest rooms which were properly furnished were occupied by Generals Sunderji, Dyal and Tirath Singh Oberoi."[21] This was immediately after the army operation. Brigadier Goraya was assigned the responsibility to escort to safety Akali Dal President and Morcha Dictator Sant Harchand Singh Longowal, Shiromani Gurdwara Parbandhak Committee chief Jathedar Gurcharan Singh Tohra and several other Akali leaders.

Then again: "Before the next meeting, our team was joined by General Tirath Singh Oberoi. He held his first meeting with the Singh Sahiban collectively in the Darshani Deodi."[22] This was in the second week of July. General Oberoi held several meetings with the Sikh leaders during that period to discuss repair to the damaged buildings.

The Operation

It was 4 pm of June 3, 1984. The atmosphere was tense with a detailed map of the Darbar Sahib (Golden Temple) complex on the wall forming the backdrop of the operations room of the 15 Division Headquarters in the Amritsar Cantonment. Senior officials from civil, police, paramilitary forces and intelligence agencies from the border district had been summoned to the emergency meeting.

"Gentlemen, we have arrived...curfew will be imposed tonight in the entire city. Anyone who violates the curfew will be shot," thundered Maj Gen Brar, the 9 Division commander, who had been entrusted with the command of Operation Bluestar. The outburst was shocking for some of those present.

"Tomorrow, we will surround the Golden Temple complex," Gen Brar went on. "We will enter the complex on the 5th evening and accomplish the task within a few hours," he asserted.

Local Intelligence Bureau chief M.P.S. Aulakh, a suave, dedicated and perceptive Indian Police Service officer, intervened making it clear the militants holed up in the complex were well entrenched and well-armed and it was too well known a fact that the mastermind in the complex was yet another former senior army officer Maj Gen Shabeg Singh who had won laurels in the 1971 war. This officer on the spot was right in his assessment that here were highly motivated people determined to die for the cause, in other words 'Warriors of Faith.' Gen Brar, blinded by arrogance who highly overrated himself, ignored the advice.

Old hand Amritsar Superintendent of Police (Intelligence) Pandit Harjit Singh interjected and told Gen Brar, "Sir, it will not be that easy." Here was an officer who too had been closely monitoring the Sikh politics and the situation associated with the rise of Sant Bhindranwale very closely for a long time. His office was located in the Kotwali police station in the Town Hall complex not far from Darbar Sahib and had his fingers on the pulse of the situation. He was brushed aside. Pandit Harjit Singh happened to be a Brahmin from one of those traditional families who wear turbans. From all appearances, they are Sikhs.

The civilian officers argued that the army entry under the given situation could also lead to communal tension. Gen Dyal retorted, "What are you talking? We will enter at 10 pm and the operation will be over by 1200 hours. Lights will be switched on by 4 am." That was the end of the matters. The civilian officers returned to their homes. None of them could sleep that night.

He ordered that anyone violating curfew should be shot. It was the BSF that had been deployed in the city. Now was the turn of BSF Deputy Inspector General G.S. Pandher who said, "We will need written permission to shoot at those violating curfew." A red-faced Gen Brar banged on the table and said, "This is open mutiny." Pandher was shocked. He was immediately told to proceed on leave, to be transferred subsequently. Operation Bluestar was on.

Earlier in Chandigarh on June 2, after the announcement of the army takeover and the appointment of Lt Gen Dyal as adviser (security) to the Punjab Governor, Gurbachan Jagat, then Deputy Inspector General of Police, was summoned to the room of the police chief Pritam Singh Bhinder on the fourth floor of the Punjab civil secretariat, then headquarters of the Punjab government. Gen Dyal was present there who had to be briefed on the situation. "On being asked my opinion, I informed him that Bhindranwale and his 130-odd followers would not surrender, but would offer stiff resistance and would rather prefer to die as 'martyrs'... (I was SSP Amritsar from April 1978 to September 1981)... Dyal was upset at this assessment and asked me a bit haughtily as to with what would the militants fight as they had only a few 'bandooks' against the fire power assembled by the army," wrote Jagat 30 years later.[23]

It was decided to take out the innocents before launching the operation. Telephones lines in the entire city had been disconnected including those of the district officials except for the hotlines with some of them. Aulakh was assigned the job of establishing contacts with some people in the Darbar Sahib complex. He reached the 15 Division headquarters next morning to establish telephonic contact with those who mattered inside the shrine and evacuate the innocents but was told to wait. One Colonel Chpora was put on duty for this purpose to facilitate communication. Aulakh was told four hours later that it was not possible to establish telephonic contact inside as the telephone lines had been physically snapped. It was conveyed that restoration of communication lines within that time was not possible and that some other method was being worked out.

Deputy Commissioner Ramesh Inder Singh reached the Kotwali police station at about 3 pm on June 4. He discussed the situation arising out of the innocents being inside the complex with other officials and it was decided to make the announcement on the loudspeaker outside the complex. The first announcement was made from the Clock Tower (Ghanta Ghar) side, the main entrance to the complex, at about 4 pm to be repeated after one hour and then again after 45 minutes. This was the period when the firing had stopped. About 140 people came out who were taken to Kotwali. They said they had not heard the announcement.

It was then decided to send somebody inside the complex and the officials zeroed in on Dr. Baldev Singh Brar, medical superintendent of the Shiromani Gurdwara Parbandhak Committee managed Guru Ram Dass Hospital, who was known to every Akali and militant leader. However, while moving towards the shrine complex, they were stopped at a CRPF naka. The CRPF officials pointed to the tank parked there that was firing at the water tank near the Akal Rest House in the shrine complex where the militants had taken up position. The Deputy Commissioner and his team returned to the circuit house. The team included Aulakh and Pandit Harjit Singh and they reported at the Division Headquarters again at 8 pm and briefed Lt Gen Dyal and Maj Gen Brar. The two senior commanders denied on the spot that tanks had been deployed. Here were the officials who had seen the tanks firing with their own eyes.

Aulakh suggested that one more attempt should be made to establish contact with those holed up in the Darbar Sahib complex. This suggestion was turned down by the army commanders arguing it was now too late.

Although the army commanders were Sikhs, they had no idea of the resolve and commitment of those who were to be their target. Sant Bhindranwale had realized the inevitability of the army action months in advance and he and his associates were prepared to face the worst, knowing fully that it would be an uneven fight. Interestingly, he did not want to waste his people. It was decided that not more than 10 people would be deployed at each of the 20 odd morchas (fortifications). "It would be massive deployment of the army. Even paratroopers might be dropped. We would give such a befitting reply that the Indian state would never forget this battle," he is reported to have said while talking to his associates in December 1983.

The total number of militants who confronted the army was not more than 200. Only the Dal Khalsa has documented the militants and others providing logistic support who were killed during Operation Bluestar. The list is not complete.

At one level, it was Sant Bhindranwale who might have been instrumental in the design to provoke army action with the objective of the creation of Khalistan with Pakistan's help and the plan was put into operation beginning with the targeted killing of six Hindus near Dhilwan. Did Indira Gandhi fall into his trap? It calls for deeper probe and research. He had resolved to make the supreme sacrifice for the Panth years ago in 1979.

When the Centre Refused Permission to Enter Darbar Sahib

Yet at another level, it was the government that had deliberately allowed the build-up as a moment had come more than a year earlier when no one would have objected to the entry of the security forces. That was the time when Jalandhar Range Deputy Inspector General of Police Avtar Singh Atwal was shot dead while coming out of the main entrance of Darbar Sahib towards the Ghanta Ghar side. His body lay right at the entrance. That was in the morning on April 25, 1983.

He had been shot by Major Singh Nagoke who was accompanied by Ram Singh Chauladha. The reason that they cited was that Atwal was responsible for the humiliation of a young Dalit woman whose brother had joined the ranks of the militants when he was the Amritsar district police chief. They got provoked when they saw Atwal. Both Nagoke and Chauladha died during Operation Bluestar.

As he came to know about Atwal being in the complex, Major Singh first went rushing to Ranjit Singh in the Nanak Niwas. He had been staying there after the assassination of Nirankari chief Gurbachan Singh. He asked for his weapon as that was more effective. However, he had dismantled it for cleaning. Later he got hold of a rifle. Atwal was accompanied by Brigadier Tejinder Singh Grewal from the Military Intelligence but he was not with him at that time.

Amritsar SSP S.S. Bains and Deputy Commissioner Sardara Singh reached the spot but they did not go near the body.

Within minutes of the incidents, Superintendent of Police Joginder Pal Birdi assembled about 100 policemen in the Kotwali police station to enter the shrine complex to arrest the culprits. That was the time when Sant Bhindranwale too could have been arrested and no one would have protested after such a grave incident. This was the first time that such a killing had taken place at the main entrance to the shrine. Birdi sought permission and waited for the orders from the state headquarters that never came.

In turn, Chief Minister Darbara Singh whose government was to be dismissed a few months later after the killing of bus passengers near Dhilwan on the night of October 5, 1983, waited for the green signal from Indira Gandhi.

He rang up P.C. Alexander, Principal Secretary to Prime Minister Indira Gandhi, at around 5 pm. He was told to wait. He started ridiculing the decision-makers at the centre saying, "What Wait..Wait.. Wait." He rang up again after some time and got the same answer. Finally, it was around 8 pm that he was told that the security forces were not to enter the complex. He was piqued at the response and started blaming Indira Gandhi for the mess in Punjab. Two other people were with him that evening in whose presence he made the last call.

This raises the basic question as to why the situation was being allowed to build up and go out of hand. Here was the most opportune moment to launch a surgical operation and the force was waiting for the order to strike. In case the effort was to harvest political benefits by ordering army action later, then Indira paid for the gamble with her life.

Tohra's Letter to Indira Gandhi

SGPC chief Gurcharan Singh Tohra protested against firing on June 1 to Indira Gandhi in a letter dated June 2, 1984. Here are the excerpts:

> It is with a sense of extreme pain and regret that I wish to draw your attention to the most brutal, most savage and most monstrous manner in which a relentless and senseless campaign of repression and suppression has been going on against Sikhs for the last about two years now. The Sikh leadership has been exercising utmost restraint in the hope that the government may see the path of reason and ultimately relent. However, the mounting fury with which the campaign continues to be pursued has completely frustrated our hopes...
>
> The climax of this ruthless and callous campaign was reached yesterday when the CRPF and the BSF, obviously at the orders of the government, launched a seven-hour long savage and shameless attack on the holy Golden Temple, killing about a dozen of the pilgrims and grievously injuring three dozen more...
>
> Madam Prime Minister, repression has never paid any government and, for sure, it is not going to pay this government either, lesser in the case of Sikhs who are known to have never bowed before force. Many a times, you have yourself eulogised the Sikhs for their courage and for their sacrifices for the freedom, defence and development of this country...
>
> I sincerely hope that you do realize that India is still too young a nation

> to afford to play with fire, but most unfortunately, fire it is with which it is playing by killing the Sikhs and by desecrating their holy shrines. I would sincerely request you to contain this fire before it attains the form of conflagration which may engulf the entire country.

He was not wrong. It was that very fire that consumed Indira Gandhi a few months later and Chief Minister Beant Singh in 1995 when police chief K.P.S. Gill claimed to have restored "peace" in the state through his killer squads.

Even before this letter reached her, Indira Gandhi was on All India Radio in the evening of June 2 justifying her subsequent action of army attack. She said:

> The reality that has emerged is not the adequacy or otherwise of the terms of settlement offered by the government on the various Akali demands, but the fact that the agitation is in the hands of a few who have scant regards for the unity and integrity of the country or concern for communal peace and harmony or the continued economic progress of Punjab. Every three or four months, a new morcha is started, and Punjab is torn by a senseless and tragic strife. Terrorists and anti-social elements have gained the upper hand. Innocent people, Sikhs and Hindus, have been killed. There is arson, looting and sabotage. Holy shrines have been turned into shelters for criminals and murderers. Their sanctity as places of worship has been underlined. A deliberate and systematic campaign is spreading bitterness and hatred between Hindus and Sikhs. And worst of all, the unity and integrity of motherland is being openly challenged by a few who find refuge in holy shrines.

Tohra had his last meeting with Sant Jarnail Singh Bhindranwale after the curfew had been imposed at 8 pm on June 3 to persuade him to leave the complex.[24]

Sant Bhindranwale convened a meeting of his associates at the Akal Takht when countdown to the showdown started giving them the option to leave the complex. "Those who want to leave would be honoured with siropas," he said. However, no one came forward to exercise this option. Here were the men in long robes who seemed to be the warriors from Sikh history but with modern weapons. The biggest weapon, however, being their commitment to the cause and their leader in the tradition of the Khalsa. Now the cause was defending the Darbar Sahib complex from the invaders.

They were the medieval warriors who seemed to have transcended space and time, resurrected from the past when the Sikhs fought for their survival for years against the rulers. And they fought till the last. They were determined to relive the times of Baba Deep Singh and Baba Gurbax Singh.

It was on June 8 morning that the first team of civilian officials entered the complex and they included Pritam Singh Bhinder and two others from the Intelligence Bureau, including Aulakh and a joint director from Delhi. Every inch of the shrine had turned red with blood. They saw the Head Priest Giani Sahib Singh crying as he was being pressured to start Maryada inside the sanctum sanctorum of Darbar Sahib while bodies were floating in the holy tank (sarovar) in the middle of which stands the shrine.

Number of Casualties

The total number of militants and Sikh devotees killed in the army attack is around 1,000 at the minimum.

The situation as on June 6 inside the Golden Temple complex has been described by Brig Goraya.

> On 6th June, Darbar Sahib complex looked like a battlefield... dead bodies were lying everywhere – in the verandahs next to the Parikarma, in most of the rooms occupied by the pilgrims in the serai complex, its courtyard and in the open spaces in front of Akal Takht. Some could be seen floating in the sarovar. I had participated in the active fighting in the 1965 and 1971 wars with Pakistan. Each lasted for about 16 days. I saw more dead bodies in the Golden Temple on June 6th than in the 32 days of both these wars put together.[25]

It was Brig Goraya, then Colonel, who was assigned the task of removal of bodies and his account gives a rough estimate of the civilians killed. He also describes the situation in the complex on June 6 and 7. He has given the figure of about 700 civilians killed within the complex. Ramesh Inder Singh estimated about 780 civilian casualties that also included those killed around the shrine in the lanes and bylanes. According to Brig Goraya, 557 bodies were lifted between June 7 and 8 from the premises of the Golden Temple. More bodies were recovered in the next four days from the basement of the Langar building, Akal Takht, Ghanta Ghar entrance and the sarovar.

Besides Brig Goraya, two other officers who were entrusted with the responsibility of disposal of bodies were Superintendent of Police Sital Das and Deputy SP Apar Singh Bajwa. Bajwa was the first to identify the body of Sant Bhindranwale and the government got the confirmation from his brother Subedar Major Harcharan Singh who was shown the body at 3.30 pm on June 7.

The Maryada (recitation of Gurbani in this case) of the sanctum sanctorum was resumed by Sikh troops of the Engineer Regiment of 9 Division.

Here is another version of the situation immediately after the army operation.

Narpinder Singh Rattan, Commissioner (Appeals), Jalandhar Division received the message from Chief Secretary K.D. Vasudeva at about 4 pm on June 7 to proceed to Amritsar. He was assigned additional charge of Commissioner, Jalandhar Division as the officer concerned had earlier proceeded on leave. Deputy Commissioner Mukul Joshi, who was with him, advised him against leaving at that time. He left for Amritsar on the morning of June 8 under army escort. Even then, it took about four hours to cover the distance of about 70 kms with the army having put up a number of barricades on the national highway, the maximum security being on the bridge on river Beas. His convoy was stopped at the Beas bridge and was allowed to proceed by the army only after getting clearance from the higher ups. From the Circuit House, the civil officers moved to the war zone.

"The Golden Temple complex was splattered with a thick layer of blood and splintered glass. Dead bodies were lying everywhere and some were floating in the holy tank. The army officers advised us to put on shoes but we went in bare foot. The scene was just horrible," recalled Rattan years later. The bodies were being loaded in trucks and tractor-trailers. They left for the 15 Division HQ where they were joined by Lt Gen Dyal and Maj Gen Brar. It was there that they got the information from Delhi that President Zail Singh was arriving at 2.30 pm. Instructions were issued to cleanse the complex immediately. He took a round of the Parikarma, paid obeisance at the sanctum sanctorum and talked to Darbar Sahib Head Granthi Giani Sahib Singh. He did not enter the Akal Takht.

At dinner in the army mess, Rattan and some other civil officers too were present. Lt Gen Dyal was heard saying while talking to another officer that in case he had soldiers with the same motivation and commitment with which the "boys" (militants) had fought, he would take over Pakistan within three days. It is pertinent to mention that the Western Command Chief General K. Sundarji too had paid similar tributes to the militants at his press conference in Chandigarh on June 6 evening.

Apar Singh Bajwa was the police officer whose virtually entire career had been in Amritsar. He had been dealing with the Sikh affairs all these years. He was earlier the City Inspector. He was tasked with cremation of the bodies.

Here is his version of the situation and number of casualties:

When I reached the temple, I saw dead bodies of Jarnail Singh

> Bhindranwale, General Shabeg Singh, Thara Singh and Amrik Singh lying there. I was asked to identify the bodies because I was familiar with all these dead men having often interacted with them as part of my duties as a police officer. The army officer in-charge then requested me to arrange the cremations. We performed these, according to Sikh rites, at the nearby Gurudwara Shaheedan.

According to the DSP, a large majority of those who died inside the Golden Temple during Operation Bluestar were common devotees who had come to the shrine on 3 June on the occasion of the fifth Sikh Guru Arjan Dev's Martyrdom Day.

> Apart from Bhindranwale's armed followers, I counted a little over 800 dead bodies inside the temple complex. I and my men were also tasked with clearing and cremating these bodies. Army and municipal officials helped transport them to the local cremation ground. While many of the innocents were killed in the crossfire between the army and the militants, it is true that the soldiers deliberately gunned down several devotees. You see they actually believed that anyone inside the temple was the 'enemy'.

The soldiers had no notion of how they should tackle an internal security situation like the one that had developed inside the Golden Temple.

Bajwa said no attempt was ever made to identify the civilians killed.

"This would have been possible if the army had involved the state police. But then at that time the soldiers were in a hurry to conclude their operation and withdraw from the Golden Temple complex. It was this kind of haste because of which scores of ordinary families not only lost their loved ones but spent months in a futile search for their dead relatives," said the DSP.[26]

Internecine War on the Eve of Bluestar

There is another aspect of the situation in the Golden Temple complex that was alarming as it was leading towards internecine war. Those who were active during the pre-Bluestar period have now no hesitation in admitting that in case the army action had been delayed by another two or three weeks, it would not have been needed at all. But then, the design, if there was any, would not have been executed. These players maintain that in the wake of internecine war, militant groups might have attacked each other and given a concrete pretext to the security forces to enter the complex.

This perception is substantiated by the developments during that period. Babbar Khalsa chief Sukhdev Singh, at a news conference on

May 21, charged Sant Bhindranwale with hatching a conspiracy to kill him and his associates. He claimed that one of the conspirators had been presented in the morning before the high priests and Sant Longowal. He put the total number of persons assigned this job at eight and disclosed their names. He claimed that four of these conspirators had been apprehended by his men.[27]

On the eve of Operation Bluestar, Babbar leaders including Mehal Singh, Anokh Singh and Babaji (UK citizen Devinder Singh) approached Bhai Amrik Singh and Rachhpal Singh to facilitate their meeting with Sant Bhindranwale who declined their request. They were short of ammunition and this was the reason for their meeting. Amrik and Rachhpal handed over some ammunition to them. They returned without meeting Sant Bhindranwale.

The total number of Babbar Khalsa activists at the start of the army operation was about 50. They had been staying in Guru Nanak Niwas. They advised Sukhdev Singh and two others to leave the complex. His reaction was he was their Jathedar and what would he do without them. He proposed that all of them should leave and prepare for the next fight. It was a conscious decision. They all agreed.

Sukhdev left along with Manmohan Singh who later planted transistor bombs in Delhi local buses in May 1985. Others left when tanks entered the Golden Temple complex on June 5.

Baba Kharak Singh, a highly respected religious leader based at Jhabal near Amritsar, was approached to start Kar Sewa for the repair of the complex. Sant Longowal who had been arrested from the complex along with Tohra had also written to the government from captivity to hand over Kar Sewa to the Sikhs. Baba Kharak Singh refused to enter the complex so long as it was under occupation forces. It was after his refusal that Nihang chief Santa Singh was drafted for the job.

The army action provoked immediate revolt amongst a section of the Sikh troops in various cantonments and many of them were killed as they tried to march towards Amritsar. The Sikh priests in military gurdwaras were the catalysts for provoking Sikh army personnel as they talked of Darbar Sahib having been destroyed. Significantly, many of these priests had their schooling in Sikh scriptures at Damdami Taksal. Rumours were believed in the absence of credible information as the press had been gagged and Punjab cut off from the rest of the world. The action lacked transparency and this was one of the major blunders.

Doctrinal Sabotage of the Sikh Struggle

The Sikh struggle, from the days of Sant Bhindranwale, was given the slant of Brahmin-Bania leadership versus the Sikhs and not as the Sikhs against the Indian state. Nobody knows whose design it was to sabotage the movement from the very first stage itself by giving this interpretation. The militant struggles going on in India at several places, especially in the North-East at that time, have been against the Indian state. In the case of the Sikh struggle, even Sant Bhindranwale used to harp on the contribution of Sikhs to the freedom struggle of the country being many times more as proportionate to their population by citing as evidence the record of the Cellular Jail at Andaman which used to be known as the 'Kala Paani.' The role of the Sikhs during the freedom struggle would be cited in the framework of discrimination and victimhood. This would some times give the impression that the struggle was merely for the redressal of some grievances.

From the very outset, the militant movement was misdirected. The struggle for a homeland cannot survive on perceived discrimination, and that too not by the state per se but by the Brahmanical leadership-dominated administration.

The political objective of the struggle during the first phase lacked clarity. This perhaps was the biggest oversight made by Sant Bhindranwale. In case the militant struggle was for the Sikh homeland, he should have spelt it out unambiguously rather than leaving it to the imagination of the Sikh people.

Sant Bhindranwale never raised the demand for Khalistan per se in unequivocal terms but that was the ultimate objective in the broader design in which General Shabeg Singh was playing the most vital strategic and tactical role. It is now learnt that his assessment was that the Golden Temple itself would be damaged during the army operation. Even one tank shell hitting the sanctum sanctorum would have been enough to provoke the Sikhs all over the world to the extreme, not just in India. That would have triggered a massive revolt among the Sikh army men and the Sikhs in general in Punjab thereby leading to total turmoil in the border state.

This could result in Sikhs crossing over to Pakistan in large numbers fearing persecution by Indian security forces thereby providing an excuse to the neighbouring country to intervene at the military level. In such a situation, he postulated that Pakistan would attack India and in that critical situation, Jammu and Kashmir could be cut off along with Punjab from India on the other side of river Beas. Kashmir has been the conflict zone between India and Pakistan since partition in 1947. This was from his experience during the Bangladesh war when refugees from East Pakistan crossed over to India.

His assessment was that as the final settlement between Sikhs and Pakistan, the Lahore area could be transferred to Khalistan in exchange for Jammu and Kashmir. The plan just failed as every precaution was taken by the army against damage to the sanctum sanctorum. What worried the army was that the militants themselves might blow up the main shrine.

It may be mentioned that during the 1965 war, Army chief General J.N. Chaudhary had favoured retreat to south of river Beas but it was Western Army Commander Lt Gen Harbaksh Singh who put his foot down and he proved right as the Indian army managed to reach the outskirts of Lahore. The map of India might have been different in case the orders of Gen Chaudhary had been carried out. General Shabeg Singh might have had that in mind.

Another dimension of his strategy is available from one of his speeches in which he gives the call to the Sikhs in villages to retaliate the moment they receive information of attack on the Golden Temple.

"We will kill one lakh (security people who attack the Golden Temple) in the first lot. You would take over by that time," he said. His expectation was that people in the rural areas would rise against the government and the Hindus. "No Chhalli Ram (the Hindu) should be seen around," he said in the same speech.

> Police are making preparations...Don't be afraid of them. Here is my request and you take this message to every village. In case the police enter (the Golden Temple complex), don't wait for my message or newspaper report. Then no Chhalli Ram should be seen around on the soil of Punjab... In case we don't fight back, the Sikhs outside would be in trouble... don't attack first...In case they attack, we would kill one lakh in the first round itself. By that time, you in villages would get into the gear by then. You would not stay silent (I hope).[28]

This was part of his speech on April 13, 1984.

His strategy was apparently two-pronged to confront the attack on the Golden Temple complex. He expected the Sikhs in the countryside to counter-attack throughout the state. The second dimension of his strategy was direct intervention by Pakistan.

However, it was not in the calculations of his military strategists that it would be a massive army operation during which the entire Punjab would be completely immobilized for 72 hours with no movement even on the rural roads. People in rural areas were not allowed to come out on the roads. Whatever efforts were made by the people were frustrated by the army. Many of those marching towards Amritsar were killed at several places in Amritsar district.

Thus neither could the Sikhs in rural areas be mobilized nor did Pakistan intervened.

Question Mark Over Timing

The reasons advanced by the government for resorting to this extreme action in the Golden Temple complex were unconvincing and proved to be self-defeating. Not only the reasons, even the strategy and tactics adopted by the army have been questionable and so was the timing. It is said the intelligence agencies planted some of the weapons after the operation was over to provide some credibility to the propaganda about a large number of weapons having been stockpiled in the shrine complex. The intelligence agencies supplied a detailed account of the weapons and the number of militants holed up in the shrine but the same was perhaps overlooked.

Sant Bhindranwale did not have more than 200 armed fighters and the rest had escaped. Moreover, their total number including that of the militants from Babbar Khalsa was never more than 300 in the shrine complex at any given time.

The timing of the army operation is also shocking as it coincided with the anniversary of the martyrdom of Guru Arjan Dev, the Fifth Guru, on June 3. It may be mentioned that Dr. Chohan announced the formation of the National Council of Khalistan on June 16, 1980 from the Darbar Sahib complex and that also happened to be the martyrdom day anniversary of Guru Arjan Dev. The edict for the socio-economic boycott of Nirankaris was issued from the Akal Takht to the Sikhs on June 10, 1978 which was the anniversary of Guru Arjan Dev's martyrdom.

Gen Brar years later attributed the urgency of the action to the fear of announcement of Khalistan by Sant Bhindranwale. But the maverick leader had never even mentioned Khalistan as demand and his speeches had remained confined to the implementation of the Anandpur Sahib Resolution which had been adopted by the Akali Dal way back in 1973. Dr. Chohan had raised this demand from British soil in the early 1970s and nothing had happened after that. The Dal Khalsa had also pressed the Khalistan demand in 1978 at the time of its formation. The preparations for this action had been going on for a long time and as such, the reasons for urgency as stated by Gen Brar are utterly unconvincing.

In the perception of Gen Brar which could be the viewpoint of the government at that time, some neighbouring country might have given recognition to Khalistan and it would have led to a situation parallel to the one in the then East Pakistan in 1971 that led to the creation of Bangladesh. Sant Bhindranwale was perceived to enjoy a mass following in the rural areas and this support base could have rebelled at the call given by him.

The UK papers trash this logic on timing.

The reasons for this extreme brutal action were perhaps somewhere else. No one has so far answered as to why this action had been timed with the martyrdom anniversary of Guru Arjan Dev when casualties of the devotees could have been the maximum.

Significantly, one major newspaper had warned against army induction to handle the situation in Punjab. In an editorial captioned 'Keep The Army Out,' it stated:

> The law and order situation in Punjab remains bad, indeed alarming. While the extremists continue to kill, burn and loot at will, the police are unable to gather the necessary intelligence, follow their movements, anticipate their criminal activities and apprehend them...But it does not follow either that those in opposition recommend a course of action that is likely to prove disastrous, or that the government panic and adopt such a course. Yet the first has already taken place; leaders of National Democratic Alliance comprising the Bharatiya Janata Party and the Lok Dal have demanded that the army be inducted into Punjab. Mrs Gandhi is not the kind of leader who either panics in the face of heavy odd, or who can miss the possible consequences of the proposal, or who is likely to look for a dangerous short-cut in Punjab. Even so the state Governor's meeting with General Dayal is bound to provoke the speculation that the government might be thinking in those terms...The army is a weapon of last resort; the government must never use it as if it was nothing more than a better equipped police force. In the case of Punjab, it is not even a weapon of last resort; it must not be used at all.[29]

And the futility of the brutal army attack had been realized within days of Operation Bluestar in the following words:

> No one in Punjab was under the illusion that the army action at Amritsar in the first week of June and the subsequent mopping up operations would lead to the elimination of terrorism in the state...It would be more sensible for the government to recognise an ugly reality. "Khalistan" has not been established on the ground; it has nevertheless begun to find a place in the minds of an increasing number in the Sikh community.[30]

The Tribune was the paper that had welcomed Operation Bluestar in the edit captioned 'A Neat Operation' that stated:

> The Sikh sentiments have been hurt cannot be denied. The Prime Minister was aware of the danger and she must have calculated the risks involved. A final judgement on this unhappy episode must be based on a balance of considerations. Would a political settlement have been possible with the killers' threat hanging over the heads of Akali leaders? Several of them have been in constant fear of their lives. Will they now be more free to negotiate for a reasonable agreement which would meet Punjab's genuine demands? This is a question which would have to be faced fairly soon. Mrs. Gandhi chose the harder option of dealing with terrorism first. The political threads cannot be picked up immediately, but they must be as soon as the pervasive dread of death from the bullet or the knife at the hands of the assassins has been removed. In fact it may be necessary not to wait for that event. The political follow-up should be possible after a reasonable period of reflection.[31]

It may be mentioned that special permission had been given to *The Indian Express* and *The Tribune* to bring out the edition at the news conference addressed by the army generals at Punjab Bhavan in Chandigarh in the afternoon of June 6.

The main target of attack during Operation Bluestar was the Akal Takht, the symbol of Sikh sovereignty in front of the Golden Temple as Sant Bhindranwale was holed up there. It was this very institution from which the call had emanated in 1948 to the Sikhs to defend the freedom of the country. The Akal Takht Jathedar in his traditional Diwali message that year had called upon the Sikhs "to get armed training for the defence of the country."[32] What went wrong over the years that the government resorted to such extreme action in 1984?

India in April 2018 has refused to provide any detail of Operation Bluestar in response to application under the Right to Information Act. Information Commissioner Divya Pradhan from the Central Information Commission said while rejecting the information that "disclosure of information will be primarily prejudicial to internal security of the nation and can be a potential cause for incitement of offences of varied nature."[33]

Information has been coming out in bits. Half-truths are more damaging.

The two gravest blunders that Indira Gandhi committed in her life as the Prime Minister were the imposition of Emergency in June 1975 and Operation Bluestar in June 1984. She survived the Emergency and returned to centre stage in 1980 after having lost elections in 1977 but paid with her life for the second blunder.

The Sikh issues are part of the political discourse in countries like Canada and the UK in 2018 and this is the fallout of Operation Bluestar.

The entire record pertaining to this army action should be de-classified.

Operation Bluestar Fails to Curb Militancy

If Operation Bluestar was the biggest shock to the Sikhs in independent India, the assassination of Indira Gandhi stunned the country. This was the biggest political assassination in independent India after that of Mahatma Gandhi in 1948 and the first of an incumbent Prime Minister.

The revival of militant struggle, however, started at another level and the two main factors that worked as a catalyst were the state repression during the hunt for militants as part of Operation Woodrose launched by the army in the countryside and mass killings of the Sikhs in Delhi and some other cities in the country following the assassination of Indira Gandhi.

The story of militant leader Wassan Singh Zaffarwal reveals how ordinary people were sucked into the struggle. He rose to be the member of the first Panthic Committee set up as an umbrella organization of militants that announced the setting up of Khalistan on April 29, 1986 from the Golden Temple complex.

He was an employee of the New Egerton Woollen Mill at Dhariwal in the border area that was amongst the oldest in the country set up by the British rulers. He belonged to a traditional Akali family whose members had taken part even in the first Punjabi Suba Morcha (agitation) in 1955. He was also vice-president of the mill workers union affiliated to the Akali Dal. The other union was controlled by the Communists.

He recalls his first encounter with Sant Bhindranwale sometime in 1983 that concered his union. The mill management was resisting the demand for revision in pay scales. Zaffarwal and his associates met Sant Bhindranwale seeking his intervention in the dispute with the management. It may be mentioned that people used to approach Sant Bhindranwale for resolution of disputes.

Sant Bhindranwale listened to their issue and told his associate Bhai Amrik Singh to give them a letter addressed to the management. Zaffarwal took the letter to the management. The revised pay scales were announced the very next morning. There was no threat to the management in the letter. This incident also brought him under the radar of the security forces.

It was Operation Bluestar that changed Zaffarwal's life. The police started conducting raids in the villages in the border districts in particular during which young Sikhs used to be rounded up and detained. Torture was normal. The army had launched search operations codenamed Operation Woodrose in the villages after Operation Bluestar. The entire village, including women and children, would be gathered in the open and made to stand under the scorching sun in the name of search operations to humiliate and demoralise them.

"I was detained twice. Before the third raid at our house, I went underground and took up arms," he told this writer.

This is the story of many of the innocent young Sikhs who went underground to escape torture by the security forces. The state repression, like at the start of the militant movement, played the vital role of the catalyst in its revival. The case of Zaffarwal is just one example.

"I got in touch with other people who had similarly gone underground. We formed a group after contacting people in 3-4 districts and named it Khalistan Liberation Army. Ours was the first major group that was organized during the post-Bluestar period," he disclosed. Zaffarwal headed this group whose other notable members included Tarsem Singh Kohar and Sukhdev Singh Kot Maulvi. Within a few months, the KLA emerged as the largest group as many of the educated young Sikhs also joined.

It was at that stage that it was decided to contact people across the border for weapons.

He was arrested on April 11, 2001 on his return to India and subsequently acquitted. He now leads a normal life in his native village.

Operation Blackthunder 1988

The militants returned to the Darbar Sahib complex in 1985 within a few months of withdrawal by the army and paramilitary forces. Their return was preceded by reorganization of the All India Sikh Students Federation whose leaders restarted their activity from the Darbar Sahib complex.

The first move that marks the cut-off date for the Darbar Sahib complex getting converted into base for the radical and militant discourse was organizing a function on January 26, 1985 in the Manji Sahib Hall to honour the families of Sant Bhindranwale, Bhai Amrik Singh and Beant Singh and Satwant Singh, both assassins of Indira

Gandhi, and several others. The leaders, who took the initiative, included Harinder Singh Kahlon and Charanjit Singh Talwandi, the convener and secretary of the AISSF respectively. Initially, Baba Joginder Singh, father of Sant Bhindranwale, who had been brought to the scene by the remnants of the radicals to provide the lead, refused to fund the function.

The organizers raised funds from the shopkeepers around the shrine complex while Manbir Singh Chaheru and some other militants contributed Rs. 1 lakh in the evening. The belated offer from Baba Joginder Singh was rejected.

Those who were honoured included families of Sant Bhindranwale (Baba Deep Singh Medal), Amrik Singh (Nawab Kapur Singh Medal), Bhai Thara Singh (Baba Naudh Singh Medal), Major General Shabeg Singh (Sardar Jassa Singh Ahluwalia Medal), Beant Singh (Bhai Sukha Singh Medal) and Satwant Singh (Bhai Mehtab Singh Medal).

An important development around this period was release of Shiromani Gurdwara Parbandhak Committee president Gurcharan Singh Tohra from Jodhpur jail on April 19, 1985. He had been arrested on June 6, 1984 from the Darbar Sahib complex after Operation Bluestar.

Tohra made an important announcement after reaching Darbar Sahib on April 22 that the Akal Takht repaired by the government by deputing Nihang chief Baba Santa Singh would be rebuilt. This announcement was to have far-reaching repercussions on the religio-political discourse. He said a memorial to those killed inside the shrine complex during the army attack would also be built.[33] The decision to construct a memorial dedicated to those killed in the army invasion of Darbar Sahib was earlier taken by the Akali Dal on October 7, 1984.[34]

It was the reconstruction of the Akal Takht that was taken over by Damdami Taksal that facilitated the return of the militants to the Darbar Sahib complex, although it might not have been the design when Tohra made the announcement.

His release was followed by that of Parkash Singh Badal on April 25. He had been detained at Pachmarhi.

The militants signed their forceful return on the Punjab scene with the assassination of Akali Dal president Sant Harchand Singh Longowal on August 20, 1985 for signing the Punjab Accord.

It was during this period that marks Phase II of the struggle that the Government of India engineered legitimacy to Operation Bluestar and that too from the Akali Dal government headed by Chief Minister Surjit Singh Barnala.[35] The legitimacy was by way of Barnala ordering a police raid on the complex on April 30, 1986.

By the time the Barnala government took over in September 1985, the radicals had returned to the Darbar Sahib complex.

The political dynamics of Punjab during the second phase of militancy beginning in July 1984 and ending with Operation Blackthunder in May 1988 is characterized by both defining of the political objective as Khalistan and at the same time its trivialization by various players in the absence of a commanding leader.

This was an action that was minutely planned unlike the blunder that was Operation Bluestar and it was carried out by special forces, not by the army. The operation was open to the media. The sanctum sanctorum this time was desecrated by the 'Khalistan Warriors' and not by the 'Indian Invaders.'

ENDNOTES

1. Harbir Singh Bhanwar was Amritsar-based part-time reporter of the UNI at that time. However, the agency had deputed a senior staffer Akhil Gautam from Chandigarh to cover the Akali event. The UNI sub-office was near the shrine. The Akali Dal had convened a political conference to announce its next programme finalized at a meeting a day earlier. The Chandigarh journalist of UNI returned to the office before the programme was to be announced by Sant Longowal. Bhanwar was there on the spot. "Even before I returned after covering the conference, this senior journalist had already filed the story without confirmation that the Akalis would not allow the games to be held", wrote Bhanwar years later.
2. Bhanwar, Harbir Singh. (2017). *Dharam Yudh Morcha*. Amritsar: Singh Brothers. p. 135.
3. The Foreign and Commonwealth office prepared the note on this request on February 3, 1983. Ref: PREM 19/1273-UK February 3, 1983 Foreign and Commonwealth Office. "The Indian intelligence coordinator... has sent an urgent request to...for advice on an Indian plan for possible action against dissident Sikhs currently occupying parts of the Golden Temple in Amritsar. The Foreign Secretary believes that the Prime Minister would wish to be aware of the approach and our proposed response.

   "Representatives of various extremist Sikh groups, over the last year or so, have taken up residence within the Golden Temple, some of them are believed to be armed. By a convention dating back to the British period in India, representatives of the Indian authorities including the police and the armed forces do not enter the temple precincts in uniform but—understand from...that a contingency plan for possible action against the extremists is being drawn up by the Indians. The Indians have requested that...to provide an expert to advise on this contingency plan.

   "The fact that this request has been made personally by...underlines not only its delicacy but the importance of the request and from what is known of the role played...it seems likely that Mrs Gandhi would have been informed before the request was made. In putting the request... made it clear that it has not been made lightly.

"The British High Commissioner in New Delhi supports the proposal...a response should be given quickly, not least because they understand that the latest developments at the temple where the rift between moderates and extremists has now widened, may soon force the Indian government's hand. BJP Fall."

4. From the UK record.
5. The complex has a fortress with two observation towers known as Bunga Ramgarhia that was built for the protection of the shrine.
6. Goraya, Onkar Singh. (2013). *Operation Blue Star.* pp. 83-84.
7. Ibid., p. 98.
8. Ibid., p. 52.
9. March 4, 1994. *The Tribune.*
10. May 14, 2017. *The Tribune.*
11. September 21, 2017. *Times of India.*
12. Bir Devinder Singh. (August 20, 2017). *Punjabi Tribune.*
13. Indira Gandhi was hailed by the opposition leader from the Right wing Jan Sangh Atal Bihari Vajpayee after the December 1971 war with Pakistan that led to creation of East Pakistan as Bangladesh.
14. Jagtar Singh. (2011). *Khalistan Struggle: A Non-movement*. Delhi: Aakar Books, pp. 153-54.
15. Ibid., pp. 168-69.
16. June 2, 1984. *The Tribune.*
17. Goraya, Onkar Singh. (2013). *Operation Bluestar*, p. 34.
18. June 4, 1984. *The Times of India.*
19. Narain Singh (ed.). (2003). *Singh Garj*. Amritsar: Gurmat Pustak Bhandar. p. 220.
20. Jagtar Singh. (2011). *Khalistan Struggle: A Non-movement*. Delhi: Aakar Books, p. 168.
21. Goraya, Onkar Singh. (2013). *Operation Bluestar and After: An Eyewitness Account*. pp. 98-99.
22. Ibid., p. 118.
23. June 6, 2014. *The Hindustan Times.*
24. Jagtar Singh. (2011). *Khalistan Struggle: A Non-movement*. Delhi: Aakar Books, p. 174.
26. Goraya, Onkar Singh. (2013). *Operation Bluestar and After: An Eyewitness Account*. pp. 83-84.
27. May 22, 1984. *The Tribune.*

28. Narain Singh (ed.). (2003). *Singh Garj*. Amritsar: Gurmat Pustak Bhandar. p. 541.
29. May 18, 1984. *The Times of India.*
30. September 14, 1984. *The Tribune.*
31. June 7, 1984. *The Tribune.*
32. Ashok, Shamsher Singh. (1982). *SGPC Da Panjah Saala Itihas*. Amritsar: SGPC. p. 244.
33. April 4, 2018. *The Times of India.*
34. April 23, 1985. *The Tribune.*
35. Jagtar Singh. (2011). *Khalistan Struggle: A Non-movement*. Delhi: Aakar Books, p. 195, cit. *The Tribune*, October 8, 1984
36. Ibid., p. 258.

7

Sikhs Avenge Operation Bluestar

Prime Minister Indira Gandhi had been forewarned that the attack on the Darbar Sahib (Golden Temple) complex would trigger the revenge psyche and rightly so. Three major actions to avenge Operation Bluestar are rooted in this historical Sikh psyche as attack on this Sikh ideological powerhouse has always sparked retaliation. These actions were her own assassination, the bombing of Air India Kanishka and the gunning down of retired army Chief General A.S. Vaidya, in that order.

Plan to Assassinate Indira Gandhi

She was gunned down within five months of the army assault on Darbar Sahib and the people who were dictated by the revenge executed the final act, they were not associated with any political outfit.

The names of all those who gunned down Indira Gandhi and those who were part of the design to kill her are in public domain. However, at least three more people besides all those known names were part of the plan to avenge Operation Bluestar.

One of them was militant leader Manbir Singh Chaheru who purchased a plot in Mohali for Bimal Kaur Khalsa, wife of Delhi police sub-inspector Beant Singh, one of the two assassins who killed Indira Gandhi.

Satwant Singh who rained bullets on her along with Beant Singh on the fateful morning of October 31, 1984 was the last to be involved.

Beant was gunned down on the spot in the firing by other security personnel while Satwant was seriously injured after they laid down their weapons and surrendered. Satwant Singh was hanged to death years later along with Kehar Singh while another accused Balbir Singh was acquitted. Beant was related to Kehar Singh. Beant and Kehar Singh were from the same Ramdasia caste.

When Beant made up his mind to kill Indira Gandhi, at the back of his mind was the future of his wife and children.

It was at this crucial juncture that he was extended assurance by Manbir. This was made possible through at least two other persons, one of whom was a bank employee while Prem Singh was with Damdami Taksal. This bank employee too was a Ramdasia.

Beant was an apolitical person and his approach towards religion was casual till Operation Bluestar. It was the army attack on the Golden Temple that transformed him and he turned into an introvert. He made up his mind but he wanted some personal issues relating to his family to be settled. Being a married man having children, his foremost worry was the future of his family. His wife Bimal was a nurse and the couple had three children including Amrit Kaur born in 1977, Sarbjeet Singh and 1983 born Jaswinder Singh. Moreover, there was also the issue of harassment of his wife post assassination and as such, some sort of protection and patronage was a must.

Manbir assured him saying, "Your children are my children". This matter ended there and then. It was Manbir who purchased a residential plot for Bimal in 1986 in Phase V of Mohali, a few months before he was arrested.

Beant had been assured of support by Manbir and Prem at a meeting in Ludhiana. The Taksal was thus in the picture in the assassination of Indira Gandhi from the planning stage. None of the main persons, who were part of the meeting where Beant Singh was assured of all help to his family is alive. Of course, this part came to be known to some others in the Taksal later when Manbir funded the residential plot for Bimal.

Manbir had joined Damdami Taksal in 1981 and became the personal bodyguard of Sant Bhindranwale. He was not in the Darbar Sahib during Operation Bluestar and organized the Khalistan Commando Force during the second phase of militancy. He was the person who headed the Khalistan Commando Force after Operation Bluestar under the name of General Hari Singh.

He was arrested on August 8, 1986 from the residence of Major Baldev Singh Ghuman in Jalandhar on the information provided by one of the All India Sikh Students Federation activists-turned-police informer. Manbir was kept in various jails in Panjab and later shifted to Bihar. His 'escape' from police custody was announced in December 1987 while he was being brought back to Punjab. The police perhaps never suspected during his long custody that he was also part of the operation to assassinate Indira Gandhi.

These people were motivated by only one factor and that was revenge. The wounds of the army attack on the Golden Temple complex were too deep. It was perceived to be an attack not just on the Golden Temple complex but the Sikh Faith itself.

It was Taksal's acting chief Baba Thakar Singh, who had undertaken the responsibility to take care of Beant Singh's family.

There is yet another aspect that has now emerged while talking to the people who were around him at that time. It was in the first week of October 1983 that bunkers and morchas started coming up in the Darbar Sahib Temple complex. That was an indication that Sant Bhindranwale, who was leading the militant struggle had by then realized the inevitability of the army attack on the shrine.

It was around this time that Kehar Singh too came out with his loud thinking that something must be done to stop this possible attack and that 'something' was the assassination of Prime Minister Indira Gandhi. However, this thinking could not be translated into action before the army attack. Kehar was working as clerical assistant with the Directorate General of Supplies and Disposal in Delhi and related to Beant. Operation Bluestar had upset both of them. Eminent preacher Prof. Darshan Singh, who was later elevated to the high office of Akal Takht Jathedar, happened to visit Delhi during this period. Both Beant and Kehar attended one of his programmes at Gurdwara Moti Bagh. Beant wept after listening to his moving discourse and was consoled by Kehar Singh, a very cool and composed person. He said, "Why do you weep? Let us do something".

The assassination plan was on. Beant needed at least one more person and they zeroed in on Satwant who was also on security duty with the Prime Minister. Satwant was taken into confidence only a few days before the assassination was to be carried out.

They decided to visit the Akal Takht on October 16 to take the pledge. Satwant, however, abstained.

Giani Puran Singh, then priest at the Akal Takht, who performed Ardas for Kehar and Beant, was not told about their design. They returned to Delhi after taking the pledge. Beant had met Sant Bhindranwale only once only casually when he visited Delhi.

Harinder Khalsa and Beant Singh

Harinder Singh Khalsa, an Indian Foreign Service Officer, was posted in Norway when Darbar Sahib was attacked by the Indian army. Beant had met him once during Indira Gandhi's visit to that country in 1983, as he had accompanied her as part of the security detail. He was distantly related to Beant Singh through his wife Satwant Kaur as they shared the same native village Maloya in the Union Territory of Chandigarh.

Harinder resigned from the Foreign Service in protest against Operation Bluestar. It was in August 1984 that three people—US-based Didar Singh Bains, Major General Jaswant Singh Bhullar (retd.) and Joginder Singh Sidhu—met him in Norway with a proposal. They were looking for a sharp shooter to avenge Operation Bluestar. They were willing to offer one lakh dollars. It may be mentioned that the name of Harinder Singh Khalsa had also surfaced in the conspiracy part at one stage along with reference to this money.

According to one account, Beant had proceeded on leave on June 26 for a few days to re-join next month. His target was to eliminate her by October 15.

He had telephoned Harinder Khalsa after the latter's resignation, saying he had earned a place in history.

It may be mentioned that the Khalistan National Organization in London on June 7, 1984 offered a reward of $50,000 for anyone bringing Indira Gandhi or Rajiv Gandhi dead or alive to the Golden Temple. Britain's Attorney General Sir Michael Wavers on March 10, 1985 ordered a probe into this announcement.[1]

The Man Who Could Not Kill Indira Gandhi

A short statured young man knocked at the door of Sukhjit Kaur Brar who used to rent out the upper storey of her house near the Putlighar area of Amritsar. This boy had joined Khalsa College and was looking for accommodation. While talking to him, Sukhjit found out that the young man happened to be her distant cousin but was much younger in age. He was accommodated in the first floor room. He was Harjinder Singh Jinda who was hanged to death along with Sukhjinder Singh Sukha in the case of the assassination of General A.S. Vaidya (retd.) in Pune on August 10, 1986. He was the Army Chief from July 31, 1983 to January 31, 1986. He settled in Pune after retirement.

She got suspicious about his activities after some time. One day when the family had gone to Delhi along with Jinda, it was revealed that he had gone for recce of the Prime Minister's house and carried a small revolver.

The day she was assassinated, Jinda was at home and as the news broke, Sukhjit told him also. He sat on the stairs and started crying. She was flabbergasted as to what had gone wrong. Suddenly, he blurted out that she was his target (*Oh taan mera shikar si*). Then he wiped his face, rushed to the neighbourhood sweets shop and bought sweets to distribute among people.

He just disappeared and nothing was heard of him till his arrest in the assassination of General Vaidya.

Jinda's mother shared with Sukhjit the happenings on the day of the hanging of Jinda and Sukha. Their families were informed at the last moment about the day of their hanging. The families met the duo, who told them to order a band to play near the jail at the time of their hanging.

Before they were taken to the gallows, they had ordered sweets to be distributed among the inmates in Pune jail. They bathed and prayed for the last time. They proceeded to the gallows shouting "Bole So Nihal, Sat Sri Akal" that reverberated through the prison. The family came to know from this that their last time had come. The families told the band to play and they started dancing to celebrate their martyrdom. Both Sukha and Jinda told the jail authorities that their faces should not be covered with black cloth as is part of the drill. They did not allow the hangman to put the noose around their necks and they did it themselves.

Their bodies were cremated by the jail authorities on the banks of the river.

Air India Kanishka Bombing

One of the most tragic incidents associated with the Sikh struggle that caught global attention was the bombing of Air India Kanishka Flight 182 that exploded mid-air over the Atlantic Ocean near the Irish coast on the fateful June 23, 1985, killing all 329 people on aboard in the Boeing 747-237 B that was on the Toronto-Montreal-London-New Delhi route.

It emerged years later that the design was not to kill people but hit India's economy by targeting this national carrier. India's economy was to be strategically targeted under this design to avenge Operation Bluestar. The action went horribly wrong. The explosive device was timed to explode after the plane had landed in London. The tragedy was collateral damage.

It was an action carried out by the people associated with Babbar Khalsa International based in Canada on their own but not by this militant organization per se.

At another level in the Sikh circles in Canada, this tragedy is perceived to be the operation of the Indian agencies to defame the Sikh struggle globally.

According to the information now available, this operation was master-minded by Talwinder Singh Parmar who was killed years later by the Punjab police. Parmar spent more than a year in hiding in the caves in the mountainous Frontier area of Pakistan bordering Afghanistan as the Canadian Sikh national of Indian origin came under the scanner and pressure of the global security agencies. This area has been known to be no man's land for centuries.

Parmar was finally named in the report of public inquiry headed by retired Supreme Court Justice Johan Major released on June 17, 2010, but not conclusively. The Commission expressed the view that "Talwinder Singh Parmar was the leader of the Babbar Khalsa, a pro-Khalistan organization at the heart of radical extremism, and it is now believed that he was the leader of the conspiracy to bomb Air India flights." All those arrested were subsequently acquitted by the court in the absence of concrete evidence.

Parmar shared the details with Babbar Khalsa leaders in Pakistan in 1990 at the time of his formal induction as the vice-president of the organization and member of the Panthic Committee.

Talwinder was from the first group of militants in Punjab who returned to Canada after his name surfaced in the encounter with the police at Daheru village near Khanna in Ludhiana district on November 19, 1981 in which a police inspector Pritam Singh Bajwa and constable Surat Singh were killed. He had migrated to that country in 1970 and resigned his job in 1978 to go back to India after the Sikh-Nirankari clash on April 13, 1978. He was associated with the Akhand Kirtani Jatha, a puritan Sikh organization.

According to the information, on target were two flights, the other being Air India Flight 301 from Tokyo to Bangkok for which the baggage carrying the time bomb was booked on the Toronto-Tokyo-Canada Pacific Flight 003 at Vancouver. The bomb on this plane exploded at New Tokyo Narita airport killing two Japanese porters shifting the luggage to the Air India flight.

The explosion at Narita took place about an hour before Kanishka went down. Both the bombs were timed to explode after the planes had landed. The luggage was to be transferred to the Air India flight at Narita. Kanishka was an hour and 40 minutes late because of a spare engine that was installed at Toronto under its left wing to be flown to India as per the normal practice.[2] Another newspaper report stated: "A bomb on board was primed to explode on the runway at Heathrow during a refuelling stop. However, there was a delay of over two hours before take-off".[3] *The Washington Post* reported: "The plane had taken off late from Toronto on Saturday night, and was again delayed in Montreal".[4] All calculations of the conspirators went wrong due to this unforeseen delay that resulted in the unprecedented tragedy. In case the take-off had not been delayed, the bomb would have exploded at London airport after the landing.

Parmar was arrested in Canada in this case in November 1985 but released in January 1986 due to lack of evidence. He was arrested again in June 1986 but released in May 1987. He left Canada again in May, 1988 as investigations progressed and the noose started tightening around him.

The Canadian investigators finally traced the case from probe into the Narita explosion in collaboration with the Japanese authorities. Canada requested the UK to extradite Inderjit Singh Reyat who was arrested on February 5, 1988. He had shifted from Canada to UK some months after the Kanishka tragedy. He was finally flown to Vancouver on December 13, 1989 to be tried there. It was Reyat's re-arrest that alarmed Parmar who then contacted his associates in Babbar Khalsa seeking protection.

It is pertinent to mention that he headed a splinter group of his own as Babbar Khalsa (Talwinder) when he planned these two bombings.

The men from Babbar Khalsa staying in Pakistan planned his hiding with the help of some arms smuggler. The ISI providing this contact to the Babbars cannot be ruled out.

One of Parmar's associates had contacted Babbars in Pakistan seeking help for him. Wadhawa Singh, the Babbar Khalsa leader in Pakistan had been associated with Parmar during the early days and thus had a soft corner for him. It was decided to extend every possible assistance to him.

He was instructed to board the flight to Bangkok via Karachi. He took the precaution of not boarding the flight from any airport in Canada and took the flight from USA. He used a fake identity and passport to travel to Pakistan. He was brought out at Karachi and taken to Lahore as per the arrangement for such covert operations. This was around May 1988.

Pakistan initially did not want to do anything with Parmar but allowed him to enter following the issue having been strongly taken up by the Panthic Committee and the Babbar Khalsa. One of his associates from Canada was also brought in by these radical Sikh organizations.

While facilitating his entry, Pakistan refused to provide him sanctuary as that could have resulted in tension with Canada. Pakistan clearly told Wadhawa and his associates to arrange a safe house for him in India or elsewhere. He stayed in the Lahore area for less than a month before he was shifted to a safe place.

It was then that a smuggler named Haji was contacted in Darra Adam Khel town in the Frontier Province of Pakistan to make arrangements for Parmar in the caves in the Frontier area bordering Afghanistan, where he stayed for more than a year and a half from 1988 to 1990, before he was brought back. He was allowed by Pakistan to stay with the Babbars for only some time after his return from the caves. Pakistan told the Babbars to push him into India.

A news report appeared in the *Punjabi Tribune* from London that Parmar was in contact with Afghan militant leader Gulbuddin Hekmatyar, who later took over as Prime Minister of that country.[5] There was no reference of his having taken shelter in caves on the Pakistan-Afghanistan border. As per this report, Hekmatyar had denied any links with the Khalistanis. However, the sources who were active in the Sikh struggle maintain the interaction was routine, if not regular.

While in the caves, he planned some major action independently that had the potential to escalate tension between India and Pakistan to a new level and create a war-like situation. He paid Rs. 40 lakhs to Haji for the purchase of a stinger missile that was to be delivered to him in Delhi after he crossed over. His planned operation got leaked to the people in the ISI who were not in favour of such action that could trigger direct confrontation between India and Pakistan. The missile was never delivered.

He formally joined the Babbar Khalsa after his return from the caves. It was in Lahore in late 1990 or early 1991 that Parmar was inducted as vice-president of the BKI and nominated to the apex Panthic Committee (Dr. Sohan Singh). He wanted to head the Babbar Khalsa, as he was from the first group of militants but the organization was in no mood to replace Sukhdev Singh. It was for this reason that he was suitably accommodated as Babbar Khalsa International's nominee on the Panthic Committee. He returned to India after that. This was the only time that Parmar formally joined the mother organization. Two of his associates were accommodated on the executive committee of the Babbar Khalsa.

Two of his associates who were in contact with the Babbars also came to Pakistan when he was to formally join the mother organization.

Also present in that hideout were Dr. Sohan Singh and Daljit Singh who headed the Sikh Students Federation.

He stayed in India for about a year and went to Bangkok through Nepal in the summer of 1992. He was there for about 2 months before heading towards Europe. It was during this period that he parted company with the Babbar Khalsa again. He contacted Babbar dissidents in Europe to rope them into his new outfit. He went to Pakistan again from Europe. One of his earlier associates from Canada, Sarmukh Singh, was with him throughout this period.

He stayed in Pakistan and sought recognition as Babbar Khalsa (Talwinder) from that country. The authorities were reluctant as Pakistan was not in favour of a split among these people. He came to India via Nepal after a short stay in Pakistan and settled in Mohali, the Punjab town bordering Chandigarh. He started mobilizing his own network in India. He went to Jammu in the first week of October to meet his contact there, who was retired Major Nanak Singh. It was during one such visit that he finally got trapped. His associates from Europe called him on October 4 on Nanak's phone. Talwinder told the man to call him again the next day.

The man called the next day but no one picked up the phone. He got suspicious.

Major Nanak Singh had told his associates in Canada later that Parmar had gone to Srinagar from Jammu and returned the following day.

According to his version, Parmar was picked up from the bus stand in Jammu as he got down from the bus on suspicion, as security was tight that day due to a bomb blast in the city. Nanak claimed that he met Parmar at the police station. He said that it was his offer of a hefty bribe (in lakhs) to the police station in charge for his release that made him suspicious. Parmar had managed to telephone Nanak with the help of a policeman about the situation in which he had landed inadvertently.

The Jammu police got in touch with the Punjab police. He was identified by the Punjab police that took over his custody.

Nanak claimed that the Jammu police started harassing him. It was at that point that Parmar's associates in Canada instructed him to move out and provided him financial assistance. He shifted to Delhi for some time from where he moved to Belgium in 1993 to land finally in Canada via Bangkok. The organization realized later that Nanak had double-crossed.

However, official sources in the know of Parmar's movement

maintain he had taken the Chhamb route to enter India that time. He stayed for some time with a contact at Jammu and went to Srinagar. It was at Jammu that he came under the radar of the Intelligence Bureau.

The man handling this operation at that time was Ajit Doval who was Inspector General of Police, in charge of operations in Kashmir in the Intelligence Bureau (IB). Doval passed on the information to Punjab Director General of Police (DGP), K.P.S. Gill, who assigned the task to the Jalandhar police. An officer of the level of Superintendent of Police from Punjab coordinated with the IB.

Additional DGP, O.P. Sharma, who headed the Punjab intelligence, later protested for having been kept out of the loop. Operation Parmar was carried out by Doval and Gill.

It was a person known to Parmar from the Goraya area nicknamed 'Sarpanch' who had come into contact with an IB. This man used to contact Parmar through a Chandigarh-based person known as 'Professor'. This so-called professor too was known to be an IB mole. It was the Goraya man who was in touch with Parmar before the encounter.

The Punjab police was passed on the information about the movement of two Maruti cars. The operation was further assigned to a Deputy Superintendent of Police (DSP) and the Station House Officer of that area. The two cars were intercepted by this police party.

The Canadian authorities visited Punjab after this encounter to get details. Yet another visit by the Royal Canadian Mounted Police officials was in 2007 as the investigation in the Kanishka blast proceeded on Parmar's role. It was during this visit that the Canadian officials met the DSP.

The Official Version of the Encounter

> Giving the details, the Director General of Police, K.P.S. Gill, told newsmen here (Jalandhar) that the Naka party posted at Kangrain village in Phillaur subdivision intercepted two Maruti cars coming from Akalpura. The occupants of the cars, finding no escape route, started firing at the Naka party. The police not only returned the fire but also chased them. The car occupants left the cars and ran to the fields. But the police gunned down three of the fleeing suspects in exchange of fire. The remaining three suspects entered the fields and hid themselves there. But when the police surrounded the fields and fired, the hiding suspects also returned the fire, which continued for two hours.
>
> The police started search operations immediately after the firing from the fields stopped and recovered six bodies. Three of the suspects

> were identified as Talwinder Singh Parmar, the originator of terrorism in Punjab, and two Pakistani nationals Habibullah Khan and Inkhab Ahmed Zia, residents of Lahore. Two passports bearing Nos H-822669 and E-090696 of the Islamic Republic of Pakistan were also recovered. The police also recovered one all-purpose machine gun, three AK-47 assault rifles, one rocket, one rocket launcher, one drum magazine and five magazines of AK 47 rifles.[6]
>
> Mr. Gill said this was for the first time that the Punjab police had obtained firsthand evidence of Pakistan's involvement in aiding abetting militancy in Punjab.

There is no mention of any policeman having been injured despite the fact that the Parmar group was heavily armed with such sophisticated weapons.

Here is the other version from sources about the two Pakistani nationals.

The two Pakistanis were from Lahore with genuine passports. One of them was a hospital employee and the other a Kashmiri, settled there. The hospital employee had come into contact with the Babbar Khalsa activist Gurdip Singh Sibia in London. Sibia finally surrendered in 1992 to the Punjab police. That surrender is a different story. This man rang Mahal Singh in Lahore from Delhi, as he had the information that Sibia too was in India and he wanted to meet him. He gave his Delhi address to be given to Sibia. Mahal telephoned Sibia at his hideout in Ahmedabad.

Sibia was in the custody of the Intelligence Bureau by that time but was asked to behave normally with his contacts. He was under constant watch and this was not known to the Babbar Khalsa people. He was shown to have surrendered and produced before newsmen in Chandigarh in the presence of chief minister Beant Singh on August 13, 1992.

The police raided the address where the two Pakistanis were staying and picked them up. They were detained in July.

Two others shown to have been killed in the encounter were Sikh hardliners from Belgium and had been taken into custody by the security agencies after they landed at the Delhi airport. They were not in touch with Talwinder earlier.

It may be mentioned that one other person who accompanied Parmar from Canada subsequently returned to Canada. He had joined him when he was inducted formally in the Babbar Khalsa.

Beant Singh's Assassination

The last major action associated with the Punjab militancy was carried out by the Babbar Khalsa. This action was the assassination of Chief Minister Beant Singh on August 31, 1995 at the main gate of the Punjab civil secretariat, the seat of the state government.

The first offer to kill Beant Singh, associated with blatant human rights violations and killings in fake encounters, was received by the Babbar Khalsa in Pakistan via USA in November 1994. Beant Singh had taken over as the Chief Minister heading the Congress government in February 1992 Assembly elections boycotted by the mainstream Akalis.

Wadhawa Singh was contacted by his associates in the USA to convey that two security personnel deployed in the Punjab Civil Secretariat had offered their services. They were Dilawar Singh and Balwant Singh Rajoana.

Wadhawa consulted one of his confidantes who expressed the apprehension that it could be a trap by Indian intelligence agencies that should better be ignored. There was no follow up action. The message, however, was repeated after some time and Wadhawa told the contact to reach Pakistan as part of the Sikh jatha on Baisakhi for a face-to-face talk

In the meantime, following the killing of Baldev Singh Hawara, the Ropar district commander of Babbar Khalsa, his second-in-command Jagtar Singh Hawara, started feeling insecure and wanted to be rescued as the noose was tightening and the main militant leaders were being killed by the security forces one after the other. He conveyed his apprehensions to the senior leaders via the contacts in USA.

The policy of Beant Singh and Director General of Police K.P.S. Gill was simple: No Prisoners.

It was decided to take Hawara and others safely via Nepal. Nepal and Bangkok were being used as the base by Babbars for such covert operations. This job was assigned to a Babbar Khalsa leader who had been carrying out such operations, as he knew how to arrange fake documents and provide authenticity. He flew to Nepal where a contact was to hand over to him pictures of five Babbar Khalsa people who were to be provided safe passage.

This contact procured fake passports and got the same stamped from the Thai immigration authorities to provide authenticity to the documents. Visas used to be stamped on arrival at Bangkok. However, a parallel system existed there for such operations and the entry visa would be genuine. These passports were stamped again by the Nepal immigration officials to provide further authenticity. Huge bribes normally facilitated such underhand operations.

These people managed to reach Nepal from where they flew to Bangkok to be taken to Lahore as per the arrangement that existed then for such operations. This operation was completed before the group of pilgrims was to reach Pakistan in April on Baisakhi 1995. They, including Hawara, were given a four-week training in assembling explosive devices in Pakistan.

The contact person from USA too reached Pakistan in April along with other pilgrims. It was then that the assassination was planned.

Hawara was taken into confidence, who agreed to facilitate the execution of this operation and return to India. It was at this point that he was given the contacts of those who had offered their services.

Hawara met Dilawar and Rajoana after his return. The plan that was chalked out in Pakistan was either to target Beant Singh or K.P.S. Gill, in that order. However, the trio finalized Beant Singh as the target.

His safe return to Chandigarh was ensured. Beant Singh was assassinated by a human bomb, Dilawar Singh on August 31, 1995, as Beant Singh sat in his car at the main gate of the Punjab civil secretariat.

ENDNOTES

1. March 11, 1985. *The Indian Express.*
2. June 23, 1985. *CBC Digital Archives.*
3. November 11, 2000. *The Irish Times.*
4. June 24, 1985. *The Washington Post.*
5. April 9, 1989. *Punjabi Tribune.*
6. October 16, 1992. *The Indian Express.*

8

Prisoner No. 141 in Faislabad in Pakistan

This was the time when the fierce storm that hit Punjab in June 1984 had started receding.

Kanwarpal Singh, a young student from Khalsa College in Amritsar on September 23, 1984 decided to cross the Radcliffe Line that divides the Indian and Pakistani Punjab. This young man was then an anonymous face in the crowd. His life changed forever as he stepped over the Radcliffe Line.

His story in a way provides some insight into the level of Pakistan's involvement over the period in the Sikh militant struggle through his multi-layered experience. However, this is just a case study and not a detailed analysis of Pakistan's role in this Sikh struggle.

Kanwarpal, now spokesman of the Dal Khalsa, was a 19-year-old student of BA Part I at the time of the army attack on Darbar Sahib (Golden Temple). He was traumatized by not only the brutality of it but also because the army had attacked the most revered shrine of the community in "free" India. Several of his collegemates also shared his deeply hurt feelings.

They would meet and discuss as to how to avenge the attack. Angry and anguished Sikh boys had started crossing over to Pakistan by that time, some to escape repression by the security forces and others dictated by the revenge psyche. They too opted for it without having even the faintest idea as to what was in store for them across the border. They succeeded in contacting a person who could facilitate their border crossing about 25 kms away from the Dera Baba Nanak sector in the adjoining Gurdaspur district.

Three of them finally made up their minds and the date fixed was September 23, 1984. Although the border with Pakistan at that time was not fenced, one had to know the way, otherwise one could get lost and even re-enter India. They were told to follow certain stars for navigation after crossing over. The smugglers on both sides used to function as the conduits. These 'boys' had been briefed but they were on their own.

They were not fortunate as after travelling some distance, the weather turned cloudy followed by heavy rain. Even in the pitch dark, they could make out that they were on the bank of a drain. There are defence drains on both sides. Drenched, they decided to spend the night there. They were spotted in the morning by the Pakistan Rangers and handed over to the intelligence agency people, who shifted them to Faislabad jail the next day after questioning them. Faisalabad was earlier Lyallpur, the second biggest town in Pakistani Punjab.

The first question they faced was as to why they had entered Pakistan. They said they had the information that Sant Jarnail Singh Bhindranwale was alive and had crossed over to that side. It was then that they came to know that it was just a rumour.

Fasialabad jail already had 138 Sikh detainees and Kanwarpal was given the number 141. About 400 more Sikh youth reached there within the next three months. Also in that jail there was Ajaib Singh Abhiyasi from Damdami Taksal. They were to spend about five months in this jail.

Jasbir Singh Rode, nephew of Sant Bhindranwale, visited Pakistan as part of the group of Sikh pilgrims in November 1984 on the occasion of the birth anniversary of Guru Nanak Dev at Nankana Sahib. Abhiyasi was taken out from jail during his visit to meet Atinder Pal Singh and Gurjeet Singh, who were staying there in a bungalow. He returned to jail after about a month.

Rode had reached Pakistan after the formation of the International Sikh Youth Federation in London that he headed. On return to jail, Abhyasi appealed to the jail inmates to join the ISYF. About 350 persons responded. Kanwarpal and his three other associates were among about 30 who refused. They were separated from them and shifted to the barrack where the Sikh hijackers were interned. It was here that he met Gajinder Singh and some others. They were the people from the Dal Khalsa who had hijacked the Delhi-Amritsar-Srinagar flight of the Indian Airlines to Lahore to protest the arrest of Sant Bhindranwale on September 20.

Nine Babbar Khalsa leaders were also in the Faislabad jail at that time. They included Manmohan Singh who was later involved in the transistor bomb blasts in Delhi.

The punishment for illegally entering Pakistan was six months. Those who did not join any organization were sent back to India, as they entered Pakistan with nothing on the record. About 400 such people were rehabilitated by the Punjab government over the period. Several of those crossing the border initially would be prosecuted, as Pakistan did not want to give the impression that the country was sheltering Sikh militants. They would be sentenced to six months in jail. Others would be kept behind four walls but without trial.

The Sikh youth had come in the hope that they would get armed training but they were rotting in jail and getting restive. Some of them decided to break out. One of them was killed and scores injured in the firing by the Pakistan jail authorities in the process. Those who managed to escape were brought back. This happened in February/ March 1985.

The militant leaders who lived outside the jail protested to the Pakistani authorities against the situation. As damage control measures, Pakistan decided to release them and hand them over to the leaders outside. Several of them opted to return to India.

Pakistan's support to the Sikh cause initially was limited, unlike Indian Kashmir. Kashmir was part of Pakistan's foreign policy but not the Sikh struggle and hence that country never publicly advocated the cause of Sikh separatists. Pakistan largely offered support to the Sikh militants that included training camps and sanctuaries, but not immediately after Operation Bluestar. Arms and ammunition were part of the strategic support.

It was around this time that Kanwarpal joined the Babbar Khalsa.

He too returned on January 13, 1986 but avoided staying at his house in Amritsar. It was in August 1987 that he, along with Jimmy Narang and Anokh Singh Babbar, were named in a case of conspiracy to target Amritsar Senior Superintendent of Police Mohammad Izhar Alam. Jimmy Narang had crossed over to India along with Kanwarpal. He was the son of Kartar Singh Narang who later took over as president of the Babbar Akali Dal.

Jimmy landed into the hands of the Jalandhar police in August 1987. Alam took him to Amritsar and it was during interrogation that Jimmy confessed about the abortive attempt. Kanwarpal had already left India for Thailand in June 1987, two months before Jimmy's arrest from where he flew to Lahore. Crossing the border subsequently became routine for him.

He received the training much later in 1990.

Pakistan Apprehensive Initially

On the record, the Sikh militant struggle initially got linked to Pakistan "by air", literally, with the first hijacking associated with militancy.

When five young Sikhs from the radical Sikh organization, Dal Khalsa, hijacked the Indian Airlines flight IC-423 from Delhi- Amritsar-Srinagar hopping flight to Lahore on September 29, 1981 in protest against the arrest of Sant Bhindranwale in the case of the assassination of Jalandhar-based newspaper owner-editor Lala Jagat Narain near Ludhiana, little did they know what was in store for them in Pakistan. They were Gajinder Singh, Satnam Singh Paonta Sahib, Tejinderpal Singh, Jasbir Singh and Karan Singh. Dal Khalsa 'boys' were not taken seriously in Punjab till then.

They were arrested and taken to military jail in Lahore Cantt where they spent about three years in solitary confinement. One hijacker each was kept in a cell and as a precaution, the next cell was kept vacant and also the third cell, so that they could not communicate with each other in any manner. These cells were without ceiling fans. It was towards the birth anniversary of Guru Nanak Dev in November that they were allowed to be together in a room for about an hour for prayers for the first time. They were given some relaxation in 1983 when the channels between Pakistan and Sant Bhindranwale became fully operational.

Pakistan was being too cautious as the country had a terrible experience in 1971 when an Indian Airlines plane on the Srinagar-Jammu route was hijacked to Lahore on January 30. The passengers and the crew were released and the plane set ablaze on February 1. India retaliated by stopping Pakistani flights over the Indian territory.

It is pertinent to mention that Pakistan at that time consisted of East Pakistan and West Pakistan divided by India. East Pakistan is now Bangladesh.

That was the time when the liberation struggle supported by India was on in East Pakistan. The two countries entered into war in December 1971 resulting in the liberation of East Pakistan as Bangladesh. Pakistan had suspected that hijacking to be an Indian covert operation to stop flights over Indian territory to the eastern part. That bitter experience initially dictated Pakistan's attitude towards the Sikh hijackers in 1981. This period in 1971 when flights over Indian territory were stopped was critical for Pakistan.

The punishment for hijacking in Pakistan at that time was death. It was after the 1981 hijacking that it was amended to include life term too. They were freed on Diwali in November 1994, after serving life term.

People like Dr. Jagjit Singh Chohan and USA-based Ganga Singh Dhillon had established contacts with Pakistan much earlier but there was nothing like the Sikh struggle in Indian Punjab at that time. It was Dr. Chohan, who had provided contacts to Sant Bhindranwale for procurement of weapons in the first stage. The channel used for this purpose was the smugglers. Yet another channel was opened through some other contacts in London, including businessmen of Pakistani origin.

Afghanistan and Pakistan had emerged as a free market for all kinds of weapons after the Soviet occupation of Afghanistan in 1979. Pakistan was the base for US operations against the Soviets in Afghanistan. Moreover, weapons have always been easily available in the Frontier areas of Pakistan.

Sophisticated weapons like AK-47 assault rifles, however, surfaced in Punjab mainly after Operation Bluestar when Pakistan got directly involved. Pakistan's involvement in the Sikh struggle subsequently became more pronounced.

The two hijackings immediately after Operation Bluestar hint at the level of Pakistan's involvement with the Sikh struggle. Both these hijackings were carried out by the All India Sikh Students Federation that functioned as the militant organization for years and was headed by Bhai Amrik Singh.

The first of these hijackings was carried out on July 5, 1984. The hijackers took the Srinagar-Delhi flight to Lahore where they were arrested and prosecuted, released after completion of the sentence. They demanded withdrawal of the army from Punjab and handing over Darbar Sahib (Golden Temple) complex to the Sikhs. They included Paraminder Singh Harfanmaula, Gurinder Singh, Harbhajan Singh, Ravinder Singh Pinka, Dalip Singh, Harminder Singh, Manjit Singh, Malagar Singh and Gurdip Singh. Significantly, former Jammu and Kashmir chief minister Farooq Abdullah had accused the Indian intelligence agencies for master-minding this hijack.[1]

They seized the Airbus A-300 at about 4.50 pm within 10 minutes after it took off from Srinagar. Pakistan initially refused permission to land but gave in after the hijackers threatened to blow it up mid-air.

This hijacking was planned by AISSF general secretary Harminder Singh Sandhu in April 1984, who deputed Harfanmaula for the job. He was to be assisted by some Sikhs settled in Srinagar but the operation could not be executed at that time. This was to protest against the ban on the AISSF imposed by the government on March 19, 1984 for indulging in subversive and anti-national activities. The plan was finally executed to protest against the army attack.

A .22 pistol was smuggled into the plane by one of the hijackers.

Five of the hijackers were from the Chandigarh-Ropar region and four from Srinagar. One of the demands included the release of Sandhu and 29 other AISSF activists arrested from the Darbar Sahib complex during Operation Bluestar.

This was followed by another hijack within days. As the Indian Airlines Boeing 737 Delhi-Chandigarh-Jammu-Srinagar flight IC 421 took off from Chandigarh for Srinagar on the morning of August 24, 1984, seven young Khalistan slogan shouting Sikhs rose from the seats, took over the plane and demanded to be taken to nearby Lahore. No one carried any weapon but they threatened to blow up the plane, posing that they carried bombs. They surrendered after a dramatic 36-hours in Dubai with a stopover at Karachi. Its call sign changed Karachi onwards from IC 421 to Khalistan Bravo Sava Lakh. No passenger was harmed.

Their demand too was the withdrawal of the army from the holiest of the holy Sikh shrine.

Some of them were undergraduate students of Sri Guru Gobind Singh College, Chandigarh. The seven were Amarinder Singh, Kamaljit Singh Sandhu, Avtar Singh, Man Singh, Devinder Singh, Tejinder Singh and Surinder Singh. Kamaljit, who financed the tickets, used to stay at the residence of Akali leader Ajaib Singh Machaki in Chandigarh.

Lahore again refused permission to land and shut down the airport. The plane kept circling over the city and permission was granted to land only when the commander threatened emergency landing due to fuel shortage. Pakistan did not want any trouble on its soil and told the commander to clear out after refuelling. They conveyed to the Pakistan authorities that they wanted to take the plane to the USA but were told that it was a short haul plane and could not fly directly to the desired destination. The next stoppage was Karachi as the commander impressed upon them to land for another refuelling as his effort was to avoid Afghanistan.

The hijackers were approached by two sets of Pakistani officials. One group consisted of officials detailed for negotiations while the other was from the ISI. They were in touch with the hijackers separately, the second group unofficially. It was during this process that the ISI officials slipped in a .32 bore revolver with enough ammunition as they realized that the hijackers did not have any weapon and exhorted them to take their fight to the logical conclusion. The nearest destinations from Karachi were in West Asian countries that included Abu Dhabi and Dubai. All three airports in the region had been shut down in view of the approaching hijacked aircraft. Finally, as fuel gauge went down, Dubai allowed it to land.

According to the information available now, officials from the USA, Soviet Union and one other country joined the negotiations. They agreed to surrender on condition of political asylum in the USA. The Dubai authorities made it clear to them that the sentence for hijacking in their country was death penalty. They negotiated a seven-day asylum for onward journey. In between, however, a different plan was being put into operation.

They were made to board a plane one by one that was supposed to be a flight bound for USA. It was not. The plane carried Indian commandoes in the guise of passengers. Dubai had agreed to hand them over to India. They were taken to the aircraft one by one, only to be overpowered by the commandoes. The plane took them to New Delhi. They were interrogated for about a month at the Red Fort interrogation centre and then shifted to Jodhpur jail for trial.

One of the passengers on that hijacked plane happened to be K. Subramanian, the international strategic affairs analyst and former Chairman of India's Joint Intelligence Committee. However, his identity was not known to the hijackers. He was a diabetic. The hijackers took proper care of him.

They were sentenced to life imprisonment. Their sentence was commuted after 12 years at the intervention of Akali Dal stalwart and Shiromani Gurdwara Parbandhak Committee president Gurcharan Singh Tohra, whom they had contacted when out on parole. In case of life sentence not involving murder, the sentence can be commuted after 10 years.

Atal Behari Vajpayee had taken over as the Prime Minister heading a minority government in 1996 to which the Akali Dal had extended unconditional support. This was Vajpayee's 13-day government. Tohra decided to use this opportunity for a cause that was associated with the Sikhs.

He took a delegation of Akali Dal MPs to the cabinet secretary. Tohra told the cabinet secretary, "This must be done". The necessary papers were moved for commuting their sentence. They were free people. Tohra allotted a ticket to Amarinder to contest the election to the general house of the SGPC from Chandigarh in 1996. Perhaps only Tohra could do that.

Pakistan's Sikh Card

Pakistan played the Sikh card on the record for the first time around

1971 after Dr. Jagjit Singh Chohan and Charan Singh Panchhi had raised the Khalistan slogan. It was Pakistan that initially provided legitimacy to Dr. Chohan and he never looked back. For years, Pakistan allowed the use of its soil to protagonists of Khalistan but within a particular framework. Yet another leader who surfaced in the Khalistan political dynamics linked to Pakistan was USA-based Ganga Singh Dhillon.

There is another global dimension to the Punjab turmoil that coincides with the Soviet invasion of Afghanistan in 1979. India was an ally of the USSR that had invaded Afghanistan. India had to be engaged on her own soil and Punjab was the soft target at that time.

Here was the convergence of the Sikh interests articulated at that time by Sant Bhindranwale and strategic interests of USA and Pakistan. Both the UK and West Germany were the countries where Khalistanis were active. This covert support from Pakistan suited Sant Bhindranwale, who otherwise perhaps might not have been aware of the deeper strategic designs. Even if he was aware, it fitted into his politics. The policy of confrontation with the Akalis by the Congress that returned to power in 1980 in both Punjab and at the Centre contributed to his build-up of the Sikh struggle. The deadly game was on in Punjab.

Sant Bhindranwale's logic was simple and down–to-earth as he welcomed everyone whose words and actions contributed to his politics that centred around what he used to articulate as "restoring the dignity of the Sikhs".

Besides Dr. Chohan, another important link between Pakistan and Sant Bhindranwale, was a UK- based group from the Akhand Kirtani Jatha (AKJ). Four in numbers, these people remained behind the scene. The person who was the most active among them, used to be addressed as Baba.

The AKJ decided to actively contribute to the Sikh struggle after the Dharamyudh Morcha was launched by the Akali Dal on August 4, 1982 from the Darbar Sahib complex. These four persons were deputed for this job in early 1983. However, only one of them would stay in Amritsar at a time.

It may be mentioned that militancy had already entered the Sikh struggle by that time. The UK chapter of the AKJ arranged a meeting between Baba and Dr. Chohan to work out modalities for extending support to the struggle in Punjab. Dr. Chohan in turn introduced him to his Pakistani contacts.

Among the four who had come from the UK, Baba was the only

person being in touch with both sides, till the end. He used to cross over to Pakistan frequently both from the Punjab and Rajasthan border. Sant facilitated his visits to Pakistan through the channels that were operated mainly by the smugglers. He had his own contacts via London across the border.

Pakistan started focusing on the Sikh struggle after the first hijacking by the Dal Khalsa. Going by the newspaper reports, the hijackers shouted Khalistan slogans. It was more than a protest against the arrest of Sant Bhindranwale in the context of the raising of Khalistan slogans. The newspaper headline screamed: "Khalistan men hijack Boeing to Lahore". The Khalistan narrative hit the global attention with this single action by young Dal Khalsa members.

The level of support by Pakistan to the Sikh radicals started going up after Babbar Khalsa leader Wadhawa Singh who had escaped to Europe was persuaded to move to Karachi for a meeting with the ISI officials in September 1983. The ISI had the impression that the Babbars were rivals of Sant Bhindranwale and hence did not like to get involved in that situation. It took Wadhawa about six months to remove this impression. The people close to the Sant had been informing the ISI about the Babbars.

Baba met Sant Bhindranwale to brief him about Pakistan's willingness to arrange weapons. Sant Bhindranwale approved the arrangement. Baba brought the first consignment before the middle of 1983 and made several rounds of Pakistan from Amritsar. It is pertinent to mention here that weapons used to be smuggled from Pakistan to India even before the start of the militant struggle in Punjab.

Baba was provided accommodation in the Darbar Sahib complex. He would not interact with other associates of Sant Bhindranwale or even the Babbars staying there, as no one was allowed to enter his room. The UK chapter of AKJ had briefed some members of the Nagoke group, the first group of militants, to take care of his security.

Baba had been under the impression that Sant Bhindranwale was sharing weapons with the Babbar Khalsa people but came to know of the reality about two months before Operation Bluestar. He protested to Sant Bhindranwale who did not respond. It was only at that time that he went to Guru Nanak Niwas Serai in the complex to meet the Babbars staying there. He disclosed his operations to the Babbars for the first time.

Baba stayed with Sukhdev after distancing himself from Sant Bhindranwale. He visited Pakistan for the last time in May before Operation Bluestar but on behalf of the Babbars. The ISI handlers agreed to supply weapons to the Babbars too, courtesy Wadhawa Singh. The consignment that was meant for the Babbars was arranged towards the end of May but did not reach the Darbar Sahib complex, as the situation had already deteriorated. The shrine complex had come under heavy fire from the security forces on January 1.

This consignment of weapons was concealed in a village near the border. It was a revolver from this consignment that was later used to kill Akali Dal chief Sant Harchand Singh Longowal on August 20, 1985.

The Babbar Khalsa people exhausted their ammunition much earlier as the action started on June 1. The security forces were targeting the Serai area. The Babbars were manning the Langar area and the Nagoke group the Nanak Niwas. They had some .303 calibre rifles too that they had snatched from a group of Nihangs that had been supplied to them by the government.

After the day-long firing ended, Baba, accompanied by Mehal Singh and Anokh Singh, went to meet Sant Bhindranwale for ammunition replenishment. However, they were refused the meeting by Bhai Amrik Singh and Rachhpal Singh, but they spared some ammunition.

With ammunition having been totally depleted, the Babbars met on June 5 around 7 pm and decided to leave the complex to prepare for the next phase of the struggle. Those present urged Babbar Khalsa chief Sukhdev Singh to leave with the first group itself. An opening had been made in the wall at the back of Nanak Niwas into Gali Baghwali, a narrow lane. Baba left in the first group and Sukhdev came out after about an hour. They took shelter in a safe house in the area till curfew was lifted.

They crossed over to Pakistan a few weeks after the Operation Bluestar.

Pakistan agencies were in contact with the select Sikh radical leaders or their representatives but the common youth who had crossed over to Pakistan did not know much till about 1987-88 about the people handling them.

They used to be confined to camps till 1987, which were more like an open jail as their movements were controlled and no interaction was allowed with the local populace. They were allowed to move out in 1987 and told about the Darra market where weapons of all sorts were openly available. The signal was to go to that market, purchase weapons and cross back to India. It was during this period that AK 47s flooded Punjab. Earlier, this assault rifle was not that common.

When Pakistan Feared Attack

As Pakistan in 1988 apprehended an attack engineered by Indian intelligence agency RAW on Sikh militants moving out in the open, their movement was again restricted and they were confined to the camps. According to those who were there at that time, Pakistan worked out an arrangement to coordinate their activities under the changed situation. It was proposed that each group could opt for one person from any other country as their representative, who would travel to Pakistan on a valid visa. These people could move about freely all over Pakistan.

With the apprehension growing about attack, they were shifted to safe houses located away from residential areas. Each safe house had about 40 to 50 militants. These locations were described by the Indian media as the training camps. The restrictions were lifted after a few months and they, for the first time, were allowed to meet media people, interact with the local population and go to gurdwaras.

This interaction was educative as they found out that Pakistanis continued to nurture the historical hangover of unprecedented bloodshed during partition in 1947 in which lakhs of people were killed on both sides. One section of the Pakistani Punjabis held the Sikhs responsible for the ghastly tragedy although people had suffered on both sides. The sense of hurt was deeper in the generation that had suffered rather than the contemporary one.

There was yet another point of distrust against the Sikhs, and it was the Sikh prayer. In the Ardas, Sikhs pray for unhindered access to the gurdwaras in Pakistan. This was viewed as a threat to the very existence of Pakistan, as the interpretation was that the Sikhs desired the return of those areas to them. The Sikh leaders concluded that for maintaining a long-term relationship, this apprehension had to be removed by convincing them that Khalistan would be no threat to Pakistan.

The Pakistanis would also refer to the paintings installed in Sikh museums and many of the gurdwaras of martyrs like Bhai Taru Singh, Bhai Sati Das, Bhai Mati Das and Bhai Dyala who were tortured to death by the Mughal rulers. Bhai Sati Das, Bhai Mati Das and Bhai Dyala had been arrested along with Guru Tegh Bahadur.

Bhai Sati Das was wrapped in cotton wool, set alight and roasted alive on November 24, 1675. Bhai Mati Das was cut vertically into two with a saw. Bhai Dyala was boiled to death in a cauldron. Bhai Taru Singh was scalped with a sharp knife and he bled to death.

The two younger sons of Guru Gobind Singh were bricked alive on the orders of Sirhind Governor Wazir Khan. They were Sahibzada Zorawar Singh and Sahibzada Fateh Singh, aged about 9 and 7, who had refused to convert to Islam. They were arrested along with their grandmother, Mata Gujri after escape from Anandpur Sahib. The paintings are part of the collective Sikh consciousness.

Those dealing with the Sikh struggle in the Pakistani establishment suggested that in case the Sikhs wanted to have cordial relations with Pakistan, history would have to be played down. But the examples of extreme torture and persecution are part of Sikh history that shaped the collective consciousness and these chapters of supreme sacrifice cannot be wished away.

The Sikh leaders pointed out during interactions on this issue that Sikhs too had been portrayed as villains in Pakistani textbooks, especially in the context of partition in 1947 and this attitude should change. In India, the Mughals are attacked as the oppressors in many of the school and college textbooks.

The discussion would veer round to the conclusion that though these writings could not be undone, there should be some damage control. Pakistan suggested to the Sikh leaders that in case such texts could not be discarded, the atrocities against the Sikhs in November 1984 should also be included in the books and paintings relating to that massacre and should also find space in the Central Sikh Museum.

The radical leaders felt there was a big communication gap that would have to be narrowed down, for which they approached the media to put across their viewpoint.

The Pakistan Sikh Gurdwara Parbandhak Committee was the by-product of this interaction.

It is pertinent to mention here that it was due to the initiative taken by SGPC chief Gurcharan Singh Tohra that Pakistan had agreed to hand over Nankana Sahib shrine to the Sikhs, whatever might be the other design as mentioned earlier. Nankana Sahib did not have a Sikh population at that time. He was instrumental in getting about 200 families from other parts of Pakistan shifted to Nankana Sahib, who started managing the shrine. These were poor families. An arrangement was worked out to support them financially and to make them economically stronger. Pakistan also agreed to renovate this shrine. Radical leader Wassan Singh Zaffarwal too had made similar efforts.

Pakistan after a stage proposed to the radicals to adopt democratic means too, to mobilize support for Khalistan as part of the strategy along with the militant struggle. At the same time, the ISI gave out unambiguous signals to the militants to undertake bigger action that included targeting security installations rather than indulging in non-strategic killing of the individuals in sporadic actions.

Pakistan Wanted Tohra or Mann to Cross Over

Pakistan was clear that mass mobilization was not possible without a known face like Gurcharan Singh Tohra or Simranjit Singh Mann. The third name mentioned was that of General Narinder Singh, although he was not a mass leader. Pakistan wanted one of them to cross over to finalize the strategy.

It was intimated that Pakistan might consider recognizing Khalistan in case approached by any of these leaders personally. This would have also raised the level of Pakistan's support to the Sikh struggle.

"Let any of them formally announce formation of Khalistan and seek recognition from us. We will accord you people due recognition", was the unambiguous message from Pakistan, the sources privy to the discussions maintain. Both Tohra and Mann had mass support at that time. Mann, however, lost that support base too fast. He was the leader who was inconsistent and shifted his stand too frequently.

Mann was the most popular but untested leader at that time with massive support as reflected in the 1989 Lok Sabha election that he won from Tarn Taran by about five lakh votes. However, this also proved to be his downfall. Here was the most crucial moment for taking the struggle to a new level by mobilizing the masses. He committed a blunder, or was made to commit one, when he refused to enter the Lok Sabha without his 3-foot sword that he used to carry at that time. He failed to grasp the deeper nuances of the demands of the politics at that time.

That was the crucial time when he could have emerged like the leaders in Kashmir who function as the front of the radical struggle. He lacked that capacity and failed.

It may be mentioned that Sant Bhindranwale at their last meeting before the army had moved into the Darbar Sahib complex had tried to convince Tohra to leave the shrine and lead the struggle from abroad. The SGPC chief expressed the view that it was Sant Bhindranwale who was the most appropriate leader to be in command and he should escape from the complex for the bigger cause. However, the maverick had resolved to sacrifice his life for the cause of the Panth, years ago.[2]

As per the information available, Inter-Services Intelligence (ISI) did not have any separate Sikh desk unlike Kashmir during those times. It was Director (Operations) headed by an officer of the rank of Brigadier, who dealt with Sikh affairs. Kashmir was and continues to be part of Pakistan's both foreign and domestic policy but the Khalistan struggle never received that support, neither political nor tactical.

The ISI had made a very clear demarcation while dealing with the Khalistanis. Providing sanctuary to militant leaders is one aspect but providing all out support is different. Pakistan had also assessed that in the absence of mobilization of Sikh masses, the militant struggle would never achieve its objective. Kashmir has been part of the people's struggle from the beginning and militancy is a later chapter. The militancy in Punjab was wiped out mainly in the absence of a mass front organization and mass support.

This issue of a mass leader also came up during the period when former AISSF leader Dr. Bhagwan Singh accompanied by one of the Panthic Committee appointed Takht Jathedar Giani Jaswant Singh and Sikh Federation faction leader Rajinder Singh Mehta visited Pakistan after the killing of AISSF general secretary Harminder Singh Sandhu in Amritsar. It was the Panthic Committee associated with Dr. Sohan Singh that had taken responsibility for the gunning down of this AISSSF leader who was arrested during Operation Bluestar from the Golden Temple complex. The killing had been executed by Paramjit Singh Panjwar and his associates. At a joint meeting, Panjwar justified the killing and refused to apologize for this action. Dr. Sohan Singh, Kanwarpal Singh and Daljit Singh Bittu were present. Jaswant Singh had crossed over to Pakistan to intervene to end internecine war among the militants. Dr. Sohan Singh and Daljit took the position that history would decide whether the killing of Sandhu was justified or not.

Mann was conveyed this message and he agreed to visit Pakistan. He arrived near the border to cross over to Pakistan to discuss this aspect. However, he was told at that very time to stay back as Dr. Sohan Singh put his foot down. It was Dr. Sohan Singh, former Director, Health Services, Punjab, who had been projected as an ideological guide of the struggle. He was among those who were instrumental in the raising of the Khalistan demand by the Panthic Committee on April 29, 1986 from the Darbar Sahib complex. His ambition was to get himself projected as the face of the Khalistan struggle, but he had never been a mass leader.

Besides the usual logistic support, the ISI would invariably confine itself mainly to making suggestions and providing inputs. "We are here to assist you. You understand the situation better"—this used to be the brief. The decision-making would be left to the Sikh militant leaders.

The militant leaders sheltered in Pakistan were confronted with a major problem after the attack on Parliament in New Delhi on December 13, 2001. Perhaps it was for the first time during this period that Pakistan came under immense pressure from the USA. The ISI people conveyed to the five main militant Sikh leaders that they could be arrested any time by the Pakistan security forces and the US intelligence people in a joint raid. The ISI made it clear that the agency could not protect them.

They were advised to go underground in Pakistan itself by using their social contacts which they had developed over the years. They spent a year while remaining underground in Pakistan. They included Wadhawa Singh, Ranjit Singh Neeta, Paramjit Singh Panjwar, Lakhbir Singh Rode and Gajinder Singh. The ISI warned that in case they were caught, they would be repatriated to India. The advice was to alert their supporters in India to arrange for legal aid in case of such an eventuality.

When Life is Too Little a Cost for Political Objective

The illegal border crossings, many a times, involve security agencies from both India and Pakistan and this service can be availed for a consideration by the people familiar with the modus operandi. These are the channels that are usually used by smugglers. As compared to the Rajasthan and Gujarat border, the border in Punjab has villages on both sides right upto the zero line. This border was fenced after 1988 on the Indian side.

Kanwarpal at one stage, was assigned the task of ensuring that the passage was safe for crossing by a senior leader. This was in the summer of 1991 when Prime Minister Chandra Shekhar opened channels for dialogue with the Sikh militants. He was the Prime Minister from November 10, 1990 and June 21, 1991. The militant leader who had come in contact with Chandra Shekhar for initiating talks was Akal Federation chief Kanwar Singh Dhami.

The government was to facilitate border crossing for Dhami to enable him to have wider consultations with the militant leaders staying in Pakistan. Wadhawa Singh from Babbar Khalsa too was to accompany him.

However, Wadhawa did not trust this channel and suspected it to be a trap. He deputed his associate Kanwarpal to go along with Dhami. He shared his apprehension with Kanwarpal and proposed he should go as a test case. He carried a cyanide capsule with him if the exercise turned out to be a trap. In case of the safe crossover, he was to convey to a contact in London: "The flight has been comfortable. Now you can come." The person who was to facilitate this exercise was a smuggler Charan Singh from Gurdaspur district.

It was arranged that Crystal Chowk in Amritsar would be the pick-up point by Charan Singh. Dhami accompanied Kanwarpal and they got there at the appointed time. In the meanwhile, an official BSF gypsy reached there. The people in that vehicle included a Deputy Superintendent of Police level BSF official who had half his face covered and his driver. He signalled them to join him and drove towards Khasa sector in Amritsar district. This sector covers the Attari-Wagha border. As they reached the area, the sun was going down. They had reached a border observation post along the fence. The fence is 100-150 metres inside Indian territory at most of the places. There are fields across the fence that are cultivated by the farmers of border villages. Gates have been installed to cross it.

The duty of the border patrol changes around this time in the evening. The new border patrol takes its position as the one on duty returns. For about half an hour, there would be no patrol party monitoring the border.

The BSF official who accompanied them did not speak all this while. He only signalled instructions to his driver.

The gate opened and they crossed over to the Pakistani side. The Pakistani post was just on the opposite side, about half an hour walking distance. They were told to walk briskly before it was dark. The Pakistanis were there to receive them.

Charan Singh charged each of them Rs. 25,000. That was the rate for facilitating crossing at that time.

The Pakistani officials later took Kanwarpal to a hotel in Lahore from where he telephoned the contact in London informing him about the safe landing. The message was conveyed and Wadhawa crossed over after a few days.

Kanwarpal did not know about the talks with Chandra Shekhar. He was there just to ensure safe crossing for his leader and fully realized the risk involved as it was not the usual crossing. Dhami shared his agenda with him later. Both of them had stayed in Pakistan earlier.

Three other militant leaders were to cross over to India after this crossing. They were Dr. Sohan Singh, Gurjit Singh and Talwinder Singh Parmar. Securing clearance for them at the post took three hours as they carried some electronic goods gifted to them from their overseas supporters. The security people had some reservations over them and hence the delay.

Dr. Sohan Singh returned to Pakistan in 1992. He was arrested in November 1993 while returning to India via the Nepal route.

Personnel from both the BSF and Pakistan Rangers used to have a tacit understanding on such crossings. Four of the Panthic Committee members crossed over to Pakistan twice in a similar manner and returned the same way during that period. The rate used to vary and at times, there could be a trap.

Move to Revive the Sikh League

Yet another idea was proposed to create a mass front for militants. The exercise to go in for the Sikh League was part of that process. It may be mentioned that the Central Sikh League was constituted by the Sikh leaders in 1919 and continued to function till 1933, before that space was taken over by the Akali Dal constituted in 1920.

This move could not be taken to the logical conclusion by the radicals. The year was 1996 when militancy had been wiped out in Punjab. The proposed Sikh League was to be on the pattern of the Muslim League that had spearheaded the demand for Pakistan, which, along with strategic geo-political factors, resulted in the partition of India and creation of the Muslim state.

The raid by the Thai police on July 15, 1996 tipped by the Indian agency officials in Thailand resulted in the premature abortion of the idea with the detention of Kanwarpal, who was later shown to have been arrested from Nepal.

The idea had been the outcome of the confabulations among Kanwarpal, one of the Dal Khalsa founders, Gajinder Singh and breakaway Babbar Khalsa associate Surinder Singh Sekhon at a picturesque beach town of Pattaya, a few kilometres away from the capital city of Bangkok. Kanwarpal had resided

there for some time after shifting his base from Pakistan under the name of Naam Singh, a Pakistani Sikh. By the time he was apprehended in Thailand, he had just resigned from the Babbar Khalsa to join the Dal Khalsa.

Having shifted his base in April 1995 to Thailand from Pakistan, Kanwarpal's relations with his parent organization soured in 1996 and Gajinder was in the know of this development. His basic point of difference was over internal dynamics of the organization. The resignation letter was forwarded to the United Kingdom headquarters of the Babbar Khalsa International. However, he had not made his resignation public.

Persuaded by Gajinder, he consented to join the Dal Khalsa and this decision too was kept under wraps. He had earlier also resigned from the BKI in 1994 for the same reason but was persuaded to stay put. However, the undercurrent of dissent and resentment continued.

Kanwarpal had decided to shift to Thailand as this South Asian country had about 30 wealthy Sikh families supporting and funding the BKI. This had been going on since 1987.

Tohra contacted Gajinder Singh during that period through Prof. Manjit Singh, then acting Jathedar of the Akal Takht and offered political space to him. He could have been put up as the Akali candidate in the Lok Sabha election from Patiala. Tohra had the information that Gajinder, who had completed his jail sentence in the hijacking case, was willing to return to India and surrender. A person is not supposed to be prosecuted twice for the same offence. However, he was reluctant to contest. The perception was that Gajinder joining the Tohra camp might have strengthened the SGPC chief vis-à-vis former Chief Minister Parkash Singh Badal with whom he had a love-hate relationship. Though Tohra never contested the State Assembly election, his ambition to become Chief Minister was too well known. Badal was the only leader who blocked his way. Tohra wanted to accommodate Gajinder in his own circle.

Under the new plan, Gajinder was to move to India and Kanwarpal to Germany. All this time, Sekhon, who was hiding in Thailand, was kept in the loop. Sekhon was given the choice to merge his BKI (Talwinder) faction in the Dal Khalsa to which he was not averse. He was to operate from the Pakistani soil.

However, Gajinder declined Tohra's offer although he was willing to return to India and surrender to complete the legal formalities. Gajinder consulted some people in India about the formation of this new outfit as the political front and the response was by and large positive.

Gajinder returned to Pakistan on July 13, 1996 from where he was to leave for Germany after two days and stay there for about two weeks. Kanwarpal was to join him there and arrange for his return to India. Gajinder was also to introduce Sekhon to Pakistani authorities and hand over his house to him.

Sekhon, who was without travel documents, travelled to Pakistan on Kanwarpal's passport which was in the name of Naam Singh. Meanwhile, Kanwarpal was left without a passport in Thailand. The plan failed as Kanwarpal was arrested on July 15 and handed over to India. He was arrested for not having the papers with him. A passport might have saved him. That was the end to the revival of the Sikh League.

Operation R.N. Kumar

Human rights activist Ram Narayan Kumar could well be one of the examples of functional understanding of agencies on both sides of the Radcliffe line.

Kumar was one of the important players in the radical political discourse who were handled by the people sitting in Lahore.

He appeared on the Punjab scene during the post Operation Bluestar period as human rights activist. His first introduction to the media in Chandigarh was by some Sikh activists, mainly from the upper strata of the Sikh society sympathetic to the struggle at the level of human rights. He subsequently co-founded the Committee for Coordination on Disappearances in Punjab (CCDP).

A Brahmin from Andhra Pradesh, he had settled in Austria. In Punjab, he worked extensively on fake encounters and involuntary disappearances. His functioning came under scrutiny some years later as he developed differences with some Chandigarh-based activists who earlier were his associates.

At one stage, he came into contact with the Babbars, first in India and later in Pakistan. This was in the context of the kidnapping of M.L. Manchanda, station director of All India Radio in Patiala on May 18, 1992. His two young daughters issued a very touching appeal for his release. The Delhi-based Punjabi lobby contacted Kumar, as he was known to be in touch with the militants.

Kumar established contact with Wadhawa Singh and proposed that Manchanda should be handed over to him. His plan that he shared with Wadhawa was to release him in Delhi at a news conference while at the same time, highlighting the cause they were fighting for. After deliberations, the top leadership of the Babbars agreed to this proposal. Manchanda was in the custody of Amrik Singh Kauli who was the main regional leader active in the Patiala-Ropar-Chandigarh belt.

Kauli contacted one of the Chandigarh-based advisers of the militants for consultations and disclosed the plan to him. The adviser rejected this idea flatly saying, "In case you release Manchanda, the government will stop taking the militants seriously and this would harm the struggle." Going against the decision of his leadership, Kauli killed Manchanda and hanged his head in Rajpura market. The killing was carried out by his associate Gurdial Singh Kauli. This was among the most gruesome killings by the militants in Punjab. The downfall of militancy-turned-terrorism started with this killing. Gurdial was gunned down by security forces within days followed by Amrik and Babbar Khalsa chief Sukhdev Singh on August 9, 1992. Those who survived escaped from India.

Meanwhile, Kumar started interacting with the Babbar leaders hereafter who included Mehal Singh, Wadhawa and Kanwarpal.

After this severe dent at every level, there was introspection in the Babbar Khalsa and the new strategy worked out. It was proposed to use the media platform in India and abroad not only to undo the damage following the Manchanda episode but also to propagate the real issues and concerns underlying the militant struggle. As Kumar had earlier offered to work for the organization in the media, he was sent the message. He agreed to take over media management but from behind the scenes.

He proposed producing documentaries and writing articles in the global media against state repression in the Indian Punjab. The Babbars provided him ample funds for this purpose.

He started with a documentary for the production of which he brought a team from Austria. He took up writing pamphlets too. Kumar was writing a book on Punjab at that time and the Babbars wanted a comprehensive perspective of the militant struggle to be projected through the book. It was at that stage that the leadership decided to have personal interaction with him for a few days to brief him thoroughly on the subject matter.

He wanted to avoid entering Pakistan on a visa as that would have triggered suspicion in India. He could not be brought in from the land route used by the militants illegally. A plan was worked out to smuggle him into Pakistan by air.

He was told to book his ticket from Vienna to Bangkok and the airline was to be Pakistan International. This flight used to be refuelled at Karachi. He was brought out at Karachi. This could not have been possible without involvement of the ISI and other agencies. He was taken to Lahore from Karachi, where he stayed for about 20 days. His exit from Pakistan was also from the same route, as he took another PIA flight from Karachi to Bangkok. He returned to Vienna from Bangkok.

This operation, however, got exposed subsequently, as he went to the Indian Embassy in Vienna after some time to add pages to his passport. It was there that an active and aware staffer caught his act. There was the time gap between the date that was stamped on his passport when he left Vienna and his exit at Bangkok. What transpired after that is not known. According to one source, that staffer was subsequently transferred from that desk. No action was taken against Kumar. This happened in 1994. His passport was returned after processing.

What he wrote later in his book was just the opposite of the briefing by Babbar Khalsa.

The Narrow Escape

Jagtar Singh Hawara and some of his associates landed in Nepal in mid-1994. These Babbar Khalsa activists operating mainly in Ropar and Chandigarh area had escaped from India to Nepal from the land route as the security forces had tightened the noose and terrorists were being killed one after the other. Crossing the Radcliffe line from the Punjab side to enter Pakistan had become very risky. It was planned to facilitate their entry to Pakistan by the air route.

Wadhawa Singh's family had also reached Kathmandu that used to be the transit for destination Pakistan. The family included his wife and young daughters. Wadhawa had decided to shift his family from his native village in Indian Punjab to Pakistani Punjab.

Hawara was one of those who were subsequently involved in the assassination of Punjab Chief Minister Beant Singh. The operation was executed by human bomb Dilawar Singh on August 31, 1995. He was arrested in December after the assassination but escaped again by digging a tunnel in Chandigarh's Burail jail, only to be re-arrested. This digging of a tunnel was virtually the repetition of *The Great Escape*, the popular World War II movie.

Kanwarpal had arranged documents for them that included fake Indian passports and reached Nepal to coordinate the plan. He specialized in such operations.

Kanwarpal had cultivated a Sikh contact in Nepal by the name of Joga Singh with whom he normally used to stay in case of not having booked a hotel. He was a sympathizer of the Sikh struggle. It was while having lunch with him at a restaurant that he suspected somebody trying to photograph them. That man ran away when Joga Singh confronted him.

However, Joga Singh being a local person recognized him as

the person whom he had earlier seen clicking pictures at a function organized by the Indian embassy in Kathmandu. He advised Kanwarpal to escape to Pakistan by the first available flight rather than going back to his hotel to pick up his luggage. He immediately contacted Pakistan International Airlines and was lucky in getting a ticket on the next flight to Karachi.

He also succeeded in contacting Wadhawa in Pakistan and told him that the Indian agencies had become suspicious and he was being trailed. He could be arrested, if he failed to escape. Wadhawa left the decision to him.

Kanwarpal rushed to Kathmandu airport. Indian intelligence was working in close coordination with Nepal security agencies. He succeeded in entering the airport. Police in civvies too rushed to the airport.

The Nepal police checked his documents and questioned him. As he had a Pakistani passport, he could not be arrested without having committed any crime in that country. In the meantime, his plane landed and he was the first to board.

However, he had to take yet another decision and that was about his own life. He had made up his mind that he would not fall into India's hands alive. The militant leaders used to carry potassium cyanide capsules and he too had taken that precaution. He carried the capsule that was to be swallowed in case caught when the security people rushed towards him at the airport while waiting for the plane. The need did not arise as they left after scrutinizing his documents.

Kanwarpal had kept the fake Indian documents for the family of Wadhawa and Hawara and his associates with Joga Singh.

Authenticity of these documents used to be managed at Bangkok airport. Kanwar had made this arrangement while staying there off and on. Indians could enter Nepal from the land route without a passport as per the arrangement between the two countries.

Joga Singh was told to send them in a group of two by air to Bangkok. It was the Bangkok immigration stamp that would authenticate these documents. This would be done by bribing the immigration people which was not uncommon. The next step would be the entry to Pakistan. Once the documents had been authenticated, this was no problem. However, here was the catch!

The airlines, if flying to nearby areas, normally get refuelled in native countries. The return to India could be on the Pakistan International Airline flight that would touch down at Karachi or any Pakistani airport. It was not a problem to take out people from Karachi airport without immigration clearance. This was part of the operation that was facilitated by Pakistan.

Hawara and his associates returned to India by the same route to execute the assassination of Beant Singh around Baisakhi in April 1995.

The Indian agencies also used virtually the same modus operandi. Kanwarpal was brought to India via Kathmandu and shown to have been arrested in Delhi.

India informed Bangkok about his presence there. The Intelligence Bureau people accompanied Thai immigration police to arrest him. However, on record he was a Pakistani national although he did not have his passport with him at that time. He had secured a Thai work permit on which his nationality was Pakistani. A Pakistani national could not be handed over to India by Thai authorities.

The IB people were certain of his real identity. They worked out an arrangement with their Thai counterparts under which he was to be deported to Pakistan. It was at this point that India succeeded in getting its operation executed.

India also succeeded in convincing the Thais to put him on the Thai Airways flight to Karachi via Nepal. It may be mentioned that some flights operate on such routes. Kanwarpal also used to facilitate his operations using such routes. He immediately understood the design and protested as to why he had not been booked on a direct flight to Karachi. His ticket for this flight had been purchased by the Indian officials.

As the plane carrying him landed at Kathmandu, India took over. He was brought down and shifted to Air India flight to Delhi. The IB people were already waiting for him in that plane.

He was shown to have been arrested only at the Delhi airport. That was on July 17, 1996.

ENDNOTES

1. Jagtar Singh. (2011). *Khalistan Struggle: A Non-movement*. Delhi: Aakar Books, p. 180.
2. Ibid., p. 201.

9

The Punjab Betrayal

The Punjab Accord was the first and the last such attempt at conflict resolution under a democratic framework within months of the Operation Bluestar. This was part of the overall strategy of Prime Minister Rajiv Gandhi to reach out to the struggling people in states like Assam in the North-East as well and not just confined to Punjab. However, the region that posed the most serious threat to the Indian state at that time was Punjab.

The Punjab Accord, following negotiations at various levels including with the militants but concluded with the Akalis, was signed on July 24, 1985 between Gandhi and Shiromani Akali Dal President Sant Harchand Singh Longowal in Delhi. The Accord was unique as it was the first such instrument signed between by the Prime Minister with the head of a political party in the country that was also ratified by the Parliament. The Accord covered almost all the issues on which the Akali Dal had been agitating till Operation Bluestar. However, this document was destined to be consigned to the dustbin of history.

This accord virtually was the betrayal with Punjab by the Akali Dal. The militants took over the Golden Temple complex again within months of signing the accord. This accord, however, achieved one purpose and that was justification to the Operation Bluestar and that too by the Akalis.[1,2]

Gandhi signed a similar Assam Accord with the All Assam Students Union on August 15, 1985. There was another similarity with Punjab. In the Assembly elections held in September 1985, the Akali Dal was facilitated into power. AASU contested elections under the banner of the Asom Gana Parishad in December 1985 and captured power. The similarity ended there.

The Punjab Accord was never implemented. Sant Longowal was gunned down on the evening of August 20, 1985 in a gurdwara at Sherpur village in his native Sangrur district for "betraying the

Panth." Former Chief Minister Parkash Singh Badal did not attend his death anniversary observed at village Longowal for about nine years. The main architect of the accord happened to be yet another leader Balwant Singh who was also subsequently assassinated by the militants in Chandigarh on July 10, 1990.[3] It was Balwant Singh who was authorized by Sant Longowal to represent him during negotiations. Longowal went to Delhi only when everything had been finalized and the accord was to be inked.

Such an accord in the absence of political will to implement it generally led to escalation in violence and the Punjab Accord was no exception. The post accord period was characterized by political gaming thereby blunting the accord as an instrument of peace.

The first interlocutor between the Prime Minister and the Akalis happened to be the senior Congress leader Sharad Pawar who years later left the party to float his Nationalist Congress Party. He made this revelation on April 3, 2015 in an otherwise nondescript Ghuman village in Gurdaspur district where had had joined the Marathi literary function dedicated to Bhagat Namdev, originally from Maharasthra, who spent his later years in this Punjab village. He disclosed that he had approached Sant Longowal, Surjit Singh Barnala and Parkash Singh Badal in jail on behalf of Rajiv Gandhi. Badal was also present at the function who later reacted in a lighter vein saying that the Congress suffered from trust deficit and subsequently he proved to be correct.

Pawar claimed that the reaction from Badal at that time was positive. All along, the impression was that the then Punjab Governor Arjun Singh was the first Congress leader who had opened channels with Akali leaders after their release from jail in 1985 who had been arrested during Operation Bluestar. However, it was Arjun Singh who took the negotiations to the logical conclusion.

As part of his strategy, Arjun Singh operated at two levels—the Akali leaders and the radicals. Badal had claimed that he spurned the offer as he did not trust the Congress. However, the fear factor cannot be ruled out. Moreover, he did not like Longowal's decision to nominate Balwant Singh as his representative for the talks. Tohra too was opposed to it but he had his own logic as he wanted all those arrested during Operation Bluestar to be released first. Those involved in the talks from the Akali side included Longowal, Balwant Singh and Barnala. The second channel was opened with the radical leaders who included the All India Sikh Students Federation President Bhai Manjit Singh and its General Secretary Harminder Singh Sandhu, then lodged in Jodhpur jail after their arrest from the Golden Temple complex during Operation Bluestar, and Dr. Bhagwan Singh.

Talks With Radicals

It is in the context of the channel having been opened with the militants that the narrative of revival of the Sikh struggle during post-Bluestar period is relevant here. The government approached two different sections of radicals while at the same time, opening channels with the Akali Dal.

It was Rajiv Gandhi's idea to involve radicals both in Punjab as well as the North-East in the democratic process. Contacts were established with Bhrigu Phukan in Assam and Manjit, Sandhu, Dr. Bhagwan Singh, Harinder Singh Kahlon and some others in Punjab.

Arrested from Darbar Sahib during Operation Bluestar, Bhai Manjit Singh was taken to the prisoners' camp in Amritsar Cantt. The prisoners had been kept in rooms with no light and denied even basic medical facilities. Their clothes were torn and dirty. The door used to be opened slightly only to push food trays. Even for that, dogs used to accompany those distributing food. The prisoners faced this hell for about a month after which the situation somewhat eased. The prisoners were screened during this period. It was like concentration camps.

According to his account, Manjit was transferred to Patiala jail in October and then shifted to Nabha jail where his interrogation started. A manager on the rolls of the Shiromani Gurdwara Parbandhak Committee, he was the brother of Bhai Amrik Singh, the second-in-command after Sant Jarnail Singh Bhindranwale and president of the AISSF.

Manjit would be taken out of his cell blindfolded for interrogation but the situation changed as he reacted against this procedure after a few days. It was then that he realized that he was being interrogated in the area where cells for condemned prisoners were located. Subsequently, his interrogation continued at the notorious Ladha Kothi interrogation centre at Nabha. Torture was routine. He would not be allowed to sleep for days. The questions that used to be asked were mainly about the source of weapons. However, till then, he was not actively involved in the militant struggle. It was here that his mother met him for the first time after the Operation Bluestar who inspired him to follow in the footsteps of his martyred brother. He was shifted to Jodhpur subsequently where all those arrested from the Golden Temple complex had been lodged.

It was at Jodhpur jail that the government initiated the move to start a dialogue with him.

The first persons to meet him in this regard included Abinashi Singh, the all-powerful personal assistant to SGPC chief Gurcharan Singh Tohra and Dr. Baldev Singh Brar, Medical Superintendent of the SGPC-run Guru Ramdas Hospital. Both of them knew almost everybody associated with the struggle, both traditional politicians and the militants. The move was to assess his mind. Manjit's initial thinking was that they might have come to him to lobby for Tohra in the power struggle. Dr. Brar asked him whom he would trust for opening a dialogue from among Tohra, Parkash Singh Badal and Jagdev Singh Talwandi. "Only the leaders who stand for Panth," was his reply. It was then that Dr. Brar came out with the real purpose, adding it was Tohra who sheltered Sant Bhindranwale at the Akal Takht. Manjit shot back, "Tohra is also responsible for the Operation Bluestar."

The officials took up the thread after Abinashi and Dr. Brar left asking who could talk to the government. He said he was willing to hold negotiations and made it clear that the only person whom he wished to be associated was Harminder Sandhu.

Meanwhile, activity to reorganize the militants and the AISSF was going on at various levels. Manjit had been appointed as the AISSF president in absentia while in Nabha jail but he had not formally taken over. It was at Nabha jail that he was pressured by Sandhu, Jasbir Singh Ghuman, Satnam Singh Akkanwali, Balwinder Singh Khojkipur and Bhupinder Longia to accept the responsibility. Five of them issued a directive to him in the capacity of 'Panj Piaras' as per the Sikh norms. Thereafter, the agencies started treating him as a political leader with whom talks could legitimately be initiated.

He was told one evening to get ready to be airlifted to Delhi for talks. He shared his information with both Sandhu and Harminder Singh Gill. Gill, another AISSF leader, was also related to Manjit. Sandhu got emotional when Manjit told him that he would trust only him to accompany him for the talks. Sandhu was suspected to be a mole of the intelligence agencies.

To overcome the legal hurdle of taking them out, they were framed in the case of the assassination of Delhi Sikh Gurdwara Management Committee president Harbans Singh Manchanda in Delhi on March 28, 1984 and transit remand taken from the court.

The people who were part of the channel that had been opened with them were Punjab Governor Arjun Singh, Prof. Sarup Singh of

Panjab University, Chandigarh and Inspector General of Police K.P.S. Gill. Gill and Sarup Singh were also related to each other. The second channel with the Akali Dal leaders was opened through Prof. Attar Singh of Panjab University.

Yet another channel operated through AISSF leader Dr. Bhagwan Singh, who was a student of Dr. Attar Singh and Kahlon who had been nominated as officiating president of the AISSF.

Both Manjit and Gill were taken to a guest house in Lodhi Estate in Delhi where K.P.S. Gill and Prof. Sarup Singh met them. Manjit refused to talk to Gill and they had some heated exchanges. Arjun Singh too joined them.

Apology from Rajiv Gandhi as Pre-Condition

Manjit set the first condition of unqualified apology from the Prime Minister for the Operation Bluestar and November 1984 massacre of Sikhs for settlement.

This was not acceptable to Gill who flared up and threatened Manjit that he would wipe out his entire family. Manjit was not to be cowed down and said this would make them part of the history while retorting, "I am also a Gill."

This happened in the presence of Arjun Singh. They were kept in Delhi for about a week and then brought back to Jodhpur to be taken to the national capital again.

Manjit questioned their legitimacy to talk to them on behalf of the government, saying they would prefer negotiations directly with Rajiv Gandhi. However, he subsequently did not insist on this condition as talks seemed to be progressing already.

Besides an apology from the Prime Minister, Manjit demanded special status for Punjab on the pattern of Jammu and Kashmir under Article 370 of the Constitution, constitutional separate nation status for the Sikhs and setting up of the tribunal to resolve the river waters dispute with the neighbouring states.

Yet another condition related to Satwant Singh and Kehar Singh who were in jail in the case of the assassination of Indira Gandhi. They insisted they should not be hanged. The government representatives agreed that both of them could be sentenced to 20 years in jail.

The attitude of the government side appeared to be positive. According to Manjit, they were told that Rajiv was not averse to an apology. However, it was opposed by Minister of State Arun Nehru, a close confidant of the Gandhi family.

Manjit proposed they should be released to take others into confidence before signing the settlement. By that time, they did not know that the government was also in talks with the Akali Dal leaders including Sant Longowal, Barnala and Balwant Singh. These Akali leaders had not put up any pre-condition unlike the radicals.

Manjit too had wanted to take Sant Longowal into confidence after his release. He had also put up the condition of return of the Sikh boys who had crossed over to Pakistan by providing them a safe passage. The talks with them were held for four times in Delhi and once each at Patiala and Amritsar.

Ironically, they were in Delhi the day Rajiv signed the Accord with Longowal. In case the Akali Dal had refused to sign unconditionally on the dotted lines, the history of Punjab would have been different. The Accord was signed on July 24, 1985 and Sant Longowal was killed by the militants on August 20, 1985 within less than a month. Longowal had signed his death warrant by signing the accord unconditionally. The minimum that he could have demanded was the release of all those arrested during Operation Bluestar, most of whom were innocent devotees.[4]

The remnants of the militants were already being reorganized by that time and the All India Sikh Students Federation reconstituted by the time the Punjab Accord was signed between Rajiv Gandhi and Sant Longowal.

According to one version, the first such meeting to revive the struggle was held at a gurdwara near Jalandhar Cantt at the initiative of the then underground former journalist Dalbir Singh who had been associated with Sant Jarnail Singh Bhindranwale. This meeting was attended by about 30 radical and militant activists.

There are yet two other versions. According to one version, the first step to reorganize the movement was taken at a meeting in Calcutta (now Kolkata), the capital of distant West Bengal, on September 20, 1984. The initiative for this meeting was taken by Charanjit Singh Talwandi alias Channi and Dr. Bhagwan Singh. This meeting was attended by Atinderpal Singh, Harpreet Singh Vichhoa, Prof. Inderpal Singh Bulara, Harinder Kahlon and several others. It was decided to begin with the revival of the AISSF that had been playing a pivotal role under the patronage of Sant Bhindranwale earlier. It was decided to nominate Kahlon as its convener. All those present were included in the ad hoc committee, besides Sarabjit Singh Jammu. This meeting was held at the residence of Kamikar Singh who happened to be president of a gurdwara committee in Calcutta. He later joined the Akali Dal led by Simranjit Singh Mann. It may be mentioned that Kahlon also attended the other meeting.

The decision to hold the meeting in Calcutta was dictated by safety considerations as the state was being governed by a non-Congress government—the CPI (M) led Left Front—and it was thought to be a safe haven. The press statement regarding the revival of the AISSF, however, was released from New Delhi. Atinderpal objected to Kahlon being appointed convener as during the pre-Bluestar organizational set up of the AISSF, he was the senior vice-president with Kahlon as the vice-president. But then the situation required a face from Punjab and not like Atinderpal who was from Bhopal in Madhya Pradesh. Later, he left for Pakistan.

Going by the third version, Kahlon had escaped to Uttar Pradesh after the Operation Bluestar. It was in August that Charanjit Talwandi and Hari Raj Singh Ghuman contacted him there. They returned to Ludhiana the same day and went to the residence of Prof. Rajinder Singh Bulara where Dr. Bhagwan Singh was also present. They discussed the future plans and revival of the movement and decided to meet in September in a village near Hoshiarpur. That meeting was attended by Kahlon, Bhagwan, Hothian, Hari Raj and some others. The statement to this effect was released from Delhi as a safety precaution.

They then shifted to Calcutta where they were provided a safe house by Kamikar Singh. Harpreet Singh Vichhoa who was in contact with Atinderpal Singh also met them there. They decided to have another meeting. Dr. Bhagwan Singh was also present. It was at this meeting that the name of Kahlon was proposed to lead the AISSF. Kahlon proposed that the statement regarding this meeting should be released simultaneously from Delhi and Amritsar. The AISSF had thus been activated by the time the centre started negotiations to settle Punjab in 1985.

Here is one version how Arjun Singh involved the militants in the negotiations. The interlocutors involved by Arjun Singh included Prof. Sarup Singh from Panjab University and Jagjit Singh Jaggi from Madhya Pradesh, an old freedom fighter and a Congress leader. Arjun Singh had been sent to Punjab from Madhya Pradesh. Both of them were known to Dr. Bhagwan Singh who had been a researcher with the Panjab University. The first meeting was arranged towards the end of March 1985 in Ludhiana to discuss the offer for talks. It was Prof. Sarup Singh who outlined the agenda. Others who attended the meeting included Talwandi and Kahlon. Talwandi was opposed to Prof. Sarup Singh being the channel.

They told Prof. Sarup Singh that their meeting should be arranged with Manjit and Sandhu so that the negotiations could be provided an element of legitimacy. Accordingly, the issue was taken up with Arjun Singh and the meeting was arranged in Delhi on May 2. In the meantime, Dr. Bhagwan Singh got in touch with Baba Joginder Singh, father of Sant Bhindranwale who had been brought in to play an active political role. His opinion was that the time was not ripe for such talks. The May 2 meeting thus did not materialize.

According to this version, Prof. Sarup Singh roped in two other leaders including Harpal Singh Pannu and Gurtej Singh who were taken to Jodhpur jail to meet Manjit and Sandhu who gave him a letter addressed to Dr. Bhagwan Singh, making it clear those outside could take the decision as they were not in touch with the situation outside. Kahlon was also provided facilities to consult the detained leaders. He also involved Jagjit Singh Rode, brother of Sant Bhindranwale. The government wanted an undertaking on maintaining the unity and integrity of the country for the talks to proceed to which they refused.

While the government laid down the condition that the AISSF should join the political mainstream and shed the tag of being a radical organization, the leaders involved in the talks rightly lay down the pre-condition of the release of those lodged in Jodhpur and other jails besides withdrawing the case against hijackers who had hijacked the plane to Dubai. There could be no midway. The demand was logical and the Akali interlocutors too should have taken a similar stand.

Manjit was expected to issue a statement in favour of the unity and integrity of the country. The AISSF leaders at that stage told Arjun Singh that they would like to take Baba Joginder Singh into confidence to which he agreed. It was decided that Manjit, Sandhu and other leaders would be taken to Moga where their meeting with Baba Joginder Singh would be arranged. K.P.S. Gill was told to facilitate the meeting. However, the need did not arise as the government arrived at the settlement with the Akalis.

Rajiv Gandhi signed the accord with Sant Longowal after more than a month long track II talks following the written communication having been exchanged between the two. The negotiations were held both in Chandigarh as well as in Delhi to sort out the irritants. The government never shared this information with the second group of interlocutors. Longowal went to Delhi only to sign the accord as the groundwork had already been done by other leaders led by Balwant Singh, the authorized representative of Sant Longowal.

Longowal went ahead to sign the accord despite advice from Tohra to first get the Jodhpur deteneus released. The Akalis signed on the dotted lines unconditionally which was a blunder. Tohra was not opposed to the negotiations per se but he wanted the centre to give some positive signals to the Sikhs at large.

Even before the talks had started, the United Akali Dal was constituted by a section of the Akalis most of whom were not from the mainstream and those active in the formation of the new party included some militant activists and their associates. The announcement of the new party with the Akal Takht Jathedar Giani Kirpal Singh as the convenor of the ad hoc committee was made on May 2, 1985. However, Giani Kirpal Singh had become a hate figure owing to his controversial statement on the state of affairs in the Darbar Sahib (Golden Temple) complex immediately after the Operation Bluestar which was aired by the official media. Baba Joginder Singh was persuaded to accept the leadership. Simranjit Singh Mann, then in jail, had been proposed as the president of the new outfit. It was this ad hoc committee which took the decision to boycott the Assembly elections in September.

The government did not want to take a chance and it was part of the tacit understanding of the Punjab Accord to facilitate the victory of the Akali Dal (Longowal) and bring in Surjit Singh Barnala as the Chief Minister. Barnala was one leader who suited the Indian state the most and he continued to be rewarded with gubernatorial office after the dismissal of the government. He was one of those Akali leaders who proved to be the best instruments for the Indian state.

(Correspondence between Rajiv Gandhi and Sant Harchand Singh Longowal: Vol. 2, Annexure 59).

ENDNOTES

1. Security forces entered the Darbar Sahib (Golden Temple) complex on April 30, 1986 when Punjab was being ruled by the Akali Dal with Surjit Singh Barnala as the Chief Minister. The ostensible provocation was declaration of Khalistan a day earlier by the 5-member Panthic Committee that was constituted as an umbrella body of militants on January 26, 1986 at Sarbat Khalsa organized by the radicals at Akal Takht.
2. Jagtar Singh. (2011). *Khalistan Struggle: A Non-movement*. Delhi: Aakar Books, pp. 258-59.
3. Ibid., p. 334.
4. Here are the details of the Punjab Accord:

   Punjab Accord

   Signed between Prime Minister Rajiv Gandhi and Akali Dal President Sant Harchand Singh Longowal on July 24, 1985:

   1. Compensation to innocent persons killed: Along with ex-gratia payment to those innocent killed in agitation or any action after

August 1, 1982. Compensation for property damaged will also be paid.

2. Army recruitment: All citizens of the country have the right to enrol in the army and merit will remain the criterion of selection.
3. Enquiry into November riots: The jurisdiction of Shri Ranganath Mishra Commission enquiring into the November riots of Delhi would be extended to cover disturbances at Bokaro and Kanpur.
4. Rehabilitation of those discharged from the army: For all those discharged efforts will be made to rehabilitate and provide gainful employment.
5. All India Gurdwara Act: The Government of India agrees to consider the formulation of an All India Gurdwara Bill. Legislation will be brought forward for this purpose in consultation with the Shiromani Akali Dal, others concerned and fulfilling all constitutional requirements.
6. Disposal of pending cases:

6.1 The notification applying the Armed Forces Special Powers Act to Punjab will be withdrawn. Existing special courts will try only cases relating to the following type of offences: (a) waging war and (b) hijacking.

6.2 All other cases will be transferred to ordinary courts and enabling legislation if necessary will be brought forward in this session of Parliament.

7. Territorial claims:

7.1 The capital project of Chandigarh will go to Punjab. Some adjoining areas which were previously part of Hindi or the Punjabi regions were included in the Union territory. With the capital region going to Punjab the areas which were added to the Union territory from the Punjabi region of the erstwhile state of Punjab will be transferred to Punjab and those from the Hindi region to Haryana. The entire Sukhna Lake will be kept part of Chandigarh and will thus go to Punjab.

7.2 It had always been maintained by Indira Gandhi that when Chandigarh is to go to Punjab, some Hindi-speaking territories in Punjab will go to Haryana. A commission will be constituted to determine the specific Hindi-speaking areas of Punjab which should go to Haryana in lieu of Chandigarh.

The principle of contiguity and linguistic affinity with a village as a unit will be the basis of such determination. The commission will be required to give its findings by December 31, 1985 and these will be binding on both sides. The work of the commission will be limited to this aspect and will be distinct from the general boundary claims which the other commissions referred to in para 7.4 will handle.

7.3 The actual transfer of Chandigarh to Punjab and areas in lieu thereof to Haryana will take place simultaneously on January 26, 1986.

7.4 There are other claims and counter claims for readjustment of the existing Punjab-Haryana boundaries. The government will appoint another commission to consider these matters and give its findings. Such findings will be binding on the concerned states. The terms of reference will be based on a village as a unit, linguistic affinity and contiguity.

8. Centre-State relations:

8.1 Shiromani Akali Dal states that the Anandpur Sahib Resolution is entirely within the framework of the Indian Constitution, that it attempts to define the concept of centre-state relations in a manner which may bring out the true federal characteristics of our unitary constitution and that the purpose of the resolution is to provide greater autonomy to the states with a view to strengthening the unity and integrity of the country, since unity in diversity forms the corner stone of our national entity.

8.2 In view of the above, the Anandpur Sahib Resolution in so far as it deals with Centre-State relations, stands referred to the Sarkaria Commission.

9. Sharing of river waters:

9.1 The farmers of Punjab, Haryana and Rajasthan will continue to get water not less than what they are using from the Ravi-Beas system as on July 1, 1985. Waters used for consumptive purposes will also remain unaffected. Quantum of usage claimed shall be verified by the tribunal referred to in para 9.2 below.

9.2 The claims of Punjab and Haryana regarding the shares in their remaining waters will be referred for adjudication to a tribunal to be presided over by a Supreme Court judge. The decision of the tribunal will be rendered within six months and would be binding on both parties. All legal and constitutional steps required in this respect will be taken expeditiously.

9.3 The construction of the SYL Canal shall continue. The canal shall be completed by August 15, 1986.

10. Representation of minorities: Existing instructions regarding protection of interests of minorities will be recirculated to the state chief ministers. (PM will write to all chief ministers).

11. Promotion of Punjabi language: The central government may take some steps for the promotion of the Punjabi language.

This settlement brings to an end a period of confrontation and ushers in an era of amity, goodwill and cooperation which will promote and strengthen the unity and integrity of India.

10

Rivers on Fire

Punjab is the only province in India where more than 70 per cent of waters from the three rivers have been diverted to the neighbouring states. This goes not only against the Riparian principle but also the internationally accepted norms of optimal use of water resources. This has also to be viewed in the context of Punjab being the granary of the country where every inch of land is under cultivation with minimum of two-crop pattern.

Total availability of water in three Punjab rivers—Satluj, Beas and Ravi—is 34.34 MAF (Million Acre Foot) out of which the home state is getting only 14.22 MAF. This is the worst form of victimization with this state that violates all canons of natural justice.

One of the most important issues in the political narrative in the region for years has been the apportionment of waters of the three rivers flowing through Punjab. This issue later entered the radical discourse and it was this militant intervention that at one time proved to be more effective. These rivers virtually remained on fire for years and the waters turned red. This issue continues to dominate the political discourse in the region.

This is one issue that has reinforced the perception of there being two laws so far as Punjab is concerned, the other one being for the rest of the country.

And the leader who earned the moniker of Defender of Punjab Waters is Congress leader Capt Amarinder Singh whose party is primarily targeted for this criminal loot of the state's river water resources.

The Akali Dal stand on this sensitive issue too has been characterized by unabashed opportunism, although this is the party that first raised its voice against this exploitation and injustice. It was mainly because of the Akali Dal's opportunism that this issue came up on the agenda of the militant organizations.

Both the Congress and the Akali Dal are responsible for this crime of divesting Punjab of its river water resources.

The dispute now, however, is just for about 1.88 MAF of water that is to flow to neighbouring Haryana through the Satluj-Yamuna Link Canal whose construction was blocked by the militants and the status quo continues for about three decades. The first right over usage that is recognized globally is a separate issue.

Technically, it is just this amount of water that set rivers in Punjab aflame. This issue continues to be the major bone of contention between Punjab and Haryana. Water from the rivers of Punjab also flows to Rajasthan, the third party to the dispute. Elections continue to be fought in Punjab and Haryana on this highly politicized sensitive and emotive issue.

At the pragmatic level, much more water can be conserved through modern techniques of water management. The reality has not been told to the people, nor have the governments taken any initiative to introduce water management techniques. Even the Supreme Court intervention where this case is being contested for years can be termed as skewed and irrational.

Yet another dimension is the criminal wastage of water in the canal systems that take off from Punjab through mismanagement, seepage and evaporation. The Rajasthan Feeder Canal is the worst example of wastage of water.

The decision of the Akali Dal government headed by Parkash Singh Badal in 1997 to provide free power to run tubewells in the farm sector has led to over-exploitation of ground water and pathetic neglect of the existing canal system. Even the waters courses in many areas have been encroached upon in the state.

Punjab is the food basket of the country but despite three rivers flowing through the state, about 70 per cent of the irrigation is by tubewells. This again is unprecedented.

The exploitation of Punjab river water in favour of Rajasthan and Haryana is described by the people in the state as colonial exploitation. Punjab is the only state in India whose entire land is under cultivation and that too with highest intensity of irrigation and cultivation.

The role of the government at the centre has been dictated by political considerations rather than pragmatism and water management. The record of the Akali Dal too, when in power in Punjab has disgustingly been dismal on this sensitive issue.

Punjab derives its name from Punj-Aab, the land of five rivers. The partition in 1947 reduced it to the land of three rivers with the

Jhelum and Chenab flowing through Jammu and Kashmir to Pakistani Punjab. The waters of even three rivers have been under dispute, beginning with Pakistan.

Going by the experts, the state could turn into a desert within less than two decades if the water table continues to fall at the present rate under the prevalent wheat-paddy cropping pattern. The issue is not just political but multidimensional.

The apportionment of the Punjab river waters among the neighbouring states is one of the most sensitive, contentious and volatile issues concerning this region but the irony is that in Punjab, it came to be identified with the Sikhs and Akali Dal despite the dubious role even of this party too on this vital issue.

This is an issue which is concerned with the economy and environment of the border state and thereby the entire country. It has nothing to do with religion or politics. However, this is one issue that the militant organizations stridently took up and successfully blocked the construction of the Satluj Yamuna Link Canal with the barrel of the gun that was started by the Akali Dal government to carry water to Haryana.

The leader who took the first concrete democratic and constitutional steps to protect the interests of Punjab was Capt Amarinder Singh when he headed the Congress government during his first term from 2002 to 2007.

Intensive farming in Punjab started with the advent of the Green Revolution in the mid-1960s that was designed by the government at the centre to provide food sovereignty to the country without going into environmental aspects about which there was no awareness at that time. Punjab (including Pakistani Punjab) has agriculturally been the most advanced region in the subcontinent having a network of canals laid by the British India government. This Green Revolution was based on high yielding varieties of wheat and paddy with cotton and sugarcane as the additional crops that replaced the traditional multi-crop farming. The entire production and marketing system witnessed major changes as the new pattern was capital and irrigation intensive. Paddy had never been the traditional Punjab crop although Amritsar and Gurdaspur have been producing fine Basmati. Punjab boasts of the best marketing system for farm produce in the country.

In order to meet the immediate demand for intensive irrigation for paddy, Punjab opted for tubewell irrigation. This is an aspect that is crucial while understanding the issue of river waters. By the time the Green Revolution was introduced, water from Punjab rivers was already flowing to neighbouring states. Haryana was carved out of Punjab in 1966 coinciding with the introduction of the Green Revolution.

According to the 2015 statistical abstract of the Punjab government, the net irrigated area of the total cultivated area in the state is 99.16 per cent, the highest among all the states in India. Out of the irrigated area, about 71 per cent is under tubewell irrigation.

As per the latest data, 100 per cent of the sown area in 2013-14 and 2014-15 was under irrigation. The data for 2014-15 shows that the area under canal irrigation was 28.53 per cent (1,1175 thousand hectares) and 71.46 per cent (2,943 thousand hectares) under tubewell irrigation. The area under canal irrigation in Punjab has been going down since 1990-91.[1] The state has failed to fully utilize even the existing availability of river waters.

This has to be seen in the context of three rivers flowing through this small state. Where is water from these three rivers of Punjab going? Of course, not flowing downstream to Pakistan where these rivers merge with the Indus (Sindh).

Waters from Punjab rivers irrigate neighbouring Haryana and arid Rajasthan and it is the apportionment to these two states that is at the root of the inter-state waters dispute. Punjab's contention ever since this issue came under focus is that this diversion to neighbouring states is in violation of the internationally accepted norms of the Riparian principle, according to which, the states through which the river flows has the first right over usage.

However, this Riparian principle was never applied in the case of Punjab and this state never objected to it for years.

This issue hit the headlines for the first time only in 1976 in the context of the dispute between Punjab and Haryana. When Prime Minister Indira Gandhi intervened during the Emergency in 1976 to adjudicate upon the division of river waters between Punjab and the successor state of Haryana under Section 78 of the Punjab Re-organization Act, 1966, little did she realize its far-reaching consequences for the agriculturally most advanced and sensitive border state in the country.

Years later, Mrs. Gandhi's decision put the Punjab river waters on fire. Instead of water, blood flowed in the semi-constructed Satluj-Yamuna Link Canal that was to carry waters to Haryana from Punjab's rivers under her 1976 award.

The role of the Akalis too on this issue has been that of repeated betrayal with the people of Punjab as evident from the facts, rhetoric of the party apart. If the Congress is blamed for looting Punjab of its waters, the Akali Dal cannot escape the charge of betrayal with the people.

Genesis of Dispute

Prior to 1966, the area that is now Haryana, then in Punjab, was already getting water through the Bhakra Main Canal while the Rajasthan Feeder taking off from the Harike barrage in Punjab was constructed exclusively for non-Riparian Rajasthan. Rajasthan was also supplied water from the Bhakra canal system. The dispute originally was not over the share that was already flowing to these two states as on November 1, 1966 and there is no change in that situation till date in 2019 but mainly of Haryana's share under the Punjab Re-organization Act. Haryana was carved out of Punjab in 1966 under this legislation. Punjab never objected to allocation to Rajasthan for decades.

Punjab and the successor state of Haryana were to mutually agree upon a settlement about their respective share in the surplus Ravi-Beas waters within two years of the re-organization under Sections 78-80 of the Punjab Re-organization Act, 1966. This Act had provision for intervention by the union government in case of the failure of the two states to arrive at a mutually agreed division within the stipulated period.

Section 78 of the Reorganization Act states:

> (1) Notwithstanding anything contained in this Act but subject to the provisions of Sections 79 and 80, all rights and liabilities of the existing State of Punjab in relation to the Bhakra-Nangal Project and Beas Project shall, on the appointed day, be the rights and liabilities of the successor states in such proportion as may be fixed, and subject to such adjustments as may be made, by agreement entered into by the said states after consultation with the Central Government or, if no such agreement is entered into within two years of the appointed day, as the Central Government may by order determine having regard to the purposes of the Projects: Provided that the order so made by the Central Government may be varied by any subsequent agreement entered into by the successor states after consultation with the Central Government.

It was the failure of Punjab and Haryana to arrive at a mutually agreed solution, which provided the pretext to Prime Minister Indira Gandhi to intervene in 1976 during the Emergency regime.

As per the March 24, 1976 notification, out of the total 7.20 MAF flow of Ravi and Beas over and above the pre-partition use, both Punjab and Haryana were allocated 3.5 MAF each with the remaining quantum allocated to Delhi to augment the drinking water supply. The entire water of the Satluj was already being used through the Bhakra and Sirhind canal systems in Punjab, Haryana and Rajasthan. Haryana was to be supplied this share by constructing a new canal that is now known as the Satluj Yamuna Link Canal. Haryana started work on the construction of this canal within its territory within no time of the 1976 award.

It is pertinent to mention here that the Akali Dal manifesto for the 1967 Assembly elections talked of Chandigarh and left out Punjabi-speaking areas but did not touch upon this sensitive issue of water sharing or repercussions of Sections 78, 79 and 80 of the Punjab Re-organization Act. The manifesto for the 1969 mid-term Assembly polls made mention of only transfer of dams stating: "The Shiromani Akali Dal would make sincere efforts for the transfer of dams and projects, left out Punjabi-speaking areas and Chandigarh to Punjab." Even this reference was missing in the 1972 manifesto. The government at the Centre after reorganization controlled all the headworks from where canals take off in Punjab.

The Akali Dal for years overlooked the far-reaching implications of Sections 78-80 of the Punjab Re-organization Act and did not question these clauses. Parkash Singh Badal was the Chief Minister of the Akali Dal government from March 27, 1970 to June 14, 1971. The Badal ministry survived the no-confidence motion moved on July 24, 1970 with the support of the Congress after the Jan Sangh had walked out of the alliance with the Akali Dal on the language issue.

It was only in the 1977 manifesto that this issue forcefully surfaced with the party emphatically demanding, "Restoration of control of the Bhakra dam, Satluj project, etc., to Punjab and annulment of arbitrary division of Ravi-Beas waters which has been done in complete detriment to the state of Punjab". Neither the Akali Dal till then demanded adjudication of river waters dispute with Haryana nor the first Akali or later the first Badal headed Akali government took it up. This party reacted only after intervention by the Prime Minister on March 24, 1976. The party even in its 1977 manifesto never raised the issue of waters flowing to Rajasthan from the Bhakra Canal system completed in 1954, the 1955 agreement that awarded 8 MAF to that state or the Bhakra Nangal Project Agreement of 1959.

Punjab and the Riparian Principle

The division of river waters emerged as one of the most important issues only when the party launched the Dharamayudh Morcha (agitation for justice) on August 4, 1982. This issue was referred to as demand No. 11 in the 15-point demand charter submitted to Indira Gandhi earlier in October, 1981 which stated: "Handing over of dams and headworks in the state to Punjab and re-distribution of river waters as per national and international rules". It was for the acceptance of this demand charter that the party launched its agitation when the radical streak in the Sikh religio-political matrix had already sharpened.

There is yet another dimension. The Akali Dal in early 1982 did not oppose water flowing to Haryana but pressed for the apportionment of surplus Ravi-Beas waters under 60:40 ratio.[2]

The first struggle was launched by the Akali Dal on the water issue on April 8 from Ghanaur in Patiala, the day when Indira Gandhi laid the foundation of the SYL Canal at nearby Kapoori village. The party started sending protesters to Kapoori from April 24 to block the construction of this channel. It was this agitation that was subsequently shifted to Amritsar under the banner of Dharamyudh Morcha by including several other demands.

Bhakra Project First Violation of Riparian Principle

The Riparian principle was never an issue, so far as the Punjab rivers are concerned even from the time the Bhakra project was conceptualized for the first time during the British period in 1919. The total command area of the Bhakra project was proposed at 4667047 acres that included 1205600 acres in the Bikaner state of Rajasthan. This project did not take off at that time and Bikaner was later supplied water from Hussainiwala barrage in Ferozepur district in Punjab through the Gang Canal. Punjab charged seigniorage on this water.

The command area of the Bhakra Canal that was completed in 1954, as a part of the Bhakra dam project included Rajasthan too. The cultivable command area of the Bhakra Canal was 84 per cent in Punjab and 16 per cent in Rajasthan. However, after re-organization of Punjab in 1966, the share of Punjab was reduced to 35 per cent with 49 per cent being that of Haryana.

The construction of this biggest project of its kind in India was started immediately after partition. It is the Bhakra project resolution No. DW-II-22(3) dated September 25, 1950 under which the Bhakra Control Board and the Bhakra Advisory Board were constituted that was the first violation of the Riparian principle. The participants in this conference at which these bodies were constituted included representatives from the central government and the governments of Punjab, PEPSU (Patiala and East Punjab States Union), Rajasthan and Bilaspur. Both Rajasthan and PEPSU were non-Riparian to Punjab rivers.

Clause IV of the functions of the Bhakra Advisory Board is the most important in the context of apportionment of water among the states concerned. It states: "To advise, at the request of the state government concerned, on the internal distribution of the allocated supplies of water from Bhakra to different areas with a view to the optimum utilization of such supplies". It is the term "optimum utilization" that calls for particular attention. Optimum utilization is basic to the utilization of river waters and besides the Riparian principle, it is this norm that has subsequently been violated with impunity.

There is yet another agreement that is relevant as it preceded the 1950 'resolution' on Bhakra. This is the 1947 agreement on the Sirhind Canal that in essence is renewal of the earlier agreement signed at the time of the construction of this canal. The 1947 agreement under the Indian Independence Act, 1947 was signed between the governments of East Punjab and PEPSU.

Its Clause (3) states: The Patiala Union shall pay to the East Punjab government an annual sum as seigniorage on the Satluj water supplies to the Patiala Feeder.[3]

Further under Clause (4): The seigniorage to be paid by the Patiala Union in consideration of the water supplied to them by the East Punjab Government will be at the rate not exceeding four annas per acre.

However, there is no mention of seigniorage on water to be supplied to Rajasthan through the Bhakra system under the 1950 resolution.

The Bhakra project originated first in a note dated November 8, 1908 prepared by Sir Louis Dane proposing two sites for storage and power development that was followed by another note in March 1910 but it was shelved. Another report was prepared in 1919. However, the first detailed project report was prepared in 1939. Another project report was prepared in 1945-46. It was revised again after the partition in 1948-49 with the final report in 1951. It was decided to start construction of the canal before the dam itself. The Bhakra Canal System was inaugurated by Pandit Nehru on July 7, 1954. It is the first system after partition that diverted water from the Punjab rivers to Rajasthan.

Yet another Bhakra Nangal Project Agreement was signed by the

Punjab and Rajasthan governments on January 13, 1959 on the sharing of cost and benefits of this project.

The 1955 Agreement

The genesis of the river waters dispute can be traced to the partition of the country in 1947 as the Radcliffe Line (geographical boundary) diagonally divided the Indus basin comprising six rivers that flow from India to Pakistan. The two countries were to negotiate their respective share as this vital issue had not been dealt with while partitioning India to create Pakistan. In this region, the partition was that of Punjab as Jammu and Kashmir was a sovereign state and subsequently negotiated its accession to India. Punjab and Kashmir are part of the Indus river system.

The Indus water basin before 1947 was the biggest zone in the world irrigated by networks of canals, and thereby the most vital hydro-strategic region.

The dispute between the two Punjabs arose for the first time immediately after partition in December 1947 on the flow of the Satluj, Ravi and Beas rivers and it was dealt with by the Punjab Partition Committee. At a meeting on December 20, 1947, the two chief engineers, each from East and West Punjab, agreed to maintain the status quo ante till March 31, 1948. This was approved by the Punjab Partition Committee. The issue was to be sorted out by that period. However, as the West Punjab government took no step to extend the agreement, East Punjab stopped the flow. The flow in these rivers around this time is usually low.

In an effort to resolve the issue, yet another meeting of the chief engineers took place at Shimla on April 18, 1948. The two agreements on the flow of these three rivers were to be ratified by the two countries. This agreement noted:

> A dispute has arisen between East Punjab and West Punjab governments regarding supply by East Punjab of water to the Central Bari Doab, Dipalpur canals in West Punjab; the contention of the East Punjab government is that under the Punjab Partition (Apportionment of Assets and Liabilities) Order, 1947, and the arbitral award, the proprietary rights in the water of rivers of East Punjab vest wholly in the East Punjab government and that the West Punjab government cannot claim any share of these waters as of right...The East Punjab government has revived the flow of water into these canals on certain conditions.[4]

There is also the Pakistani version of the story.

Pakistani writer Ayesha Siddiqa presented the issue in a different perspective. The version is as follows:

The biggest problem, of course, lay with the partitioning of the state of Punjab, as it contained a complex irrigation system built by the British to be run under a single administration. The task was eventually delegated to the Chief Engineers of East Punjab (India) and West Punjab (Pakistan) who agreed to allow the existing water sharing systems to continue until the following year. This Standstill Agreement between India and Pakistan expired on March 31, 1948. On the following day, Indian Punjab cut off water flow to Pakistan.

The conflict in Kashmir overlapped with the water disputes, and by January 1948 India had taken the Kashmir issue to the United Nations Security Council (UNSC). On April 21, 1948, a resolution calling for a ceasefire and withdrawal of all troops was passed.

The Kashmir dispute and disputes over the sharing of water resources are intertwined. From independence to the present day, they remain the two biggest challenges when it comes to normalising relations between the states of India and Pakistan.[5]

Further, "In the early days of independence, the fact that India was able to shut off the Central Bari Doab Canals at the time of the sowing season, causing significant damage to Pakistan's crops, exposed a central weakness and vulnerability in the newly created state that was desperately trying to establish its independence. As noted by one British general on a visit to the area in 1948, the dispute centres around the "water insecurity" of Pakistan, as all of its rivers either originate in or pass through India."

Experts agreed, saying that resolving water disputes under the auspices of the World Bank was 'one way to reduce hostility'over Kashmir.

Here is yet another Pakistani viewpoint: "The Inter-Dominion Agreement on the Canal Water Dispute, signed by India and Pakistan at New Delhi on May 4, 1948, restored the canal water flows that India had choked off. Through this agreement, India made clear its intent to use all of the water of the rivers in question; the agreement merely allowed Pakistan time to find alternative sources to replace the lost water."

To make matters worse for Pakistan, its West Punjab government was notified by India's East Punjab government that this agreement would be discontinued on Sept. 4, 1948. Pakistan's foreign minister appealed to the Indian Prime Minister, Jawaharlal Nehru, to continue water supplies to West Punjab and to the Sindh irrigation systems until the two governments could reach a final agreement. Nehru responded that supplies would be continued temporarily, and with no commitment for the future.

A few weeks later, on Oct. 24, 1948, Nehru informed the Pakistani government by telegram that the East Punjab government was under no obligation to continue the supply of water to West Punjab, and that in any future discussion of the matter full right of the East Punjab government to reduce the supplies at will must be recognized.

A further indication of India's intentions came when construction work

> began in late 1948 on the Harike Barrage, upstream of the Ferozepur Barrage, at the confluence of the Beas and Sutlej. It was clear that the Harike Barrage would make it possible for India to completely abandon the Ferozepur Barrage and shut down supplies of water to Pakistan's Sutlej Valley canals. Pakistan tried to appeal to the International Court of Justice in June 1949, but India refused to participate. Instead, India urged that the Inter-Dominion Agreement of May 4, 1948, be made permanent.[6]

It was in this background that the World Bank president Eugene Black offered the services of his organization in 1952 to settle the dispute as it had the potential to escalate.

The first intervention was made in 1954 which stated that India should have exclusive right over the use of the Ravi, Beas and Satluj rivers with similar rights to Pakistan over the Indus, Jhelum and Chenab.

The Jhelum and Chenab flow through Jammu and Kashmir to West Punjab to merge with the Indus downstream. The settlement was to be over division of waters of these six rivers, including the five flowing though original Punjab. Both the countries accepted the proposal. The Indus Water Treaty was signed between India's Prime Minister Jawaharlal Nehru and Pakistan President General Ayub Khan on September 19, 1960 at Karachi.

Before completing the formalities, the World Bank team decided to tour the Indus basin in 1954.This aspect is important in the context of the 1955 apportionment in India on which the Indus Water Treaty was based.

The World Bank had signalled that the "allocation of waters to the two countries would depend on their relative utilization potential for these waters and both countries were to establish over a period of time their capacity to absorb the river waters to feed canal irrigation systems."[7]

This gave a significant twist to the situation. It is at this point that Rajasthan came into the picture. "We had to be vigilant during the visit to emphasize the urgency and importance of irrigation development in the Indus basin in India...I urged, therefore, that the work should begin immediately on the construction of the Rajasthan canal. This will furnish the best possible proof of India's needs."[8]

However, there is another vital aspect of the water sharing proposal.

"The Government of India immediately wrote to the states concerned to give their requirement, based on specific areas which could be irrigated by gravity flow. *Lift areas were not to be included.*"[9]

It is the aspect of gravity flow that is all the more important as it was this dimension that was subsequently violated.

A meeting of the chief engineers from Punjab, PEPSU and Rajasthan was held on November 23, 1954 in the framework of the Centre's instructions. Only such areas were to be included which could be irrigated by gravity flow. The total requirement of the area was assessed at 19.50 MAF with 5.99 MAF for Punjab, 11.97 MAF for Rajasthan, 1.16 MAF for Pepsu and 0.38 MAF for Jammu and Kashmir. As against this requirement, the dependable flow of Ravi and Beas was around 15.74 MAF and total mean supplies 19.27 MAF. The report was finalized by the Central Water and Power Commission.

However, this aspect of gravity flow was violated going by the lifts on the Rajasthan Canal. Irrigation on one side of the canal is by gravity flow but by lifts on the other. A total of seven lift canals were to take off from the Rajasthan Feeder.

There is yet another dimension as this feeder canal project was originally finalized on October 29, 1948. The work on the Harike Barrage from where this channel was to take off was completed in 1952. The barrage had been designed for a canal to take off from this point. The barrage was constructed by the Punjab government. The project report was already there when the 1955 allocation was decided. This allocation to Rajasthan is now justified on the logic of protecting India's interests against that of Pakistan. However, the project had already been conceived.

The total availability of the waters of Satluj, Beas and Ravi on the basis of 1921-22 to 1945-46 flow series at that time was 32.58 MAF that included Satluj with 13.30 MAF, Beas having 12.85 MAF and Ravi with 6.43 MAF. The dependable availability was about 26.9 MAF. The Bhakra project had already been conceptualized and partly implemented by that time to use the entire Satluj waters. The issue was with the Ravi and Beas rivers with a total flow of 19.28 MAF.

The meeting of the inter-state conference on the development and utilization of waters of the rivers Ravi and Beas in the context of the above flow assessment was held in Delhi on January 29, 1955. Contrary to what the Akali Dal has maintained for years, this meeting was attended by Punjab Irrigation and Finance Minister Chaudhary Lahiri Singh, besides irrigation ministers from PEPSU (later merged with Punjab), Rajasthan and Jammu and Kashmir and presided over by the Union Minister for Irrigation and Power.

That was the time when Punjab should have planned a new network of the canal system. The Indian Punjab mainly had the Upper

Bari Doab Canal on the Ravi taking off from the Madhopur, Sirhind Canal system on the Satluj from the Ropar and Western Yamuna Canal from Yamuna from Tajewala, now in Haryana. Punjab was under gravity flow. All these three canals were from the pre-partition period. It was only the Bhakra project that was undertaken during the post-partition period.

Punjab and PEPSU were allocated 7.2 MAF, Rajasthan 8 MAF and J&K 0.65 MAF from Ravi and Beas over and above the actual pre-partition utilization based on the flow series pertaining to the period 1921-22 to 1945-46 under the 1955 agreement. The Indus Waters Treaty with Pakistan was signed in 1960 on this basis under which Satluj, Beas and Ravi became available to India for unrestricted use after March 31, 1970.

Two of the clauses under the 1955 allocations are important: Clause (I): "In case of any variation in total supplies, the shares shall be changed pro-rata on the above allocations subject to the condition that no change shall be made in the allocation for Kashmir state which shall remain as 0.65 MAF." and Clause (V): "The question of allocation of the cost of water including the cost of storage and other works may be taken up separately as the conference was concerned only with the distribution of supplies."

It was on the basis of Clause (V) that Punjab demanded royalty from Haryana and Rajasthan. The resolution adopted unanimously by the Punjab Assembly on November 17, 2016 is as follows:

> It is a historical truth that before Independence a Riparian state used to get royalty for sharing water with the non-Riparian state. For example, during the British rule, river water of Punjab was twice allocated to other states. Water was given to Patiala, Nabha and Jind states in 1873 and it was clearly specified that Punjab being a Riparian state had right over these waters and accordingly, these states had to pay royalty in lieu of water till 1945-46.
>
> For the second time, the water was released to the Bikaner state through Gang Canal on the request of Maharaja Ganga Singh of Bikaner and the Bikaner state paid royalty to Punjab.
>
> Therefore, considering the aforesaid facts, this House strongly directs Punjab government to immediately take up the matter with the central government, Haryana, Rajasthan and Delhi, regarding securing cost/royalty in lieu of river water...so as to undo the injustice meted out to the state for decades by Congress-led governments in Punjab and at the Centre.
>
> However, the Inter-State River Waters Disputes Act adopted in 1956 dropped the royalty clause. This clause states: "Prohibition of levy

> of seigniorage: (I) No State Government shall, by reason only of the fact that any works for the conservation, regulation or utilization of water resources of an inter-State river have been constructed within the limits of the State, impose, or authorise the imposition of any seigniorage or additional rate or fee (by whatever name called) in respect of the use of such water by any other State or the inhabitants thereof.

Work on the Rajasthan Feeder was formally inaugurated on March 31, 1958 by Union Home Minister G.B. Pant and water released on October 11, 1961. That was Phase I of the project that is now known as the Indira Gandhi Canal project in Rajasthan.

According to the information provided by the Punjab government, the 1955 agreement was never ratified by the state cabinet. Punjab presented no other plan to utilise these waters.

There is another significant aspect to this apportionment, as Haryana had not come into existence at that time.

> In the areas given by Punjab, no area from any district, which later became part of Haryana, was included because the areas which could be irrigated by gravity in these districts were already in the Western Yamuna Canal and the Bhakra Canal. There were good arable lands in these districts. But these lands could be provided irrigation only by lift and as such, in accordance with the instructions from the Government of India, were not included in Punjab.[10]

Food Security and Haryana

The situation, however, changed in the mid-1960s following the report by the Food and Agriculture Organization (FAO) that showed what Kanwar Sain describes as an, "Alarming picture of population explosion" in less developed regions in Haryana. It recommended that every acre of arable land should be brought under irrigation to meet the food requirement, including the lift system.

As per the White Paper released by the Punjab government in 1982, the Food Committee on land and water use in Punjab was constituted on January 12, 1965 to recommend rational redistribution of surplus Ravi-Beas waters in the state. The committee recommended in February 1966 that 4.56 MAF water be allocated to the region that later formed Haryana, overlooking the earlier gravity flow principle. No decision was taken on this report. Haryana came into existence on November 1, 1966 following re-organization of Punjab. This report of the Food Committee was to later become the basis for allocation to Haryana as the successor state.

Another important aspect was deliberately overlooked in the context of the sharing of waters between Punjab, Rajasthan and Haryana. River Yamuna flowed through Punjab till its re-organization in 1966 and this river was not included in the divisible pool when the issue of Haryana cropped up. There is no mention of the share of Punjab in the Yamuna despite the fact that the state was Riparian till 1966. Yamuna merges with Ganga and is part of that river basin.

Punjab raised this issue at the 10th National Conference of Water Resources and Irrigation Ministers at New Delhi on September 21, 1992 where Irrigation and Power Minister Harcharan Singh Brar demanded: "Punjab should be provided its legitimate share in the unutilized waters of all the rivers of Punjab at the time of its division in 1966."

His articulation on the waters sharing issue was important. He said,

> I would like to begin by drawing the attention of all the members present here, to the mistaken though popular belief that Punjab has an enormous water resource that it grudges sharing with its neighbours. The fact of the matter is, however, that against our requirement of 39.75 MAF of water, we at present have only 14.54 MAF as surface water and for irrigation over and above this, we have to resort to tube wells. More specifically, 40 per cent of the area we presently irrigate through canals and 60 per cent with the help of tubewells. Irrigation through electricity is nine times more expensive and through diesel pumps 22 times more expensive than canal irrigation. In other words, our rightful natural resource, which has not been allocated on equitable basis, is not available to us and Punjab has to bear an enormous financial burden on artificial means of irrigation. It might surprise most of you to know that the quantity of water given by the Riparian states of the country put together, to other non-Riparian states, is less than 20 per cent of what Punjab alone has been compelled to give of its water to its neighbouring states. I wonder how many of you would see reason in Punjab having nothing to do with Yamuna waters because its geographical area does not form part of the Yamuna basin.

Kanwar Sain Recommended Reopening of the 1955 Agreement

Haryana Chief Minister Bansi Lal set up a technical review board headed by Kanwar Sain in the context of the FAO Report, which held its first meeting in February-March, 1969. This board assessed the water requirement of the state at 23.6 MAF. As against this assessment, the available supply from the Yamuna was 3.26 MAF and from the Satluj 4.37 MAF. Additional water requirement for providing irrigation even for one crop worked out at 16 MAF.

This is where the situation starts changing and the Punjab Re-organization Act comes in. Total availability of water for Haryana was calculated at 8.54 MAF including 4.80 MAF from Ravi and Beas. Undivided Punjab had been allotted 7.2 MAF under the 1955 agreement from the surplus Ravi-Beas waters. However, the Haryana area not under gravity flow had been left out under the 1955 agreement.

It was in this context that Kanwar Sain recommended years later in his write up in *The Indian Express* that "the Government of India must, therefore, agree to re-open the 1955 agreement for review by a tribunal to be set up under the Inter-State River Waters Disputes Act, 1956."

His argument was that the Punjab government "has no legal right to deprive specific areas of Punjab and PEPSU of the water earmarked for them in the 1955 agreement. No part of 7.2 MAF allotted to Punjab and PEPSU under the 1955 agreement could be given to the Haryana areas not considered in the 1955 agreement. If these areas in Haryana were to be supplied water, the 1955 agreement should be re-opened."[11]

According to this recommendation, it is the allocation to Rajasthan that would have been cut in favour of Haryana.

There could not be a stronger case in favour of Punjab. Kanwar Sain was Chief Engineer of Bikaner state and later headed several organizations. The Rajasthan Feeder taking off from Harike was his idea that originated way back in 1940.

There is yet another intriguing aspect. The Satluj waters were in use under the Sirhind Canal and Bhakra Canal systems. It is the Ravi and Beas waters that were to be allocated. Waters of Ravi can be brought neither to Haryana nor Rajasthan directly. Harike is at the confluence of the Satluj and Beas. Ravi is in upper areas touching Pakistan and only its limited water is diverted to Beas through the Madhopur Link. Under the Bhakra Nangal project, Beas waters were diverted to Satluj from Pandoh Dam in Mandi district. The basic reason for this diversion was that the water flow in Satluj was less than the total designed capacity of the Bhakra reservoir.

There is also the agreement signed by the governments of Punjab and Rajasthan on January 13, 1959 that is known as the Bhakra Nangal project agreement about sharing the cost and benefits of the Bhakra Nangal project. It is a very detailed agreement which had nothing to do with the 1955 agreement.

Work on the Bhakra project had been initiated after the signing of the agreement between the Punjab government and the Raja of Bilaspur in 1945.

The Riparian principle finds no mention while conceptualizing the Bhakra dam project, even in 1921. This was never an issue in case of the Punjab rivers even during the British period.

This Riparian issue was never raised by Punjab all along till 1976.

Indira Gandhi Award of 1976

Haryana claimed 4.8 MAF in 1967-68 under the Punjab Re-organization Act which was rejected by Punjab. As the two states failed to reach an agreement within the stipulated period of two years, the Government of India constituted a committee in April 1970 to determine the share of the two states which recommended 3.78 MAF for Haryana. The Planning Committee, in March 1973, recommended 3.74 MAF for Haryana but that again was not acceptable to both the states as Haryana staked its claim to 4.8 MAF. The Central Water Commission in 1974 recommended sharing of the Beas project waters on a 50:50 basis. The Centre intervened and Prime Minister Indira Gandhi issued her award on March 24, 1976 allocating 3.5 MAF each to Punjab and Haryana out of the total surplus Ravi-Beas waters of 7.2 MAF, with Delhi getting 0.2 MAF for drinking water supply on the recommendation of the Central Water Commission.

According to the details given in the White Paper, Punjab first protested against the decision on July 6, 1976 and this is also corroborated from the record obtained from the state government under the Right to Information Act.

As per the information provided by the Punjab government under RTI Act, the first formal protest against the apportionment of river waters was lodged by Chief Minister Giani Zail Singh on November 19, 1976 who headed the Congress government in Punjab from 1972-1977. This is communication No. 10178-IW (1) 76/34437 dated November 19, 1976. The Chief Minister referred to the protest earlier lodged by the state government on July 6 and the reply received from the Centre. He sought the personal attention of Indira Gandhi. He referred to the adjournment motion, the notice for which was given by some MLAs in the Assembly. However, the same was rejected by the Assembly Speaker. Instead, the Speaker convened a meeting of leaders from all parties and groups in the Assembly in his chamber on September 3, 1976. The Speaker informed about the view that emerged at the meeting to the Chief Minister. It was felt that grave injustice had been done to Punjab and the matter should be taken up with the Prime Minister. Giani Zail Singh referred to a note prepared by the ministry concerned of the Government of India whereby it had been pointed out as to how a part of the land then under canal irrigation would turn barren in case Haryana was given this share.[12]

There is yet another reference to the Punjab Congress lodging a protest against this award with Indira Gandhi.[13] According to subsequent disclosures, Giani Zail Singh had made it clear to Mrs. Gandhi that he could not continue as the Chief Minister in case he was compelled to implement the decision.[14]

A July 1995 note of the Punjab irrigation department too refers to the protest lodged by the Punjab government in November 1976 demanding review of the March 1976 award.

This award favoured Haryana as the rivers flow through Punjab and division of waters of river Yamuna was not included in the divisible pool. There was no mention of Yamuna flowing through Haryana in the Punjab Re-organization Act, which was part of Punjab before re-organization. This was a blatant case of discrimination against Punjab in the Re-organization Act itself. Yamuna should have been included in the divisible assets between the two states. This Act was flawed.

No Protest by the Badal Government in 1977

The Akali Dal government headed by Parkash Singh Badal that came into power in 1977 did not lodge any formal protest, which is proof of the betrayal by the party on this sensitive issue at that time. The Akali Dal was part of the Janata government at the Centre that succeeded the Congress government in 1977. His problem was that it was his friend Chaudhary Devi Lal who had formed the government in Haryana.

This river water dispute is a sad commentary on the opportunistic role of traitors and political traders. The Congress traded this issue in Haryana for political gains. The Akali Dal betrayed the people while publicly taking a tough stand against what used to be described as the loot of Punjab river waters while the practice was diametrically opposite. The Badal government rather collaborated with the Devi Lal government by way of initiating steps to start work on the Satluj Yamuna Link Canal project to supply water to Haryana.

Here are the facts that speak for themselves.

Three days before Giani Zail Singh lodged his government's protest, the Haryana government released Rs. 1 crore to Punjab on November 16, 1976 for taking up the construction of the canal that was to carry the share of the state under the 1976 award.

This payment was preceded by a letter with DO No. 9798-IPWII-76/39166 written by Haryana Chief Minister Banarsi Das Gupta to his Punjab counterpart stating,

> When I met you on the evening of 5th of November, you were good enough to my suggestion that work should be started immediately in the reach on which there is no difference of opinion among the chief engineers of the two states. I shall be grateful if you would kindly issue orders to the department to take action accordingly. I am directing my irrigation department to place a sum of Rs. 1 crore, for the time being, at the disposal of the Punjab government, so that the necessary organization is set up and work started.

The political situation was to change during the subsequent period.

The Assembly elections were held on June 12, 1977. The Congress lost and Parkash Singh Badal headed the Akali Dal-Janata Party government in Punjab and he had his family friend Devi Lal in Haryana. The Badal government wrote letter No. 7/78–IW (I) -78/23617 dated July 4, 1978 to Haryana seeking Rs 3 crore for starting this project. In case Badal was opposed to the 1976 apportionment, how was this letter written? The Haryana government sent another cheque for Rs. 1 crore on March 31, 1979. Before writing the letter, the Punjab government issued notices No. 113/5/SYL and No. 121/5/ SYL February 20, 1978 for the acquisition of land for this project under Section 4 of the Land Acquisition Act, 1894. The money sought was for land acquisition.

Not only that. This notification invoked an urgency provision stating, "Further in exercise of the powers under the said Act, the Governor of Punjab is pleased to direct that action under Section 17 of the aforesaid, shall be taken in this case on the grounds of urgency and provisions of Sections 5(a) will not apply with regard to acquisition of the said land."

This notification invoking Section 17 reinforces the revelations made by Gurcharan Singh Tohra that Badal had colluded with Devi Lal to lay the foundation stone of this canal. It was Tohra who had stonewalled this move after Devi Lal shared the information with him in the Central Hall of Parliament while inviting him to preside over the function. This speaks volumes about Badal's double standards on the river waters issue.

The Haryana Assembly record corroborates Badal's complicity in laying the foundation stone for this canal much before Indira Gandhi. The Governor announced in his Address on the opening day of the budget session of the Haryana Assembly on February 27, 1978: "It is hoped that work on this project would be speeded up as process for land acquisition has already been initiated." He was referring to land acquisition in Punjab.

Then there is the statement of Haryana Chief Minister Chaudhary Devi Lal on March 1, 1978 in the Assembly:

> Mr. Speaker, I want to draw attention of Rao Sahib through you that his Congress (Party) has been in power in Punjab, Haryana and the Centre for the last seven years but failed to resolve this issue. So much so that no decision could be arrived at even to acquire land. The result of our personal relations (Between Devi Lal and Badal) is before you as they have issued notification for land acquisition...The notification states: 'Whereas it appears to the Governor of Punjab that land is likely to be acquired for public purpose namely for construction of Satluj Yamuna Link canal in village Kamalpur and Sarala Kalan, Tehsil Rajpura, district Patiala'.

Rao Birender Singh: This notification is under what section?

Chaudhary Devi Lal: This is Sections 4 and 17 notification. I would also like to inform Rao Sahib that I were to preside over the function and Badal Sahib was to inaugurate it but has been delayed due to the session." This was the function to lay the foundation stone for the SYL Canal.[15]

Ironically, the Akali Dal has all along blamed the Congress on this sensitive issue while Badal's friend Devi Lal attacked that party for having failed to resolve it. What a contradiction.

It was after the foundation stone laying ceremony was dumped at Tohra's intervention that Haryana moved the Supreme Court on April 30, 1979 for the implementation of the 1976 award. Punjab also approached the apex court on July 11, 1979 challenging ultra vires of Section 78 to 80 of the Punjab Re-organization Act as well as the 1976 apportionment. Punjab approached the Supreme Court only after Haryana sought judicial intervention. This dispute had entered a new phase. The Badal government was dismissed on February 17, 1980.

The role of the Akali Dal is characterized by extreme opportunism on the river waters issue during this period.

While Badal had tied up with Devi Lal to lay the foundation stone of this canal, the 1995 note prepared by the Punjab government makes an interesting observation according to which Haryana was already drawing 1.99 MAF through the Bhakra Main Line over and above the waters flowing through the channel from its 1976 share. The SYL Canal was not needed at all. This was known even in 1986 going by the newspaper report. "Haryana is already drawing around 1.9 MAF of its share through the Bhakra main line."[16]

Badal also stands exposed in the White Paper on the Ravi-Beas Agreement 1981 that states:

> The then Chief Minister of Haryana and the then Chief Minister of Punjab agreed that the construction work on the Satluj-Yamuna Link Canal in the Punjab Territory would be inaugurated by the former chief minister of Punjab, Sardar Parkash Singh Badal and the function would be presided over by then Chief Minister of Haryana Chaudhary Devi Lal. This was confirmed in the official communications as also in the proceedings of Haryana Vidhan Sabha dated 1st March, 7th March and 10th March 1978."

According to a note prepared by the Punjab irrigation department in July 1995, the work on the project was initiated in 1978-79, the period when the Akali Dal ruled the state. The SYL Canal project in Punjab envisaged a 121 km long carrier channel to carry 6500 cusecs of waters to Haryana. Two power houses of 50 MW capacity were to come up on this channel in Punjab. The canal was to irrigate 1.28 lakh hectares in the Ropar and Patiala districts of Punjab as well.

Years later in 1994, Capt Amarinder Singh, then part of the Akali Dal, urged Badal to clarify his position on this issue at Akal Takht. He wrote,

> "What we have said many times in the past is that Mr Badal must put at rest this unnecessary speculation...as to whether he did or did not agree to Punjab's water being given to Haryana—the SYL canal saga. He says he did not. What we have suggested is that he should make the same statement at Akal Takht and then everyone will accept it. That will put at rest this endless controversy once and for all."[17] But then the record clearly establish Badal's role in initiating construction of SYL canal.

The Badal government was dismissed on February 17, 1980 with Congress winning the next Assembly election. Darbara Singh took over as the Chief Minister on June 6, 1980. With Congress in power in Punjab, Indira Gandhi opted for out-of-court settlement of the river waters apportionment. Her choice was dictated by the forthcoming Assembly elections in Haryana in May 1982.

Indira Gandhi forced Darbara Singh to sign the revised accord with his Haryana and Rajasthan counterparts on December 31, 1981 on the basis of what was given as the revised flow series of 1921-59, according to which the surplus was estimated to be at 17.17 MAF as against 15.85 MAF on the basis of the earlier 1921-45 flow series. Punjab's share was notionally enhanced from 3.50 MAF to 4.22 MAF in 1981.

Darbara Singh was threatened to sign on the dotted line or resign. He succumbed to the pressure. The SYL Canal in Punjab was to be completed by December 31, 1983 under this 'agreement'. The Akali Dal needed an issue and here was one. Badal's dubious role in the move to construct the SYL Canal had not surfaced in the political discourse by that time.

It is the role of Indira Gandhi to pressurize the Punjab Chief Minister that is highly questionable as the judicial intervention should have been allowed to settle the issue, which would have been binding on all the parties. She laid the foundation stone of the SYL Canal on April 8, 1982 at Kapoori in Patiala district near the state's border with Haryana to harvest political advantage, thereby setting Punjab aflame. The election in Haryana was held in May 1982.

However, the religio-political dynamics was changing in Punjab as militancy had already hit the state and warring Akali factions entered the competitive mode. The Akali Dal launched an agitation against this canal at Kapoori from April 24 to block its digging. This agitation on river waters initially failed to gain momentum till more demands, including religious ones, were added and the morcha re-launched from Amritsar on August 4, 1982 as the Dharamyudh Morcha. River waters apportionment was one of the main issues. The rest is history.

Haryana had completed its 91 km portion of the SYL Canal by June 1980 at a cost of Rs. 30 crores, the work on which had been started immediately after the 1976 award.

The SYL Canal was to take off from the tail end of the Anandpur Hydel channel that runs parallel to the Nangal Hydel channel till Lohand Khad where it discharges its water to flow down to the Satluj again after generating power at two power houses.

Since Punjab was also to derive incidental benefits from the SYL Canal by way of power generation and irrigation, the cost was to be shared between Punjab and Haryana in the ratio of 1:5 on an ad hoc basis. The total cost incurred on this project till March, 1995 was 521 crores as against the 1993 revised cost of Rs 601.25 crores.

When Rajiv Gandhi took over as the Prime Minister after the assassination of his mother Indira Gandhi, he opted to end confrontation with the Sikhs and initiated the reconciliation process that ended up in the signing of the Punjab Accord between him and Akali Dal chief Sant Harchand Singh Longowal on July 24, 1985.

The construction of the SYL Canal resumed under this accord at the time when Punjab had the Akali Dal government headed by Surjit Singh Barnala. The alignment of this canal had earlier been finalized when Badal was the Chief Minister and construction had started during the Barnala regime. It was the Akali Dal commitment to complete this canal by August 13, 1986-87. Here was another act of treachery with the people in the state by the Akali Dal.

The 1981 agreement had superseded the 1976 award while the Punjab Accord replaced the 1981 agreement.

Para 9 of the Punjab Accord on Waters

9.1 The farmers of Punjab, Haryana and Rajasthan will continue to get water not less than what they are using from the Ravi Beas system as on July 1, 1985. Water used for consumptive purposes will also remain unaffected. Quantum of usage claimed shall be verified by the Tribunal referred to in para 9.2 below.

9.2 The claims of Punjab and Haryana regarding the share of their remainder waters will be referred to for adjudication to a Tribunal to be presided over by a Supreme Court judge. The decision of this Tribunal will be rendered within six months and would be binding on both parties. All legal and constitutional steps in this respect to be taken expeditiously.

9.3 The construction of the SYL Canal shall continue. The canal shall be completed by August 13, 1986-87.

In order to bring the accord under the purview of the Inter-State River Waters Disputes, 1956, an amendment was inserted through an amendment bill in Parliament and this was Section 14 empowering the Centre to constitute the Tribunal. The Ravi-Beas Tribunal that is also known as the Eradi Tribunal was constituted on April 2, 1986 and it submitted its interim report on January 30, 1987 under which Punjab was awarded 5.00 MAF and Haryana 3.83 MAF while keeping the share of Rajasthan, Jammu and Kashmir and Delhi unchanged. The Punjab government took the stand that the Eradi panel had not followed the terms of reference and made its position clear through a communication in July 1992.

The Punjab Assembly adopted a resolution on November 5, 1985 declaring the 1981 agreement as redundant and rejecting the White Paper released on April 23, 1982 by the Darbara Singh government.

The resolution moved by Chief Minister Surjit Singh Barnala stated:

> Whereas a memorandum of settlement was signed between the Prime Minister Shri Rajiv Gandhi and late Sant Harchand Singh Longowal, President, Shiromani Akali Dal, on July 24, 1985 covering inter alia, the aspects of interstate disputes on allocation of surplus Ravi-Beas water and whereas this is the final Accord in suppression of all previous settlements in this regard, the previous Ravi-Beas Agreement, 1981 has become redundant and irrelevant. Moreover, this House feels that the observations made in the said white paper were not correct. Now,

> therefore, this House resolves that the aforesaid white paper be and is hereby annulled and rejected.

It was for the first time that the water apportionment had been ratified in the Punjab Assembly.

The work on this canal was abandoned due to the gunning down of its chief engineer M.L. Sekhri and superintending engineer Avtar Singh Aulakh by the militants on July 23, 1990 in their office in Chandigarh. By that time, about 90 per cent of the work had already been completed.

The action was planned by four militant organizations associated with the Panthic Committee (Dr. Sohan Singh) and assigned to the Khalistan Commando Force but was carried out by the Babbar Khalsa. The idea had originated with a dominant faction of the Bharti Kisan Union.

Beant Singh Government for Annulment of All Accords

The Congress returned to power amidst boycott by the Akali Dal in the February 1992 election and Beant Singh took over as the Chief Minister. This government took up the issue of the share from the Yamuna that was riparian to Punjab till 1966 and staked claim to 1.48 MAF in various communications in July, September and November 1992. Yamuna water was allocated among Haryana, Uttar Pradesh, Rajasthan, Himachal Pradesh and Delhi following which Punjab lodged its protest in July 1994 reiterating the need for equal and equitable application of one single acceptable principle for the resolution of the river water issue. Through another communication in September, 1994, the Punjab government demanded that the share of 4.65 MAF of Haryana under the Yamuna Waters Agreement be apportioned between Punjab and Haryana in the 60:40 ratio. This claim was rejected by the Centre in a communication dated November 1, 1994 on the logic that there was no such provision under Section 78 of the Punjab Re-organization Act.

The Punjab government shot back on December 29, 1994 and February 10, 1995 asserting that under the said Act, only Beas waters were to be apportioned and Ravi waters did not form a component of the Beas project. The diversion of Ravi waters to Harike via the Madhopur Link was meant for Rajasthan even before the Beas project was commissioned and as such, Ravi waters could not be construed to be part of the Beas project.

This government reviewed the situation at a meeting in July 1995. The note circulated at this meeting stated:

> The state government is of the view that all the decisions taken and averments made after the state re-organization in 1966 should be scrapped and the entire water issue examined de-novo. The state government feels that if the apportionment is made as per the provisions of the Re-organization Act, the share of Haryana could be delivered through the existing Bhakra Canal and the construction of the SYL Canal might not be required.

It was following this meeting that Haryana released its note on July 30, 1995.

Chief Minister Beant Singh was killed down on August 31, 1995. Badal, who took over as the Chief Minister in March, 1997, never initiated any action on the recommendation to annul all the awards and accords.

Various options were considered by the Centre to complete the construction of the career channel, including the one to be handed over to the central security forces. However, the risk was too high. Finally, the Supreme Court intervened and issued directions on June 4, 2004 to re-start work on this canal by July 15, 2004. The Congress had formed the government in Punjab in March 2002.

Amarinder Government Annuls Water Awards and Accords

It was Chief Minister Capt. Amarinder Singh heading the Congress government in the state at that time who took the bold step and abrogated all awards and accords with the adoption of the Punjab Termination of Agreements Act, 2004. However, while this Act scuttled the completion of the Satluj Yamuna Link Canal in Punjab territory, Section V of the same provided constitutional guarantee to the waters already flowing to the neighbouring states. This section states: "Notwithstanding anything contained in Sections 3 and 4 of this Act, all existing and actual utilizations through the existing systems shall remain protected and unaffected." This bill was unanimously adopted in the Assembly.

Badal later promised to abrogate Section V after forming the government. He formed the government in the 2007 election and the party retained power in 2012 creating history but he, as usual, backtracked from this promise.

Both Prime Minister Dr. Manmohan Singh and Congress President Sonia Gandhi were livid and they vent their ire on Capt Singh. "Although he does not lose his temper easily, Dr. Singh is learnt to have pulled up the Punjab Chief Minister in no uncertain terms at yesterday's meeting. "What do you think... whatever your logic for taking this step, I am not going to endorse it," a fuming Prime Minister is reported to have told Capt Amarinder Singh. He also upbraided him for the fact that he kept him and the Congress President in the dark on this issue. "Are we running a country or what? We will not allow the mockery of the Constitution," he reportedly added.[18] The Congress high command preferred not to declare Capt Amarinder Singh as the chief ministerial candidate in the 2007 Assembly elections and paid a heavy price as he turned indifferent.

Former Prime Minister and senior BJP leader Atal Behari Vajpayee too questioned the Punjab government action saying, "Every state, every political party has a right to take a stand in the democracy. That is not the issue. However, democracy only functions by mutual consent, not by arbitrary action... I urge all of us to treat this as a national problem that could degenerate into a crisis, and seek amicable answers to the dangerous questions.[19]

The President of India referred the Waters Termination Act to the Supreme Court under Presidential Reference. The 5-judge bench of the Supreme Court gave its observation on November 10, 2016 that stated: "We are of the view that the Punjab Act cannot be considered to be legal and valid and the State of Punjab cannot absolve itself from its duties/liabilities arising out of the Agreement in question." The court ruled that the 2004 Act was in violation of the constitutional provisions, the Inter-State River Waters Disputes Act, 1956 and the Punjab Re-organization Act, 1966.[20]

The decision of the President to refer the legislation to the Supreme Court triggered unprecedented activity in Punjab. The case came up for hearing in the Supreme Court in February 2016. With the start of the hearing in the Supreme Court, Badal moved a resolution in the State Assembly on March 10, 2016.

This resolution stated:

> Punjab is an agrarian state and river water is its life-line. However, Punjab has been meted out injustice on this extremely sensitive issue since the partition of the country. As per Riparian principles, Punjab has total right on its river water. Despite that, from the beginning itself, daylight robbery on Punjab river water has been committed through various awards and accords. Despite being owners of river water, Punjab farmers have to get 73 per cent of the water using tubewells, due to which the water table has been going down continuously. The situation has reached such a critical juncture that acceptance of this injustice would amount to signing death warrant for Punjab and Punjabis. Punjab does not have even a drop of water to spare for others. This House hereby unanimously resolves that

> no anti-Punjab decision on river water would be acceptable. No decision on the completion of Satluj Yamuna Link Canal to forcibly divest Punjab of its Ravi-Beas waters by violating the Riparian principle would be tolerated. This House unanimously resolves to defend the interests of Punjabis rising above party lines and personal differences.

This resolution was adopted unanimously.

It was while winding up the debate on this resolution, Badal announced to de-notify the canal land and return the same to the owners. Accordingly, the Punjab Satluj Yamuna Link Canal Land (Transfer of Property Rights) Bill was adopted on March 14, 2016 unanimously. The Bill provided for returning free of cost 3,928 acres of land acquired for this canal to the original owners. However, the legislation did not get assent from Governor Kaptan Singh Solanki.

The Supreme Court sought details of the legislation the same day and stayed the operation of this legislation on March 17 while ordering the status quo.

In an apparent attempt to counter the Supreme Court, yet another resolution was adopted on March 18, 2016 in the Punjab Assembly asserting, "Punjab is facing an acute water crisis. It does not have a single drop to give from its rivers. Neither was there any need in the past, nor there is any need now to construct the SYL Canal. The House unanimously decides that the canal will not be allowed at any cost."

Within hours of the Supreme Court having delivered its final ruling on November 10, 2016, the 42 Congress MLAs in the state handed over their resignation from the Assembly. State party Chief Capt Amarinder Singh, the MP from Amritsar, resigned from the Lok Sabha.[21] The Supreme Court ruled that Punjab was bound to share Ravi-Beas waters with Haryana and Rajasthan and complete the SYL Canal.

The Punjab cabinet on November 15 decided to de-notify the 5,376 acres of land that had been acquired for this canal and return to its original owners free of cost. This was followed by a special session of the Assembly on November 16 to adopt another resolution and demand royalty on water already flowing to Rajasthan and Haryana.

The text of the resolution:

> It is a historical truth that before independence whenever water was released by one state to another state, which had no right as per the Riparian principle, the royalty was given to the Riparian state for the same. For example, during the British rule, the river waters of Punjab was given twice to another states. Earlier, water of Satluj river was given to Patiala, Nabha and Jind states in 1873 and it was clearly specified in

> the decision taken that Punjab being a Riparian state, has the rights over these waters. Therefore, Patiala, Nabha and Jind states will have to pay royalty in lieu of water and these states had paid this royalty upto 1945-46. Similarly, for the second time water released to Bikaner state through Gang canal on the request of Maharaja Ganga Singh of Bikaner and the Bikaner state paid royalty to the state of Punjab in lieu of that. Therefore, while considering the aforesaid facts, this House strongly recommends to the State government to immediately take up the matter with the central government regarding securing cost from non-Riparian states in lieu of releasing of river waters to these states without securing anything for the same, so as to undo the injustice and the highhandedness meted out to the state for decades by Congress-led governments in Punjab and at centre.

The issue is with the Supreme Court.

Environmental Degradation Caused by the Rajasthan Feeder

The aspect of severe environmental damage caused by the Rajasthan Feeder in the desert state is an aspect that has been ignored all along.

Six lift canals take off from the Rajasthan Feeder that include Sahwa, Gajner, Kolayat, Bangarsar, Phalodi and Pokaran canals adding to the cost of water.

The Rajasthan Feeder has several aspects including its cost-benefit analysis. Here is a study quoted in a research thesis on this canal that states,

> A comprehensive study by Mott MacDonald (a consultant agency for State Government of Rajasthan for Indira Gandhi Nahar Project) indicated that in year 1995-96 around 10% of Culturable Command Area (CCA) of Stage-I became waterlogged (water table within 0-1 meters from surface) and that potentially sensitive area (water table within 1-6 meters from surface) increased from 9% in 1981 to 25% in 1990, and expressed the fear that by year 2000, extent of potentially sensitive area may go up to about 50% of the Stage-I, if no drainage solutions are provided for (MacDonald and Dalal, 1999).[22]

Here is another study about this canal: "Initially, the project area had a deep water table, and the provision of drainage was not included in the original development plan. The IGNP was conceived in the 1950s when the Environmental Impact Assessment (EIA) was not considered important, nor was an EIA ever made. Monitoring of the water table was also not a high priority."

Therefore, it took till 1973 for awareness of the problem to reach the stage whereby systematic monitoring began, and the monitoring network was considerably expanded in the early 1980s. As per the irrigation terminology (Sharma, 1999), about 54% of the Stage I area was "potentially sensitive", 4% of the area "critical" and 3% of the area waterlogged during the year 1998. The mean water table rise is 1.1 m year" and nearly 3,960 kms will be liable to waterlogging by the end of 2001 (Sharma and Mathur, 1991). However, a far more serious waterlogging problem is likely to appear in Stage II. Owing to an underground hard substratum of gypsum within 10 m of the surface, about 34% of the area (1,205 kms) is vulnerable to waterlogging (Rahmanai and Soni, 1997).

According to Chouhan (1988), thousands of hectares of land will be submerged in 25 to 30 years. In Lune-ki-dhani, Dabli Kalan, Dabli Khurd and Rampur villages in Stage I and near Madasar village in Stage II, 0.6-3.5 m water is standing in the cultivated fields. The houses have collapsed and villages have been abandoned. The impact of waterlogging in IGNP is mainly on the individual farmers whose land is affected.[23]

Waterlogging is acute in some areas. The worst affected are the villages including Naurangdesar, Silvana, Lakhuwali and other areas where agriculture activity has almost completely stopped. Pilibanga and Badopal also have a similar problem. About 44,625 hectares of land in the north of the canal has become waterlogged.

More than 40 per cent of the water in this canal is wasted due to seepage and evaporation.

Fresh cost benefit analysis of the Rajasthan Canal and the SYL Canal needs to be undertaken in terms of treating cost of water per unit supplied for irrigation. This cost should be treated as cost of input for the crop. The world over, the basic principle is to use every input in a way that the output is the highest. Exception has to be made in case of water for drinking purposes. However, taking water from a river hundreds of miles away and then lifting it to the parched fields goes against all canons of optimal utilization. River waters should not be politicized and turned into an emotive issue. What is needed is a pragmatic approach.

However, it is the real issue that has to be addressed. The Haryana government admitted way back in 1995 that the state was drawing 1.99 MAF out of its share of SYL Canal share of 3.5 MAF through the existing Bhakra canal system. Punjab rivers have been on fire for all those years. But the issue was about just 1.41 MAF of waters, going by this record.

The memorandum submitted by an all-party delegation led by Chief Minister Manohar Lal Khattar that called on President Pranab

Mukherjee on November 29, 2016 is self-explanatory. Khattar said after the meeting: "Haryana should get its due share of water. The state is asking for its rightful share and not Punjab's share. Both states had been allotted an equal share of 3.5 million acre feet (MAF) water under a water sharing agreement, but Haryana was getting only 1.62 MAF. Since 1981, Punjab has been utilizing 1.88MAF water that rightfully belongs to us".[24]

According to Haryana, the two states have thus been engaged in a bitter war over just 1.88 MAF of river water.

Much more water can now be made available to Haryana itself through modern water harvesting techniques. Why should precious water be allowed to go waste in Rajasthan?

Haryana can be supplied more water by remodelling the Bhakra Main Line (BML) Canal, only if it is available. Haryana, all along, has been drawing excess water depending on the needs through BML. However, it had been brought on the record for the first time. It was in this context that the SYL Canal is not needed.

The SYL Canal is more of a political project.

Chandigarh: City of Discord

Chandigarh, the most modern city in India that was planned and constructed as the Capital of then Punjab, is now a disputed territory since 1966.

Lahore, the capital of Punjab, became part of Pakistan during partition of the country in 1947. The Indian Punjab was without its Capital. It was planned to go in for a new city. Prime Minister Jawaharlal Nehru supervised the coming up of this dream project. Chandigarh has been a Union Territory since 1966 housing the governments of both Punjab and Haryana. Chandigarh turning into a city of discord is rooted in the re-organization of Punjab in 1966 that was supposed to be on a linguistic basis.

The transfer of Chandigarh to Punjab has been one of the issues that formed the core of the Akali struggles since 1966.

Punjab was re-organized on the basis of the controversial 1961 census in which the Punjabi Hindus by and large opted for Hindi as their mother tongue. In Chandigarh, the issue took yet another turn as the migrant construction workers from Hindi-speaking states who had shifted here changed the character of this city from Punjabi-speaking to Hindi-speaking. The land for this city had been acquired by uprooting the Punjabi population, mainly the farmers.

Punjab had opposed re-organization on the basis of the 1961

census. This issue divided even Hindu and Sikh MLAs in the Congress in the Punjabi region.

It is pertinent to mention here that the court language before the British annexed Punjab was Persian. It was replaced by English and Urdu. The Sikh religious texts were in Gurmukhi script while Punjabi also used to be written in Shahmukhi that is also known as the Urdu script.

Hindi entered Punjab coinciding with the Arya Samaj movement taking roots here. This movement was just religious but also changed the linguistic complexion of the region.

The regional formula known as the Sachar formula was the basis for dividing Punjab into Punjabi and Hindi zones and notification was issued to this effect on July 24, 1957.

The capital project area of Chandigarh was included neither in the Punjabi nor Hindi zone. This is the root cause of the dispute over this city that had been constructed as the Capital of Punjab.

The Shah Commission that was formed in 1966 for re-organization of Punjab recommended the transfer of Chandigarh to the proposed state of Haryana on the logic that the area was Hindi-speaking. Chandigarh was part of the Kharar tehsil.

However, the Centre decided to retain it as a Union Territory housing the Capitals of both Punjab for which it was built and the successor state of Haryana. This was the first case of reorganization in India in which the Capital had not been transferred to the parent state.

This provoked the Akali Dal to launch another agitation demanding transfer of Chandigarh to Punjab.

Prime Minister Indira Gandhi offered a solution that failed to satisfy neither Punjab nor Haryana. She announced the formula on January 29, 1970 under which Chandigarh was to be transferred to Punjab while Fazilka and Abohar along with 104 villages from Punjab to Haryana. As this area was not contiguous to Punjab separated by Punjabi-speaking Kandukhera village, it was to be linked by a 200 metre wide and about seven kilometres long corridor that was just unprecedented. A Commission was to be set up to settle the remaining territorial claims. Haryana was to be given a grant of Rs. 100 crores by the Centre to build its new capital.

This solution was junked by both the parties to the dispute.

The transfer of Chandigarh and left out Punjabi-speaking areas to Punjab was one of the demands on which the Akali Dal launched an agitation from August 4, 1982. The transfer of Chandigarh to Punjab was again part of the Punjab Accord signed between Prime Minister

Rajiv Gandhi and Akali Dal president Sant Harchand Singh Longowal on July 24, 1985.

This accord stated:

> 7.1 The Capital project of Chandigarh will go to Punjab. Some adjoining areas, which were previously part of Hindi or the Punjabi regions were included in the Union territory. With the capital region going to Punjab the areas which were added to the Union territory from the Punjabi region of the erstwhile state of Punjab will be transferred to Punjab and those from Hindi region to Haryana. The entire Sukhna lake will be kept part of Chandigarh and will thus go to Punjab.
>
> 7.2 It had always been maintained by Smt. Indira Gandhi that when Chandigarh is to go to Punjab, some Hindi speaking territories in Punjab will go to Haryana. A commission will be constituted to determine the specific Hindi speaking areas of Punjab which should go to Haryana in lieu of Chandigarh.
>
> The principle of contiguity and linguistic affinity with a village as a unit will be the basis of such determination. The commission will be required to give its findings by 31st December, 1985 and these will be binding on both sides. The work of the commission will be limited to this aspect and will be distinct from the general boundary claims which the other commissions referred to in para 7.4 will handle.
>
> 7.3 The actual transfer of Chandigarh to Punjab and areas in lieu thereof to Haryana will take place simultaneously on 26th January, 1986.
>
> 7.4 There are other claims and counter claims for readjustment of the existing Punjab-Haryana boundaries. The government will appoint another commission to consider these matters and give its findings. Such findings will be binding on the concerned states. The terms of reference will be based on a village as a unit, linguistic affinity and contiguity.

Rajiv Gandhi on January 23 or 24, 1986 subsequently conveyed to Punjab Chief Minister Surjit Singh Barnala late at night his inability to transfer Chandigarh on January 26 citing Haryana's compulsion. Barnala conveyed to Finance Minister Balwant Singh who rushed to his residence around 11 pm and advised him to resign. Barnala refused and that was the end of it.

Chandigarh continues to be a Union Territory.

ENDNOTES

1. June 12, 2018. *The Tribune.*
2. Jagtar Singh. (2011). *Khalistan Struggle: A Non-movement*. Delhi: Aakar Books, p. 74.
3. Central Water Commission. (1995). *Legal Instruments of Rivers in Punjab,* Volume III, Agreements on Inter-State Rivers, New Delhi, p. 22.

4. The Punjab River Water Dispute, Council of Sikh Affairs, Chandigarh, p. 6.
5. Ayesha Siddiqa, *Al Jazeera*, August 1, 2011.
6. Khaled Ahmad, *Newsweek*, August 01, 2013 based upon Saiyad Ali Naqvi's *Indus Waters and Social Change*: *The Evolution and Transition of Agrarian Society in Pakistan*, Oxford University Press, Karachi.
7. White Paper, Government of Punjab, 1982.
8. Gulhati, N.D. (1973). *Indus-Water Treaty*. Bombay: Allied Publishers. p. 178.
9. Sain, Kanwar. (February 15, 1983). Sharing of Ravi and Beas Waters. *The Indian Express*.
10. Ibid.
11. Ibid.
12. August 2, 1993. *Daily Ajit*.
13. August 14, 1978. *The Tribune*.
14. September 1, 1983. *The Tribune*.
15. From the record of Haryana Assembly.
16. February 8, 1986. *The Indian Express*.
17. March 30, 1994. *The Tribune*.
18. July 15, 2004. *The Tribune*.
19. August 10, 2004. *The Tribune*.
20. November 11, 2016. *The Tribune*.
21. November 12, 2016. *Hindustan Times*.
22. Bhaskar, Rajesh: Analysis of Hydrogeological System and Land Cover for Assessment of Risks to Irrigated Agriculture in Thar Desert: Charanwala System of the Indira Gandhi Canal Project, International Institute for Geo-Information Science and Earth Observation, Enschede, The Netherlands & Indian Institute of Remote Sensing, National Remote Sensing Agency (NRSA), Department of Space, Government of India, Dehradun, India.
23. Sharma, K.D., Indira Gandhi Nahar Pariyojana—Lessons Learnt from Past Management Practices in the Indian Arid Zone, Central Arid Zone Research Institute, Jodhpur.
24. November 30, 2016. *Hindustan Times*.

11

Democratic Mandate to Kill

The guns fell silent by the end of 1995 after a free-for-all for about four years when the violence peaked and Punjab turned into a vast killing field. While the militant struggle got criminalized, the security personnel too turned terrorists with the mandate to kill. Unlike the militants, the security forces are supposed to function under the law but every law was violated with impunity in Punjab with the one objective: to restore peace and normalcy. The security forces succeeded but it was the peace of the graveyard.

According to a Punjab police press note, the monthly average killings of civilians that was 216 in 1991 came down to 127 in 1992 and four in 1993 while the police encounters during 1992 were the highest ever at 1,330 followed by 570 in 1993. January 1994 witnessed zero killing of civilians.

The security forces were given what can be termed as the democratic mandate to kill by facilitating Congress into power by engineering boycott by the mainstream Akali factions of the assembly elections held on February 20, 1992. The Congress government headed by Beant Singh that took over gave a free hand to the security forces. This free hand was the licence to kill. The policy was simple—no prisoners. The face of the Indian state in this battle was the Director General of Police K.P.S. Gill who subsequently claimed that the boycott was his design.

On the surface, however, this boycott was dictated by the militants. The boycott story has thus two sides. The poll boycott was the one issue on which the interests of a major section of the Sikh militants and the Indian government converged, though for different reasons.

The installation of the Congress government was the design of the Indian government as part of the strategy to confront Sikh radicals using boycott as a tool. The dominant pro-boycott lobby among the radicals walked straight into the trap.

The militants had their own logic and one of the reasons that were advanced in favour of boycott was the fear of civil war among Sikhs in case of pro-radical factions coming to power. This apprehension was based on the killing of 29 Akali candidates by the pro-boycott lobby in the aborted June 1991 elections. Any Akali faction and associates coming to power would have led to confrontation with the militants as happened in 1985 when the Akali Dal formed the government with Surjit Singh Barnala as the chief minister.

Militancy in Punjab was already witnessing internecine killings and civil war could have been the next stage.

Pakistan too had conveyed concern to the militant leaders over these killings, especially with reference to that of Baldev Singh Lang who was a candidate from Akali Dal (Mann). The responsibility of his killing was claimed by Babbar Khalsa on June 5, 1991 saying he was collecting money in the name of militants. The press note claiming responsibility was issued in the name of Amrik Singh Kauli.

One of the arguments advanced in favour of poll boycott was that since they had rejected the Indian Constitution, how could they contest election under it? The election could be contested after constituting a front organization that possibly would have included Akali Dal (Mann), AISSF (Manjit) and representatives of Damdami Taksal. Distrust already existed between dominant militant organizations, various factions and their leaders.

The feeling among the militant leaders, most of whom were then in Pakistan, was that the government formed by these people would be part of the system and they would become the target. This would lead to retaliation and hence intensification of internecine war with those in power.

One of the arguments was that one should get killed at the hands of the security forces under a non-Sikh government rather than by "government of one's own people."

Moreover, leaders like Manjit Singh belonged to the families of martyrs and any retaliation against them would have proved counter-productive as this could have given the impression that they were targeting families of those who had made sacrifices for the Panth. The best course to avoid such civil war was to deny power to the politically ambitious section.

The radicals associated with militant leader Gurbachan Singh Manochahal, All India Sikh Students Federation and Akali Dal (Amritsar) headed by former IPS officer Simranjit Singh Mann favoured participation. The logic advanced was using democratic tools for the achievement of Khalistan.

Some sort of credibility to this election boycotted by all the main Akali factions was secured by the government by roping in the Akali faction associated with Capt Amarinder Singh. He subsequently returned to the Congress, his mother party that he had left in protest against the storming of Darbar Sahib by the army in June 1984.

Yet another leader who was persuaded to put up candidates was former minister Sukhjinder Singh who at one time was a Khalistan supporter but backed out subsequently. Here is his justification for entering the poll fray:

> Having given a deliberate thought and serious consideration without prejudice and false prestige, I am veered to the idea that the recent decision of the boycott of Punjab election by various Akali factions is impolitic, illogic and erroneous and that no useful purpose will be served to the interests of the Sikhs, State of Punjab and even the militants through this negative approach. On the other hand, it will facilitate anti-Sikh forces to easily capture state apparatus and continue with the repressive policy already in vogue with greater vigour... The Sikhs are a Nation as such they are entitled to 'Right to Self Determination' according to the established principles of international law... the only solution to the existing Sikh problem is the formation of a State of their own as envisaged in the Sarbat Khalsa Resolution.
>
> World history is a testimony to the fact that this goal is achievable through struggle on two fronts. Since militants are already struggling on one front and Sikh masses do not want the other front i.e. Parliamentary Struggle to be left abandoned, therefore, according to the wishes of the people, we have come forward to fight on the Parliamentary front against the nefarious designs of the Congress to give relief and respite to the people from the clutches of the most arrogant, corrupt and repressive government machinery...I, therefore, invite all those who subscribe to this political ideology, irrespective of the party affiliation to join me in this sacred mission and get in touch with me without any loss of time.

The poll percentage in 1992 was 23.82.

The blunder that was the boycott of the February 1992 assembly elections by the mainstream Akali Dal was a turning point in the militant struggle that precipitated its countdown.

The security forces launched an all-out offensive to eliminate militant leaders one after the other backed by this manufactured democratic mandate within no time of the Beant Singh government taking over in the state.

The boycott coincided with fratricidal killings among the contesting and competing militant groups. Punjab was rid of political violence within about two years of this election. It is a different issue that Beant Singh himself became a victim of militant violence on August 31, 1995 at the main gate of the Punjab Civil Secretariat in Chandigarh that happened to be the last major action during that phase that had started in 1980.

Poll Boycott as State Tool

The intervention by way of boycott of elections in Punjab by Akalis and militant organizations has played a crucial role in the political discourse of the state from time to time beginning with the 1985 assembly elections held after the signing of the Punjab Accord between Prime Minister Rajiv Gandhi and Akali Dal chief Sant Harchand Singh Longowal. It was boycott by the United Akali Dal articulating the voice of the militants that facilitated into power the Akali Dal government headed by Surjit Singh Barnala.

The Barnala government sent security forces into the Darbar Sahib complex on April 30, 1986 following the declaration of Khalistan that amounted to providing ipso facto legitimacy to the decision of the Indira Gandhi government to attack the shrine in June 1984.[1]

Boycott of assembly election was back on the agenda of the militants before the aborted June 1991 assembly elections. The same discourse was carried forward to the February 1992 elections.

1991 Elections Boycott Discourse

The 1985 boycott paved the way for the implementation of the tacit understanding behind the Punjab Accord that was installation of the puppet Akali Dal government commanded by Surjit Singh Barnala. The main instrument in this strategy was Baba Joginder Singh and one cannot say whether he was conscious or not of the state design.

Baba Joginder Singh, father of Sant Jarnail Singh Bhindranwale, had been brought on the scene by the radicals as most of the senior Akali leaders were in jail after Operation Bluestar and he was perceived to be the rallying point. The outfit that Joginder Singh headed was known as the United Akali Dal. The formation of this new party was announced on May 2, 1985 along with a 7-member ad hoc committee headed by Akal Takht Jathedar Giani Kirpal Singh.

Keeping in view objections to Giani Kirpal Singh heading the committee, it was Simranjit Singh Mann who replaced him and in his absence, Baba Joginder Singh agreed to take over as convener. The All India Sikh Students Federation too had been revived as a political party.

As the election agenda came up at the UAD meeting, AISSF convener Harinder Singh Kahlon favoured participation on the logic that in case of getting a majority, resolution could be adopted in the assembly as a step towards achievement of the political objective.

It may be mentioned that going by the Sikh sentiment prevailing at that time in the backdrop of the army attack on the Darbar Sahib complex in June 1984, Operation Bluestar had reduced the traditional Akali Dal to irrelevance. The perception was that the candidates from the radical stream could capture power and this would not suit the government in Delhi. It was for this reason that a strategy was worked out to facilitate traditional Akalis into power.

The Sikhs by and large had rejected the Accord. Sant Longowal had been assassinated on August 20, 1985 within less than a month of signing the accord. The UAD dominated assembly could have adopted the Khalistan resolution and then sought recognition from other countries. The Centre feared such a situation again in 1991.

It was Baba Joginder Singh who was instrumental in forcing the boycott decision. He was fed the disinformation that Sant Bhindranwale was alive, having crossed over to Pakistan and that he had sent the message against joining the poll fray. The two persons who were made to believe and spread the information that Sant Bhindranwale was alive and kicking were Baba Joginder Singh and Baba Thakar Singh.

The decision to boycott elections was formalized at the next meeting at Jalandhar. Kahlon had made it clear that he would not contest but the party must not opt for boycott. He was overruled.

The two Babas, consciously or unconsciously, were playing into the hands of intelligence agencies from day one itself when they announced that Sant Bhindranwale was alive. The three players being manipulated by the Indian state at that time included both these Babas on one side of the Sikh religio-political spectrum and Barnala on the other.

It is now a well-known fact as brought out by former intelligence agency officials in their books that militancy in Punjab, especially during the post Operation Bluestar period was partly state designed.

The 1989 Lok Sabha election is relevant to the boycott narrative as this was one election in which the candidates supported by the radicals won with massive margins, resulting in total marginalization of the Akali Dal. Inder Kumar Gujral who later rose to be the Prime Minister was elected from Jalandhar.

The mass support at that time was an interesting phenomenon

as the fall of militancy was perceived to have started with Operation Blackthunder-II in May 1988 during which the so-called Khalistan warriors had defiled the sanctum sanctorum filling people with revulsion against this section. The one important aspect of the post-1988 period was that militancy was dominated by the Babbar Khalsa and associated bodies.

Out of the total 13 seats, three seats had gone to the Congress. Simranjit Singh Mann won from Tarn Taran with a record margin of more than four lakh votes. This was the area which was one of the worst hit by state repression, and also by militancy. However, Mann's shoulders could not carry this heavy mandate and he succumbed.

There is yet another aspect of the selection of candidates for the 1989 Lok Sabha election. Bhai Manjit Singh, who had been released from Jodhpur jail, took over as the AISSF chief.

Originally, it was Bhai Manjit Singh who was to contest from Tarn Taran as his village Bhure Kone was part of that constituency. Mann's name had been proposed from Patiala. That was not to be.

Mann's sister Daljit Kaur met Manjit and pleaded that her brother be fielded from Tarn Taran as this was perceived to be the safest seat for him. Manjit agreed and he decided against contesting himself. Atinder Pal Singh, another militant leader who was also in jail, was put up from Patiala. This was the only election in which the AISSF supported candidates won with huge margins.

Manjit was also approached by a family member of Chaudhary Devi Lal from Haryana and offered Rs. 20 lakhs for a ticket from Punjab. He refused. Devi Lal was close to Punjab Akali Dal leader Parkash Singh Badal. Devi Lal contested from Ferozepur but lost to Dhian Singh Mand supported by AISSF.

The agenda of election boycott entered the discourse of radical politics again at the time of the aborted June 1991 assembly election. The 1992 election boycott by the mainstream Akalis too was rooted in the 1991 decision.

There was no central command representing the radical organizations and the issue of participation in the assembly election further sharpened the division in the otherwise fragmented radical political stream. While a major section of militants favoured boycott, one faction was for using the electoral platform as a tool to carry forward the struggle. It may be mentioned that there were several groups that were functioning at the local level all over Punjab. It was this situation that resulted in the gunning down of 29 Akali candidates of various shades and the election was cancelled hours before the polling was to start on June 22. The election was announced on April 12, 1991 and notification issued on April 18. The last date for filing nomination papers was April 26. The Akalis too were in disarray while the political discourse was being dictated by the militants.

Mann announced at the Baisakhi conference on April 14 at Talwandi Sabo where the boycott call was first given by the Babbar Khalsa and associates that elections would be contested on the agenda of a sovereign and independent state.[2] He was hackled by the supporters of the militants. The Babbar Akali Dal in Chandigarh reiterated the call for poll boycott on April 24 on the logic that the elections would divide the Sikhs and weaken the struggle.

The Khalistan Commando Force led by Wassan Singh Zaffarwal on April 24 opposed the boycott line saying, "It would be a big mistake and defeat for the Sikh movement to adopt the boycott line this time too. The militant movement had been let down by the Barnala government and it was possible that it would be let down again by the so-called Akali leaders and their supporters unless the candidates put up by them were challenged and defeated."[3]

Gurbachan Singh Manochahal asserted on May 21 that the assembly elections would be used as a vote for Khalistan, saying the Sikhs were anxious to "throw away the shackles of slavery" and that the elections would be used as a weapon to achieve that objective.[4]

The Babbar Akali Dal, formed by people sympathetic to Babbar Khalsa, attacked Manochahal, saying he and Manjit had been trapped by the intelligence agencies. The party's logic was that no Sikh government could stay in power under the Indian Constitution. This line was in consonance with the decision taken by the Babbar Khalsa and others to go in for poll boycott. For Mann, the agenda for elections was to be the sovereign Sikh state that was to be a buffer between India and Pakistan.

The first meeting on the agenda of the 1991 assembly elections was held in Chandigarh some time in April that was attended by Sukhdev Singh and Wadhawa Singh from Babbar Khalsa and leaders from several other factions. Sukhdev apprehended multiplicity of militants' candidates keeping in view the clash of interests among various groups. The militants were a divided lot even otherwise. Under this situation, he was not in favour of participation in the democratic process. Senior journalist Karamjit Singh, who was in that circle, however, was of the opinion that the decision should be taken on principles rather than being driven by other reasons.

The perception among pro-boycott militant leaders was that as

Khalistan would be a reality in the not too distant a future, there was no need to jump into the electoral fray. Here was a major miscalculation. The next meeting was held after a few days at Amritsar which was also attended by Major General Narinder Singh (retd) and militant leader Gurjant Singh Budhsinghwala. The dominant view at this meeting tilted towards boycott. However, no final decision was taken.

Babbar Akali Dal president Kartar Singh Narang opposed participation in the election process on the logic that free and fair polls would not be possible under the prevailing state terrorism. He was addressing a gathering at Bir Baba Budha at Jhabal near Amritsar.[5]

It was around this period that Dr. Sohan Singh returned from Pakistan while Daljit continued to stay back. Dr. Sohan Singh was in favour of participation in the democratic political process. The main militant leaders in Pakistan at that time included Wadhawa, Daljit, Zaffarwal and Kanwar Singh Dhami. They had met before the return of Dr. Sohan Singh to India. Also present at that meeting was an official from the ISI.

The ISI official was for participation in the polls by setting up some front while others except Dr. Sohan Singh held views to the contrary. Dr. Sohan Singh decided to return to India. The person officiating as assistant to Dr. Sohan Singh at that time was Harjit Singh from the Sikh Students Federation. He accompanied Dr. Sohan Singh to India. He was to keep an eye on his activities.

Ludhiana was the venue of the third meeting held at the residence of Mohkam Singh from Akhand Kirtani Jatha that was attended by Sukhdev Singh, Dr. Sohan Singh, Gurjant Singh, Maj Gen Narinder Singh (retd), Talwinder Singh Parmar and Karamjit who was the common link in all these meetings.

Talwinder questioned the poll boycott logic while Sukhdev echoed the boycott line. At this stage, Dr. Sohan Singh walked out in protest. However, Maj Gen Singh and Karamjit brought him back. Finally, a stamp was put on the poll boycott decision.

In continuation with this line, yet another meeting was held at Amritsar which, among others, was also attended by Paramjit Singh Panjwar. It may be mentioned that Dr. Sohan Singh used to stay in touch with the contacts of Panjwar who had been functioning on the two sides of the border. It was he who pressured Dr. Sohan Singh to toe the boycott line. Daljit, who was also contacted in Pakistan, too agreed. The decision was now final.

Daljit and Sukhdev never met each other.

Three different press notes were issued by these organizations in

April 1991 advocating boycott of elections. Stressing this line, the first press note stated:

> This bait of elections thrown by the Brahmins is a testing time for the militants. In case you have decided not to take the bait and you have no conscious or unconscious, direct or indirect role in the deal that is on in Delhi, then we militants, despite differences, are part of the eternal unity. We are eager to know your stand on this issue as the discerning Khalsa Panth is now looking towards us as to how we react to the offer. In case you become victim of this move of the Brahmin, then the Khalsa Panth has a right to expect that valiant and ever-awakened militant leadership is still to take birth.

The boycott call was articulated in *Awaz-e-Punjab*, the two-page handwritten mouthpiece of the militant organizations associated with the Babbar Khalsa whose only three issues were brought out. This pamphlet was distributed at the political conference on Baisakhi on April 13, 1991 at Takht Damdama Sahib, Talwandi Sabo. These militant organizations also gave a call for setting up 'mini Khalistans' by way of organizing Khalsa Panchayats in villages. No member of any militant organization was to be a part of the Khalsa panchayats. All disputes, even murder cases, were to be adjudicated upon by these panchayats. The effort was to ensure complete boycott of the state administration. At the same time, dissolution of the existing panchayats was part of the design as it was stressed that all the elected members must resign within a month.

The problem with the militants was that they were not talking of the polls being held by the Indian state but by the Brahmins (read rulers). The fight was supposed to be against the Indian state and not any particular community but this distinction always remained blurred. The militants or those providing them the so-called ideological lead did not draw clear cut battle lines. Half the battle is lost when one cannot identify and quantify one's enemies. The perception on both these major issues suffered not only from total distortion and perverted thinking but also lack of ideological framework.

Indira Gandhi was a Brahmin married to a Parsi. One of her daughters-in-law was a Sikh and the other a Christian. By no stretch of the imagination could the family of this "Brahmani," as she used to be referred to by Sant Bhindranwale in his speeches, be fitted in the traditional communal framework going by this diversity in her family. The problem with those trying to guide the militant struggle was that they failed to analyse the character of the Indian state which is not defined by "Banias (mercantile class) and Brahmins" (The upper

Hindu priestly class whose members do not enjoy that high status in Punjab). These organizations appealed to Damdami Taksal acting chief Baba Thakar Singh to set up a coordination committee to ensure poll boycott. However, Damdami Taksal refused to play this role.

Dr. Sohan Singh parted company with the Babbars after his return to India in May 1991. The Panthic Committee associated with his name was reorganized. In the reorganized panel, Daljit and one Shahbaz Singh replaced Babbar leaders Mahal Singh and Wadhawa Singh. Shahbaz was the name given to human rights activist Jaspal Singh Dhillon.

The press note released to this effect on June 3 spelled out differences with the Babbar Khalsa. It was stated that the Babbar Khalsa had refused to withdraw one of its two representatives as had been agreed earlier. This panel opposed the floating of a political front by Babbar Khalsa that was known as the Babbar Akali Dal. Moreover, the Babbar Khalsa had failed to dissolve the 'government in exile' based in the UK. This statement was released in the names of Panthic Committee members Dr. Sohan Singh, Harinder Singh Sultanwind, Satinderpal Singh, Daljit Singh and Shahbaz Singh and militant leaders Gurjant Singh Budhsinghwala (Khalistan Liberation Force), Paramjit Singh (Khalistan Commando Force), Rachhpal Singh Chhandran (Bhindranwale Tiger Force) and Daljit Singh (Sikh Students Federation). It was silent on elections.[6]

The Babbar Khalsa hit back on June 5, accusing Dr. Sohan Singh of unilaterally taking a decision to enter into negotiations with Prime Minister Chandra Shekhar while reiterating that it was opposed to participation in elections under the Constitution.[7]

While these militant organizations gave the call for boycott of June 22, 1991 elections, a section of the militants owing allegiance to Gurbachan Singh Manochahal, the AISSF (Bhai Manjit Singh) and Akali Dal (Mann) decided to jump into the fray, including the traditional Shiromani Akali Dal. The Congress, the CPI and the CPI (M) boarded the boycott wagon, though for different reasons. However, the CPI revised its decision on June 15 as only seven out of 25 members of its executive committee voted for boycott. The pro-boycott brigade was led by senior party leader Satya Pal Dang. The BJP too decided to stay away with the decision having been announced on June 13.

When Badal Wanted to Join AISSF in 1991

The traditional Akali leaders had realized the futility of contesting elections in case even a section of the militant organizations decided to participate. They initially made a beeline for Manjit who was also the front man again for the Manochahal camp.

The most important Akali leader who pleaded for a ticket with Manjit was Parkash Singh Badal, then two-time chief minister.

"In fact, Badal sought to be admitted to the AISSF saying a Sikh, by definition, is a student all through life," Manjit disclosed years later in February 2017. Badal also suggested only those persons should be given tickets who had made sacrifices for the Panth.

The Akali leader who played the crucial role of a mediator at that time between Manjit and Badal was former minister Sukhjinder Singh.

By the time Badal approached him, less than 12 seats were left for which candidates had not been finalized. Manjit was coming under pressure.

According to Manjit, Sukhjinder and his son Sukhpal Singh Khaira were finally taken to Manochahal who was underground. Some other leaders including Harminder Singh Gill, Ghuman and Professor Sarup Singh were also there. Sukhpal used to trim his beard to which Manochahal objected. Sukhjinder had also sought a ticket for his son.

Manochahal agreed to give 10 tickets to Akali Dal. Badal wanted the Majitha constituency also among these 10 seats. However, Manochahal backed out the next day. Badal suspected that it was Manjit who had sabotaged this arrangement. Badal then put up his own candidates.

Manochahal's agenda was to get the Khalistan resolution passed in the assembly as winning the election was not an issue under that situation. This got leaked out and the centre called off the election hours before start of polling.

Boycott Discourse the During Post-June 1991 Period

The boycott narrative continued even after the June 22 election was aborted at the last minute. Now it was Tohra who expressed himself against participation during an informal interaction. He was not the SGPC chief at that time as he had yielded that space to Baldev Singh Sibia.[8] He favoured setting up a joint committee to fight state repression.

The predominant view to boycott elections was articulated again by various militant groups who sent their opinions in writing to the Anandpur Sahib conclave of various Akali and Sikh Student Federation factions and human rights organizations convened by Sibia on September 1, 1991.

One of the persons who worked at the grassroots in favour of poll boycott happened to be Bharti Kisan Union President Ajmer Singh Lakhowal. BKU (Lakhowal) pressed for boycott at the September 1, 1991 meeting and subsequently zealously campaigned to implement this agenda. This faction of the farmers' organization articulated concerns of the militants and human rights organizations for some time. Rather this was the main vehicle to carry forward the boycott campaign. Yet at another level, it was Babbar Akali Dal President Narang who had been actively advocating this line among the Akali faction. This Akali Dal faction later phased out as it lacked any following and had failed to evolve as an effective front organization of the Babbar Khalsa.

It was the nine-hour meeting on September 1 at Anandpur Sahib that was quoted by Badal on January 5, 1992 while favouring boycott. The only Akali faction that participated in the election was Akali Dal (Kabul Singh) of which Captain Amarinder Singh was the dominating leader but managed to win only three seats. The boycott was formally announced by the four main Akali factions at Ludhiana on January 19, 1992. The election was held on February 19 and the results declared on February 21. It was a clean sweep for the Congress in this farcical election.

One statement received at the September 1 meeting was in the name of Khalistan Commando Force chief Paramjit Singh Panjwar, Khalistan Liberation Force chief Gurjant Singh Budhsinghwala, Bhindranwale Tiger Force of Khalistan chief Rachhpal Singh Chhandran and Sikh Students Federation president Daljit Singh. The joint statement stated: "We expect from you to first ratify rejection of the constitution from this land representing Sikh sovereignty and freedom and announce that you would not even dream of contesting parliamentary or assembly elections under it."[9]

The Babbar Khalsa statement was released in the names of Sukhdev Singh, Talwinder Singh, Wadhawa Singh, Mehal Singh and Kulwant Singh. The call was to "pass a resolution in favour of Khalistan after announcing boycott of elections forever and rejection of the constitution."

Then there is yet another articulation under the names of Panjwar, Daljit Singh, Chhandran and Budhsinghwala. It may be mentioned that some of these names had appeared in other statements too. This statement too called for election boycott saying, "We can't even dream of contesting parliamentary or assembly election under the Indian Constitution."

The two persons who initially opposed the poll boycott at this meeting were Badal and Capt Amarinder Singh. After some time, Badal came out of the hall and when he returned after a few minutes, he was a changed person and joined the boycott chorus. It was at this meeting that a nine-member committee headed by human rights leader Jaspal Singh Dhillon was constituted for unity among various Akali factions and Sikh organizations.

K.P.S. Gill and Poll Boycott

According to the sources, at another level, the strategy to make Akali Dal boycott the polls was fine-tuned by the police chief K.P.S. Gill to facilitate non-Akali government to power.

> There was also a realization to build consensus against terrorism among political parties. Political actors also realized that democracy was the only antidote to terrorism. The earlier redundant moderate political parties faced the dilemma of democracy, that is, it would lead to revival of competition for legislative power. It is pertinent to note that there was an understanding to encourage Akalis to boycott the elections and allow the Congress to form the government and fight terrorism...This generally unknown aspect of the 1992 "boycott" of assembly elections by Akali Dal came to light through our interactions with several key political actors, importantly, K.P.S. Gill, the police chief of Punjab in August and September 1991. Gill was the ardent supporter of building consensus against terrorism and was convinced that an unhealthy competition should be avoided. Hence the boycott by the Akalis was encouraged and perhaps engineered...There was an understanding to encourage Akalis to boycott the elections and allow the Congress to form the government and fight terrorism.[10]

This period of interaction coincides with timing of Anandpur Sahib meeting.

It is pertinent to mention here that a statement was issued in 1990 by academics who included Prof. Manoranjan Mohanty and Dr. Pramod Kumar stressing the need for democratic intervention in Punjab affairs.

It stated:

> While early elections are a must, elections should not be seen as the only democratic exercise nor should they be restricted to sending representatives to the Lok Sabha and the state assembly. Every other elected body, right up to the village level, should choose their own representatives, in what can only be a state-wide gigantic but vigorous and health-giving democratic exercise. Incidentally, any opposition to holding elections now or in the immediate future suffers from an inbuilt flaw and also contains a danger. The danger comes from stalling a democratic process compounded by

> shutting out popular participation. For this it is imperative to restore people's confidence and create conditions for removing fear psychosis for holding free and fair elections...We believe that we are on the threshold of a historic possibility in Punjab. We urge that this opportunity must not be lost. This is time therefore to take comprehensive democratic initiatives involving a set of interdependent measures. Nothing short of genuine and fearless participation of common people in strengthening the democratic political process in the state can help resolve the contemporary crisis.

This thesis of the design behind boycott is supported by a chain of political developments during that period. There was another section that was for elections and opposed the boycott move when the meetings for the boycott of the February 1992 polls started. However, the strategy to get the elections boycotted by the mainstream Akali Dal had already been unleashed.

Lakhowal's BKU turned out to be the most potent tool in the process. Besides the Akali Dal, it was this organization that had a following across Punjab and that too among the Sikh peasantry. BKU had submitted its views at the Anandpur Sahib meeting in writing. It stated, "Participating in elections is meaningless till the resolution of the Punjab problem. Therefore, elections should be boycotted. The representatives of the organizations in the parliament and other such committees should exhibit a spirit of sacrifice and resign to contribute to the ongoing struggle. Those leaders who have sought government protection should return their security." The last sentence was targeted at the traditional Akali leaders.

The decision to boycott the election was announced by Baldev Singh Sibia after the meeting.

> At a stormy 9-hour meeting which was attended by all the Akali Dals, the action committee (of the Sikh organizations) decided to boycott elections till the state repression was stopped, political prisoners released, black laws withdrawn, paramilitary forces recalled and atrocities on Sikhs outside Punjab stopped. Briefing newsmen after the meeting, the SGPC President, Mr Baldev Singh Sibia, said the meeting was of the opinion that the Sikhs were being subjected to police repression without parallel even during the Moghul period, the Sikh youth were being killed in fake encounters and the families of the militants were being eliminated.[11]

The one militant leader who vociferously opposed the election boycott was Manochahal. His views were conveyed at a meeting of the representatives from various Akali factions, and All India Sikh Students Federation. The leaders present included Badal and Baba Joginder Singh.

Manochahal's logic proved to be prophetic. According to Bhai Manjit Singh, Manochahal was of the opinion that this strategy would finish the militants both physically and politically. He was clear that the militant struggle could not be carried forward without political support from the Sikh masses. A front organization was a precondition for the success of the militant struggle. Elections could be one of the tools to be used by the front organizations.

The militant movement was almost wiped out virtually within a year after the formation of the Congress government. Akali Dal (Mann) and AISSF too favoured contesting the election. It was the boycott line that prevailed.

Panjwar's Threat for Boycott from Pakistan

One of the militant leaders whose threatening intervention dictated the poll boycott decision at the final stage was Paramjit Singh Panjwar based in Lahore in Pakistan at that time. The day was January 3, 1992 when a meeting of various Akali factions and AISSF was going on at Punjab Bhawan in Chandigarh. Those present included Badal, Mann, Narang, Baba Joginder Singh, Bhai Manjit Singh and others. Manjit got a message from the Punjab Bhawan reception about the telephone call. It was Panjwar on the other side. The threat had the desired effect. He repeated this warning again before the formal announcement.

Manjit conveyed to this author off the record while returning to the meeting hall that elections would be boycotted and the decision would be formally announced at the appropriate time.

> One of the leaders who attended the meeting said on condition of anonymity that the meeting decided to boycott the elections in the prevailing situation. He said the decision would stand even if the government accepted the four demands of the Akalis including withdrawal of the army, end to police excesses, punishment to those guilty of November 1984 riots and release of arrested Sikh youths as these were only for creating conducive atmosphere for initiating a dialogue to find a solution to Punjab problem.[12]

The formal decision was announced by Badal at a meeting of various Akali factions and AISSF at Ludhiana on January 18, 1992 after announcement by the election commission. Bhai Manjit Singh sat next to Badal when he announced the boycott decision.

Manjit personally was for contesting elections at the time of the Chandigarh meeting on the logic that the boycott would prove to be suicidal for the Sikh struggle. Like Manochahal, he too was for using the election as the stepping stone for the achievement of the political objective. He succeeded in getting this meeting postponed with

Ludhiana being the venue of the second meeting despite the threat from Panjwar. Manjit was aligned with Manochahal who was for use of the ballot box but at the same time wanted every candidate to confirm in writing at the Akal Takht to adopt the Khalistan resolution in the assembly.

He decided against attending this meeting. However, the leaders from Babbar Khalsa, SSF chief Daljit Singh Bittu and Panjwar started putting pressure on him. And finally, it was Baba Thakar Singh who was brought into the picture who was accompanied by Bhai Mohkam Singh and Gajjan Singh. Baba Thakar Singh opted for an emotional approach to clinch the issue and asked Manjit: "Are you my son or not?" Bhai Manjit Singh gave in and decided to attend the Ludhiana meeting. According to him, both Badal and Simranjit Mann were already in favour of the boycott. Manjit had been left with no option after he had given an undertaking to Baba Thakar Singh as all the others were for boycott.

Here is yet another version.

Dr. Sohan Singh, Daljit Bittu, Babbar Khalsa leader Wadhawa Singh and Akal Federation chief Kanwar Singh Dhami were in Pakistan before the election. Babbar Khalsa chief Sukhdev Singh, Gurjant Singh Budhsinghwala and Talwinder Singh Parmar who were in India favoured election boycott as per the 1991 decision. However, Dr. Sohan Singh was in favour of participation and so was Pakistan.

The ISI officials met Dr. Sohan Singh and wanted him to organize some sort of political front for which he decided to return to India. Daljit too crossed over to India during that period.

Dr. Sohan Singh had a meeting with the militant leaders to persuade them to contest but they were stubborn. There were heated arguments. Gurjant threatened that whoever participated would be killed. According to one version, Gurjant had been seen coming out of Badal's residence in Chandigarh earlier. Dr. Sohan Singh finally gave in.

As per the information available with the insiders, Daljit told Mann to boycott, Paramjit Panjwar to Manjit and Babbars to Tohra and Mann.

The Indian government, in an attempt to provide some sort of legitimacy, also tried to rope in the Akali Dal (Babbar) and offered Rs. 2 crores to Kartar Singh Narang besides the release of his son arrested in the transistor bomb blasts in Delhi buses. All the candidates were also to be provided financial help. He discussed the proposal with Wadhawa Singh who rejected it.

Tohra had at one stage lobbied with Babbars and others in favour of participation in the polls. He contacted them through his young associate Karnail Singh Panjoli and the meeting was fixed at a place near Shahabad about 20 kms from Ambala Cantt. He was of the opinion that boycott would prove to be disastrous for the struggle.

He pleaded with the Babbars that the poll boycott would leave the field open to the Congress. "Don't bring in the Congress," he pleaded. It may be mentioned that at one stage, he favoured poll boycott.

Those present included Sukhdev, Wadhawa, Balwinder Singh Jatana and Kulwant Singh.

The top militant leaders were targeted one after the other within days of the Congress forming the government in the state. Tohra was not wrong. Beant Singh opted for allout suppression of even democratic activity by the Akalis.

The next strategy after forming the government was to get democratic legitimacy for this government. This was achieved through elections to the urban local bodies. This was part of the overall strategy. Akali Dal participated in these elections but the results were rigged, not the polling as such. In the election to the panchayat bodies, the candidates of an Akali shade were not even allowed to contest.

Meeting at Mehta Chowk

There is yet another version according to which, the first meeting on the election issue was held at Damdami Taksal headquarters at Mehta Chowk that was attended by all six Akali factions including Akali Dal (Mann), Baba Joginder Singh Akali Dal, Bhai Manjit Singh faction of the AISSF, Babbar Akali Dal and Badal and Jagdev Singh Talwandi factions. Senior Akali leaders Ranjit Singh Brahmpura, Ujagar Singh Sekhwan and Parkash Singh Majithia were present, besides representatives of Damdami Taksal. Three more such meetings were held subsequently. Besides Taksal, those who favoured polls included Bhai Manjit Singh and Mann. However, Badal, Talwandi and Narang pressed for boycott. Damdami Taksal, AISSF and Jagjit Singh Rode group opted for participation in the polls while Sukhdev, Daljit and Gurjant were for boycott.

It was around this period that Mohkam tried to convince Panjwar of the need to join the election process but he expressed his helplessness. Gurjant finally threatened very coolly: "We will kill whoever participates in elections." This was what Panjwar had conveyed to Manjit.

The decision proved to be suicidal for the militants.

At another level, Badal would not have been the chief minister in 1992 as there were several others powerful aspirants. Badal had exercised the right choice. After all, politics is the game of exercising the right choice at the right time.

Badal and Babbars

Several such under currents characterize the Sikh struggle similar to Badal approaching Bhai Manjit Singh with the proposal to function unitedly under democratic domain. Badal had got in touch with Babbar Khalsa leader Wadhawa Singh too some time in 1995 after the assassination of Chief Minister Beant Singh.

Badal had the apprehensions that the militants might threaten poll boycott again and he wanted to sort out that issue before the 1996 Lok Sabha polls. The message Badal conveyed was simple and in unambiguous terms. He stated: "The Sikhs have suffered much. Lok Sabha elections are not far off. Please don't disrupt the process this time. We will cooperate at every level and adjust your candidates. Let us form the government." Badal wanted assurance on peaceful elections.

He offered one Lok Sabha and 10 assembly seats to Babbar Khalsa nominees.

Further talks, however, were to be held overseas involving one representative from each side.

According to the people privy to this interaction, the deal was finalized. Before putting the final seal on this deal, Wadhawa consulted Dal Khalsa chief Gajinder Singh. Badal's representative proposed that Pakistan should be part of the deal indirectly to ensure violence free polls.

These talks took place between September and December 1995. However, Badal changed his attitude suddenly after the arrest of Jagtar Singh Hawara and others in the case of the assassination of Chief Minister Beant Singh on August 31, 1995 by human bomb Dilawar Singh. This assassination had been carried out by Babbar Khalsa.

Sukha, Jinda Letter

An important development before decline of the militant movement started after the installation of the Beant Singh government was the hanging of Harjinder Singh Jinda and Sukhjinder Singh Sukha on October 9, 1992 in the assassination case of former army chief General A.S. Vaidya. Their bhog (prayer) ceremony was performed at the Akal Takht on October 18 where they were declared martyrs of the Sikh nation. Their death anniversary continues to be observed at the Akal Takht by the Shiromani Gurdwara Parbandhak Committee. They walked to the gallows like heroes.

These two developments, the other being the poll boycott, brought about a paradigm shift in the militant movement.

Punjab and Chandigarh got terrified like never before.

What triggered this panic was the letter released under the signatures of Sukha and Jinda, the detailed excerpts of which, about one page, appeared in *The Indian Express* on July 27, 1990. The way it was released created a total scare on the one hand and electrified the militant movement, though briefly, on the other. Punjab came under an unprecedented fear psychosis. At one level, this letter was part of the inner struggle among the militants.

This letter had actually been planned when the Amarjit Singh Chawla and Rajinder Singh Mehta faction of the Sikh Students Federation announced Jinda as the chief of this outfit as part of the design to sideline Daljit Singh Bittu. He was startled. A meeting was facilitated between him and Karamjit at Gurdwara Dukhniwaran Sahib, Patiala. Two letters were planned by them as part of the strategic move. Apart from this one, the second was to be released later in the name of Satwant Singh and Kehar Singh, lodged in Tihar Jail, Delhi and later hanged in the case of Indira Gandhi's assassination.

The basic problem was how to get the same carried by newspapers verbatim. It was Daljit who took upon himself this responsibility as only the fear of the gun could force the Chandigarh newspapers and news agencies, apart from correspondents of other papers stationed there, to carry the complete text.

Karamjit undertook the responsibility of drafting this letter. He went through letters written by Shaheed Bhagat Singh from jail, besides other sources. Karamjit took about 15 days to finish the job and consulted books from *The Tribune* library as he was Assistant Editor with the *Punjabi Tribune*. This letter reflected extensive knowledge of the writer on both the Sikh doctrine as well as Marxism. While Onkar Singh, brother of Jathedar Prof. Manjit Singh, typed the letter, it was Dr. Gurbhagat Singh of Punjabi University, Patiala, who translated it into English. However, only the handwritten signed Punjabi version was released along with the threat letter. Each page of the letter dated May 4, 1990 carried their signatures.

Here is an important aspect how this letter was smuggled into Pune jail to get it signed from Sukha and Jinda and the newspapers were forced to carry it verbatim.

Justice Ajit Singh Bains (retd), who headed the Punjab Human Rights Organization, had a good rapport with Karamjit who broached the subject with him. Justice Bains agreed to accompany Karamjit to Pune in January end or early February 1990. They were given just Rs. 5,000 besides air tickets with the understanding that they would go by air and return by rail. Amarjit Chawla and a brother of Jinda also happened to travel that day to Pune by the same flight they boarded from Delhi.

It was normal practice that intelligence agencies used to track Sikh passengers after they landed in Pune. They first went to a gurdwara and then moved to a hotel for the night to reach the jail the next morning. That happened to be the day on which relatives and other acquaintances were allowed to meet prisoners. Chawla and family members of Sukha and Jinda were also there. Karamjit, however, wanted to meet them separately. He approached the jail superintendent and disclosed his professional identity. He was refused permission. Justice Bains had no problem due to his status of being a retired high court judge. Karamjit handed over to him the envelop carrying the statement that was in Punjabi. On second thoughts, he took it back.

As Karamjit was leaving the room, the jail superintendent suggested a way out and it was to seek permission from the trial court that had convicted them. He did not suspect the motive. Karamjit took a three-wheeler and reached the court 15 kms away and talked to their two lawyers. However, much to his misfortune, the lawyers were on strike that day. They said they could move the court after seeking permission from their bar president. Finally, they took Karamjit to the judge concerned. As he was told that they wanted his permission for Karamjit to meet Sukha and Jinda, the judge got scared and without saying anything, retired to his chamber. Then he sent his peon with a message allowing Karamjit to meet them.

As he reached there again, the intelligence agencies took him to a tent. An intelligence agency officer talked to him about his antecedents. By that time, Justice Bains came out. Karamjit suddenly changed his mind and they both returned. Chawla did them a favour by buying them return air tickets. The letter was then sent by post. That was how they got it signed.

One part of the intricate and risky operation was over. Then started the next and more important part and that was the publication of the letter verbatim, something that had never happened earlier in the history of the Indian media, at least in this part. It was a 10-page handwritten text with about 550 words on each page. It also carried a four-page addendum.

The issue was discussed at a meeting of the four militant organizations led by Babbar Khalsa including Khalistan Commando Force and Sikh Students Federation under whose name this letter was to be sent. This letter was accompanied by a separate threatening letter addressed to every journalist or editor to whom it was delivered, with complete information about his/her leanings and professional conduct, to create terror. The Babbar Khalsa took this responsibility and entrusted this duty to its regional commander Balwinder Singh Jatana who belonged to Ropar district and whose entire family was later wiped out, including his handicapped sister the very night when Chandigarh Senior Superintendent of Police Sumedh Singh Saini survived a bomb attack in Sector 17, Chandigarh. That inhuman operation was carried out by Nihang Ajit Singh Poohla and his men who were working for Saini.

However, the attack on Sani had not been carried out by Jatana and his associates but by the Khalistan Liberation Force with which militants including Devinder Pal Singh Bhullar were associated. One of the Akhand Kirtani Jatha members who was in custody of Chandigarh police had earlier confessed during interrogation that it was Jatana who was planning the attack. It was for this reason that retaliation was immediate although Jatana was not involved.

The letter was delivered as per the plans. *The Indian Express* used almost the entire text on one page with some deletions. *The Tribune* carried about one-eighth of the text. *Punjabi Tribune* Editor Shingara Singh Bhullar consulted Karamjit on how to go about it. The *Punjabi Tribune* carried a major portion of the letter. The drama started the next day.

The Tribune and *The Indian Express* were the only two English dailies published from Chandigarh at that time. Jatana was furious. He went to meet *The Tribune* General Manager S.D. Bhambri at his residence but not from the front door. He climbed over the boundary wall and knocked at his back door. He threatened to carry the entire text in *The Tribune* group of papers with an apology on the front page for not complying with the instructions on the first day.

An emergent meeting of The Tribune Trust was held amidst tight security in the office. The militant struggle was to enter a new phase. *The Tribune* acted as required while *Dainik Tribune* carried a full statement in instalments.

As the full text appeared in *The Tribune*, the state was engulfed in fear psychosis due to the shock waves it triggered. The Fourth Estate crumbled overnight. There was yet another significant aspect. In the words of Karamjit, the ideological powerhouse had been unleashed with the publication of this letter. The letter was perhaps the best articulation of the aims and objectives of the militant struggle.

This was the also the time when mistrust took roots in the movement, especially between Daljit and Babbars. General Narinder Singh and Karamjit were to sort out the irritants. It was resolved that the Babbars would be consulted on all policy matters, especially while issuing statements.

The press notes used to be posted from the Sector 17 post office and later from Kharar as a precautionary measure during that period. The intelligence agencies were so alert that any person buying more than three or four newspapers from vendors in Sector 22 used to be put under watch. This sector was the main distribution point for newspapers.

Jinda and Sukha were hanged on October 9, 1992 in the Pune jail. Their last wish was that sweets should be distributed in the jail after their hanging.

ENDNOTES

1. Jagtar Singh. (2011). *Khalistan Struggle: A Non-movement*. Delhi: Aakar Books, pp. 258-59.
2. April 15, 1991. *The Indian Express.*
3. April 25, 1991. *The Indian Express.*
4. May 22, 1991. The Indian Express.
5. April 15, 1991. *The Times of India.*
6. June 4, 1991. *Daily Ajit.*
7. June 6, 1991. *The Times of India.*
8. July 18, 1991. *The Indian Express.*
9. Press Note.
10. Pramod Kumar. (2017). "Punjab Politics-Contesting Identities and Forging Coalitions", *Economic and Political Weekly*, Vol. 52, No 3.
11. September 2, 1991. *The Indian Express.*
12. January 5, 1992. *The Indian Express.*

12

Not Rooted Out

Punjab represents an interesting paradox. This state is least suitable for armed struggle but the phenomenon of violent political conflicts here is cyclical.

The terrain here is homogeneously plain and the socio-religious fabric despite being rooted in a composite culture is characterized by demographic heterogeneity. Both these dimensions are hostile to militancy associated with any religious formation.

The social fabric in Indian Punjab comprises mainly Sikhs and Hindus and the Dalit identity assertion is a recent phenomenon. The Dalits, otherwise, are associated mainly with the Sikh or the Hindu formations.

The Sikhs constitute about 64 per cent with the Hindus being about 35 per cent. The Dalits are included in these demographic boundaries.

It is the Sikh section that has a long history of struggles in pre-partition Punjab unlike the Hindu formation that is characterized mostly by socio-political passivity during that long period. The Sikhs fought their own battles for survival. The Sikhs were at peace for such a long time only during the reign of Maharaja Ranjit Singh whose government functioned as Sarkar-e-Khalsa.

The Sikhs did not compromise to their subjection by the British in 1849 unlike the two other demographic formations in the region. Maharaj Singh had started mobilizing Sikhs even before the start of the Second Anglo-Sikh War in 1849.[1,2]

(The Namdharis too had started the struggle for the Sikh Raj. The Namdhari or Kuka movement was started by a Sikh preacher Baba Ram Singh, which was originally religious in content. However, in 1869, the Kukas of Ferozepur proclaimed the Sikh Raj.[3] Baba Ram Singh was arrested in 1872 and deported to jail in Burma where he died in 1885. The gurdwara liberation started in 1920. Sikhs were the first to oppose the Pakistan Resolution in 1940.)

It is this historical background that continues to impact the religio-political dynamics characterizing Indian Punjab post-partition. The Sikh concerns are perceived to be disruptions by the other section of population. Even the demand for declaring Amritsar as a holy city on the pattern of some Hindu pilgrimage centres was opposed by the Punjabi Hindus.

From the time of the Sikh-Nirankari clash of 1978, the positioning by the Sikh bodies were perceived to be a threat to peace by the majority of Hindu leaders. The Hindus became the target as the leaders started identifying with the forces with which the Sikhs had come into confrontation, despite the fact that it was not a Sikh-Hindu tension.

This precisely is the reason that the peaceful agitation launched under the banner of Bargari Insaaf Morcha in June, 2018 demanding action against culprits of sacrilege of the Guru Granth Sahib came to be viewed as a threat to peace by the non-Sikh sections.[4]

This demographic characteristic is the antithesis to militancy associated with one faith. The Hindu formation in Punjab completely identifies itself with the Indian state. The militant struggle got isolated from a major section of the Sikh population too after a stage.

These two are among the main factors this armed struggle had to confront and was contained through unprecedented brutal and unconstitutional police methods. These methods succeeded in the absence of mass support. The struggle in Kashmir is backed by strong mass support.

There is one important dimension leading to the steep fall of militancy and this was its brutalization. This was in the context of the kidnapping of M.L. Manchanda, station director of All India Radio at Patiala on May 18, 1992. He was beheaded by his kidnappers from the Babbar Khalsa militant outfit and his head was displayed in the Rajpura market.

Yet another factor was the lack of mass support from the Sikhs to this struggle. Despite hundreds of killings in fake encounters and forced disappearances, there were few mass protests. Moreover, no effective leader emerged in this domain after the killing of Sant Jarnail Singh Bhindranwale.

The 1989 Lok Sabha election was the first mass assertion in support of the militants in which almost all the candidates supported by the AISSF won. These candidates included Simranjit Singh Mann. However, he refused to enter the Lok Sabha without his long sword and that was his undoing. He would have survived like the political leaders in Kashmir, if he had entered the Lok Sabha at that critical juncture. The Kashmir struggle is rooted in masses. Mann would have replaced the traditional Akali leaders. These leaders at one stage provided him total space but he failed to function because of his earlier blunder.

It was the failure of these leaders elected to the Lok Sabha in general and Simranjit Singh Mann in particular that was among one of the reasons for lack of a mass front for the radical politics. This resulted in total thrust on armed struggle and increase in level of violence.

The political objective has to be clear and also the enemy for any struggle to succeed. The militant struggle lacked on both these articulations. Autonomy within India cannot be the objective of armed struggle. It is different in case of Kashmir as that state had joined India as part of the conditional accession treaty and Article 370 granting special status to that state was diluted over the years.

The militants failed to articulate their case convincingly to even a major section of the Sikhs, which had certain grievances, nothing more than that. Every struggle must have a convincing narrative. The grievances can be redressed. One of the grievances was that 93 per cent of those who were hanged during the freedom struggle were the Sikhs. Most of those who were sentenced to life term and deported to the penal settlement at Andaman too were Sikhs. However, they were denied a proportionate share in political power.

It is not without reason that most of the issues on which the Akali Dal launched the struggle on August 4, 1982 are no more relevant. The Anandpur Sahib Resolution was part of the agenda of this Akali struggle that was taken up by Sant Bhindranwale. It was referred to a Commission in 1985 and that was the end of it. The Khalistan narrative dominated the militant discourse from 1986.

Pakistan's intervention in support of this Sikh militant struggle was limited to providing sanctuary and supply of weapons. Pakistan never extended open political support to the Sikh struggle. That limited intervention continues.

Among others, the three factors that hit the militants-cum-terrorists hard were the coordination between the army and the state security agencies when the state was handed over to the army in 1990-91, infiltration by the state agencies and criminals in their ranks and lack of ammunition. However, the most important was their complete alienation from the Sikh masses.

State Repression as a Tool

The Supreme Court verdict on creation of just three cremation grounds in Amritsar district is a telling commentary on the strategy adopted by the security agencies to confront militancy-cum-terrorism in Punjab. This approach that was in brazen violation of every constitutional norm and the law succeeded in curbing violence associated with Sikh militancy, not the political struggle. The demand for dignified space for the Sikhs is attracting more supporters now at the global level.

The case relating to cremation of unidentified bodies also provides one estimate of killings by the security forces. This can assist in assessing the total loss of human life in this violence till 1995. This is a very important dimension of this conflict as not even a near exact count of the loss of human lives is available. This is a must for studying various dimensions of this struggle.

The Supreme Court observed in its November 15, 1995 order, "This Court cannot close its eyes to the contents of the press note dated January 16, 1995 stated to be investigated by Khalra and Dhillon. In case it is found that the facts stated in the press note are correct—even partially—it would be a gory tale of human-rights violations. It is horrifying to visualize that dead-bodies of a large number of persons—allegedly thousands—could be cremated by the police unceremoniously with a label "unidentified". Our faith in democracy and rule of law assures us that nothing of the type can ever happen in this country but the allegations in the press-note—horrendous as they are—need thorough investigation."

This press note was released by human rights activists Jaswant Singh Khalra and Jaspal Singh Dhillon quoting the record of three cremation grounds in Amritsar district—Durgiana Mandir in Amritsar, Tarn Taran and Patti.

The Supreme Court referred the matter following the CBI probe to the National Human Rights Commission (NHRC). The case involved cremation of 2,097 dead bodies. However, no probe was ever ordered into such cremations in other parts of the state. The probe upheld these cremations.

According to the submission made by the Punjab government counsel Altaf Ahmed before the NHRC, 11,696 civilians were killed in terrorist related violence.

The NHRC states in its April, 2012 report: "Shri Altaf Ahmed, learned Senior Counsel assisted by Shri R.S. Suri, appearing for the state of Punjab... submitted that the state... lost as many ... 300 family members of police and para-military forces besides as many as 11,694 civilians as a result of terrorist-related violence."

The Punjab Advocacy and Documentation Group, a non-government organization, has put the total number of disappearances and killings in fake encounters at 8,257 from 1980 to 1985. The group included A.K. Ganguly, retired Supreme Court judge; Colin Gonsalves, senior advocate of the Supreme Court; and Paramjit Kaur Khalra of the Khalra Mission Organization. The investigation by this group was spread over seven years. (*The Hindustan Times*, December 3, 2017).

The Punjab government came out with the year-wise killings of civilians from 1982-95 in 2005. This was in a written reply to unstarred question No. 194 dated October 14, 2005 from Congress MLA Tarlochan Singh, according to which, 11,336 civilians were killed by the militants during this period.

The Punjab police released a press note on February 5, 1994 releasing some figures from 1988 to January 31, 1994.

Violence in Punjab (Punjab Police Press Note February 4, 1994)

	1988	*1989*	*1990*	*1991*	*1992*	*1993*	*1994 (Jan 31)*
Monthly average of civilian killings	162	97	206	216	127	4	0
Hardcore terrorists killed	56	102	92	132	139	59	2
Non-hardcore and others	3819	2497	1642	1973	1971	741	11
Police encounters	461	582	746	1282	1330	570	12

As per this press release, the 'monthly average of civilian killings' was 162 (1988), 97 (1989), 206 (1990), 216 (1991), 127 (1992) and 4 (1993).

The 'hardcore' terrorists killed were 56 (1988), 102 (1989), 92 (1990), 132 (1991), 127 (1992), 57 (1993) and 2 (January 31, 1994).

The 'non-hardcore and others' killed were 3,819 (1988), 2,497 (1989), 1,642 (1990), 1,973 (1991), 1,971 (1992), 741 (1993) and 11 (January 31, 1994).

The police encounters were 461 (1988), 582 (1989), 746 (1990), 1,282 (1991), 1,330 (1992), 570 (1993) and 12 (January 31, 1994).

It is the figure relating to 'non-hardcore and others' that provides insight into the killings by the security forces.

The press note states, "The year 1993 was indeed a year of peace during which terrorist crime in Punjab, which had started registering a decline from the mid of 1992 neatly tapered off to zero level. As against the killing of 1,504 civilians including 252 security men during 1992, there were only 48 killing of civilians, 25 of them being security men during the year 1993."

The last para of this press note is a commentary on the vast operational area of Punjab militants. The press release claimed, "A series of operational-cum-hiding bases of the terrorist outfits like the KLF and the Babbars outside Punjab (Haryana, Delhi, Bihar, West Bengal, Orissa, Madhya Pradesh, southern parts of UP, Maharashtra and Gujarat) were exposed and sanitized by the Punjab police during extended anti-terrorist operations."

This press note was released during the media interaction of K.P.S. Gill at the Chandigarh Press Club on February 4, 1994.

Here is another tabulation of the killings:

Violence in Punjab, 1981-94

	Civilians and Police Killed	*Police Killed*	*Extremists Killed*	*Total Killed*	*Extremists Arrested*
1981	13	[2]	14	27	84
1982	13	[2]	7	20	178
1983	75	[20]	13	88	296
1984	359	[20]	77	436	1,630
1985	63	[8]	2	65	491
1986	520	[42]	78	598	1,581
1987	910	[95]	328	1,238	3,750
1988	1,949	[110]	373	2,322	3,882
1989	1,168	[201]	703	1,871	2,466
1990	2,467	[506]	1,320	3,787	1,759
1991	2,591	[497]	2,177	4,768	1,977
1992	1,518	[252]	2,111	3,629	1,502
1993*	38	[21]	472	510	454
Totals	**11,684**	**1,776**	**7,675**	**1,935**	**20,050**

*1993 data from January 1 - September 10 only.
(Paul Wallace: *Khalistan Movement: Fragmented But Reviving*? 2017)

Hindus and Sikhs Killed by Terrorists in Punjab, 1981-91

	No. of Hindus	*% of Hindus*	*No. of Sikhs*	*% of Sikhs*
1981	10	77	3	23
1982	8	62	5	38
1983	35	47	40	53
1984	237	66	122	34
1985	45	73	17	27
1986	324	63	193	37
1987	425	47	478	54
1988	858	45	1,044	55
1989	442	38	734	62
1990	743	30	1,694	70
1991	744	29	1,847	71
Totals	**3,871**		**6,177**	

Source: Data reported in *The Times of India*, February 9, 1992, p. 15 from the Ministry of Home Affairs, Government of India.

Punjab Chief Minister Capt Amarinder Singh in 2018 put the death toll at 35,000 in a different way stating, "To Mr. Badal goes the credit for the 35,000 deaths in Punjab during 80s-90s."[5] This cannot be rejected as just a political statement.

However, this violence was not confined to Punjab.

The transistor bomb blast killings in Delhi in reaction to the Sikh carnage of November 1984 is just one example. Moreover, all the killings during this massacre of Sikhs at various places in the country cannot be excluded. The militants carried out killings in several other states in the country.

The Punjab government detailed the number of killings by the terrorists in a written reply to an unstarred question by Congress MLA Tarlochan Singh on October 14, 2005. As per this detailed information, a total of 11,336 persons were killed by the militants in Punjab during the period 1982-95. The police district-wise killings were 822 (Amritsar), 1,599 (Tarn Taran), 1,185 (Majitha), 408 (Gurdaspur), 1,026 (Batala), 712 (Jalandhar), 383 (Hoshiarpur), 260 (Kapurthala), 160 (Nawanshahar), 451 (Patiala), 331 (Sangrur), 331 (Barnala), 147 (Fatehgarh Sahib), 572 (Ludhiana), 477 (Jagraon), 83 (Khanna), 408

(Ropar), 723 (Ferozepur), 72 (Muktsar), 363 (Moga), 145 (Faridkot), 245 (Bathinda), 188 (Mansa) and 245 (GRP).

These numbers vary and at least an approximate figure should be worked out by the Union Home Ministry.

The Punjab militant struggle, however, is not just numbers as this is only one dimension. The numbers, of course, are an indication of the loss of human lives. What is more important is that these numbers continue to add up.

The period from 1990 to 1993 witnessed the highest intensity of killings during the entire period of militancy in Punjab. The downward trend in killings started within six months of the February 1992 elections. Punjab virtually turned into a vast killing field with free for all.

The observation made in the monthly Punjab intelligence report on the situation in October 1991 is very significant. It states: "Matter of concern is not that October registered highest killings during the year but due to the fact that the terrorists have the mobility and capacity to strike. They killed 43 members of policemen's families besides killing 51 securitymen. They killed railway patrol party after blasting the train. They murdered six ITBP men in Amritsar. Six Nirankaris were killed in Faridkot. Two prominent leaders of the BJP and the Congress were murdered. Torching of 31 village banks revealed the weakness of area security. Outside Punjab, four Punjab terrorists joined hands with four terrorists of UP to carry out bomb blasts in Rudarpur in which 50 persons were killed. They belonged to Bhindranwale Saffron Tiger Force of Swaran Singh Jawanda of Batala. Death squads were sent to UP, West Bengal, Maharashtra and Delhi to eliminate political targets by Babbars, KLF and KCF (Panjwar). Next two months preceding elections are very critical from law and order point of view."

This was also the period when some of the militant leaders had realized that all was not well with their strategy and tactics. The statement released by Babbar Khalsa chief Sukhdev Singh Babbar was an indication that something was terribly wrong. He strongly condemned the brutal killings of innocent family members including women, children and relatives of policemen. He said such indiscriminate killings, setting on fire the houses of policemen and kidnappings of their children had given a major setback to their struggle. This statement also warned policemen against killing of Sikh youth in fake encounters and committing atrocities on their family members.

The Panthic Committee (Manochahal) too opposed killings of families of policemen.

The period 1990-93 is also the period when the gangs patronized by the police moved about in the garb of militants. Punjab police chief S.S. Virk admitted in February 2007 that former militants were pressed in this battle against militancy and he put the number of such people at about 300. Neither honour nor life was safe in Punjab's countryside during this period.

Then there were mass killings of bus and rail passengers including the areas in neighbouring Haryana.

It was under this situation that the security forces were sanctioned the 'democratic' mandate to kill by engineering a boycott of the February 1992 assembly elections.

This too was the period when the militants received the maximum support from various Akali factions and the culmination was the memorandum demanding Khalistan submitted to the UN Secretary General in April 1992 that was signed by the leaders like SGPC chief Gurcharan Singh Tohra and two-time Chief Minister Parkash Singh Badal along with Simranjit Singh Mann.

The 1989 Lok Sabha elections can safely be taken as a cut-off date for this increased political back up from various Akali factions. It started with this period that the fear of the unknown engulfed the state. This was the only time when the militants received unstinted support from virtually all the Sikh organizations including the Akali factions.

> For the first time since the start of the armed struggle in Punjab and at the time when the tide had started turning against militancy, various Akali factions, farmers and human rights organizations, at a convention organized at Anandpur Sahib on August 11 (1991), exhibited consolidation in support of the militant movement and resolved that only the militants had the right to negotiate with the government as they had the primary role to play under the given situation.[6]

This mandate to the militants by the Sikh organizations was confronted by the Indian state with a 'democratic' mandate to kill to the security forces by engineering the installation of the Beant Singh led Congress government in February 1992. The Indian state succeeded in crushing this struggle using methods that were unconstitutional.

This total brutalization witnessed in Punjab during this later period to "restore normalcy" is also reflected at another level. The Sikhs are now the most scared people in India and this dimension provides some insight into the strategy of the security forces to deal with militancy purely as a law and order problem. "The Sikhs today are the community who fear police the most as per the study on religion-wise distribution of police fear. The report has observed that this can have a possible connection to the particular history of Punjab in the last four decades." (*The Times of India*, June 12, 2018).

The only political initiative at conflict management taken by the government was the 1985 jinxed accord. This struggle was dealt with mainly at the law and order level. But then those spearheading this struggle too had failed to project this struggle as a political conflict between India and the Sikhs.

Confusion Over Political Objective

The militant struggle has to have a well-defined political objective along with strategy to achieve that and clearly identified adversary.

A very significant dimension of militancy in Punjab is that it did not surface in the religio-political domain to achieve a political objective but as a part of revenge psyche that is a part of the broader Sikh psyche. The political objective made its entry later. This is one of the reasons that this struggle could not be projected and articulated as the political conflict against the Indian state. The political objective initially was not the establishment of a sovereign Sikh state and the struggle was not targeted against the Indian state per se. The revenge psyche initially got unleashed mainly to target members of the heterodox Nirankari sect and its supporters. The "enemy" was subsequently identified as the 'Brahmanical order' that can broadly be interpreted as the Hindu hegemony.

Sant Bhindranwale at one stage summed up the objective in the context of a separate Sikh identity. He stated:

> The Sikhs are mainly striving for an identity. By identity, I mean the political, religious and cultural recognition of the community.[7] Sant Longowal, on the same day, elaborated the Sikh Nation concept that he said was reinforced by cultural, social and historical heritage of the Sikhs. He clarified that "India was a multi-nation country, adding that Sikhs were one of the nation therein. Referring to the demand for greater autonomy of states, Sant Longowal said the concept of greater autonomy for states was in no way opposed to the concept of a strong Centre.

Absence of a Commanding Leader in Phase II

The first phase witnessed the emergence of Sant Bhindranwale as the most dominant leader in the radical stream. It was only his legacy that was there to fill that space during the second phase that failed to throw up even a single commanding leader who could have some semblance of following. These people were too small and lacked in vision needed for struggle of such a magnitude. One can objectively assess the size of these leaders now when several of them who survived are leading a normal life.

Militant struggle cannot be perpetuated by legacy alone in the absence of credible and visionary leadership. It was because of the absence of a commanding leader that factionalism dominated the struggle in Phase II.

Significantly, the Babbar Khalsa had parted company with Sant Bhindranwale too in December 1983 when differences between the two militant groups came out in the open. The situation took a serious turn when Babbar Khalsa chief Sukhdev Singh charged Sant Bhindranwale with "hatching a conspiracy to murder me and my close associates... (a few months ago) Sant had commissioned Kala Singh to kill me. He was given a revolver and 32 cartridges."[8]

However, the Babbar Khalsa admitted years later in a statement dated February 13, 1993 that this confrontation was part of a conspiracy hatched by some people from within the organization. "Some people from amongst us created differences with Sant Bhindranwale, who left Guru Nanak Niwas and shifted to Akal Takht. Later these very people joined the Barnala government and became chairman. They then settled in UK through the Indian High Commission and started spying on us. Now we have realized as to how these people sabotaged us." The press note was signed by Wadhawa Singh, Harminder Singh Toni, Baldev Singh Halwarekalan, Jagtar Singh Panjola and Kulwant Singh. One of the persons being hinted at here was Inderjit Singh Baghi, who was considered close to Bibi Amarjit Kaur.

Sant Bhindranwale, despite such differences, represented a unified command that was missing in the post-Bluestar period.

This lack of a unified command and organizational structure was pointed out by Pakistan too from time to time.[9]

Three killings in the context of mutual mistrust and internecine tussles are important to be mentioned here.

Abinashi Singh, the all-powerful personal assistant to Shiromani Gurdwara Parbandhak Committee chief Gurcharan Singh Tohra for years and Dr. Baldev Singh Brar, medical superintendent of Sri Guru Ram Das Hospital run by this body, went missing on the evening of March 31, 1987. Both of them were in touch with almost every militant leader who counted and vice versa. Their whereabouts could never be traced.

AISSF leader Gurjit Singh who was also the son-in-law of Sant Bhindranwale's brother, was perceived to be too ambitious by several of his associates and it was suspected that he could be accessed by the government due to this weakness. It may be mentioned here that most of the members of Sant Bhindranwale's extended family have been known to be vulnerable and this has been brought on record by a retired officer of the spy agency, Intelligence Bureau, in the context of Jasbir Singh Rode, nephew of Sant Bhindranwale.

It was suspected that Gurjit was in touch with the Centre through Abinashi Singh. When confronted by Charanjit Singh Talwandi, he denied that he was talking to the Centre. It was decided that Abinashi Singh too should be questioned. Gurjit was assigned the job to bring Abinashi. However, the problem was of taking him out without arousing any suspicion. This was how the name of Dr. Brar entered. Both were close to each other.

Gurjit took Dr. Brar along to bring Abinashi Singh. They were taken from their houses on the pretext of some meeting but never returned. Nothing is known as to what transpired at the meeting. The bodies of Dr. Brar and Abinashi Singh were never recovered. Both Talwandi and Daljit Singh from SSF were present at the place where they were taken.

The next victim in this internecine war was Tarlochan Singh Riyasti, a Congress leader who earlier was one of the intermediaries between Indira Gandhi and Sant Bhindranwale and continued to be active. His half-burnt body along with another person was recovered from a car in Ludhiana on January 9, 1988. This action too was executed by Gurjit Singh.

The most shocking, however, was the gunning down of Harminder Singh Sandhu who was among the most powerful people close to Sant Bhindranwale and general secretary of the All India Sikh Students Federation. He was assassinated at his residence in Amritsar on January 24, 1990. This action was carried out by Paramjit Singh Panjwar and his associates.

According to the information with the state agencies on February 1990, the hit list of militants included about 20 leaders from Taksal, AISSF (Manjit), Akali Dal (Mann) and conventional Akalis.

The killing of 29 candidates from Sikh parties in the aborted June 1991 assembly election is yet another evidence of the sharp divisions that had hit the militant struggle.

Virtually unlimited availability of sophisticated weapons like AK-47 from across the border further added to this chaos. The leaders started losing control over the cadre.

Here is how the situation was perceived at one stage: "Officials are assassinated, criminal gangs flourish and, most wrenching to the hard-working Sikh community, Sikhs have begun killing each other as divisions among them deepen."[10]

A statement that appeared in the media in July, 1991 on internecine war was a detailed analysis on the situation. Issued in the name of the Panthic Committee (Dr. Sohan Singh), it stated: "They are the people who are responsible for diverting the Sikh struggle from its real objective. It is these people who are responsible for internecine war among the Sikhs."[11]

Anti-social Activities Under This Cover

The post Bluestar phase witnessed the shift from militancy to criminalized and brutalized militancy that can also be termed as militant terrorism. It was this multi-dimensional shift that was among the factors that explain the fall of this struggle.

It was with January 26, 1986 Sarbat Khalsa that the militants reclaimed control of the Golden Temple complex as despite having formed the government, the mainstream Akali Dal was being pushed to the margins and losing its relevance. The split in the Akali Dal on the issue of police entry into the Golden Temple complex after the announcement of Khalistan strengthened the radicals as SGPC chief Tohra too opposed this action of the state government.

However, anti-social elements too infiltrated the ranks of the militants. Summoning people to the office of the Sikh Students Federation in the Golden Temple complex for extortion became too common. It was during this period that the agencies penetrated the ranks of the militants.

A total of 46 decomposed bodies, both of men and women, were recovered from the big heap of debris that had come up between the Langar building and Manji Sahib Diwan Hall. This was the rubble of government constructed Akal Takht brought down by the radicals to be rebuilt through 'Kar Sewa'.

Under whose command, in case there was any, such activities were going on in the holiest of the holy shrine of the Sikhs? Room numbers 45 and 46 in the parikarma of the Golden Temple were notoriously known as the torture rooms. No militant organization ever provided an explanation for this pile up of bodies.

According to one estimate, more than 30 groups functioned independently in Punjab by June 1988 when Operation Blackthunder II was carried out in the Golden Temple complex to flush out these people again. This time, the Sikhs did not protest.

This operation had shocked the Sikhs for the reasons that were different, not due to any action of the government. The people who defiled the Golden Temple this time were the so-called freedom fighters of Khalistan. These elements did not spare even the sanctum sanctorum of the shrine where utensils full of human excreta were recovered when they surrendered. These people had taken shelter there for about three days.

Operation Blackthunder was the watershed and beginning of the downfall but at the same time, the following years were the worst, so far as killings were concerned and also the enigmatic mass support, including from all the main Akali factions.

No militant organization ever came out with explanation for such despicable behaviour and killings. The Golden Temple was under the control of the militants and as such, it is the militant organizations whose explanation was called for. This heap of dead bodies under the Akal Takht debris and using sanctum sanctorum as toilet could not be blamed on government agents. If nothing else, at least an apology was called for.

The recovery of dead bodies from the debris of Akal Takht in front of Langar building was one stinking aspect of this struggle during Phase II. There was another one related to the domain of morality and ethics. It is an open secret that the intelligence agencies used the situation to every advantage to defame the militants. The dignity and honour of the Punjabis got compromised. A section within the militant ranks was resorting to rapes and molestation of women and that too belonging to the families that would shelter them. The agencies had only exploited the space provided by criminalised section of militants. This resulted in their total alienation.

Notice of such anti-social activities by people under the garb of militants was taken by a section of the militants in 1990. The statement issued in the name of Panthic Committee stated: "Time has come for us to rise above factions and identify those elements, who are indulging in extortions, lootings and violating all norms of morality and ethics. They oppose such activities in statements and talk, but in fact are creating fear among the people with their AK-47s. These people have blemished the lofty traditions of the Khalsa".[12] This statement was issued in the name of the Panthic Committee whose members mentioned included Dr. Sohan Singh, Mahal Singh, Satinderpal Singh, Wadhawa Singh and Harminder Singh Sultanwind. Other names mentioned were those of Sukhdev Singh, Paramjit Singh Panjwar, Daljit Singh and Gurjant Singh Budhsinghwala.

The July 5, 1992 Panthic Committee statement made a candid admission of this dark side that stated:

> The criminal activities under the name of militant struggle has impacted entire Punjab but the situation is the worst in Majha region. Numerous groups have come up in this area that loot Sikh families and even resort to immoral activities. A time came when these non-ideological groups resorted to such terror and lootings and it became unbearable for the Sikhs to live in villages. Many of the Sikh families migrated to cities. Not only life and property, even honour of Sikh families is not safe.

This statement also talked of infiltration of militant organizations by anti-social elements. But then, it was the Sikh struggle that was stigmatized.[13]

The Panthic Committee in its July 29, 1992 statement issued warning saying, "The Panthic Committee, hereby, makes it clear to the people that the militant organizations working under it do not believe in extortions to collect money for ongoing struggle... It is the responsibility of the chiefs of these three organizations to end such extortions."[14] The statement was issued in the name of Dr. Sohan Singh, Shahbaz Singh, Satinderpal Singh, Harminder Singh Sultanwind and Daljit Singh Khalsa.

Earlier, the Khalistan Liberation Army (KLA) and Akal Federation in a statement on January 21, 1991 stated: "Robbers and killers are agents of the government and enemies of the Sikhs. Black cats and the Indian National Army are government agents." This statement was released under the names of Shamsher Singh, acting convener, Akal Federation and Kapoor Singh Jamraud, chief general of the KLA. Kapoor Singh Jamraud was the pseudo name of Narain Singh Chaura.[15]

Another statement from the Panthic Committee associated with the name of Dr. Sohan Singh stated on July 29, 1992: "Three militant organizations under this panel make it clear they don't resort to extortions to carry on struggle. Contact any of these organizations, in case you get extortion letter."

Here was yet another murkier dimension as the Babbar Khalsa issued a warning on May 2, 1992 to extortionists using the name of this organization even in West Bengal. However, Babbar Khalsa chief Sukhdev Singh Babbar had realized that the situation could not be rectified by just issuing two or three statements.

The counter-insurgency strategy of the security agencies, who had penetrated the ranks of militants succeeded in creating terror among the leaders who started withdrawing from the scene. The situation worsened when the militants started targeting families of the policemen. This situation led to a no-holds-barred retaliation by the security forces.

Militancy and Mass Support

Among the main reasons for the collapse of the militant movement was the absence of mass front to provide the much-needed strategic support to sustain it.

The Akali factions that came out in support of the struggle from time to time could not be mobilized as mass front to carry forward the cause using democratic means. This support, of course, was reflected through two major political mobilizations but that was never institutionalized.

Thousands of people hit the streets in support of the militants in Kashmir almost every day but that was never the case in Punjab despite the fact that the killings by the police in fake encounters and torture and humiliation of the family members of the militants, even women, was too common.

The traditional Akalis had no sympathy for the cause of the militant struggle despite supporting several of their calls including boycott of elections in February 1992. Leaders like Parkash Singh Badal supported even the demand for Khalistan on record. The statements rejecting the Indian Constitution or supporting Khalistan were not translated into democratic action programmes to supplement the militant struggle. It was a love-hate relationship between the Akalis and the radicals.

There was yet another aspect. The Akalis wanted the Congress government to confront the militants and clear the field for them to rule later in the next election. This was one of the aspects of the 1992 election boycott, besides other reasons.

The United Akali Dal had come up as the political party organized by the radicals and the traditional Akali Dal had extended unstinted support to this output. However, this body disintegrated within months with the dominant democratic space again taken over by the traditional Akali Dal. The second phase was when Simranjit Singh Mann came out of jail after winning the 1989 Lok Sabha election with a massive margin.

The situation at one stage had moved towards formation of a mass front beginning with overwhelming mandate, with which the candidates supported by the radicals, mainly the All India Sikh Students Federation, won the 1989 Lok Sabha election. It was in this election that former police officer Simranjit Singh Mann won from Tarn Taran by a margin of about 4.8 lakh votes. However, Mann failed miserably to evolve as an effective leader to function in the democratic domain. The former Indian Police Service officer was not just over-ambitious, he lacked vision and political experience. He failed to deliver at that crucial stage. None of those elected to the Lok Sabha with the support of the hardliners played any major role in the religio-political dynamics of that period.

The February 1992 Assembly election boycotted by the main Akali parties facilitated installation of the Congress government headed by Beant Singh. The security agencies were given unfettered power with the Congress government functioning as the shield. There were no democratic mass mobilizations against blatant violations of human rights by the security forces. The poll boycott decision boomeranged. It is these mobilizations that could have sustained the struggle. The Beant Singh government adopted the policy of 'No Prisoners'.

The militant organizations never evolved any strategy to mobilize mass support to sustain the struggle. The might of the state in a big country like India cannot be confronted mainly through armed struggle and that too in a terrain that is flat. The counter-strategy was missing.

Fear cannot command respect. The militants had little connect with the Sikh masses.

Even the poll boycott was not matched by post-poll strategy unlike the Indian state. It was the poll boycott that was used by the state against the militants. The government lacking people's mandate lacked legitimacy. The Indian state had already chalked out the strategy to fill this gap through municipal and panchayat elections to seek legitimacy for this manufactured mandate.

On the other hand, the militants failed to carry forward this support to the boycott after the election in the absence of any strategy.

As the security forces launched a crackdown on the militants many of whom had turned criminals, the Akali leaders waited in the wings for them to be eliminated.

It was yet another event, years later in 2015 that to an extent provided the answer as to how the mass support that had got mobilized without any effort petered out within no time. This was the massive turnout on the call of the hardliners to protest against the failure of the Akali Dal government headed by Parkash Singh Badal to check incidents of desecration of Guru Granth Sahib beginning with Bargari.

The organizers included some of the very people who had been instrumental in organizing the Sarbat Khalsa at the Akal Takht on January 26, 1986 that witnessed the militants taking over the Golden Temple complex again.

Punjab witnessed such a massive gathering after years at Chabba near Amritsar on November 10, 2015 and the same mistakes were repeated as that of 1986. This gathering announced parallel chiefs of five Sikh Takhts (Religio-temporal seats) with Jagtar Singh Hawara, under detention in the case of assassination of then Chief Minister Beant Singh, as the Akal Takht Jathedar. This massive mobilization on a sensitive religious issue stood sabotaged. The diktat for this move had come from some NRI hardliners. The support fizzled out within no time.

The Panthic Committee clarification on the issue of mass front in a statement dated October 29, 1991 is self-explanatory. It stated: "Some of our brothers think that we don't believe in a mass movement. We believe such propaganda is being resorted to by those people who want to denounce these four organizations as dictatorial, one-sided, single track or parochial. Therefore, we want to further clarify this aspect. The question is that of mass movement for what. Any mass movement bereft of a political objective would ultimately lead to nowhere. In case it is a farmers' based mass movement, it would end up bargaining on higher prices for crops. The employees' front would end up by getting higher pay and emergence of some as leaders. Any mass front under the Indian constitution might claim to be heading towards the final aim by getting elected as MLAs and MPs. These forms of mass struggle do not touch the fringe of the spirit of such struggle. We want to keep people out of this Leftist explanation of mass movement." The statement was issued in the name of Dr. Sohan Singh, Satinderpal Singh, Harminder Singh Sultanwind, Daljit Singh and Shahbaz Singh.[16]

However, Babbar Khalsa International differed on this issue as evident from its September 1, 1991 statement. This organization stated:

> The militants are engaged in armed struggle. They are fighting for independent and sovereign Khalistan. However, they don't overlook importance of mass struggle. We want coordination in these two forms of struggle. We should unite after rejecting the Indian constitution for the achievement of Khalistan. International situation is now in our favour. We should not be in any dilemma. You can launch peaceful struggle for Khalistan. India is presently in deep economic and political crisis. We should exploit this situation to our advantage. We should make the Khalistan struggle mass based... Everybody should contribute to this struggle and we definitely seek you contribution.

It was a policy statement released in the name of Sukhdev Singh, Talwinder Singh, Wadhawa Singh, Mahal Singh and Kulwant Singh.[17]

Another group of militant organizations too, in a separate statement on September 1, 1991 favoured mass struggle. This statement was issued in the name of Paramjit Singh Panjwar (Khalistan Commando Force), Gurjant Singh Budhsinghwala (Khalistan Liberation Force), Rachhpal Singh Chhandran (Bhindranwale Tiger Force of Khalistan) and Daljit Singh (Sikh Students Federation). These statements were released at the September 1, 1991 meeting of various Akali factions, human rights bodies, farmers unions and other Sikh bodies held at Anandpur Sahib.

However, the mass front failed to come up, as there was no organized effort.

Pakistan on the Sikh Struggle

Hamid Gul, the former chief of the ISI, shared his views on the Sikh struggle with some of the Sikh activists in Lahore after his retirement in the mid-1990s. The ISI chief is not known to interact with the Sikh militant leaders directly, as the junior officials designated as handlers maintain contact with them. He was an Islamic scholar too and brainchild behind organizing Tehrik-e-Taliban.

He was of the opinion that Operation Bluestar had outlived its utility as the factor to sustain the Sikh struggle after a few years. The struggle needed a new agenda and programme from time to time.

He suggested to the Sikh leaders to globalize their struggle by coordinating with other militant organizations and widen their support base. Kashmiris have their voice in the UN but not the Sikhs. This was possible only in case the Sikh struggle has lobbies in foreign governments that is different from having official support.

The Sikh struggle has never been formally adopted even by Pakistan as part of its policy and it is nothing more than limited proxy war. It was for this reason that Pakistan's all out support was missing all along. The money and material that came from Pakistan too was limited, mainly to sustain the struggle. The militants resorted to bank robberies precisely because of this reason. Of course, several militant leaders continue to be sheltered by Pakistan.

The insiders maintain the militant leaders staying in Pakistan failed to convince their handlers that they were capable of delivering result by intensifying the struggle.

The struggle seems to have revived at the political level among the Sikhs abroad. However, they do not have much of a connect with those whose cause in Punjab they espouse.

A new factor has emerged at the global level relating to the Sikh struggle. Hundreds of families of militants managed to shift to other countries to escape persecution. Majority of these families are those of the militants who were killed by the security forces. They are now settled in countries like Canada, USA, Germany, Italy and UK.

Changing Dynamics of India's Relationship with the Sikhs

Discrimination against the Sikhs has been part of the Akali narrative for years. Here is a demand that was part of the list prepared by the Akali Dal working committee at its meeting on September 11, 1980 to be submitted to the Prime Minister: "2-Protest against discrimination against Sikh officials in general and an eminent doctor like Dr. Jaswant Singh Neki in particular."

The grievance was that the Sikhs were being ignored in promotion to the higher echelons of civil services and armed forces.

That situation has now changed. India had a Sikh Prime Minister in Dr. Manmohan Singh who completed two terms from 2004-2014. Two Sikh generals have been army chief. That narrative now stands diluted. Giani Zail Singh, of course, was elevated to the highest office of President of India but then Operation Bluestar was during his tenure.

The Sikh struggle now survives in Punjab mainly as agenda of some fringe organizations. Its protagonists are now active mainly in other countries where the Sikhs are settled in sizeable numbers. The radical discourse earlier too was introduced by the fringe organizations but with one difference. The space to the radical discourse was provided by the Akali narrative. Now the main support to this discourse is from the globalized Sikh radicals whose agenda is Khalistan.

The Indian state continues to perceive a threat from the radical Sikhs.

The basic issue is that the narrative relating to that period continues to be a part of the political discourse in one context or the other. It is this narrative that continues to fuel the radical ideology at the global level, not the original demands that are no more relevant.

The Closure

India's Punjab Tragedy continues to await closure even 35 years after Operation Bluestar.

Operation Bluestar, however, is just one part. Punjab turned into a killing field in 1990-91 and although violence rooted in that deadly politics petered out after 1993 with assassination of Chief Minister

Beant Singh on August 31, 1995 being the last major action, people continue to die in sporadic incidents.

Sikh identity issues have forcefully surfaced in the countries where the members of this community are settled in large numbers. The thrust now is on maintaining the purity of the Sikh religion. This issue cannot be viewed in isolation with the Sikh religio-political discourse rooted in the politics of 1980s in Punjab.

When about 10,000 Sikh men, women and children chanting Khalistan Zindabad slogans marched through the streets in London on June 2, 2019 to mark anniversary of Operation Bluestar, the signal was loud and clear. The Sikh radical political discourse has survived overtime.

India has never taken a single step towards the closure of that tragedy. It is the accountability and not just apology that would initiate the closure. The tragedy demands justice, justice for everybody.

Congress President Sonia Gandhi for the first time offered what was interpreted as regret while addressing an election rally in Chandigarh in January 1998 during the Lok Sabha election.

Here are excerpts from a report datelined January 25, 1998 that appeared in *The Hindu*

"Mrs Sonia Gandhi today came pretty close to apologizing for Operation Bluestar. Addressing an election rally at Chandigarh, she referred to the "June 6, 1984 events" and observed that she "understood" hurt to the Sikh psyche; but in the same breath also added that her family was also "hurt".

Prefacing that "she did not want to rake up old issues" and that "sometimes an expression of sympathy was not enough of a salve," Sonia Gandhi indirectly referred to the anti-Sikh violence in the wake of the assassination of Indira Gandhi.

> As a widow and as a mother, I empathize with the victims; this should have never happened. My husband also felt that way...I can understand the pain terrorism can inflict; my husband and my mother-in-law were both victims of terrorist violence. I have been the face of hatred. I have experienced the pain of sadness of the loss of dear ones.

Prime Minister Dr. Manmohan Singh issued formal apology for November 1984 anti-Sikh pogrom on August 11, 2005. He said,

> I apologize not only to the Sikh community but to the whole nation, because what took place in 1984 is a negation of the concept of nationhood enshrined in our Constitution. I am not standing on any false prestige. On

behalf of our government, on behalf of the entire people of this country, I bow my head in shame.[18]

Rahul Gandhi said in 2014: "The Prime Minister of the UPA has apologized and the President of the Congress party (has) expressed regrets. I share their sentiments completely." (*The Indian Express*, March 17, 2014).

The apology is for only the November 1984 planned massacre of Sikhs and this is only one part. Apology even for the entire situation would be meaningless without accountability. The basic issue is the deadly politics that produced the Punjab tragedy. It is this politics for which accountability must be fixed for which modalities should be worked out. The role of individual leaders must be brought out. The entire record with the government relating to the Punjab based militant struggle must be made public, at least till the November 1984 carnage of Sikhs.

The Sikhs might have moved on, but there is no closure and moreover, the struggle continues.

ENDNOTES

1. He was arrested and deported to Singapore that was a penal settlement at that time. He died there on July 5, 1856. "The first person who revolted against the new regime was Bhai Maharaj Singh. After the battle of Gujrat, when all the other Sikh chiefs, not listening to the suggestion of the Bhai to fight yet another battle either at Rawalpindi or Panja Sahib, surrendered to the British in March, 1949, Maharaj Singh abruptly and secretly left them and went underground to prepare the Khalsa for a general rebellion against the foreign rule".
2. Ganda Singh (ed.). *The Panjab Past and Present* (Vol. 4). Patiala: Punjabi University. p. 288.
3. Ibid., p. 290.
4. Former chief minister Parkash Singh Badal and Akali Dal chief Sukhbir Singh Badal too opposed had similar perception but that was because of the fact that these incidents related to the period when they were in power in 2015
5. December 19, 2018. *The Tribune.*
6. Jagtar Singh. (2011). *Khalistan Struggle: A Non-movement*. Delhi: Aakar Books, p. 362.
7. November 26, 1982. *The Indian Express.*
8. May 22, 1984. *The Tribune.*
9. Mohinder Singh. (2009). *Neeh Rakhi Gayee.* Amritsar: Panth Khalsa Parkashan, p. 279.
10. December 22, 1990. *Chicago Tribune.*

11. July 5, 1991. *Daily Ajit*.
12. From the press note.
13. From the press note.
14. From the press note.
15. From the press note.
16. Press note.
17. Press note.
18. August 12, 2005. *The Tribune*.

13

SGPC: The Most Peaceful Struggle

The Sikh history at times has been characterized by the most peaceful struggles even in the face of brutal state repression. The struggle for the liberation of gurdwaras beginning 1919 that continued till 1925 during the British rule represented this other extreme. The statutory status of the Shiromani Gurdwara Parbandhak Committee evolved during this agitation. The Sikh Gurdwara Act 1925 was the product of this agitation that ended up more than just for the liberation of the gurdwaras.

This vital aspect of the Sikh struggles cannot be overlooked while analysing the period of militancy beginning 1978.

Shiromani Gurdwara Parbandhak Committee (SGPC), the unique statutory body of the Sikhs in the world set up for the management of the notified shrines of the community in the land of the Sikhs that was Punjab, is rooted deep in the religio-political dynamics of what has been left of that state with the name remaining the same. Created on November 15, 1920 by the Sikhs, this body acquired the statutory status in 1925 with the enactment of the Sikh Gurdwara Act, 1925.

This struggle was anti-imperialist in content that witnessed the first biggest democratic mobilization of this vibrant community during the British rule. This struggle at one stage attracted world attention for being extremely peaceful even in the face of brutal state repression.

The genesis of separate and exclusive Sikh identity is traced to this gurdwara liberation struggle. The militant struggle years later was ideologically rooted in this assertion. This is besides the fact that Sikhism was created as a new religion by Guru Nanak Dev having unique and separate content and character.

The SGPC was the first statutory body in India that granted voting rights to women having attained the age of 21 in 1925 as against 1928 in the UK. This dimension was revolutionary in itself at that time.

This was the first statutory body in India that opposed the Pakistan Resolution adopted by the Muslim League in 1940.

It was the SGPC that called for the carving out of the Sikh state.

It again was the SGPC that resolved at one stage to "provide ideological lead to the Sikh community in the historical crusade for preserving its political identity as a nation."[1]

The creation of the democratically elected SGPC at a representative gathering on November 15, 1920 to take over and manage shrines of the community was the watershed development in the Sikh religio-political domain in the 20th century. The five-year phase till this body acquired statutory status in 1925 is the period of the most peaceful struggle by the Sikhs for the liberation of their shrines from the degenerated and corrupt priestly class patronized by the British that turned into confrontation against the British rulers.

> The Sikhs declared a peaceful war against unjust and immoral laws that governed the management of the gurdwaras and offered a challenge to the government to do its worst to maintain such laws. The Sikhs call it the 'Third Sikh War.' On account of the treachery of their ministers and generals, the Sikhs were defeated in two Sikh wars fought against the British in the middle of the last century. But in this their 'Third War' they were a bit more careful and more determined. The stakes here were their gurdwaras and their religion.[2]

This distinct Sikh institution did not remain confined to its statutory role of management of notified shrines as it donned political role at crucial moments despite the Akali Dal having been set up by this body within less than a month of its creation on December 14, 1920. The prefix Shiromani was added to the Akali Dal later at a party meeting on March 29, 1922.

At the political level, it was after the formation of the SGPC and the Akali Dal that the Sikhs who once ruled this land emerged as the third distinct entity at the political level under the new dispenzation. "It was only after and as a consequence of the Gurdwara Reform Movement and the formation of the Shiromani Akali Dal as a political party that the Sikhs came to be counted and constituted a distinct community to be considered and consulted."[3]

This body was accorded statutory status with the enactment of the Sikh Gurdwara Act on July 7, 1925 by the Punjab Legislative Council. This is the first organization in the world for the management of shrines that that is democratically elected in the election conducted by the government with every Sikh man and woman having attained the age of 21 years eligible to become a voter in the region under its jurisdiction.

Originally, it was set up as a nominated body that later evolved its election procedure by involving local gurdwara committees in Punjab. The Sikh religion is not individualistic and Gurdwara is the institution that represents core values of the Sikh ethos. The institution of Sangat (Sikhs' gathering) is symbol of participatory democracy and democratic functioning is part of the Sikh doctrine.

The main objective of the struggle was transfer of control of the shrines to Sikhs and not enactment of the Sikh Gurdwara legislation per se that emerged as the solution during the stir.

This struggle was multi-layered in the sense that it posed a direct challenge to the British rule in this part of the country. Punjab had already become cradle of freedom movement by the time the agitation for the liberation of their shrines was launched by the Sikhs.

It is pertinent to mention that the Congress Party was set up on December 28, 1885 to act as a bridge between the British Government and the Indian elite with the idea proposed by retired British civil servant Allan Octavian Hume. In Punjab, the Sikh elite set up Chief Khalsa Diwan on October 30, 1902 for almost the same purpose and this body kept itself aloof not only from gurdwara liberation struggle but also the freedom movement. At one level, the Shiromani Akali Dal, the second oldest political party, can claim to be the first political party in the country set up by the Indians themselves unlike the Congress.

The management of the Sikh shrines had degenerated to such an extent that the priests of several Sikh shrines had denounced even the freedom fighters of the Ghadar Party and Komagata Maru as non-Sikhs. The extreme was the honouring at the Akal Takht of Brigadier R.E.H. Dyer who had ordered firing on peaceful protesters in Jallianwala Bagh on April 13, 1919 in Amritsar killing hundreds of men, women and children. It was under this revolting situation that the Sikhs decided to liberate their shrines from these priests.

The priests by and large had become instruments of the British rulers. Within no time of Punjab having been annexed, the British rulers had understood the importance of having control over them. This religion is unique as it is religio-political in content with the Khalsa (the pure), the baptised form of Sikhs, created by the 10th Lord, Guru Gobind Singh, being synergy of 'Saint-Soldier.'

Hindu Rituals Enter Gurdwaras

Years before the mobilization of Sikhs started to claim right to the management of their shrines, protests had started erupting against the priests for introducing non-Sikh practices in gurdwaras, including installation of idols of Hindu gods and goddesses.

It may be mentioned that at the time when the Sikhs were being hunted and persecuted by the Mughal rulers with bounty on their heads forcing them to retreat to the jungles and desert of Rajasthan, their shrines passed into the hands of people from Udasi and Nirmala Sikh sects. In the process, the management of the gurdwaras turned dynastic leading to degeneration and distortions.

Darbar Sahib came under the management of the Sikhs for some time when they rebuilt the shrine that was razed by the forces of the Afghan invader Ahmad Shah Abdali first in 1757 and again in 1762.

The distortions in Sikh religion became more pronounced as the management of the Darbar Sahib complex changed hands during the reign of Maharaja Ranjit Singh after the death of Akali Phoola Singh in 1823. The Harmandar Sahib, also known as Darbar Sahib, turned into the Golden Temple under Sikh rule when Maharaja Ranjit Singh who decided to beautify the shrine with gold work. Guru Nanak had created Sikh religion as a religion of the ordinary people without any distinction and Darbar Sahib, over the years, came up as a place for socio-spiritual solace on the principle of universal brotherhood and egalitarianism. Sikhism rejected the existing social order.

It may be mentioned that it was Akali Phoola Singh who had summoned Maharaja Ranjit Singh at the Akal Takht. That was the start of the decline of this institution and end to the democratic ethos of the Sikh doctrine. Akali Phoola Singh had taken over the management of Darbar Sahib complex in 1800 heading a fighting force of about 2,000 Nihangs following complaints of mismanagement. He was subsequently appointed general in the army of Mahara Ranjit Singh and given the command to expand the Sikh Empire on the Peshawar side. The management of the shrine subsequently passed on to the priestly class.

The Dogra courtiers from Jammu, who dominated the court of Maharja Ranjit Singh, too were instrumental in this deterioration. The Dogras were Hindus. The Dogra courtiers started patronising the 'mahants' who introduced Hindu religious practices in the Darbar Sahib complex. It was during this period that idols of Hindu gods and goddesses appeared in the Darbar Sahib complex. The paintings of Hindu deities appeared on the walls of Akal Takht and Baba Atal shrine. "The idols of Hindu elephant deity Ganesh were installed by Darbar Sahib Head Granthi Giani Sant Singh and Akal Takht priest Gurmukh Singh."[4]

British Administration and Sikh Shrines

The British rulers understood the strategic importance of the Sikh shrines in Punjab's religio-political dynamics within no time of the annexation of Punjab.

The Sikhs were the only community in India in the running of whose religious institutions the British rulers got keenly involved. This unusual interest was rooted in the fact that the Sikh struggle for freedom had started within no time of the annexation of Punjab in 1849 and the first leader to raise the banner of revolt was Bhai Maharaj Singh. His objective was the restoration of the Sikh Empire. He used the platform of gurdwaras by establishing contacts with Sikh religious leaders in the state and sought their cooperation as his reputation was that of a religious person. The British rulers thus at the very beginning realized the significance of maintaining control over Sikh shrines as gurdwaras were a ready platform to mobilize the Sikhs against the government.

It is in this background that the British administration unleashed its design to control Sikh religious institutions. "Realizing that religion was a great factor in the Sikh struggle for freedom, they not only tried to control religious affairs of the Sikhs and inculcate among them the spirit of loyalty towards the British rule through Sikh religious institutions but also viewed with suspicion any socio-religious reform movement among them."[5]

The 'mahants' managing the shrines became willing instruments in the hands of the British rulers who too patronised the system of hereditary priests. It was this patronage that led to the confrontation between the Sikhs and the British rulers.

The British India government formally intervened in the management of the Darbar Sahib complex on December 22, 1869 with the constitution of a management committee headed by Teja Singh, the general in the Sikh army who had betrayed in the 1849 Anglo-Sikh war and colluded with the invaders. It was this committee that prepared 'Dastur-ul-Amal' (norms) for the functioning of the Darbar Sahib. Teja Singh was otherwise a Brahmin. The British administration also patronised Udasis and Nirmalas.

The Singh Sabha movement was the first step towards Sikh awakening. The first Singh Sabha was founded on October 1, 1873 at Amritsar to counter the growing influence of the reformist Hindu organization Arya Samaj.

The Sikhs started reacting to the malpractices by the hereditary priests managing the shrines. There is reference to the arrangement that was worked out around 1895 for the Nankana Sahib shrine as part of the initiative by Mehar Singh Chawla of Lahore to end malpractices.

> Public subscriptions were raised for extending the building and gold plating two central domes of the Janam Ashtan, providing certain rooms to the Baradari and a well to the Bal Lila. After sometime, it was proposed that a representative committee should be appointed to control all the gurdwaras at Nankana Sahib. On a fixed day a meeting was held, which was attended by many Sikh leaders and 'mahants' of the local gurdwaras. The Deputy Commissioner of Lahore, Mr Hallifax, was also present. After some discussions the 'mahants,' who were present, agreed that the gurdwaras were the property of the Panth and they would serve under a committee of control. They signed a document to this effect.[6]

The mahants later backtracked "on the advice of a Hindu tehsildar."

Removal of Hindu Idols from Darbar Sahib

The mismanagement and departure from Sikh practices in the gurdwaras were not confined to Punjab alone.

There is the 1905 case of a gurdwara in the memory of Seventh Master Guru Har Rai in Kabul in Afghanistan whose Brahmin priest installed idols of Hindu gods and goddesses provoking the Sikhs. The case went to Amir of Kabul who ruled against the Brahmin priests. The idols were removed.

It was in 1905 that idols were removed from the Darbar Sahib complex following the government's intervention sought by the Akal Takht Sarabrah Aroor Singh.

The Chief Khalsa Diwan adopted a resolution in 1906 demanding that the control of the Darbar Sahib be handed over to the Sikhs. A proposal came up in May 1907 for the setting up of a "Gurdwara Sambhal Committee" for this purpose. The Sikh bodies earlier urged the government in 1906 that they should be allowed to appoint the Darbar Sahib custodian (Sarabrah).

However, the flashpoint was the Gurdwara Rakab Ganj case in Delhi that triggered the first organized protests by the Sikhs. This shrine where headless body of the 9th Sikh Lord Guru Tegh Bahadur was cremated after his martyrdom on the orders of Emperor Aurangzeb was constructed by General Baghel Singh who captured Delhi on March 11, 1783 and unfurled the Khalsa flag from the ramparts of the Red Fort.

The 'mahant' of this historic gurdwara had sold part of the land to the government to facilitate construction of a straight road to the Viceroy House, now the Rashtrapati Bhavan. The government demolished the boundary wall of this shrine on January 14, 1914. A futile attempt was made by two Sikh leaders, Master Sunder Singh and Harchand Singh, to raise this issue during the three-day Sikh Education Conference beginning April 10, 1914 at Jalandhar. They were thrown out. This land was restored in December 1920 after World War I.

The seeds of the SGPC were sown during this agitation when a committee to manage this shrine was constituted in July 1914. This followed a meeting of the representatives of the Sikh organizations convened by the Darbar Sahib Sarabrah Aroor Singh at Amritsar on May 3, 1914. Aroor Singh had summoned this meeting at the instance of the government. This meeting adopted six resolutions.

> "Acting on one of the resolutions, the Chief Khalsa Diwan, on June 21, 1914, drew the constitution of the Khalsa Gurdwara Committee, Delhi. The Committee was to consist of seven members to be elected as follows:
>
> 1. Four members from Delhi Province to be elected by the Delhi Khalsa Sangat (Sikhs of Delhi);
>
> 2. Three members to be elected or nominated as under:
>
> a. One member to be returned by Sri Darbar Sahib (Amritsar) and the four Takhts — Akal Bunga Sahib (Amritsar), Sri Kesgarh Sahib (Anandpur), Patna Sahib (Patna) and Hazoor Sahib Nanded (Deccan);
>
> b. One member to be nominated by the Darbars of Patiala, Jind, Nabha, Kapurthala and Faridkot states;
>
> Note: The representatives of the States will be nominated by the States in turn as under :
>
> Patiala for two years; Jind, Nabha, Kapurthala and Faridkot for one year each; and in case any State does not exercise its right within two months, then the next state in turn will have the right to return a member.
>
> 3. One member to be elected by the Khalsa Diwan and Singh Sabhas affiliated to the Chief Khalsa Diwan.
>
> Pursuant to the constitution, early in July 1914, four members of Delhi to the proposed committee were elected at an ordinary Singh Sabha meeting in Delhi. Shortly, the Committee started functioning."[7]

The construction on the Capital project was suspended by the government in view of the start of World War I and resumed only in 1918. The government not only returned the original land but also ceded some extra land under an agreement signed on March 1, 1920, between the Deputy Commissioner (Delhi) and Chief Engineer on behalf of the Government and the Khalsa Gurdwara Committee through its representative Sardar Bahadur Sobha Singh. The Government imposed a condition that the Sikhs would not construct any other building there without its prior permission. The outer wall of the area ceded to Gurdwara Rakab Ganj, as also the inner wall, were constructed by the Khalsa Gurdwara Committee by end of 1920 after Sardul Singh Caveeshar in the daily *Akali* of September 2, 1920, asked for 100 self-sacrificing volunteers to construct these walls.

The Delhi Sikh Gurdwara Management Committee came up in 1971.

Start of Liberation Struggle in Punjab

Among the most prominent early leaders spearheading the gurdwara liberation struggle was Kartar Singh Jhabbar belonging to Sheikhupura district, now in Pakistan, who had entered the religio-political domain as a Sikh preacher in 1909 after his three-year training. An activist of Singh Sabha, he founded the organization known as Khalsa Diwan Khara Sauda in 1912.

The turning point in his life was the Jallianwala Bagh massacre at Amritsar on April 13, 1919. This carnage of innocent men, women and children who had joined a political conference at this place near the Darbar Sahib had triggered strong protest with the people sabotaging railway lines and communication system. He was arrested along with several other protesters from Chuharkana in Sheikhupura district. Seven of them were sentenced to death, including Jhabbar on May 22, 1919. However, on the day he was to be hanged on May 30, his sentence was converted to life imprisonment, to be jailed at Andaman, known as Kalapani.

It was during his stay at the Cellular Jail that he also came to realize the extreme of degeneration that had hit management of Sikh shrines and institutions including Darbar Sahib and Akal Takht. In the early morning hours, he would hear prisoners reciting Gurbani. They were the freedom fighters and not criminals but priests at Akal Takht had passed edict against them. Some of them had at one time aspired to go to Canada but the voyage turned into tragedy that is known as Komagata Maru, the name of the Japanese ship they had hired from Hong Kong. The activists of the Ghadar Party had returned from the USA to overthrow the British India government through armed struggle. Many of them were Amritdharis.

He also came across a writing of Ghadar Party leader Lala Hardayal advocating Hindi as the national language and using objectionable language against Guru Tegh Bahadur, the Ninth Sikh Guru.[8] His detention in Cellular Jail was his period of awakening.

He was released in March 1920 when rest of his sentence was

commuted as part of the political settlement between the Congress and the British government. Jhabbar had now emerged as a political leader.

The Sikh League had already been organized by that time at a meeting on December 27, 1919 at Amritsar. The League had demanded that the Darbar Sahib complex should be handed over to a committee of representative Sikhs which would subsequently be an elected one. However, no follow-up action was taken on this issue.

A notable development during that period was the three-day conference of the Sikh League at Lahore beginning October 18, 1920 under the presidency of Baba Kharak Singh. The leaders were conveyed by Risaldar Gopal Singh Bhagowalia at this conference that the government was willing to concede demands like transfer of the control of Sikh shrines, freedom to carry kirpan, reservation of 33 per cent seats in the provincial council for Sikhs and release of political prisoners subject to the condition that resolution of non-cooperation against the British government should not be adopted at the conference. The offer was rejected. The effort of the rulers was to keep the Sikhs away from the freedom movement as Punjab happened to be the main recruiting ground for the armed forces.

It may be mentioned that the movement for the liberation of gurdwaras had already gained momentum coinciding almost with the start of publication of the *Akali* daily newspaper from May 21, 1920.

Jhabbar made two significant points in his two-hour speech on October 19. One, participate in the freedom struggle but do not join the Congress till the party assured the Sikhs of their rights. Second, the non-cooperation resolution should be passed before Mahatma Gandhi's speech as otherwise, it would be construed to have been influenced by him.[9] However, the non-cooperation resolution was passed after his address. The issue of bargaining with the Congress had thus entered the Sikh political discourse at the first stage itself. This conference was also attended by Mohammad Ali, Shaukat Ali and Maulana Abul Kalam Azad.

A part of Gandhi's speech at this conference is very important in the context of the gurdwara liberation struggle. Gandhi has been quoted as saying, "I have come to know that some Sikh youths are forcibly taking over gurdwaras and it is not proper. To take over gurdwaras by throwing out 'mahants' amounts to despotism."[10]

The Jallianwala Bagh massacre had intensified political activity in the Sikh domain with conferences being organized at various places, although the people who had been fired upon by the security forces were from all the three religious shades. Some Sikh leaders like the Darbar Sahib Sarabrah Aroor Singh, who supported the British administration, came under attack at such conclaves. Of particular significance was the resolution for the boycott of such leaders adopted at the conference at Faizlapur now in Pakistan. This undated resolution states:

"This conference of the Khalsa excommunicates those Sikhs who had honoured Punjab Governor Michael O Dwyer at his farewell. They are Sardar Bahadur Sunder Singh Majithia, Sardar Aroor Singh, Sarabrah, Sri Darbar Sahib, Sardar Bahadur Gajjan Singhji of Ludhiana and Risaldar Gopal Singhji Bhagowalia. No Sikh should inter-act with them."[11] Dwyer was Punjab Lt Governor at the time of the Jallianwala massacre. In a way, this was the start of the gurdwara liberation movement. A number of such conferences were organized during this period before the gurdwara liberation agitation was formally launched.

The first gurdwara to be liberated was Babe Di Ber in Sialkot district in Pakistan. Jhabbar proposed a nine-member committee headed by Kharak Singh to manage this shrine. However, according to another reference, the committee was set up on October 5, 1920 had 13 members.[12]

There is yet another reference about Gurdwara Chomala Sahib, Lahore, being the first to come under control of the Sikhs on September 27, 1920 followed by Gurdwara Babe Di Ber on October 5. A 12-member committee was constituted for Gurdwara Chomala Sahib.

The focus then shifted to Darbar Sahib. At the time of the annexation of Punjab in 1849, the Darbar Sahib management was with a committee of baptised Sikhs along with the priests. A meeting of some Sikh Sardars (members of the elite) was called at the house of Raja Teja Singh at Amritsar in 1859 to settle certain issues with the priests. The Amritsar Deputy Commissioner was also present. It was at this meeting that the issue of management of this shrine by the Sikhs themselves was taken up without the help of the government. It was decided to set up a nine-member committee of baptised Sikhs with government appointed president who was known as Sarabrah.[13] The duty of the Sarbrah was to carry out instructions of the committee. However, this committee was dropped in 1883 with the Sarbrah emerging as the all-powerful custodian.

Entire octroi revenue of Amritsar at that time was dedicated to the Darbar Sahib. Slowly, the share was slashed to only six pies a rupee. This share too was subsequently taken away. Only canal water and lighting charges were left to be paid from the municipal funds. Despite huge money at his disposal, the Sarbrah had never given any account to the Sikhs as he was accountable only to the deputy commissioner. However, some of the priests had a share in income.[14]

Meanwhile, the management started degenerating. "The precincts (of Golden Temple) began to be used by Pandits and astrologers for the propagation of superstitious practices. Idols were openly worshipped in the holy compound. Dirty booklets were sold and shops of all sorts were opened in the premises. On Basant and holy days, licentious songs were sung by musicians inside the temple. Rogues roamed about harassing women."[15]

The movement to end such distortions started in 1905 with the first action being the removal of idols of Hindu gods and goddesses. This was followed by a resolution moved by former Sarbrah Sardar Bahadur Arjan Singh adopted at a meeting of the Chief Khalsa Diwan to amend Dastur-ul-Amal of the Darbar Sahib.

Objections were subsequently raised to the practice of the government appointing Sarbrah while reverting to the earlier committee system. It was the Sikh Youngmen Association of Quetta that on December 22, 1906 resolved that the management of the Darbar Sahib should be handed over to the Chief Khalsa Diwan. The demand was raised in May 1907 for nomination of a "Gurdwara Sambhal Committee." However, the campaign could not be carried forward.

The movement to take over the management of the Darbar Sahib revived in 1919 after the war and taking the initiative this time was the Sikh League. The Sikhs of Basra, Baghdad and Maymyo too sent resolutions to the government on this issue.

The government, on July 14, 1920, took the position reiterating reply given to a question on April 13, 1920 in the Legislative Council that stated: "The question of management of the Golden Temple at Amritsar has been under the consideration of the government for some time. It has been decided to defer the action until the Reforms Scheme has been brought into operation. The elected representatives of Sikh constituencies will then be consulted for any changes which may be contemplated."[16]

The big push came in 1920.

The liberation struggle got intensified with the Sikhs taking over the control of the Darbar Sahib complex on October 12, 1920. The very first resolution adopted that day at the congregation was revocation of excommunication of the Sikhs arrested in Ghadar struggle and under detention at Andaman. At the same time, it was resolved that Aroor Singh was not a true Sikh (Guru Da Sikh Nahin). The Sarabrah (custodian) of the Darbar Sahib appointed by the British administration at the time of its takeover was Sunder Singh. A 25-member committee was set up headed by Teja Singh Bhuchhar for the management of the Darbar Sahib complex.

It may be mentioned that Sikhs from lower castes were not allowed to offer Parsad at the Darbar Sahib by the then priests despite the fact that Sikh religion recognises no caste, creed or class. The Khalsa Brotherhood led a procession of these newly baptised Sikhs to Darbar Sahib who were Dalits. The priests refused to offer prayer for them but ultimately relented under pressure. In the meantime, the priests at the Akal Takht, feeling threatened by this action, fled. The Sikhs took over their holiest of the holy complex.

Jhabbar and his associates, who had taken over the shrine, received invitation from the Deputy Commissioner through Sunder Singh Ramgarhia on October 14 for talks. The delegation included Dharam Singh, Basant Singh, Teja Singh Bhuchhar, Teja Singh Chuharkana and Jhabbar. Professors Kashmira Singh and Bawa Harkishan Singh from Khalsa College also joined them, mainly as interpreters. The Deputy Commissioner made it clear that the management of the shrine was an internal affair of the Sikhs and the administration would not like to intervene hereafter. It was proposed that a committee should be constituted that would be handed over the control formally. By that time, hundreds of Sikhs had gathered outside the meeting venue. Jhabbar came out to discuss the proposal with the gathering.

The names proposed included Sunder Singh Ramgarhia, Jhabbar, Bhuchhar, Baba Kehar Singh, Mukand Singh, Deva Singh, Bahadur Singh, Prof. Teja Singh and Prof. Bawa Harkishan Singh. The control was transferred to a nine-member committee and the announcement to this effect made at the Akal Takht at 3 pm. The names finalized for this committee included Ramgarhia, Profs Teja Singh and Bawa Harkishan Singh, Bhuchhar, Jhabbar, Dr. Gurbaksh Singh, Bhai Chanda Singh Editor, Deva Singh and Hakim Bahadur Singh.

Setting Up of the SGPC in 1920

Meanwhile, these Sikh leaders decided to convene representative Panthic gathering at the Akal Takht on November 15 to work out permanent arrangement. The invitation was issued under the seal of the Akal Takht and signed by Dr. Gurbaksh Singh. Norms were specified for the participants besides the number of representatives from different Sikh bodies. Significantly, this invitation had also been extended to the Sikh regiments.

The representation given to the Sikh bodies for this conclave was as follows

Four Takhts (six representatives each); Gurdwaras (one representative each); Khalsa College Amritsar- managing committee (one), staff (two) and students (two); G.N. College, Gujranwala–managing committee (one), staff (two) students (two); Akal College, Mastuana–managing committee (one), staff (two) students (two); Khalsa high schools, middle schools and primary schools (one each from the managing committee, staff and students); Sikh states (five each); mixed Sikh cavalries (two each); mixed Sikh regiments (two each); purely Sikh cavalries (five each); purely Sikh Regiments (five each) and Nihang Jathas whose duty had been protection of shrines (five each for 100 members).

However, the government was still not willing to lose its indirect control over the shrine and in a move to preempt the November 15 conclave, announced a 36-member committee on November 13 in consultation with Maharaja Bhupinder Singh of Patiala and others. The members of this committee included Maharaja Bhupinder Singh, Nihal Singh (Judge Patiala), Bachittar Singh (Judge Jind), Beant Singh (Judge Nabha), Puran Singh (Kapurthala), Inder Singh (Faridkot), Bhag Singh Kalsia and Fateh Singh Granthi, Amritsar etc.

There were certain other developments too preceding the formation of the committee. Several Sikh leaders and teachers and students of the Khalsa College, Amritsar met in October end on the college premises to discuss modalities for the management of the shrines. The meeting adopted a resolution moved by Prof. Bawa Harkishan Singh to take up this issue with the Chief Khalsa Diwan. The thinking was that this body could be handed over this responsibility after changing its bylaws.

A committee was set up to talk to the Diwan leaders. The members included Kharak Singh Raees (Sialkot), Harchand Singh (Lyallpuri), Gurdial Singh Bhaini, Master Tara Singh, Bhai Jodh Singh, Prof. Teja Singh (Mastuana), Prof. Bawa Harkishan Singh, Prof. Naranjan Singh, Lal Singh (Ludhiana), Ujjal Singh (Mian Channu), Amar Singh Dayal (Jhabal), Sunder Singh Chawla (Lahore), Teja Singh Samundari, Sardool Singh Kaveeshar, Master Sunder Singh Lyallpuri, Giani Sher Singh, Kartar Singh Jhabbar, Amar Singh Lyall Gazette, Bakhshish Singh Samundari, Teja Singh Bhuchhar, Charan Singh

(Nabha), Joginder Singh (Patiala), Shamsher Singh Advocate, Avtar Singh Barrister (Gujranwala), Harnam Singh Chawinda, Arjan Singh Dhirka, Ram Singh Editor Panch, Master Chanda Singh Editor, Dan Singh Vachhoa, Master Mota Singh and Akali Mangal Singh. This committee was briefed to submit its report on November 15 after taking the Diwan leadership. However, the talks ended in a fiasco.[17] Its report was discussed at a meeting on November 7 that came to the conclusion to set up a committee at the November 15 meeting.

The two-day meeting beginning November 15, 1920 decided to constitute 175-member committee that also included 36 members announced by the government. Presided over by Principal Teja Singh, this conclave was attended by about 10,000 persons. The criterion adopted was to make selection by inviting five members from each district. The committee was finalized late in the night on November 15. Members were also included to represent Sikh states and Sikh bodies in Burma, Malaya (now Malayasia), China and USA. The effort was to give it a global character. Initially as a stopgap arrangement, Harbans Singh Attari was elected president with Sunder Singh Ramgarhia as manager.[18]

However, according to another version, Sunder Singh Majithia was elected its president, Harbans Singh Attari as vice-president and Sunder Singh Ramgarhia as secretary. Before getting elected, Majithia sought apology for his any act of omission or commission.[19] All these three office-bearers were close to the government. The executive committee had Jodh Singh, Teja Singh, Buta Singh Vakil, Harbans Singh Charan Singh, Amar Singh Lyall Gazette and Baba Kehar Singh Patti as members.

A five-member committee was constituted to scrutinise members that included Jathedar Balwant Singh, Prof. Bawa Harkishan Singh, Master Mota Singh, Jathedar Teja Singh Bhuchhar and Prof. Teja Singh Mastuana. Bhai Jodh Singh was co-opted in the absence of Master Mota Singh. The executive members included Jodh Singh, Teja Singh, Buta Singh Vakil, Harbans Singh, Charan Singh, Amar Singh and Kehar Singh Patti.

According to Teja Singh, the inaugural meeting of the new body was held on December 12, 1920. The names of the new members were read and they were taken to first floor of the Akal Takht to be subjected to scrutiny as per the criteria laid down by the five-member committee (Panj Piaras). The members of this committee included Bhai Teja Singh, Principal, Akal College, Bhai Teja Singh Bhuchhar Majha Diwan, Bhai Balwant Singh Kulla, Bhai Mota Singh and

Prof. Harkishan Singh, Khalsa College. After scrutiny, they were presented before the congregation.

> The scrutiny over, all members headed by five Panj Piaras, clad in black and carrying their kirpans on their shoulders came down singing shabads and presented themselves before the Sangat. The scene was the most impressive when assistant secretary Bawa Harkishan Singh read out names of those who were declared duly inaugurated specifying the respective confessions of those who were found short in any respect. The attention of the audience became most rapt when the name of Sardar Bahadur Sardar Sunder Singh Majithia was announced. The Assistant Secretary explained in detail the position of the Honourable Sardar. He said that in view of the fact that certain members of the Panth were displeased with the Sardar Bahadur, he had been asked to say in the presence of the Guru, before His very throne, whether or not he had been prompted in all he had done, as Secretary of the Chief Khalsa Diwan or as representative of the Panth, by motives which in any way aimed not at the unalloyed welfare of his community. With perfect humility and dignified serenity Sardar Sunder Singh said that in the presence of the Guru he solemnly affirmed that whatever he did he did to the best of his ability and understanding in the best interests of the community and not at all actuated by any selfish or unworthy motives that were attributed to him. Still however, he said, he implored the indulgence of the forgiving Panth.[20]

Majithia was then elected president with Harbans Singh Attari as vice-president and Sunder Singh Ramgarhia as secretary of this body. A sub-committee including the office-bearers was formed for drafting a new constitution and Dastur-al-Amal of the Darbar Sahib. The members of this sub-committee, besides the executive committee, included Bhai Jodh Singh, Principal Teja Singh, Buta Singh Vakil, Prof. Harbans Singh, Charan Singh, Amar Singh Editor and Kehar Singh Patti. This committee was given three weeks to finalize rules and regulations.

According to the other version, Harbans Singh Attari replaced him when Sunder Singh Majithia was inducted as member of the executive council.

An important decision taken at this meeting was to stop the Hindu practice of applying tilak daily to Guru Granth Sahib in the Darbar Sahib.[21]

This body was registered as a society under Section XXI of the Companies Act, 1860 by H. Calvert, Registrar of Joint Stock Companies, Punjab on April 30, 1921.

The First Election

A very significant aspect of the SGPC is that within months, its character changed from being a nominated to an elected body. The organization had evolved its own election system involving the entire community not only in Punjab but also the Sikh regiments. This system was part of the constitution that was adopted by this body. The new constitution provided for four-fifth of elected members and remaining one-fifth to be nominated by them. Districts were apportioned a fixed number of seats proportionate to population of Sikhs and religious importance. The Sikh states too were given representation. One fourth of the seats in such states were to be filled up by the Maharaja. Every initiated Sikh not less than 21 years of age was entitled to vote.

The first election on the basis of this constitution was held in July 1921 for which polling officers were deputed by the parent body. The procedure was to convene a meet of the eligible Sikhs and then seek nominations. The voters would be asked to write names of the candidates on a slip and hand over the same to the polling officer.

The first meeting of the house elected under this system was held on August 14, 1921 at the Akal Takht in which nominated seats were filled up. The nominated members included such eminent persons as Bhai Kahan Singh Nabha, Harbans Singh Attari, Prof. Jodh Singh, Baba Gurdial Singh, Baba Partap Singh, Baba Jaswant Singh Bedi, Bhai Sangat Singh Kamalla, Bhai Hira Singh Ragi, Sardar Man Singh Vakil and Sardar Ram Singh Kabuli. Another meeting was called on August 27 to elect office-bearers.

The provision of co-opted members was made to accommodate scholars and other eminent persons who otherwise would not contest election and thereby give wider representation.

Baba Kharak Singh was elected president, Sunder Singh Ramgarhia vice-president and Sardar Bahadur Mehtab Singh as honorary secretary. The 31-member executive committee was also elected. This executive committee a few days later constituted a seven-member working committee and local committees for Darbar Sahib, Amritsar, Darbar Sahib Tarn Taran and Nankana Sahib. Every affiliated gurdwara was to contribute one-tenth of its offerings to the SGPC but this was not binding on shrines having less offerings.

The system of co-option was carried forward under the Sikh Gurdwara Act but now rather than nominating persons of eminence, it is the politicians who mainly fill up this quota. The original purpose has been lost in the process.

Baba Kharak Singh retained presidency in the next election held on July 16, 1922 while Amar Singh Jhabal and Jaswant Singh were elected vice-president and secretary respectively.

Formation of the Akali Dal

Within days of the formation of the SGPC, the Sikhs took over gurdwara Panja Sahib and it was during this action that the seeds were sown for the launching of the Shiromani Akali Dal with a proposal having been mooted by Jhabbar to keep a volunteer force of about 200 men and women ready at Amritsar to facilitate liberation of gurdwaras in case of any resistance by the non-Sikhs. The Hindus of Panja Sahib had opposed management of this shrine passing into the hands of the Sikhs. This idea regarding volunteer force named as Gurdwara Sewa Dal was published in the *Akali* newspaper that used to carry daily diary of Jhabbar.

At the meeting of the SGPC called on December 14, 1920 for this purpose, the proposal was mooted by Jhabbar, according to which about 100 volunteers were to remain stationed at Amritsar to be sent wherever needed for the liberation of gurdwaras. This volunteer force was called Akali Dal but the name was to be finalized later. Similar units were set up at several other districts.

The name Akali Dal was given the final approval at another meeting on January 23, 1921 at the Akal Takht. Arjan Singh Dhirke had proposed the name Gurdwara Sewa Dal. Sarmukh Singh Jhabal was elected first president of the Akali Dal at this meeting. Shiromani was added at a meeting on March 29, 1922.

This force was specified two objectives:

1. To serve the Panth by carrying along all Akali Jathas; and 2. To implement the directive from the SGPC for managing the gurdwaras.

Proposal for Gurdwara Legislation

The SGPC finally acquired statutory status with the enactment of Sikh Gurdwara Act, 1925. The first legislation mooted by the government in 1921 was rejected.

This legislation was not as much the formal demand of the Sikhs as is now being made out going by certain developments associated with the adoption and implementation of this legislation but had evolved during negotiations with the British rulers over the period. The then British rulers were faced with yet another hurdle after the adoption of the 1925 Act and it was getting this legislation endorsed and accepted by the Sikh leaders, many of whom had been incarcerated in the Lahore fort after the Shiromani Gurdwara Parbandhak Committee and the Shiromani Akali Dal had been banned on October 12, 1923.

The Act envisaged the constitution of a central board for the management of shrines in Punjab with every Sikh, both men and women, having attained the age of 21, being eligible to vote, subject to other qualifications. At the doctrinal level in the Sikh philosophy, women enjoy equal status with men.

Adoption of the Sikh Gurdwara Act 1925

Moved as a private member's Bill by Tara Singh Moga on May 7, 1925, it was discussed by a select committee on June 20 and adopted on July 7 at a special session of the Punjab Legislative Council at Shimla. After having been given approval by the Governor General on July 28, it was notified on August 7 and implemented with effect from November 1, 1925. The body known as the Central Gurdwara Board, thus constituted, was authorised to change its name with three-fifth majority. The statutory elected body subsequently reverted to its original name of the SGPC at its very first general body meeting.

The board was to have 120 elected members with chiefs of the Darbar Sahib, Akal Takht, Takht Keshgarh Sahib, Takht Hazur Sahib and Takht Patna Sahib being its ex-officio members. Fourteen members were to be co-opted from outside Punjab from the rest of the country while 12 members were to be nominated by the rulers of the Sikh princely states which included Patiala, Nabha, Faridkot, Jind and Kalsia. Despite this representation, this Act was not to apply to the Sikh princely states.

At the time this legislation was enacted, 56 Akali leaders were in jail under Sections 120B, 120A and 124A of the IPC for conspiracy to dislodge the British government. Baba Kharak Singh, then among the most commanding Akali leaders, was already detained in Dera Gazi Khan jail since 1922 and had been sentenced in two different cases. Only the leaders jailed in Lahore fort had been framed in the conspiracy case. The government put up the condition of endorsement of this Act for the release of these leaders. Sixteen of them refused to accept this pre-condition and they included Teja Singh Samundari, Master Tara Singh, Bhag Singh Advocate, Gurcharan Singh Advocate, Gopal Singh Qaumi, Sarmukh Singh Jhabal, Sohan Singh Josh, Sewa Singh Thikriwala, Babu Tript Singh Lyallpur, Teja Singh Akarpuri, Santa Singh Sultanwind, Teja Singh Ghawind, Hari Singh Jalandhari, Hari Singh Editor Akali, Rai Singh (Daljit) and Teja Singh Chuharkana. However, Chuharkana backtracked and came out leaving 15 in jail.

The Sikh Gurdwara Act had been enacted by the government as

an escape route to end confrontation with the Sikhs over liberation of gurdwaras as the apprehension was that the unprecedented repression let loose on the peaceful protesters had started affecting the psyche and morale of the soldiers in the Sikh regiments of the Indian army.

These leaders refused to come out on this condition. There was no need to put up this condition in case the legislation was the achievement of this glorious Sikh struggle. Clearly, the government had some apprehension. Moreover, these leaders could have come out even on this condition in case they had perceived it to be their achievement. The legislation at one level was part of the Machiavellian tactics of the British rulers to buy peace. The sacrifices the Sikhs had made were unparalleled but the same were for the liberation of gurdwaras as a part of the struggle under the already existing non-statutory SGPC and not for the enactment of this legislation per se that was its by-product. The struggle was for transfer of gurdwaras to this body constituted in 1920. The formal demand for legislation had been made only at a later stage that was never on the agenda of the struggle.

It may be mentioned that in 2014 when the Haryana government adopted the Haryana Sikh Gurdwara Management Act on July 11 to end jurisdiction of the SGPC over the shrines in the neighbouring state of Haryana, it was stiffly opposed by Punjab Chief Minister Parkash Singh Badal, Akal Takht Jathedar Giani Gurbachan Singh, SGPC chief Avtar Singh Makkar and Shiromani Akali Dal President Sukhbir Singh Badal alleging direct interference in the religious affairs of the Sikhs by the Congress government in the neighbouring state. The jurisdiction of the SGPC also extended to Haryana and Himachal Pradesh, the two states carved out of Punjab following its re-organization in 1966 to create Punjabi Suba on the demand of the Akali Dal. These leaders asserted they would not allow bifurcation of the SGPC for the formation of which the Akali Dal had made big sacrifices. However, as per the history, these sacrifices were for the liberation of the Sikh shrines for which the SGPC had been constituted in 1920, not for getting it statutory status in 1925.

Interestingly, the SGPC inserted an advertisement in the newspapers on July 30, 2014 whose last para stated: "The SGPC makes a humble appeal to all the Sikhs who have faith in Guru Hargobind Sahib not to fall prey to the evil designs and forces who have always tried to belittle Sikh history, Sikh glory and Sikh institutions. The community should unitedly obey all "hukamnamas" and directives issued by Shri Akal Takhat Sahib." Such an advertisement was unprecedented. Ironically, it was Badal who was accused of violating the 'Hukamnama' issued by then Akal Takht Jathedar Bhai Ranjit Singh on December 31, 1998 to maintain unity in Akali Dal to observe the Khalsa Tercentenary falling in April, 1999. That had led to the split in the Akali Dal with Jathedar Gurcharan Singh Tohra raising this slogan "Akal Takht Mahaan Hai, Sikh Panth Dee Shaan Hai". This very slogan was heard again in 2014 and this time, it was raised by the Badal men opposing the Haryana gurdwara panel. History sometimes repeats itself in strange ways. The Akal Takht Jathedar Giani Gurbachan Singh too had opposed formation of the Haryana gurdwara panel.

The Shiromani Akali Dal has always accused the Congress of interfering in the religious affairs of the Sikhs. However, the party was in for a shock when the BJP-led government of Maharashtra amended Takht Sri Hazur Sahib Nanded Board Act, 1956 through a notification in February, 2015 empowering the state government to appoint President of the board managing this historical shrine. Earlier, the board constituted under the Act used to elect its President. The state government nominated BJP MLA from Mulund in Mumbai, Tara Singh as the President, evoking strong reaction from SGPC chief Avtar Singh Makkar who dubbed it as a direct interference in the religious affairs of the Sikhs. He went on to say that the Maharashtra government had made a mockery of the institution by appointing a non-baptised Sikh as the President. The BJP-led government in Maharashtra refused to yield to Badal.

There is another important aspect relating to the very first election of this body. A section of the leaders of SGPC entered the electoral fray as a party under this very banner in the first general election held on June 18, 1926 under the Sikh Gurdwara Act. This group had the tacit support of Maharaja Bhupinder Singh of Patiala, otherwise an ally of the British. The other party was the Akali Dal led by the so-called hardliners, who had refused to pledge support to the legislation as a precondition to come out of jail and the third group was of the Sikhs directly in league with the government. "Every tactic was resorted to in this election, which are now being used in the Assembly and the Lok Sabha elections. Every type of corrupt practice was adopted to win by hook or by crook. The main aim was to win the election irrespective of the methods involved as the perception was that winning the election was going to be the single most spectacular achievement."[22]

Significantly, Maharaja Bhupinder Singh as an ally of the British had played important role in saving Jhabbar at one point during the gurdwara liberation struggle. Jhabbar was the man who was instrumental in 1920s in the reconstruction of Gurdwara Kartarpur Sahib, now in Pakistan, where Guru Nanak had spent his last years. This gurdwara had been badly damaged due to floods, as it is situated near river Ravi.

Launch of the Gurdwara Liberation Struggle

This first elected house of 120 members had 85 members from the Akali Dal, 26 from the SGPC group, five from the pro-government group and four independents. The name of the body constituted under the Sikh Gurdwara Act was Central Gurdwara Board was reverted to the SGPC at its very first meeting on November 4, 1926, as the Act carried this provision. The elected body resolved to recommend to the government to extend the jurisdiction of this Act to all the princely states and rest of the country. The seeds for the Akali Dal's demand of the All India gurdwara legislation had been sown at this first meeting itself.

It is necessary to go into the short history of this legislation as the first move had been initiated in 1921 itself.

The Sikh shrines, at one stage, had gone under the control of the 'mahants' (hereditary priests) who had introduced distortions in the Sikh way of life. The 'mahants' were only the managers initially but when the British rulers updated the revenue records by way of land settlement, these people managed to get the gurdwara properties transferred in their own names.

The British government in 1859 set up a committee of trustees presided over by its nominee (Sarabrah) for the management of the Golden Temple. This committee system was later dropped in 1883 while retaining Sarabrah who was to report directly to the Amritsar Deputy Commissioner.

The issue of allowing the Sikhs to appoint Sarabrah was first taken up by the Singh Sabhas and then Chief Khalsa Diwan in 1906. The Diwan also adopted a resolution that Dastur-al-Amal of Darbar Sahib should be revised in consultation with the Panth. The Diwan also formed a sub-committee for the reform of gurdwaras but this body was essentially of the Sikh elite. This organization brought out a pamphlet in 1915 for circulation among the Sikhs to seek suggestions on liberation of shrines. The matter was dropped as impracticable.[23]

It may be mentioned that the Sikh shrines at far off places like Baghdad in the West and Dhaka and Chittagong in the East were mainly associated with Guru Nanak or Guru Tegh Bahadur who had travelled extensively to preach Sikhism. The reach of this religion at one time was far and wide. The Sikhs in Baghdad set up a Central Sikh Committee on October 10, 1920 for proper management of gurdwaras and for taking up their concerns with the Mesopotamian (now Iraq) government. This committee resolved that the Sikh literature should be translated in Arabic and English for free distribution in that country. Jagat Singh was the secretary of this committee.

The conduct of Darbar Sahib priest, Partap Singh, by way of his opposition to the enactment of the Anand Marriage Act, 1909 governing the Sikh marriages, too provoked the Sikhs.

It was the Sikh League constituted on December 27, 1919 that for the first time called for transfer of management of Darbar Sahib to a "representative body of the Sikhs, constituted on an elective basis and responsible to the Panth."[24]

The demand for the transfer of management of Sikh shrines was picking up. "Even the Sikhs of Basra, Baghdad and Maymyo sent resolutions to the government to withdraw from the control of Darbar Sahib."[25]

The first indication of the government thinking on this issue is evident from the reply given to a question in the Punjab Legislative Council on March 13, 1920 that stated:

> The question of management of Golden Temple has been under the consideration of the government for some time. It has been decided to defer the action until the Reforms Scheme has been brought into operation. The elected representatives of the Sikh constituencies will then be consulted for any changes that may be contemplated... The government intends to consult these gentlemen at an early date after the conclusion of election. With their assistance, a committee will be selected in whose hands the appointment of the manager and security of accounts will thereafter rest. When committee is constituted, it is the intention of government to stand aside from the management entirely, in future.[26]

However, this reply was not to the satisfaction of the Sikhs. The action was on. After a meeting at the nearby Jallianwala Bagh, the Sikhs took over the control of Darbar Sahib and Akal Takht on October 12, 1920. The provocation was the refusal of the priests to offer a prayer for the newly baptised Sikhs from lower castes. The Deputy Commissioner called a meeting of the priests and Sikh leaders the next day to work out the arrangement for management of Darbar Sahib. The priests did not attend. The outcome was a 9-member committee. At the political level, the Sikh League gave a call for non-cooperation with the government in October 1920.

British Rule and Sikh Institutions

The British rulers got highly concerned when the call was given from Akal Takht to the Sikh representatives for a meeting on November 15, 1920 on the issue of liberation and management of gurdwaras. It was for the first time after the annexation of the Sikh Empire in 1849 that such a big gathering of the community representatives was being held. The SGPC was born at this conclave.

It was after the takeover of Nankana Sahib Gurdwara by the Sikhs that the government came out with two-pronged strategy to deal with the situation. The first was to enact legislation and thereby legalise government intervention in the gurdwara affairs. The second was to crush the Akali agitation. The massacre of 130 Sikhs at Nankana Sahib by goons of Mahant Narain Das took place on February 20, 1921 that proved to be the watershed in the gurdwara liberation movement. The SGPC was under pressure from the common Sikhs to come up with some concrete strategy.

There is yet another aspect of the takeover of gurdwara Nankana Sahib. As Mahant Narain Das had rightly assessed, the takeover of the shrine was on the list of the Sikhs, as there had been numerous complaints of every sort against him. He approached the Hindu leaders in Lahore including Lala Lajpat Rai who used to bring out a newspaper 'Vande Matram'. He donated Rs. 3,000 to the newspaper in return for help. It was a huge amount at that time. The meeting was held at the residence of Lala Lajpat Rai where it was decided to set up a Trust of Hindu leaders for Nankana Sahib and get it registered. The Mahant objected to all of the trustees being from Lahore asking who would resist the Akalis at Nankana. Lala replied that confronting Akalis was not their responsibility. The Mahant dropped the idea of Trust but did not take back the money donated to the newspaper.[27]

Mahatma Gandhi and Shaukat Ali, younger brother of Mohammad Ali Jinnah, visited Nankana Sahib on March 3, 1921 after one of the biggest tragedies during gurdwara liberation struggle as the goons of the Mahant attacked the unarmed Sikhs. Gandhi proposed that the Sikhs should boycott the trial relating to the Nankana Sahib tragedy as no justice could be expected from the British administration. He was seconded by Lala Lajpat Rai. The proposal was adopted at a formal meeting of the SGPC on March 6, 1921 and conveyed to the government. Gandhi offered to head a non-official committee to probe the tragedy.

The Punjab Governor summoned a meeting on March 8 of Sikh leaders including Harchand Singh Lyallpur and Kharak Singh Sialkot from Sikh League, Shivdev Singh and Harbans Singh from Chief Khalsa Diwan and Teja Singh Bhuchhar and Jhabbar from the Akali Dal. Sardar Bahadar Mehtab Singh also joined them but Harchand Singh and Kharak Singh abstained. Three ministers including Majithia, Lala Harkishan Lal and Mian Fazal Hussain were there from the government side to assist the Governor.

The Governor told them to stop forcible takeover of the gurdwaras and seek judicial intervention. Jhabbar said, "You promise the enactment of a law for this purpose and we will stop forcible takeover as otherwise, there is no legal provision for approaching the courts."

Lala Harkishan Lal intervened saying how could the government transfer control of gurdwaras to the Sikhs through legislation that were under the control of 'mahants'. Jhabbar advanced the logic that the gurdwaras were the property of the Panth and not of these 'mahants'. He and several of his associates were arrested on March 12 for taking over the Nankana Sahib shrine. A special court was set up for this trial.

Several Sikh leaders supported the suggestion made by Gandhi for non-cooperation to the trial. This trial was of the Sikhs who had been arrested from Nankana Sahib after take-over of the shrine. However, Jhabbar differed on the logic that theirs' was not a political struggle but a religious one. He told them that they would state truthfully that after coming out of the jail, they would continue with their struggle. The Congress leaders dissociated themselves and did not support their cause. At the end of 6-month trial, Jhabbar was sentenced to 18 years in jail and others were awarded varying sentences. The liberation struggle petered out for the time being.

Finally, Majithia and Chief Khalsa Diwan intervened for the release of these detainees. The government agreed for their release subject to individual written undertaking that the person would not incite others in future to take over the control of gurdwaras. These conditions were humiliating but Jhabbar and some of his associates gave in and came out in September 1921. Only six of these convicted Akalis refused to give written undertaking. Jhabbar perhaps committed a blunder, as it was after this undertaking that he started getting marginalized.

The First Bill

The very first Bill that was proposed in April, 1921 by the government to counter the Akali struggle was opposed even by Sikh members of the Legislative Council. The 'mahants' too persuaded a section of the Hindus (Sanatani Hindus) to send telegrams to the government opposing this Bill. The government had announced the formation of a committee to prepare the draft on February 16, 1921.

Education Minister Mian Fazal Hussain on March 14, 1921 moved the following resolution in the legislative council:

> That this council moves the Local Government to take early steps to introduce a Bill overhauling the law relating to charitable and religious endowments in the province and pending the presentation and passing of the legislation, it moves the Governor-General to make and promulgate an Ordinance on the subjects so that the movement to alter and reform the existing management of such endowments may cease to threaten the peace and good governance of province; provided that on the expiry of the ordinance the jurisdiction of the civil courts, or of such courts as the Bill which it is proposed to introduce may establish, shall not be ousted.[28]

The Gurdwara Commission was to consist of three members with two of them being non-official Sikhs. Some Hindu members raised the issue of the so-called Sikh sects and demanded representation for them too. The Sikh members protested against the wording of the resolution and repudiated the argument that there were any sects among the Sikhs. They had reservations about the Ordinance as it made no distinction between ordinary charitable trusts and Sikh gurdwaras. The resolution was adopted amidst boycott from them. However, under the circumstances, the government decided against promulgating the Ordinance and opted for the Bill for which the Council was adjourned till April 5. The government sought suggestions from the Sikhs for the Bill.

The government was concerned about the fall out of the liberation of gurdwaras as evident from the decision to increase the strength of the police.

> The government proposed a demand of Rs. 1,15,217 for an additional force of police necessitated, as alleged, by the disturbed state of the central Punjab, and particularly by the disputes regarding the management of gurdwaras. In vain did Sardar Mehtab Singh protest against the use of police in gurdwaras which gave rise to nothing but misrepresentation and repression of Sikhs. In vain did he appeal to the government that the Sikhs were the same who had shed their life's blood in Britain's cause all over the world. The demand was sanctioned.[29]

The SGPC convened a meeting of the Sikh organizations at Akal Takht on March 20, 1921 in which several resolutions were adopted. The following are some of these articulations:

That all Sikhs arrested by the authorities in connection with the gurdwaras should be released.

That the Panth strongly resents and condemns the action of the authorities concerned in arresting the Sikhs from gurdwaras in various places and handing over the same to their previous 'mahants' and 'pujaris'.

That pending enactment of legislation on the lines suggested by the SGPC for the management of gurdwaras and other religious and charitable institutions of the Sikhs, the control and management of gurdwaras be left in the hands of those who were exercising such control at the time when the arrests of the Sikhs began in various places.

All efforts of the Panth to make the government alive to the pressing need for reform in Sikh gurdwaras and charitable institutions having failed, the Panth standing before the Akal Takht in the presence of Guru, resolves solemnly that if the innocent Sikhs arrested are not released and satisfactory legislation of the gurdwaras is not passed by the April 10, 1921, the Sikhs will consider it an interference with their religious rights and will be compelled to all necessary means of reforming the gurdwaras themselves.

The Guru Panth calls upon every Sikh to join the Akali 'Jathas' to effect the reformation of their gurdwaras.

As by the grace of the Guru, the Sikhs during this hour of trial have shown the greatest fortitude and self-control, so the Guru Panth ordains that in future, too, they should similarly maintain their calmness and self-restraint in the face of even greater hardships and should never be prompted by an idea of revenge or retaliation. Thus, they should remain faithful to Sikhism upto the last breath.

The Shiromani Committee requests all Sikhs not to interfere in the existing management of any new gurdwara upto April 10 next.[30]

It was decided to set up a 12-member committee at this meeting to discuss the proposed legislation with the government and members of the Legislative Council. The draft Bill that was published on April 8 left the SGPC and other Sikh organizations disappointed. This was the first formal demand for the enactment of the legislation.

The statement of objects and reasons of the proposed Bill stated:

> Recent events have brought into prominence the fact that the management of Sikh Gurdwaras and shrines leaves much to be desired. The object of this Bill is to obtain by the appointment of a Board of Commissioners information relating to the foundation, past management, rights or succession, titles in property and other necessary matters relating to such institutions so as to enable government, the legislature and the public to know on what matter legislature is necessary to ensure that in the future

> these gurdwaras and shrines shall perform their proper functions, viz.,the maintenance and furtherance of the Sikh religion. The Commissioners who will be appointed under the Bill, besides enquiring and reporting are, in order to prevent further tension, empowered to take possession of Gurdwaras and shrines which are notified as disputed and manage them during the period of their office; and at the same time by powers conferred on them to entertain compromises and settlements in respect of particular Gurdwaras entered into by parties disputing.[31]

The Board of Commissioners headed by a non-Sikh as President appointed by the government was to be constituted under the proposed Bill. A Sikh commissioner was to be nominated by the government while two Sikh members were to be selected by the Sikh members of the Council. The term was to be two years and the salary was to be paid from the gurdwara funds. According to another version, there was a provision to give representation to the 'mahants' too. This clause was dropped in the amended draft that was referred to the select committee. The Sikh members of the committee raised several objections, including payment of salary from gurdwara funds. These select committee members included Dasaundha Singh, Kartar Singh, Harnam Singh and Mehtab Singh. The Bill did not recognise gurdwaras as the property of the Panth and left the arbitration to the commission.

There was another significant development and that was the reaction from a section of the Hindus. The Punjab Hindu Sabha wrote to other Hindu bodies on April 4, 1921 "emphasising that no changes should be allowed in the system of worship and other conditions prevailing in the gurdwaras and that if a Gurdwara Commission be appointed, sufficient representation should be granted to the Hindus."[32] However, Hindu leaders like Shankracharya of Shardha Peeth supported the Sikh cause.

As the deadline of April 10 passed, the SGPC met on April 11 to reject the draft and set up a 7-member committee to chalk out a line of action. The members included Kharak Singh, Harbans Singh Attari, Prof. Jodh Singh, Prof. Harkishan Singh, Bhai Tara Singh, Batan Singh Canadian and Teja Singh Samundari. The committee decided to intensify the struggle and started enlisting Sikhs for the purpose.

The Bill was presented in the Council on April 16 but its consideration postponed to May 9. In the meanwhile, the government called a meeting of the SGPC and representatives of 'mahants'. Several ministers, members of the Council and other Sikh leaders also attended.

Three points emerged at this meeting. Only those 'mahants' with good character could continue with the management of shrines. The gurdwaras belong to the Panth and therefore, should be under Panthic committees. Accounts of the gurdwaras should be made public.

Yet another meeting was held on April 26, 1921 to take the final call. It was at this meeting that certain irreconcilable issues cropped up. One of the contentious issues was insistence against any change in the form of worship prevalent in 1920. This amounted to stonewalling reforms and it was not acceptable to the Sikh representatives. The next issue was the composition of the Board of Commissioners.

The Sikh representatives came down from their earlier demand and agreed to have president of the board appointed by the government subject to the condition of his being a Sikh. The 'mahants' insisted that the President must be European and not a Sikh.

The meeting of the Council scheduled for May 9 was postponed. The SGPC executive committee at the two-day meeting beginning May 10, 1921 rejected the Bill. The Sikhs and the government were now heading towards confrontation. The SGPC, while opposing the Bill, resolved as follows:

To resort to passive resistance so far as possession of the gurdwaras that had already come under the Panthic control was concerned; and

As a preparation for this to resort to a process of self-purification, otherwise called non-cooperation, by

> Boycotting intoxicants like liquor,
> Fostering the use of Swadeshi goods, and
> Organizing and availing of panchayats.

In the meanwhile, the SGPC elections had taken place and the new body at its meeting on August 28, 1921 confirmed the decisions taken at the May 10 meeting.

This meeting gave a call to the Sikh members of the Legislative Council to resign their seats in protest against repressive measures adopted by the government against gurdwara liberation movement. However, they ignored this call.

The government dropped the idea of adopting the Bill and issued a communiqué in which "it advised the Sikhs to carry out reforms by persuasion and the legitimate pressure of public opinion, or by resort to law, which was now discovered by government to contain provisions, which go a considerable way towards achieving the objects in question."[33]

However, in a knee-jerk reaction, the government took back

the keys of Darbar Sahib in September thereby triggering another confrontation.

Call to Boycott the Prince of Wales

The government, on April 20, 1921 had announced the handing over of the control of Darbar Sahib complex to the Sikhs. However, the keys of Toshakhana (treasury) were with the government appointed Sarabrah (custodian) Sunder Singh Ramgarhia, who otherwise was fully cooperating with the SGPC. A section of the Sikhs favoured total control of the SGPC over the shrine with the keys being handed over to chief Baba Kharak Singh. However, the government took back the keys from the Sarabrah evoking strong reaction.

This action of the government was based on an intelligence report in which apprehension had been expressed that the objective of the hard-line Sikhs was to take over the shrine treasury and use this money for political struggle.

It was in the context of this agitation that the SGPC in early December, 1921 gave a call to the Sikhs to boycott the Prince of Wales (British Crown Prince) during his forthcoming visit to Punjab and observe strike in Amritsar on the day he landed in India. No gurdwara was to accept offerings from him, honour him with a 'siropa' or perform 'ardas' (Prayer) in his name. The Guru Nanak Dev birth anniversary on November 15 was not to be celebrated. It was decided against accepting any conditions for getting the keys back.

The intensification of the agitation started worrying the government at another level and that was likely to impact the Sikh regiments too. The government got further alarmed when retired Captain Ram Singh of Patiala and Risaldar Sunder Singh of Sialkot announced their decision to participate in the agitation.

The government was so worried about the repercussions of the Sikh agitation on the Sikh troops that it transferred two Sikh regiments from Jalandhar. At the same time, instructions were issued to take adequate steps and frame those under sedition charge who tried to mislead Sikhs in the armed forces.

The government proposed to hand over the Darbar Sahib complex to Maharaja Patiala while at the same time, constituting a central committee to deliver the keys.[34] As every move of the government failed, it was decided to return keys to the SGPC but the same was rejected by it raising the pre-condition of release of Akalis arrested as a part of this agitation.

The government announced in the Legislative Council on January

11, 1922 to dissociate from management of Darbar Sahib complex and release the detained Akalis. The keys were passed on to Baba Kharak Singh on January 19 by the district magistrate at a huge gathering in front of the Akal Takht. He had been released from Dera Gazi Khan jail on January 17.

It was this victory that was described as the "First victory in the struggle for the freedom of the country" by Mahatma Gandhi. However, the government had not released all the agitators and as such, the Akalis were continuing their agitation by way of organizing conferences. The government issued instructions on March 6, 1922 to 13 Deputy Commissioners to crush the agitation and the action started on March 20.

A group of retired senior Sikh army officers called on the Prince of Wales during his visit to Lahore with a request to transfer management and control of gurdwaras to the SGPC. It was during this period that black colour turned into a symbol of protest as the government started targeting those donning black turbans. It was in this background that representatives of the government and the SGPC met on March 8, 1922 to discuss another gurdwara legislation.

Second Proposed Gurdwara Legislation

The draft Bill in circulation at that time authorised the SGPC to nominate members to the governing board but now the government wanted to change this provision. The SGPC had turned irrelevant and weak in the perception of the government and hence the change in attitude.

One of the most vociferous opponents of the Gurdwara Bill was Dr. Tej Bahadur Sapru, member for law affairs, when the issue cropped up in the Viceroy's Council arguing it was unprecedented. His logic was that

> This sets up a very dangerous precedent. Communal representation is different. We should seriously ponder over before acceding to the demand for appointing judges on communal basis. Moreover, it is the power of the Crown and the executive to appoint judges. Such disputes could also arise in case of Hindu or Muslim shrines. Is the government prepared to enact similar legislation for them too? I can't agree with this proposal either as a lawyer or politician.[35]

However, before any decision could be taken on the second draft, the Akali agitation entered yet another phase with the launching of Guru Ka Bagh Morcha in August, 1922.

The Guru Ka Bagh Morcha was launched when the 'mahant' of that shrine stopped Sikhs from cutting wood from the land attached to it for 'langar' and lodged a complaint with the police. The police arrested five Sikhs on August 9, 1922. Sikh volunteers would march from Akal Takht to Guru Ka Bagh, about 20 km on Amritsar-Ajnala road, where they would be stopped by the police and lathi-charged mercilessly till they fell down. This went on day after day.

As this morcha started, the government got worried again about its impact on Sikh regiments. Discontent among the Sikh defence personnel could destabilize the British grip over India as the Sikhs were the vital component of the Indian defence forces. The Punjab countryside was the fertile recruiting ground for the British Indian army, which also happened to be the support base of the Akali agitation being fought under the SGPC.

According to one report, the percentage of ex-servicemen in Akali Dal in Punjab was 12.9 and thus a cause of worry.[36]

Even extreme repression had failed to demoralize the Akalis and it had rather proved counter-productive. India had never witnessed such a peaceful agitation and that too which the government had been trying to crush brutally. The brutality shocked the entire country. The government stopped lathi-charging the peaceful agitators on September 13. The Congress set-up a committee on September 27, 1922 headed by S. Ayanger to probe police atrocities during Guru Ka Bagh Morcha.

The situation was discussed at a high-level meeting convened on October 3, 1922 which, among others, was attended by the Viceroy, the Punjab Governor, Dr. Sapru, Sunder Singh Majithia, Mian Fazal Hussain and Lala Harkishan Lal. It was at this meeting that the proposal for another Bill was considered. The draft prepared by the Chief Khalsa Diwan was introduced in the meeting by Majithia. This Bill favoured that the 'mahants' should continue to manage the gurdwaras subject to certain conditions. The draft proposed the following clauses:

-The 'mahants' would not treat gurdwaras as their personal property.

-They would strictly adhere to the Sikh norms as per Guru Granth Sahib. They would have to maintain and publish accounts.

-A 3-member committee would be set up for every shrine with the 'mahant' as its member-secretary. One member would be nominated by the SGPC and the second was to be elected by the local Sikhs.

-The 'mahant' could not be removed without proving that the

person indulged in immoral activities. A tribunal was to be set up to go into such complaints and take decision.[37]

The draft did not envisage any central body.

At the same time, the government revised its own draft known as "Sikh Gurdwara and Mandir (Inquiry) Bill" which earlier had been rejected by the SGPC. The thinking was to adopt this Bill with certain changes without caring for the approval from the SGPC as the basic objective was to contain discontent in the Sikh regiments. Thus, two Bills were under consideration of the government.

The issue cropped up again at the executive council meeting on November 3, 1922 and the predominant view favoured the above draft. Majithia again strongly advocated the Chief Khalsa Diwan draft while opposing the Fazal Hussain draft in writing. His logic was that it was his Bill that would weaken the Akali agitation and thereby restore peace. The proposal to have a gurdwara Bill had first been advocated by the government after the Nankana Sahib massacre, then after the Chabian Da Morcha and now when the Guru Ka Bagh agitation was on. At the same time, the perception in the government was that this could provoke the Hindus as well as the Muslims in demanding similar legislations for their shrines.

The Majithia Bill proposed a 5-member central board with one representation from the SGPC besides local committees. This Bill was opposed by the Sikhs.

The government finally rejected the draft submitted by the Chief Khalsa Diwan and opted for the second version drafted by Mian Fazal Hussain. This Bill was moved in the Council on November 7, 1922. The Sikh members of the Legislative Council boycotted the proposed Bill and refused to cooperate even in the select committee. The SGPC and all other Sikh organizations were opposed to the Bill, which envisaged setting up of a Board of Commissioners. A separate judicial tribunal was to be constituted for the management of the disputed shrines till the adjudication about their status of being Sikh shrines. However, the main aim of the government was to use it as a propaganda tool to check growing discontent in the Sikh regiments and find a way out of the Guru Ka Bagh agitation. The Bill was adopted on November 16, 1922 with 41 members in favour and 33 against.[38] Those opposed to the Bill included all the Sikh and Hindu members of the council along with three Muslim members.

The government had got alarmed at an intelligence report filed by Deputy Superintendent of Police Sant Singh on March 7, 1922 which stated, "According to my information, the Akali agitators have succeeded to a large extent in penetrating the Sikh regiments. The Sikh units are in constant touch, overtly or covertly, with the SGPC. They consult the SGPC on issues that are cropping up in these regiments."[39]

What shook the government was the decision of the ex-servicemen to join the Akali agitation at Guru Ka Bagh. The first group of 101 such volunteers was led by Subedar Major Amar Singh on October 22. They were in uniform, not of the army but of their own with long black robes, black turbans, saffron waste band, etc and marched to Guru Ka Bagh in military precision. They were arrested and humiliated by disrobing them, allowing only the undergarments. The second group of 103 volunteers led by Risaldar Ranjodh Singh marched to Guru Ka Bagh on November 12. He had fought for the British government in France and had lost an eye in the war. This group included three commissioned officers, several havaldars and other ranks. Two of them had lost their leg each in the war. The ex-servicemen joining the Akali agitation came as a big boost for the SGPC while it had demoralising effect on the government.

> Photographs of beating of Akalis, including the military pensioners, and other Akali propaganda material had reached some of the Sikh units in spite of tight measures by the army authorities to prevent the leakage of such information. The very real danger was that the Sikh soldiers would be affected and the rumours that the Sikh graduates of Khalsa College, Amritsar, were being asked to join the 'jathas' to Guru-Ka-Bagh brought home to the authorities the imperative need for an immediate solution.[40]

Despite every effort, the government could not insulate Sikh regiments from repercussions of the Akali agitation. Some of the armed forces personnel started donning black turbans and wearing 'kirpans' for which they were punished. The government deputed Deputy Commissioner of Shahpur on November 6, 1922 to tour the Sikh regiments from November 7, as he was well-versed with Punjabi language. He submitted his report to the government on December 26, 1922.

Reference to gurdwara legislation cropped up during interaction between Amritsar Deputy Commissioner J.M. Dunnet and Subedar Major Amar Singh. The group led by the Subedar Major was stopped by Dunnet while proceeding to Guru Ka Bagh. Going by the version of the converzation available, Dunnet proposed three solutions to Amar Singh. One was judicial; the second was talks across the table and third was the gurdwara legislation.[41] This group was arrested on October 25.

The Guru Ka Bagh Morcha ended when Sir Gangaram, a renowned

philanthropist of Lahore, intervened to take the disputed land on lease from the 'mahant' for a year and allow the Sikhs to collect wood from there for the gurdwara 'langar'. Here was an escape route for the government acceptable to all.

SGPC and Akali Dal Banned

The draft Bill was rejected by the Sikh organizations at a meeting in front of the Akal Takht on November 19, 1922 and resolved that any Sikh accepting nomination as commissioner under the Bill would be dubbed as traitor of the Panth. The meeting put the pre-condition of release of all Akali leaders arrested during the Guru Ka Bagh morcha for the SGPC entering into any dialogue with the government. The perception was that the government had indirectly retained control of the shrines and it was precisely for this reason that it was opposed by Sikh members of the Legislative Council too. The government approached several Sikh lawyers to nominate them as commissioners under the Gurdwara Bill but they declined.

There was yet another significant development during this period that further alarmed the Punjab government and it was the launch of the militant Babbar Akali movement. "The activities of the Babbar Akalis in the Jullundur Doab and the terror they created among the loyalists and pro-government elements in the Panjab villages added further to the worries of the high authorities in India."[42]

The Punjab government banned the SGPC and the Akali Dal on October 12, 1923. Sixty members of the SGPC attending a meeting were arrested and charged with conspiring against the state. This came to be known as the Conspiracy Case. Fifty-six Akali activists were charged under Sections 120B, 121A, 124A, 17A and 17C. These sections related to the conspiracy to overthrow the British government and set-up Sikh Raj. The takeover of gurdwaras was cited to in this context. The SGPC was perceived to be associating itself with political struggles. The decision of the SGPC to boycott Prince of Wales was also referred to in this context. In an effort to further the cause, the SGPC had set-up panchayats at several places, it was stated.[43]

New members were nominated to the SGPC and after their arrest, yet another set of activists came forward to run the affairs. The new executive committee met on November 4, 1923 and resolved as follows:

> This new executive committee of the SGPC lays on record its firm conviction after careful consideration that it is the duty of every Sikh to protect these religious rights for the defence of which the SGPC and the Shiromani Akali Dal, the representative bodies of the nation, have been

declared unlawful by the government. The new executive declares its firm and unalterable determination to uphold these rights.

The new executive committee believes firmly that the government by declaring the SGPC and the Shiromani Akali Dal as unlawful has levelled a mean attack against the sacred rights of association in regard to Sikh religious matters and this meeting expresses its sense of disgust at this attitude of the government.[44]

The police arrested 62 members of the new committee on January 7, 1924. They courted arrested on the Ghanta Ghar entrance as the Akali workers frustrated the entry of the police with shoes on, from the back entrance of Akal Takht.

The government finally stopped arresting SGPC members, as they used to be replaced and this body continued to function. The government instructed rulers of the Sikh states too to crush Akali struggle and they complied with faithfully.

Earlier, the Akali Dal had started the Jaito Morcha in September, 1923. Both Guru Ka Bagh and Jaito agitations had attracted countrywide attention. The decision to launch Jaito Morcha was taken by the SGPC at its meeting on September 29, 1923. Initially, a group of 25 Sikhs used to be sent to Jaito to court arrest. They would face police 'lathis'. This went on for months. It was decided to intensify the agitation and accordingly, the first Shaheedi Jatha of Akalis started for Jaito from Akal Takht on February 9, 1924. It was this 'jatha' that was fired at on February 21 after reaching Jaito.

This agitation was launched by the Akali Dal in protest against the decision of the British government to dethrone Maharaja Ripudaman Singh of Nabha who had been supporting the Akalis. He had started donning black turban in protest against atrocities against Akali agitators during Guru Ka Bagh morcha and the earlier killing of the Sikhs by Mahant Narain Das at Nankana Sahib.

The Jaito agitation for restoring throne to Maharaja Ripudaman Singh took another turn when the Akhand Path (Uninterrupted recitation of entire Guru Granth Sahib) on this issue organized by the Akalis at Gurdwara Gangsar at Jaito was interrupted by the police that was considered to be an act of desecration.

The Maharaja of Patiala wrote to the Agent of the Governor General on February 23 fully supporting the police action in which 13 people had been killed on the spot while some seriously injured died later at Jaito. He justified police firing as being in self-defence and he blamed the Akalis for attacking police. He went to the extent of saying that the Akalis were provoking revolt against the government in the country.[45]

The issue was raised in the Central Assembly by Pandit Madan Mohan Malviya on February 26, 1924. It reached the Parliament in London too.

It was the Jaito agitation in which 'Jathas' (groups of volunteers) from abroad also courted arrest. A 'jatha' of 11 Sikhs from Canada started on July 17, 1924 by sea, reached Calcutta on September 14 and courted arrest at Jaito on February 21, 1925. Similarly, a 'jatha' from Hong Kong reached Amritsar on February 24, 1925 and from Shangai on July 15 to participate in the agitation.

The issue of the gurdwara Bill again cropped up during the Jaito agitation as the government initiated moves to normalise relations with the Sikhs. Honorary magistrate and Delhi contractor Sobha Singh happened to be one of the interlocutors detailed by the government to arrive at a settlement with the Sikhs. He was the nephew of SGPC chief Sardar Bahadur Mehtab Singh, then in jail. Sobha Singh made certain recommendations to the government after meeting Mehtab Singh that included amendment to the existing legislation to make it acceptable to the Sikhs or enactment of a new legislation. His second meeting with the Sikh leaders detained in Lahore Fort on March 10, 1924 remained inconclusive.

The authorities deputed General William Birdwood, Commander-in-Chief of the Northern Command to negotiate with the Sikhs. He sought the help of Bhai Jodh Singh to negotiate with the Akali leaders in Lahore Fort and outside to work out a solution. Bhai Jodh Singh, who too had been member of the SGPC, was against confrontation between the Sikhs and the British India government. He held nine meetings with the Akalis lodged in the Lahore Fort under the conspiracy case. However, this initiative ended in stalemate on June 2, 1924 as the Akali leaders set up the precondition of unconditional release of all the jailed leaders and completion of 101 Akhand Paths at Gurdwara Gangsar.[46]

However, going by his earlier experience as Member (Home) in the Viceroy's Council, the Governor opted for repressive policies to crush the Sikhs. "Hailey was not interested in negotiating with the Akali leadership till the whole Sikh attitude had been transformed and made more pliable...Real peace was not possible till the government was able to dictate terms to the Sikhs."[47] He mooted the idea of forming Reforms Committees of the Sikh elite at the district level to weaken the Akalis. It was for this reason that the government did not want the credit for gurdwara legislation to go to the Akalis. He was not in favour of the gurdwaras being passed on to the hardliners through this legislation. That was the time when the remaining members of the SGPC considered to be moderates favoured settlement with the government.

On the other hand, the Gurdwara legislation was again referred to in the letter that the Akali leaders wrote to Mahatma Gandhi in April, 1924 during the Jaito agitation. This was in reply to Gandhi's earlier letter. The April 20, 1924 letter made it clear that the Akalis were for a legislation that provided for transferring management of all historical gurdwaras to a central body elected by the Sikhs.[48]

Intervention by Jinnah and Malviya:

The intervention to break the deadlock came from Pt Madan Mohan Malviya and Mohammad Ali Jinnah forcing Hailey to start negotiations with the Akalis.

> At this critical juncture, national leaders like Madan Mohan Malaviya and Mohammad Ali Jinnah came to the rescue of the Akalis. Realizing that the new Governor was not prepared to negotiate with the Akali leadership or the nationalists and was cleverly encouraging anti-Akali associations to draft a Bill on the lines quite unfavourable to them, Pandit Malvaiya tried to take the wind out of Hailey's sails by drafting a Bill of his own in consultation with the Akali leadership and by asking the Sikh members of the Panjab Legislative Council to move the Bill and the Hindu members to support it.[49]

Malviya proposed in November 1924 that a private member's Bill be adopted in the Punjab Legislative Council acceptable to the Akalis. However, in case the Council rejected the Bill, then the same should be passed by the Central Legislative Council. Malviya himself proposed to move the Bill in the Central Legislative Council on the logic that there were gurdwaras outside Punjab too and hence the need for all-India gurdwara legislation.

The strategy of the government at that time was to create the impression that the SGPC was not the sole representative body of the Sikhs. The government had set up the so-called reform committees as its puppets parallel to the SGPC. The other part of the strategy was to create conditions in which the SGPC and other organizations approached the government for the enactment of legislation. Hailey was looking for some honourable escape route as the Akali agitation had intensified and even extreme repression failed to crush it. The issue of torture of Sikh prisoners especially in Nabha jail had been raised in the Parliament in London. Malviya approached both the Sikh and Hindu members of the Punjab Legislative Council on this issue.

> The moves of Malviya and Jinnah seem to have compelled Hailey to change his earlier policy of allowing the movement to prolong itself indefinitely and not to compromise with the Akalis on the Gurdwara Bill issue. Thus, on the one hand, he tried to persuade the Viceroy and Members of his Council not to allow the nationalist leaders to negotiate on behalf of the Akali leadership, while on the other, he opened negotiations with the Sikh members of the Panjab Legislative Council through E.W. Emerson and F.H. Puckle... It was under these circumstances that Sardar Tara Singh, a Sikh MLC from Moga, was asked to introduce the Bill drafted by him, the detailed provisions of which had been discussed both with the Akali leaders in the Lahore Fort jail and the government officials in Lahore and Delhi, before its introduction in Punjab Legislative Council on 7 May 1925.[50]

Tara Singh summoned a meeting of the Sikh members of the Legislative Council and set up a sub-committee which included Tara Singh, Jodh Singh, Narain Singh, Gurbaksh Singh and Mangal Singh. It was this committee, which acted as the intermediary between the government and the SGPC. No pre-conditions were laid down for talks.

The priority was gurdwara legislation. Several meetings were held between this committee and the government in which the framework of the gurdwara legislation was finalized. Both the SGPC as well as the government had now converged on the enactment of the gurdwara legislation but for different reasons. The SGPC backtracked from its pre-condition of release of all the arrested leaders, which paved the way for the introduction of the Sikh Gurdwara Bill.

The Sikh members of the Council entrusted the preparation of the final draft to another five-member committee with tacit approval of the government. They included Narain Singh Advocate, Tara Singh Moga, Gurbaksh Singh Advocate, Mangal Singh Mann Kotshera and Prof. Jodh Singh. None of them had ever participated in the gurdwara liberation struggle.

The SGPC got approval from the leaders detained in the Lahore Fort jail for giving green signal to this committee for finalizing the draft of gurdwara legislation. The government was represented by Deputy Commissioners of Amritsar and Lahore and two legal experts, including Kanwar Dalip Singh Barrister and Viesley. They were to discuss four basic issues.

The first problem was the identification of shrine as gurdwara, mode of announcement of the same as gurdwara and how to bring them under a new management. The second was the identification of the gurdwara properties and settlement of the same. The third issue related to the compenzation to those who were going to be hit with the change in gurdwara management and fourthly, what type of management was to be proposed for the shrines declared as gurdwaras and with whom was this authority to vest.

The government allowed open access for consultation with those lodged in Lahore Fort jail. Each and every proposal was discussed by the committee members with the Lahore detainees and also the SGPC leaders outside. In the first list, 232 gurdwaras were identified. However, the select committee dropped 17 gurdwaras from this list and included 29 others. The list was published with a directive to current managements to provide the list of properties attached to these shrines, which they claimed to be their personal within 60 days of the notification of the Bill. In the second list, the number of gurdwaras was brought down to 224 and after discussion in the select committee, 95 of these were dropped while three new included.

The government came out with the draft of the Gurdwara Bill on January 21, 1925. The government was not originally in favour of giving voting right to the Sikh women under the Act. Women in England were not entitled to vote in Parliamentary elections till then.[51]

According to one proposal, the government favoured constitution of local committees for the management of shrines like Akal Takht and Takht Keshgarh Sahib to weaken the central committee. However, this was not acceptable to the Sikh leaders, especially those lodged in the Lahore fort jail. They stressed the need for high-powered central management rather than decentralization.

Voting Right to Sikh Women

The SGPC at its meeting at the Akal Takht on April 27 resolved to recommend three amendments. The management of Akal Takht and Takht Keshgarh Sahib was to remain with the central body. Women would have the right to vote. The income of the gurdwaras would be used only for the propagation of religion, education and help to the needy. The decentralization move was opposed by six of the Akali leaders lodged in the Lahore Fort jail who pressed for total control with central board.

The government was opposed to giving voting rights to women but finally gave in under pressure. This was for the first time that women had been given the right to vote in India in any statutory elected body. This can be seen as the first step in India for the empowerment of women. It was the most progressive step at that time.

Bhai Jodh Singh was apprehensive of the attitude of 'hardliners' towards implementation of this Act. In his perception, while Akalis in Malwa and Doaba were moderates and favoured legislation, the leaders from Majha were 'radicals' who opposed any settlement with the government. He was of the opinion that in case the moderates failed, the situation might get complicated.

His reservation about the voting right to women was also questionable, as he felt this could pose a serious threat to the moderates. Women were considered to be more sympathetic to the radicals and the perception was that majority of them might convince their husbands to support the hardliners.[52]

Adoption of the Sikh Gurdwara Act

Moved by Tara Singh on May 7, the Bill was finally adopted on July 7, 1925. This was a victory for the Akalis at one level as despite such brutal repression, the government had come under pressure to arrive at a settlement with them, of which this Act was the outcome. With the implementation of this Act, the SGPC acquired a statutory status and thus virtually became a state within a state, although the struggle was not for this legislation per se but for restoring management of the gurdwaras to the Sikh bodies with no interference from the government.

The proposal for the legislation had first been mooted by the government as an escape route and to counter the likely disaffection among the Sikh troops against state repression. The Act was thus the by-product of the gurdwara liberation struggle. However, the government was still apprehensive about acceptability of this legislation by the Sikhs whose views were articulated by the SGPC.

Ironically, it is this Act that has provisions for indirect government interference. The power to appoint gurdwara judicial commission vests with the state government. This commission has been manouevred by the government from time to time. The Akali Dal government headed by Parkash Singh Badal used this body against the then SGPC chief Gurcharan Singh Tohra during the factional fight in 1999 leading to split in the party.

Hailey announced in the Legislative Council on July 9 that only those leaders would be released from Lahore Fort jail who give undertaking to facilitate implementation of the Act and not takeover any gurdwara or the related properties forcibly henceforth. He also announced that the ban imposed on the SGPC and the Akali Dal on October 12, 1923 would be lifted only after the new central board was constituted by holding elections.[53]

The SGPC executive committee, at its meeting on July 13, 1925 rejected these pre-conditions for the release of the detained Akali leaders as "totally unnecessary, unjust and humiliating". A day earlier, the Akali Dal had stated that these conditions had been put up to humiliate the Sikhs and no honourable Sikh would accept them for release from detention. Meetings were being organized all over Punjab against these conditions and when the SGPC executive committee's three-day meeting started on October 4, 1925, the situation in the state was surcharged. These conditions were being perceived as a big challenge to the Akali struggle.[54]

At the same time, the executive committee hailed the Act as "acceptance of basic demands of the Sikh struggle" and stated that as the leaders detained in Lahore Fort jail had given their nod, therefore, the Sikhs were being appealed to extend all help in its implementation.[55] However, Mangal Singh moved an amendment that the implementation of this resolution should be deferred for a month. This was done mainly to study all aspects of the Act to remove any apprehension of any trap having been laid down by the government. The basic demand was the transfer of the management of their shrines to the Sikhs.

There is yet another version of this meeting.

> The general committee of the SGPC at a meeting on October 4, 1925 to consider its reaction towards the gurdwara Act, found itself divided into three different camps: The first party favoured acceptance of the Gurdwara Act and ending all actions without waiting for the release of the Akali prisoners, the second wanted to reject the Act unless the government released the Akali prisoners unconditionally, and the third was for postponing the decision on the question till detailed rules under the Act were published.[56]

Some members of the Gadgaj Akali Jatha and Central Majha Diwan who opposed this legislation tried to gate-crash in the SGPC general body meeting that started at Akal Takht on October 4. Their logic was if Tara Singh, Narain Singh and Jodh Singh—all three Council members—could participate in the meeting, they also had the right. The council members had been invited by the SGPC to seek certain clarifications.

However, those detained in the Lahore Fort jail were getting divided on the issue of ratification of the Act as precondition for release, despite a resolution adopted by them that priority should be the implementation of the Act and not their release.

The group led by Mehtab Singh that articulated moderate opinion favoured coming out after accepting government conditions. Those who opposed conditional release were of the opinion that the decision of 19 of them of coming out by giving written undertaking would be "detrimental to the Panth, divisive and strengthen the government to crush us."[57] Resolutions were being adopted in Punjab for unconditional release of Akali leaders and elections to SGPC. Even the Sikh members of the Legislative Council pressed for unconditional release and it was resolved that one office of the Minister under the Sikh quota lying vacant would not be accepted by any of them under that situation.

However, Risaldar Sunder Singh and Risaldar Ranjodh Singh succumbed to the pressure and came out of jail after signing the undertaking on January 21, 1926. The government withdrew the conspiracy case against them.

This was followed by the undertaking given by Bawa Harkishan Singh in the court on January 25, 1926. He was supported by 19 other leaders who made similar statements in the court. They were released within no time. They included Bawa Harkishan Singh, Sardar Bahadur Mehtab Singh, Gurdit Singh Bahlolpur, Giani Sher Singh, Pritam Singh Anandpur Sahib, Gurdit Singh, Editor, Nation, Headmaster Mehtab Singh Tarn Taran, Gurbaksh Singh Dilli, Gopal Singh Sagri, Captain Ram Singh, Piara Singh Canadian, Kirpal Singh Amritsar, Kishan Singh Amritsar, Kishan Singh, Bal Singh Canadian, Dan Singh Vichhoa, Bakhshish Singh Ludhiana, Bhagat Jaswant Singh, Mit Singh Canadian and Prof. Sahib Singh. Sixteen leaders still in Lahore Fort jail continued to face the conspiracy case of mutiny against the King. Within fourteen days, Teja Singh Chuharkana also fell in line. However, these leaders were not welcomed by the Sikhs after their release.

A general body meeting of the already existing SGPC was held within five days of the release of its President Mehtab Singh, which was attended by 140 members. It was resolved to hold the election of the office bearers in the same meeting. The moderates put up Mehtab Singh while Bhag Singh Canadian was the candidate from the hardliners. Mehtab Singh won. The Sikhs were getting divided and the Akali Dal perceived to be hardliner was coming into confrontation with the moderate faction in the SGPC.

This was the time when the Akali Dal started distancing itself from the SGPC leadership.

Akali Conference Rejects Legislation, Section 144 in Darbar Sahib

There was another significant development. The Akali Dal decided to go ahead with the two-day Sarbat Conference beginning June 10, 1926. Significantly, this conference rejected the Sikh Gurdwara Act and constituted a 21-member committee to take over gurdwaras from the SGPC. This conference was dominated by the representatives from Gadgaj Akali Diwan and Central Majha Diwan, who were instrumental in these decisions. The Akali Dal was caught in a situation, which was not of its making as these resolutions were not in accordance with the party policy. Baba Gurdit Singh was Chairman of the reception committee of this conclave.

In accordance with the decisions taken at this conference, a small group of leaders led by Mool Singh Chawinda and Risaldar Tara Singh that also included representatives of the Gadgaj Akali Diwan started from Akal Takht on the evening of June 17 to take over the SGPC office resulting in a scuffle. The very next day, scores of Akalis went to Akal Takht and demanded the keys of Darbar Sahib. Several persons were injured in the fight between the two groups. Prof. Jodh Singh and Giani Sher Singh sought police intervention. The Deputy Commissioner led the police to the Akal Takht and imposed Section 144 in the Golden Temple complex and arrested 62 Akalis from the shrine. The government accepted the request of the SGPC to deploy police for some time within the complex on payment.

This was the first case of Section 144 having been imposed in the shrine complex and deployment of police there on the request of the SGPC. Significantly, during the post-1947 period, Punjab Chief Minister Bhim Sen Sachar had to resign for sending police to the complex on July 5, 1955 during the first Punjabi Suba morcha. Such was the anger among the Sikhs that he appeared at Akal Takht on November 10 to apologize for the action. This was not appreciated by the Congress leadership and he had to resign in January, 1956.

In the first ever election to the statutory SGPC held on June 18, 1926, then known as the Central Gurdwara Board, means were not important as the only aim was to win. Even some nomination papers were rejected on flimsy grounds including that of Sarbar Bahadur Mehtab Singh, Master Tara Singh and Amar Singh Vasu. In the 3-cornered contest, two of the groups were more or less considered to be close to the government, which included the SGPC groups led by Mehtab Singh and the other being the reformists while the Akali Dal represented the third dimension. The SGPC funds were misused along with the employees by the dominant group. The Akali Dal returned with a majority. Three of the Lahore detainees, Bhag Singh, Gurcharan Singh and Teja Singh were among those who won. Out of the 120 seats, the Akali Dal captured 85, Mehtab Singh group bagged 26 and reforms group won five and four went to independents. The people had rejected the leaders who had come out of jail after giving undertaking to the government despite their sacrifices during the gurdwara liberation struggle. They were dubbed as pro-government. The very first election of the statutory body was not without interference by the government.

Meanwhile, Teja Singh Samundari died under detention. His body was taken in a procession from Lahore to Amritsar, which was the recognition of the sacrifices made by him for the Panth. He was just 44.

The government lifted the ban on the SGPC and the Akali Dal on September 13, 1926 as it had become redundant after the election of the central board resulting in the unconditional release of the 15 detainees from the Lahore Fort by September 27. However, Sewa Singh Thikriwala was re-arrested in Patiala state where he died in jail.

The first meeting of the central board was held on September 4, 1926 in the Town Hall chaired by the Deputy Commissioner as provided under the Act. The agenda was to elect presiding officer and co-option of 14 members. The two names which were proposed included Joginder Singh from the Mehtab Singh group and Mangal Singh put up by the Akali Dal. Mangal Singh was declared elected with 82 votes while his rival polled 53 votes. In the co-option, the share of the Akali Dal was nine members with five members from the opposition.

The first formal meeting of the statutory Central Gurdwara Board was held on October 2, 1926 in which nominated member Hazara Singh Jamarai resigned to pave way for co-option of Master Tara Singh. Baba Kharak Singh was elected as the first President with Master Tara Singh as the Vice-President. Baba Kharak Singh was elected in absentia as he had not been released from jail by that time. His name was proposed by Baba Gurdit Singh.

The meeting was adjourned for half an hour and Master Tara Singh presided as the acting President in the absence of Baba Kharak Singh when the session resumed. Those elected to the executive included Mangal Singh, Bhag Singh, Jaswant Singh Jhabal, Man Singh Sargodha, Kundan Singh Thekedar, Mohinder Singh Sidhwan, Giani Sher Singh and Bachittar Singh.[58] However, according to Josh, seven persons were elected to the executive and he did not include the name of Bachittar Singh. According to him, the eighth nominee had lost the election.

It was resolved that the Central Board would be known by the earlier name of the Shiromani Gurdwara Parbandhak Committee. A provision to this effect had been made in the Act. Through another resolution, this body demanded the release of all the detained Akalis including those in princely states who had been arrested as part of the gurdwara liberation struggle. Significantly, a resolution was adopted at this meeting congratulating those who had refused to come out of jails by accepting the government conditions.

Punjabi in Gurmukhi script was to be the official language of the SGPC. It was at this very meeting that seeds were sown for the demand of the all India Gurdwara legislation from which the Akali Dal subsequently backtracked when it was under the control of Badal and his son Sukhbir Singh Badal 2007 onwards. Introducing hereditary politics in the Akali Dal, Badal later passed on the baton to Sukhbir on January 31, 2008 ending internal democracy in the party for which it was known.

The statutory Central Gurdwara Board renamed SGPC took formal charge of the gurdwaras on November 27, 1926. The SGPC had emerged as a 'mini state.' The gurdwara liberation struggle was over, although several leaders including Baba Kharak Singh were still in jail. The Akali Dal at its general body meeting on December 5 adopted a resolution to make every effort, though peaceful, to get them released.

The Sikh Gurdwara Act was applicable to Punjab and later its jurisdiction came to be extended to the Sikh princely states. This arrangement continued till the reorganization of Punjab in 1966 when Haryana and Himachal Pradesh were carved out of the mother state to meet the Akali Dal's demand for a Punjabi-speaking state, which essentially was a Sikh majority state. However, the Sikh Gurdwara Act continued to be a common link between the three states and the SGPC acquired the status of an inter-state body corporate with the power to amend it having passed on to the Parliament. The Union Home Ministry was vested with the authority to function as the nodal agency. Any amendment could be adopted only by the Parliament. However, rather than following the parliamentary route, the home ministry started issuing executive orders to amend this Act.

Two notable orders include reservation of 30 seats for women by increasing the total strength of the house by 30 and withdrawal of voting rights to the Sehajdharis in 2003. The Union Home Ministry of the then BJP-led NDA government in which the Akali Dal was the partner issued a notification taking back the voting rights of the Sehajdhari Sikhs on October 8, 2003 following a resolution passed at the general house of the SGPC on March 30, 2002.

Women were to be elected from the seats which were declared double and this was to be done by rotation. The procedure adopted for this amendment was in gross violation of the Act. The withdrawal of voting rights to the Sehajdharis had been affected by an amendment in the Punjab Assembly in 1959 and the same could not be withdrawn by an executive order. This came to be challenged in the court and a situation arose when the Supreme Court put under suspended animation the newly-elected house in 2011, allowing only the executive committee to perform day-to-day functions. The situation was unprecedented. The Act was finally amended on April 25, 2016 to withdraw voting right to Sehajdharis. The Supreme Court on September 15, 2016 re-installed the general house elected in 2011 on the basis of this amendment. The functioning of the 2011 general house had been stayed by the Punjab and Haryana High Court declaring the October 8, 2003 notification as null and void.

Yet another major development was the move to have separate gurdwara body for Haryana. The Punjab Re-organization Act of 1966 made a provision under Section 72 allowing Haryana to have its own gurdwara management body and it was under this provision that the Haryana government went ahead in 2014 to come up with the Haryana Sikh Gurdwara Management Act to meet the demands of the Sikhs of that state. Badal dubbed it yet another attack on the Sikhs by the Congress asserting the Akali Dal would not allow the SGPC to be diluted for the formation of which the Sikhs had made unprecedented sacrifices. But the sacrifices were for the liberation of the gurdwaras and not for the Sikh Gurdwara Act, 1925 per se.

Badal as the chief minister wrote an article (it appeared under his name) in the *Hindustan Times* on July 26, 2014 opposing the Haryana gurdwara panel in which he stated:

> If the move to break this historic institution is not opposed and effectively stopped, then the Khalsa Panth will lose the single and united religious rallying point. The SGPC is not just a managing institution for historic gurdwaras but is also a global democratic religious platform through which the Sikh community articulates its spiritual values, safeguards its religious legacy and fights any ideological or other attack on the religion. The conspiracy is aimed at ensuring that the community should disintegrate into separate centres and even parts in different states, districts and even villages.

But then he must share the blame as this situation would not have arisen in case the Akali Dal under his command had got the All India Gurdwara Act enacted during the National Democratic Alliance (led by the BJP) rule at the Centre from 1999 to 2004 in which his party was the partner. However, his apprehension was that such a legislation might end his monopoly over the affairs of this body.

Akali Dal had reacted strongly when Pakistan government formed the Pakistan Sikh Gurdwara Parbandhak Committee in 1999. However, the Delhi Akali Dal led by Paramjit Singh Sarna and Delhi Sikh Gurdwara Management Committee had differed with Badal on this issue. The SGPC recognised the PSGPC years later.

It may be mentioned that the shrines in Delhi were brought under the Delhi Sikh Gurdwara Management Committee with the adoption of the Delhi Sikh Gurdwara Act in 1971. Takht Hazur Sahib, Nanded in Maharashtra is managed by a separate board constituted under the Takht Sri Hazur Abchalnagar Sahib Board Act, 1956 and so is the case with Takht Patna Sahib for which a committee was constituted in 1956 under the rules then got approved from the district administration. The Maharashtra government in a decision on August 22, 2014 reduced the representation of the SGPC in the Hazur Sahib Board from four to one on the demand of the local Sikhs articulated by the Bhatia Committee.

In Jammu and Kashmir, gurdwaras are managed under the State Sikh Gurdwaras Parbandhak Board Jammu and Kashmir constituted under the Jammu and Kashmir Sikh Gurdwaras and Religious Endowment Act, 1973 (Act XV of 1973).

The SGPC and the Akali Dal have been losing their global character over the years especially after Badal emerged as the supreme leader in the Sikh religio-political matrix.

The situation has come to such a pass that neither Badal nor his son and Shiromani Akali Dal President Sukhbir Singh Badal dare visit countries like USA or Canada publicly or address a gathering in any of the gurdwaras there. Sukhbir had to cancel his 10-day tour to Canada on August 23, 2013 as the NGO Canadian Sikh Coalition had threatened to file suit against him in the court for "war crimes and crimes against humanity." A similar case against his father registered in a Wisconsin court in the USA was dismissed on December 24, 2013. The last senior Akali leader who continued to visit these countries was Jathedar Gurcharan Singh Tohra. He was the only Sikh leader who went abroad after 1984 and faced the Sikhs who had turned hostile to the traditional Akali leaders. That hostility continues unabated.

What is more ironic that the Akali Dal has virtually shrunk to Punjab at the time when the Sikhs have turned global. It was only after about a decade that the Akali Dal staged a comeback in the Delhi Sikh Gurdwara Management Committee elections in 2013 and retained power in the February 2017 election.

The Sikhs in other states have different issues facing them. With the formation of the DSGMC, the Sikhs emerged as a powerful group in the national capital who could negotiate with other political parties on their own terms.

The interests of the Sikh farmers in Haryana are in contradiction with those of the Punjab farmers so far as the river water dispute between the two states is concerned. The Akali Dal had been opposing the flow of water to Haryana through the Satluj-Yamuna Link Canal and this was one of the major issues on which the party launched the Dharamyudh Morcha on August 4, 1982 from the Akal Takht. It was the Akali Dal which had been bargaining on behalf of the Haryana Sikhs with the political parties in that state and this bargaining depended upon the interests of Badal and his family rather than of the Panth.

It is in this context that the Sikhs in Haryana started demanding their own gurdwara management committee as this would provide them the platform to assert themselves. Despite the fact that Haryana had the highest Sikh population after Punjab followed by Delhi, they were ignored by the successive governments at every level. With the formation of the Haryana Sikh Gurdwara Management Committee, the Sikhs have emerged as a powerful group having capacity to alter the fortunes of any political party in 22 of the total 90 assembly seats in that state. This new body betrays their identity assertion. It is for this reason that Badal had been opposing tooth and nail as it weakens his bargaining position in Haryana where his family has business interests. Akali Dal is now like any other political party with the space for a Panthic party being vacant. Sikh identity assertion has ceased to be an issue with the Akali Dal and this agenda has now passed on to the Sikhs outside India. But the problem with the Diaspora is that they continue to be frozen in a time warp, not acknowledging the fact that Punjab has moved on.

The SGPC should have been the institution uniting the Sikhs but its role has turned divisive, especially in the context of the issues like the Nanakshahi calendar. The SGPC has backtracked from the original almanac implemented in 2003. The Pakistan and US gurdwara panels follow the original almanac according to which, most of the events relating to the Sikhs fall on different dates.

The SGPC committed yet another blunder when its executive committee on August 25, 2018 rejected Justice Ranjit Singh Commission report on the sacrilege of Guru Granth Sahib during 2015 when Badal was the chief minister.[59] That was tabled later in the Punjab Assembly on August 27.

In an unprecedented move, the Punjab Assembly on August 28, 2018 passed a unanimous resolution against the SGPC for breach of privilege by rejecting the report that was yet to be tabled. This report indicted Badal.

Despite these failings, the SGPC is the best model of management of shrines of any community in the world in the context of its being based upon participatory democracy with every Sikh man and woman as per the qualifications of a voter under the Act having the right to vote.

The SGPC should start playing larger role in the global Sikh discourse rather than being the instrument of the Akali Dal leadership. This body has played this role for years earlier that now stands diluted. A beginning should be made with the co-option of eminent personalities to give it a global character.

The Sikh Gurdwara Act should be amended to bar political parties from contesting elections to its general house. The candidates should contest in individual capacity and not candidates of any political party. This would go a long way in ending hegemonic control over this body by the political leadership.

ENDNOTES

1. Gurdwara Gazette, July 1979, p. 7.
2. Parm Bakhshish Singh and Devinder Kumar Verma. (1998). *Punjab and the Freedom Struggle*. Patiala: Punjabi University. p. 243.
3. Sarhadi, Ajit Sing. *Punjabi Suba*. Delhi: UC Kapur & Sons. p. 60.
4. Dilgeer, Harjinder Singh. (2014). *Sikh Tawarikh*, Part III. Amritsar: Singh Brothers. pp. 25-26.
5. Ganda Singh (ed.). *The Panjab Past and Present*, Vol. IV. Patiala: Punjabi University. p. 289.
6. Teja Singh. (2000). *The Gurdwara Reform Movement and the Sikh Awakening*. Amritsar: SGPC. pp. 61-62.
7. Kharak Singh (ed.). (1997). *On Gurdwara Legislation*. Chandigarh: Institute of Sikh Studies. pp. 74-75.
8. Narain Singh. (1998). *Akali Morche te Jhabbar*. Amritsar: SGPC. p. 48.
9. Ibid., p. 77.
10. Ibid.

11. Ibid., p. 56.
12. Sohan Singh Josh. (1974). *Akali Morchon Ka Itihas*. New Delhi: PPH. p. 35.
13. Teja Singh. (2000). *The Gurdwara Reform Movement and the Sikh Awakening*. SGPC. p. 95.
14. Ibid.
15. Ibid., p. 96.
16. Ibid., p. 99.
17. Dilgeer, Harjinder Singh. (2014). *Sikh Tawarikh*, Part III. Amritsar: Singh Brothers. pp. 126-27.
18. Teja Singh. (2000). *The Gurdwara Movement and the Sikh Awakening*. Amrtisar: SGPC. p. 111.
19. Sohan Singh Josh. (1974). *Akali Morchon Ka Itihas*. Delhi: PPH. p. 53.
20. Teja Singh. (2000). *The Gurdwara Movement and the Sikh Awakening*. Amrtisar: SGPC. p. 112.
21. Dilgeer, Harjinder Singh. (2012). *Shiromani Gurdwara Parbandhak Committee Kiven Bani*. Amritsar: SGPC. p . 398.
22. Sohan Singh Josh. (1974). *Akali Morchon Ka Itihaas*. New Delhi: PPH. p. 483.
23. Teja Singh. (2000). *The Gurdwara Reform Movement and the Sikh Awakening*. Amritsar: SGPC. p. 66.
24. Ibid., p. 79.
25. Ibid., p. 99.
26. Ibid., pp. 99-100.
27. Narain Singh. (1988). *Akali Morche Ate Jhabbar*. SGPC, p. 102.
28. Teja Singh. (2000). *The Gurdwara Reform Movement and the Sikh Awakening* (3rd Edition). SGPC. p. 204.
29. Ibid., p. 205.
30. Ibid., p. 207.
31. Ibid., p. 216.
32. Ibid.
33. Ibid., pp. 223-24.
34. Sohan Singh Josh. *Akali Morchon Ka Itihas*. New Delhi: PPH. pp. 138-39.
35. Ibid., p. 168 quoted from General Observations on the Bill File No. 644
36. Sidhu, Gurdev Singh. (2016). *Directory Akali Lehar (1921-25) Vich Shamal Saabka Sainik*. Patiala: Punjabi University. p. 20.
37. Sohan Singh Josh. *Akali Morchon Ka Itihaas*. New Delhi: PPH, pp. 200-03.
38. Ibid., p. 218.
39. Ibid., p. 149.
40. Mohinder Singh. (2015). *The Akali Movement*. Patiala: Punjabi University. pp. 65-66.
41. Gurdev Singh Sidhu. (2016). *Directory Akali Lehar (1921-25) Vich Shamal*

Saabka Sainik. Patiala: Punjabi University. p. 64.

42. Mohinder Singh. (2015). *The Akali Movement*. Patiala: Punjabi University. p. 118.
43. Sohan Singh Josh. *Akali Morchon Ka Itihaas*. New Delhi: PPH. pp. 310-11
44. Mohinder Singh. (2015). *The Akali Movement*. Patiala: Punjabi University, p. 122 quoted from The Civil and Military Gazette, January 9, 1924.
45. Sohan Singh Josh. *Akali Morchon Ka Itihaas*. New Delhi: PPH. pp. 335-36.
46. Mohinder Singh. (2015). *The Akali Movement*. Patiala: Punjabi University, p. 150.
47. Ibid., p. 153.
48. Sohan Singh Josh. *Akali Morchon Ka Itihaas*. New Delhi: PPH. p. 390.
49. Mohinder Singh. (2015). *The Akali Movement*. Patiala: Punjabi University, p. 154, cit. Hailey's letter dated October 29, 1924 to Alexander Muddiman, Hailey's Papers, Mss Eur @220/6-C, IOL, London.
50. Mohinder Singh. (2015). *The Akali Movement*. Patiala: Punjabi University. pp. 153-54.
51. Sohan Singh Josh. *Akali Morchon Ka Itihaas*. New Delhi: PPH, p. 438.
52. Ibid., p. 443.
53. Ibid.
54. Ibid., p. 453.
55. Ibid., p. 454.
56. Mohinder Singh. (2015). *The Akali Movement*. Patiala: Punjabi University, p. 128.
57. Sohan Singh Josh. *Akali Morchon Ka Itihaas*, New Delhi: PPH. p. 465.
58. Shamsher Singh Ashok. (1982). *SGPC Daa Panjaah Saala Itihas*. Amritsar: SGPC, p. 30.
59. August 26, 2018. *The Tribune*.

APPENDIX

Among the Performers

They are the actors who played distinct roles assigned to them by the directors but did not dominate the struggle at the political level. They appeared on the stage at a particular time.

Women had little command and direct role in this struggle. At the political level, the most prominent face was that of Bimal Kaur Khalsa, widow of Beant Singh who had gunned down Indira Gandhi. She was elected to the Lok Sabha in 1989.

The only woman who crossed the border was Kulbir Kaur who had accompanied her brother-in-law Kanwar Singh Dhami who headed the Akal Federation. They subsequently got married in Pakistan.

Another woman who is a known face associated with that struggle, is Sandeep Kaur who runs a foundation for orphans and abandoned children, mainly girls.

General Shabeg Singh: From Being an Indian Patriot to Sikh Martyr

When Brigadier Shabeg Singh was entrusted with the responsibility of organizing underground resistance under the banner of Mukti Bahini in East Pakistan that is now Bangladesh, he would never have even imagined that he would end up in a role that was of strategizing yet another liberation war but that was to be against the very Indian army of which he was the part. The highly decorated officer of the Indian army faced ignominy but finally his journey ended up as a martyr of the community he belonged to—the Sikhs.

He was the General Officer Commanding-in-Chief of the Army of Sant Jarnail Singh Bhindranwale at the time of Operation Bluestar.

His turbulent journey reinforces the Sikh perception of discrimination and victimhood at the hands of the Indian state. He entered the Akali Dal political arena through the Shiromani Gurdwara Parbandhak Committee president Gurcharan Singh Tohra and was active during Dharamyudh morcha. He subsequently came closer to Sant Bhindranwale.

Belonging to Khiala village in Amritsar district and a graduate of Government College, Lahore, Shabeg joined the Indian army as an officer in 1940 during World War II and was commissioned in the 2nd Punjab Regiment as 2nd lieutenant. His regiment was moved to Burma that was part of war theatre against the Japanese enemy. As the army was re-organized after 1947 partition, he was posted with 1st Para. He saw action in Jammu and Kashmir in 1947 against Pakistan. He was GSO –J (Intelligence) in the 4 Corps in the North-East during the 1962 war with China.

Thereafter he held several positions including that of instructor at the Dehradun military academy. He saw action again in the 1965 war with Pakistan when he was posted in the Haji Pir area in Jammu & Kashmir. It was during this period that his father expired but he decided against leaving the station at that crucial period, as his battalion was to go into offensive the next day, such was his dedication. It was after the war that he took leave to be with his family.

His next posting was as Deputy GOC of 8 Mountain Div in the Eastern sector for counter-insurgency operations in that volatile region.

He was selected for a strategic role and that was planning, organizing and executing underground operations under the cover of Mukti Bahini for the liberation of East Pakistan as the struggle was already on in that region. The Bengali officers and other ranks who had deserted the Pakistan army were put under his command.

India never admitted direct involvement in insurgency operations in that region till the surrender by the Pakistan Army in East Pakistan. It was the Mukti Bahini that cleared the ground for the Indian army to launch the main offensive in November 1971 and enter Dacca without much resistance. He was the hero of the Bangladesh war.

Shabeg was promoted to the next rank of Major General after the war with headquarters at Jabalpur and awarded the Param Vashisht Sewa Medal. The Pakistani prisoners of war were under his command. However, it was during this period that the situation started changing against him. The government ordered a probe against him after posting him as GOC in another command. He was charged with corruption and court of inquiry ordered against him. He was framed as he had pointed out corruption at the highest level in the army. He was unceremoniously dismissed from service on May 30, 1976, a day before his retirement on May 31, 1976. Here was a hero of Bangladesh war, who had been dishonoured and disgraced.

His honour was finally restored by the Supreme Court in December 1983 but it was too late by then. He had already taken over the command of yet another army of warriors based in the Darbar Sahib (Golden Temple) complex and he died during that war fighting against that very army, which honoured him as hero once but to be thrown out as villain and that too on phony charges. Now, he is revered as a martyr of the Sikh nation along with Sant Bhindranwale and others.

Dr. Jagjit Singh Chohan

Dr. Jagjit Singh Chohan, a popular medical practitioner, was elected to the Punjab Assembly for the first time from Tanda in Hoshiarpur district on Republican Party of India ticket in 1967 and became Deputy Speaker of the Assembly when the first-ever Akali Dal-led coalition government headed by Justice Gurnam Singh (Retd.) took over in the state. However, as Lachhman Singh Gill replaced Justice Gurnam Singh after a split in the party, Dr. Chohan extended him support and was inducted as the Finance Minister. He lost in the 1969 assembly elections. He had played a major role in the former Akali leader Darshan Singh Pheruman's undertaking fast unto death on August 15, 1969 for transfer of Chandigarh to Punjab who died on October 27 on the 74th day of his fast. Pheruman raised the issue of "Azad Panth-Sikh Homeland" in "Azad Hindustan", his will.

A new chapter in the Sikh religio-political dynamics started unfolding as Dr. Chohan shifted to England. A Sikh group there had already raised the demand for Khalistan. The Sikh Homeland slogan was first raised by the founding president of UK, Akali Dal, Charan Singh Panchhi and his group included Giani Bakshish Singh and Sohan Singh Birmingham. Among their associates were Gulwant S Sandhu, Swaran Singh, Onkar Singh, Sohan Singh, Avtar Singh Azad, Jaswant Singh Dhadi and Sohan Singh Dhesi. Some of them later joined Dr. Chohan who landed in the UK in 1970 as the Akali Dal general secretary.

There is yet another version. Davindar Singh Parmar was the first person to raise the Sikh homeland demand. A breakaway group from the newly formed UK Akali Dal set up the Sikh Homeland Front that included Parmar and Panchhi.

Dr. Chohan placed a half-page advertisement in *The New York Times* of October 13, 1971, on Punjab as a Sikh homeland, stating:

"At the time of partition of the Indian subcontinent in 1947 it was agreed that the Sikhs shall have an area in which they will have complete freedom to shape their lives according to their beliefs. On the basis of the assurances received, the Sikhs agreed to throw their lot with India, hoping for the fulfilment of their dream of an independent, sovereign Sikh homeland, the Punjab."

Here is a version as reported by Dr. Darshan Singh Tatla:

> Dr. Chohan won little sympathy from ordinary Sikhs. The Khalsa Diwan Society [KDS] Vancouver and a Leeds gurdwara in Britain were first to pass strictures against Dr. Chohan in December 1971. Other gurdwaras followed, censuring Chohan's anti-Indian activities. Dr. A. K. S. Aujala, Akali Dal leader, warned against 'traitors' implying clearly the activities of Dr. Chohan and his associates by placing a full-page advertisement through the Punjabi media. To show its displeasure with the ideas of Sikh separatism and perhaps to strengthen the hand of moderate Akalis in Britain, Indian authorities arrested Chohan's supporter Giani Bakhshish Singh during his Punjab visit on 15 November 1972. Detained for a year without trial, he was released only after the intervention of the British government.

The Sikh Homeland advocates in UK intensified their activities.

Charan Singh Panchhi underscored: Sikhs have to realize that there is no future in India dominated by Hindus. The honour and prestige of the community cannot be maintained without state power. Sooner, we realize this challenge better it will be for us to set our objective of establishing a sovereign Sikh state in the Punjab. We cannot keep ourselves in bondage forever... [*Des Pardes*, December 12, 1971]. UK was the country in which the Sikh Homeland demand was first raised. (Dr. Darshan Singh Tatla: *Imagining Punjab: Narratives of Nationhood and Homeland Among the Sikh Diaspora*).

Harsimran Singh who was among the Dal Khalsa founders, shared that Sikh leaders from UK contacted him around 1972 and they included Giani Bakhshish Singh, Iqbal Singh and Sohan Singh Patara. Bakhshish Singh visited India in 1972 and met Harsimran who was already active along with senior leader Hargurnad Singh.

Dr. Chohan and Panchhi were taken to Pakistan in 1971 during Indo-Pak war to use them in the psychological war. This psychological war was related to Nankana Sahib shrine, the birthplace of Guru Nanak Dev. The Pakistan authorities wanted to give an impression that the Nankana Sahib shrine had been handed over to the Sikhs. Pakistan TV telecast the handing over ceremony with Dr. Chohan as the custodian of the shrine. At the same time, he made an appeal to the Sikh soldiers in the Indian Army to rebel against India as Pakistan had done such a big favour to the Sikhs. However, there was nothing like Sikh struggle on the ground in Indian Punjab at that time and his appeal went unnoticed. Nankana Sahib was the launching pad for Dr. Chohan.

Dr. Chohan returned to Punjab in 1977 to stay for about two years. He had two meetings with Sant Jarnail Singh Bhindranwale to "test him". These meetings were arranged by a retired Punjab police officer who had mainly served in Amritsar district.

He later returned to the UK where he stayed till 2001. He was back in India in June 2001 and died in Tanda on April 4, 2007.

K.P.S. Gill: The Competitive Terrorist

The second phase of militancy post Operation Bluestar is characterized by criminalization of both militancy and policing. K.P.S. Gill, who was inducted the face of anti-militancy offensive during this period, earned the sobriquet of supercop but ended up with a stigma. Here was an officer who was associated with almost every vice—best known for wine and women.

A 1958 batch Punjab born Assam cadre Indian Police Service officer, he came on deputation to Punjab in September 1984 as Inspector General of Police (Operations) in the Punjab Armed Police.

He took over as the DGP in May 1988 to continue till December 1990. He hit the limelight during Operation Blackthunder in 1988 that was launched to flush out the militants from the Golden Temple complex for the second time.

He was brought back again in 1991 and continued till his retirement in 1995.

When he was shifted to Punjab, his one apparent quality was his dashing personality. A tall Jat Sikh used to heavy drinking is not unusual for Punjabis, but he would be the first to reach the spot of encounter (fake or genuine) in the morning. Gill was the police officer who restored legitimacy of the instruments of the state that had become irrelevant. He combined political tools with police methods to win the war in competitive terrorism. However, the supercop ended up as a villain.

He used structured violence to outcompete violence by non-state actors. However, his own actions came under scrutiny by the very people whom he had made relevant. At the time when all organs of the state including judiciary had become irrelevant, he was the man who commanded the police from the front to protect these organs.

He was part of the team along with then Governor Arjun Singh who crafted the Punjab Accord between Prime Minister Rajiv Gandhi and Shiromani Akali Dal President Sant Harchand Singh Longowal in July, 1985. He had opened the channel with the militant leaders Bhai Manjit Singh and Harminder Singh Sandhu then lodged in Jodhpur jail, besides some other leaders who were over-ground.

His final assault on militants was after Beant Singh took over as the Chief Minister in Punjab heading a Congress government in the February 2002 election that was boycotted by the mainstream Akali Dal. The political tool that he mixed with the police methods was manoeuvring the Akalis into boycott. His political strategy was to build consensus against terrorism through the Congress. Both Beant Singh and Gill became hate symbols in the process in one section of the Punjabi society while both of them emerged as 'Heroes' and 'Saviours of the Nation' at another level. Gill's biggest failure was the assassination of Beant Singh in 1995 by a human bomb at the main entrance to the Punjab Civil Secretariat. He was the state police chief at that time.

He went to the extent of brutalizing the state police to confront brutalities by the militants. The state acts under the constitution and when state actors abdicate constitutional methods, the actions come under question. He fine-tuned competitive terrorism as part of strategy and tactics.

Punjab turned into cremation ground for bodies that were unidentified and that was mainly during his two tenures. His popularity came to be overshadowed by the molestation charge levelled against him by Punjab IAS officer Rupan Deol Bajaj, the case in which he was convicted in 1996. It was this conviction of the national hero and poster boy of the fight against militancy in Punjab that phased him out into anonymity. He died in 2017 in Delhi.

Dr. Sohan Singh

Dr. Sohan Singh, who retired as Director, health services, Punjab in 1974, was perceived to be among the top ideologues of the Sikh militants.

It is not known as to what stage in his career he tilted towards secessionism, as Khalistan did not constitute even a noticeable component of the Sikh religio-political dynamics at the time of his retirement.

What is on the record is that he raised the demand for Khalistan from the platform that was an annual conference of the All India Sikh Students Federation on May 26, 1976 at Amritsar.

He floated the Sikh Sophisticates Forum in September 1979 in Chandigarh, where he was based and used to organize seminars. In the government record, he was first arrested in October 1981.

As Sant Jarnail Singh Bhindranwale came into the limelight, he started visiting him. Dr. Singh would advise Sant Bhindrawale to raise the demand for Khalistan that the latter always refused. It was during this period that he came in contact with the other associates of Sant Bhindranwale.

He renewed his activity a few months after Operation Bluestar with his first intervention being around the time the Taksal people decided to organize Sarbat Khalsa on January 26, 1986 at the Akal Takht. He was among those who pressed for including the demand for Khalistan as the political objective in the resolution to be adopted at that conclave. He faced stiff resistance.

The demand for Khalistan was finally raised by the Panthic Committee set up at Sarbat Khalsa on April 29, 1986 from the Darbar Sahib complex.

Later he drifted towards the Babbar Khalsa and his name came to be associated with Panthic Committee, as the main body split.

He crossed over to Pakistan in February 1990 and stayed there till April 1991. As per the government record, it was during this period that he met Afghan resistance leader Gulbuddin Hekmatyar. It is pertinent to mention here that the first among the Sikh militant leaders to meet him was Gurdip Singh Sibia, secretary of the BKI in UK, who was in Pakistan for about a year to coordinate the activities of his associates from India.

He attended several meetings of the militant leaders on the issue of boycott of June, 1991 assembly election in Punjab that was aborted a few hours before polling and again in the run-up to the February 1992 election.

Dr. Sohan Singh returned to Pakistan in 1993. He decided to go to the USA from there after a few months. However, Pakistan had been taking certain precautions while sheltering Sikh militants. They were not allowed to board the flight from any Pakistani airport to destinations in Europe, USA or Canada. They could take a flight to nearby places like Nepal and Bangkok.

It was under part of this arrangement that Dr. Sohan Singh landed in Nepal. He was accompanied by three others, one of whom was related to a police officer in Punjab. He informed his relative that they were in Nepal. While in Nepal, Dr. Sohan Singh was accommodated at the residence of a member of the Sikh community, while his associates stayed in a hotel. The police officer was S.P.S. Basra. It was Basra, who headed the police party to Nepal. The Punjab team informed Nepal police and Dr. Sohan Singh was nabbed from his hideout. One Joga Singh, a Nepali Sikh, was alerted from Lahore to confirm the arrest. He was permitted to arrange food for Dr. Sohan Singh but not allowed a meeting. It was after two days that it was known that Dr. Singh had been handed over to Punjab police. His arrest was formally announced after a day of his arrival in Chandigarh. He was sentenced under National Security Act and released after about two years.

Although, he was shown to have been arrested from Mohali on November 3, 1993. He was 78 at the time of his arrest and remained in jail till 1995. He went into hibernation after his release.

He died on October 31, 2012.

Gajinder Singh: The Stateless Militant

Gajinder Singh was among the 20 terrorists in the list that was submitted by India to Pakistan after the attack on Parliament in December 2001. He is among the founders of the radical Sikh organization Dal Khalsa that continues with its agenda of sovereign Sikh state of Khalistan. Although living in Pakistan, Gajinder is stateless, as Pakistan does not acknowledge his presence in that country.

He became part of the Sikh Homeland narrative for the first time when he shouted slogans at a rally addressed by then Prime Minister Indira Gandhi in 1971 at Dera Bassi, about 20 kms from Chandigarh. He was an activist of the All India Sikh Students Federation at that time. The protest by his group was against backtracking of the ruling Congress at the Centre from the promises made to the Sikhs before partition of the country. His family had shifted to Chandigarh in 1960.

He was arrested in 1972 and framed under the Arms Act. He started penning poetry while in jail, the anthology was named "Panj Teer Hor" (Another Five Arrows) in Punjabi advocating the Sikh Homeland.[1]

When a group of young Sikhs decided to float Dal Khalsa in 1978 borrowing this name from the Sikh history, Gajinder was among its five founding members.

He hit the limelight when he and his associates hijacked the Indian

1. When Guru Gobind Singh, the Tenth Sikh Guru, deputed Baba Banda Singh Bahadur to Punjab from Naded in Maharashtra during his last days, he gifted him with five of his signature arrows as a symbol of his authority. Baba Banda Bahadur subsequently defeated the Mughals to lay the foundation of the Sikh Rule.

Airlines plane to Lahore on September 29, 1982 in protest against the arrest of Sat Jarnail Singh Bhindranwale. All the five hijackers faced trial in Pakistan and were sentenced to life imprisonment. They were released in 1994.

Out of jail, his life entered yet another phase. His option was to return to India and pass all the legal hurdles as other two of them had done, only to face another trial. He decided to stay back in Pakistan. Pakistan, however, refused him asylum and denied travel papers.

He took a flight to Germany in July 1996 on fake documents but was caught. He was deported to the point of his embarking the plane and the country was Pakistan. India wanted Germany to send him to New Delhi while the Indian Diaspora campaigned for his asylum there.

When India handed over the list of 20 wanted terrorist leaders to Pakistan after the Parliament attack, his name was on the list. Pakistan denied his very existence in Pakistan. However, that is a technicality.

A section of the Sikh Diaspora active in radical political domain has lobbied hard with Pakistan for getting Gajinder political asylum. As his very existence has been denied, he cannot get travel papers to leave the country. He continues to be stateless.

Gajinder is the oldest Khalistani activist on the Pakistani soil.

Main Militant Outfits

- Dal Khalsa
- All India Sikh Students Federation
- Akal Regiment (Wing of AISSF)
- Babbar Khalsa
- Khalistan Commando Force
- Khalistan Commando Force (Panjwar)
- Khalistan Commando Force (Yadwinder Singh Yadu)
- Khalistan Commando Force (Rachhpal Singh Fauji)
- Khalistan Liberation Force
- Bhindranwale Tiger Force of Khalistan (Gurbachan Singh Manochahal)
- BTFK (Sangha)
- Khalistan Armed Force
- Khalistan Liberation Army
- Dusht Daman Brigade
- Khalistan National Army
- Akal Federation
- Sikh Students Federation

- Bhindranwale Saffron Tigers Force
- Dashmesh Khalistan Commando Force
- Sikh Army of Khalistan
- Khalistan Guerrilla Force
- Khalistan Armed Force
- Khalistan Mukti Vahini Force
- Dusht Sodh Commando Force
- Liberation Tigers of Khalistan
- Kamagata Maru Dal of Khalistan
- National Tigers of Khalistan
- Sikh United Army
- Khalistan Security Force

Socio-Economic and Educational Background of Militants

The radical political and militant dynamics attracted Sikhs from varied cross-sections and socio-economic backgrounds. They were inducted into the struggle by what can be termed as the 'Pull Factor', the people who were totally dedicated to the cause.

Major General Shabeg Singh and Major General Narinder Singh were from the Indian army background.

Militants like Devinderpal Singh Bhullar (Lecturer, Guru Nanak Engineering College, Ludhiana), Dharambir Singh Kamoke (Doctorate in Economics), Navneet Singh Qadian, Ranjit Singh Kukki, Dr. Gurpreet Singh Virk, Dr. Pritam Singh Sekhon, Kanwarjit Singh Sultanwind, Sukhwinder Singh Sangha, Dr. Gurnam Singh Butter and several others were all well educated.

The list of those who came from economically affluent families is long while some of them came from abroad to contribute to the struggle. Talwinder Singh Parmar settled in Canada and returned to join and organize the struggle. At least, three of those from the group of militants had come from the Punjab police.

Index